The Criminal Law Library

FRAUD

The Criminal Law Library

Editor-in-Chief:

Rt. Hon. Lord Elwyn-Jones, PC, CH

General Editor:

Gavin McFarlane, LLM(Sheffield), PhD(Lond),
Barrister and Harmsworth Scholar of the Middle Temple

The Criminal Law Library—No. 1

FRAUD

ANTHONY J. ARLIDGE, MA (Cantab),
One of Her Majesty's Counsel,
Barrister of the Middle Temple, Recorder

and

JACQUES PARRY, BCL, MA(Oxon),
Barrister of the Middle Temple,
Lecturer in Law at the University of East Anglia

WATERLOW PUBLISHERS LIMITED

First Edition 1985
© A. J. Arlidge and J. H. Parry 1985

Waterlow Publishers Limited
Maxwell House
74 Worship Street
London EC2A 2EN
A member of the British Printing & Communication Corporation PLC

ISBN 0 08 039163 X

British Library Cataloguing in Publication Data

Arlidge, Anthony
    Fraud.—(The Criminal law library; no. 1)
    1. Fraud—England
    I. Title   II. Parry, Jacques H.   III. Series
    344.205′263   KD8000

In memory of
Alfred William Parry
(1914–1984)

Printed in Great Britain by
A. Wheaton & Co Ltd, Exeter, Devon

Preface to the Series

BY THE RT. HON. LORD ELWYN-JONES, PC, CH

After half a century in the law, I find that one of the most striking changes has been the enormous increase in criminal work coming before the Courts. There has been a lamentable increase in the number of crimes, both major and minor, which have been committed, particularly in recent years, and the volume of both trial and appellate work, at all judicial levels, has increased greatly.

English criminal law, which is an uncodified mixture of common law and statute law, has in my time increased both in quantity and complexity. Although most crimes are now defined by Act of Parliament, many are still offences at common law.

The law is a living law which has had to be adjusted to the changes in our society. A great deal of law reform has been generated by the Law Commissions and the Law Revision Committee. Parliament and Ministers have produced a flow of Acts of Parliament and Statutory Instruments to meet the demands for revision and reform. Criminals, for their part, have been adept in exploiting commercial, industrial and technical change. Fraud is no longer a fairly simple matter of falsifying entries in manuscript ledgers. Computer systems may be tampered with so that accounts can be milked on an international scale. When I was called to the Bar in Grays Inn in 1935 it took four days to cross the Atlantic by the fastest liner from Southampton to New York. Today a determined drug dealer or fraudsman can have visited four continents in that time. New criminal offences have had to be made, in piecemeal fashion, to catch up with offenders of all ages. New procedures have had to be introduced in the Courts to cope with the ever-increasing backlog of work. Conflicting lines of authority abound, perhaps inevitably when the sheer volume of case law being produced is so immense.

The law's penal provisions have also been greatly changed. Courts are exhorted to regard imprisonment as a last resort method of dealing with offenders. A considerable array of alternatives to imprisonment have been introduced into our penal system.

It is perhaps surprising that against this background criminal law has not received the same concentrated attention from specialised textbooks as many other major branches of the law. There are series of practitioners' texts for example in common law, conveyancing, local government and shipping law, but until now there has not been available a series of specialised books for the practitioner analysing in depth the major topics of criminal law on an individual basis. It is I think timely that such a comprehensive and accessible series should now be published and it is good that Waterlow Publishers are to fill this lacuna with their Criminal Law Library.

Elwyn-Jones

Foreword

BY THE RIGHT HONOURABLE THE LORD ROSKILL, PC

I am delighted to help launch this new venture with a preface to the volume devoted to fraud. Hardly a day passes without some reference in the media to yet another fraud or alleged fraud. Successive governments encourage ordinary families to invest their savings and one government at least has cherished the idea of "an equity-owning democracy". But too often one also reads of the sinister side of modern financial life, of those who, having persuaded the thrifty to part with the savings of their lives with specious promises of lucrative returns of capital or income or of both, fulfil their obligations by decamping with those savings to some country from which extradition is either impossible or at best impracticable. Allegations of fraud have been widespread in markets whose members have for generations prided themselves upon their commercial integrity. This alas is the commonplace of today.

When I recently saw in a national newspaper the question asked— "When did a professional fraudster last receive a seven-year sentence?", my reaction was, when indeed? The older of us can recall memories, either of our own or of our predecessors, of the swift and condign punishment inflicted on the Bottomleys, the Hatrys and others of that ilk half a century or more ago. Others still relate how Whittaker Wright only escaped his long sentence of penal servitude by a dramatic suicide in the Royal Courts of Justice.

What of today? The modern fraudster can and does use modern technology to aid his wits and how does our system of criminal justice intend to deal with frauds facilitated by switching millions of pounds or dollars around the world through several countries in succession all in a matter of seconds?

Trials lasting three to six months or even a year now regularly take place. A month's trial in a fraud case is almost a short cause. Difficulties of proof, of getting reluctant witnesses from abroad, alleged deliberate protraction of committal proceedings or of trials and suggestions that the system of criminal justice has been played to the advantage of crooks and the disadvantage of society are among the problems of today. Is it a harsh truth, as some say, that our tribulations in this field are due to a system of criminal justice which is archaic, cumbersome and unreliable? Does that system offer an open invitation to blatant delay and abuse?

I must not anticipate any recommendations which the Fraud Trials Committee, of which I am Chairman, may make. But only the most myopic of lawyers could find the existing system incapable of improvement and it may be that the necessary improvements require to be of a radical nature.

I welcome Mr Arlidge and Mr Parry's book and I hope it will help those to whose lot it falls to prepare, present and try fraud cases of all kinds the better to understand them and will at the same time hopefully simplify their conduct.

House of Lords   *Roskill*
June 1985

Preface

It is customary for a preface to begin by defending the decision to write the book in the first place. On this score, at least, we make no apology. There are of course already on the market a number of excellent books on the criminal law in general, some written for practitioners and some for students; but these works are by their nature unable to deal with every topic in equal depth. Monographs on specific areas, on the other hand, are (by comparison with other fields of law) somewhat thin on the ground. The law on a particular point can therefore prove hard to find. Hence we conceived the idea of a co-ordinated series of volumes on different aspects of the criminal law, intended primarily for the practitioner but with the academic and the student also in mind; and we are pleased that the idea has been adopted by Waterlows under the editorship of a former Lord Chancellor, Lord Elwyn-Jones. Given the aims of the series, fraud was an obvious title. It is a theme which is central to the protection of property rights by the criminal law. The offences embraced by it are many and various, ranging from the broad sweep of the Theft Acts to the complexities of the Companies Acts, as well as some vestiges of the common law; but we hope the reader will agree that the connections between them justify bringing them together in one volume.

The book appears against a background of controversy. It has been suggested that the criminal law in general, and the system of jury trial in particular, have become increasingly unable to deal with large-scale frauds. This concern has led to the establishment of a committee under the chairmanship of Lord Roskill to consider the conduct of fraud trials, and the committee's report is due to be published at about the same time as this book. We have not sought to enter that debate. Obviously the Roskill Committee will receive wider evidence, and have greater analytical skills at its disposal, than we can muster. But this preface may perhaps be an appropriate place to give a broad indication of our own views. It would, in our opinion, take a very strong case indeed to justify the abolition of the right to trial by jury in any case of serious crime. Jury trial is a constitutional bulwark which should not be relinquished unless there is simply no alternative. Fraud cases are largely concerned with questions of honesty and dishonesty, questions which a jury (as the representative of the community at large) is uniquely qualified to resolve.

Jurors come fresh to the arena; they are not case-hardened. This serves to minimise the risk of an innocent person being convicted by the acquired scepticism of the tribunal. Moreover, quite apart from the difficulty of distinguishing those frauds which are unsuitable for jury trial, it would be hard to justify trying serious robberies (for example) by jury but serious frauds in some other way.

Criticism has justifiably been made of the length of fraud trials and the burden they place on juries; but for the most part juries seem content to undertake this heavy responsibility. In one case at the Central Criminal Court where a defendant was discharged through illness the jury volunteered to return and try him when he was better, because they knew so much about the case already. That jury included a milkman whose additions regularly beat the lawyers' calculators. It has been suggested that juries are more ready to acquit in fraud cases because they cannot understand them. Our personal experience, and such statistics of which we are aware, suggest that this is not the case; on the contrary, our impression is that a guilty defendant is if anything *less* likely to be acquitted in a fraud case, because it is easier to impugn the testimony of an eye-witness than to explain away what the defendant himself has committed to paper. The suggestion has also been made that in some cases prosecutions have not been brought because of the complexity of the case and the length of time it would take. But if such cases exist they must be very much the exception.

Clearly, however, something urgently needs to be done to make fraud trials more manageable. It may be that the legal profession is ready to enter the twentieth century. Judges who try long frauds at present have no secretarial help, although the burden on them is considerable. The greatest delays result from the taking of longhand notes by the judge and from the necessity for the jury to hunt through enormous bundles of exhibits. Is it unthinkable that courts might be equipped for the presentation of documents on visual display panels, or even that judges might be encouraged to learn speedhand?

Apart from such practicalities there are broader issues of policy at stake. Central to any change in procedure is the question of how far (if at all) the right to silence should be curtailed. It dates from the days when most serious crimes carried the death penalty. We feel that the time has come, if jury trial is to be preserved, when defendants should be compelled to disclose which allegations they admit and which they deny, and possibly also the general nature of their defence. Provided this is done when they have had a proper opportunity to consider the prosecution case on paper and to take legal advice, we can see no vice and much virtue in it.

Having thus stated our position on these matters in the barest outline, we leave them (not without relief) to the consideration of others. Our brief is the exposition of the law of fraud as it now stands—a substantial enough undertaking in itself. We have been fortunate to receive invaluable help from various quarters. Lord Roskill has kindly agreed to contribute a foreword, for which we are most grateful. Our thanks go also to those friends and colleagues who have patiently read one or more chapters in draft, answered our questions and assisted in other ways too numerous to mention: notably **Robert Burgess, Alex Noel-Tod, Gillian Parry, Helen Rogers, Ian Smith and Rhidian Thomas.** For help with typing we are grateful to Carolyn Bassett, Elizabeth Edser, Sally Hallam, Jennifer Humphries and Angela Schuter. The errors that remain are of course our own responsibility; we would, nevertheless, be grateful to have them pointed out. Finally we must express our appreciation to Dr Gavin McFarlane for his encouragement, advice and support, and also to the staff of Waterlows. Their patience as the original deadline receded into the mists of history was positively stoic.

We have endeavoured to state the law as at 1 May 1985, except that we have anticipated the coming into force of the Companies Act 1985 and the Company Securities (Insider Dealing) Act 1985, and have incorporated a few later developments at proof stage.

A.J.A.
J.H.P.

Contents

Table of Cases

Prosecutions brought by the Crown, the Director of Public Prosecutions and the Metropolitan Police Commissioner are listed under the name of the defendant. Paragraph references in bold type indicate that the case in question is given substantial discussion in the text.

xix

Table of Statutes

Paragraph references in bold type indicate that the provision in question is quoted (in full or in part) in the text.

CHAPTER 1

The Concept of Criminal Fraud

1.01 Contrary to popular belief, English law knows no crime by the name of fraud. Instead it boasts a bewildering variety of offences which might be committed in the course of what a layman (or for that matter a lawyer) would describe as a fraud; and this book deals with some of the most important of these offences. What the law does possess, however, is a *concept* of fraud, a broad notion (broader, indeed, than the layman's) of what it means to defraud someone. There are several reasons for undertaking a preliminary survey of this general concept before descending to specifics. In the first place it obviously represents a common theme uniting the offences considered, although it is in no sense a definition of the scope of the book: many of the offences we discuss do not strictly require proof of fraud at all. On the other hand many of them do. It has in the past been common for an express requirement of "fraud", or a requirement that something be done "fraudulently" or "with intent to defraud", to be included in the definition of an offence. Admittedly the modern trend is to eschew these expressions in favour of more everyday language; but in many cases (*e.g.* the redefinition of forgery,[1] or the replacement of larceny with theft[2]) the change is one of terminology rather than substance.

1.02 Sometimes, indeed, the element of fraud is not merely an essential requirement but is in fact the gist of the offence. This is arguably so in the case of section 458 of the Companies Act 1985,[3] which makes it an offence for a company to carry on business for any fraudulent purpose; but, as we shall see, it is doubtful whether this offence is quite as wide as the wording would suggest. A clearer example is the common law offence of conspiracy to defraud, which (at common law) consisted simply of an agreement between two or more people to do something falling within the legal concept of fraud. There was no need for the conduct agreed upon to constitute an offence in itself,[4] and conspiracy to defraud has traditionally served as a substitute for the general fraud offence which we do

---

1 Forgery and Counterfeiting Act 1981; *infra*, para. 6.03ff.
2 Theft Act 1968 s. 1(1); *infra*, para. 3.02ff.
3 Replacing Companies Act 1948 s. 332(3) with effect from 1 July 1985; *infra*, para. 9.03ff.
4 *Warburton* (1870) L.R. 1 C.C.R. 274.

1

not have. Fraud may not be illegal *per se*, but joint fraud is. In practical terms conspiracy to defraud has been virtually abolished by the Criminal Law Act 1977,[5] the effect of which (according to the House of Lords in *Ayres*[6] and the Court of Appeal in *Tonner*[7]) is that if an agreement involves the commission of any substantive offence it must be charged as a conspiracy to commit that offence and not as a conspiracy to defraud.[8] The range of substantive offences is so wide that it will be a rare event for a charge of conspiracy to defraud to succeed. But even if the common law charge has lost its practical utility, it retains its theoretical significance for the law of fraud. Any agreement which formerly amounted to a conspiracy to defraud is still a criminal conspiracy, though it will usually have to be charged under the Criminal Law Act rather than at common law; therefore, in the rare case where fraudulent conduct involves no substantive offence, it will be conspiracy to defraud (and therefore the legal concept of fraud) which defines the outer limits of criminal liability.

1.03   Moreover the courts have shown a tendency to standardise the interpretation given to the requirement of "fraud" (and its cognates) in various contexts, so that for most purposes it is not an over-simplification to speak of *the* concept of criminal fraud rather than of a variety of different senses. In *Scott v. Metropolitan Police Commissioner*,[9] for example, Viscount Dilhorne (with whose speech the other Lords agreed) referred to Lord Radcliffe's analysis in *Welham v. D.P.P.*[10] of the "intent to defraud" then required by the law of forgery, and, although it was unnecessary for him to express a view, went on:

> ". . . for myself I see no reason why what was said by Lord Radcliffe in relation to forgery should not equally apply in relation to conspiracy to defraud."[11]

More recently Viscount Dilhorne's exposition of conspiracy to defraud has in turn been applied[12] to the offence of fraudulent evasion of a Customs and Excise prohibition;[13] the reasoning in *Welham* has been applied by the House of Lords[14] to the offence of fraudulently using an excise licence,[15] and by the Court of Appeal to that of fraudulent trading;[16] and it now seems that the test of dishonesty, a requirement

5   s. 5(1), (2).
6   [1984] A.C. 447.
7   [1985] 1 W.L.R. 344.
8   *Infra*, para. 12.34ff.
9   [1975] A.C. 819.
10 [1961] A.C. 103.
11 [1975] A.C. 819 at p. 839.
12 *Attorney-General's Reference (No. 1 of 1981)* [1982] Q.B. 848.
13 Customs and Excise Management Act 1979 s. 170(2); *infra*, para. 10.14.
14 *Terry* [1984] A.C. 374.
15 Vehicles (Excise) Act 1971 s. 26(1).
16 *Grantham* [1984] Q.B. 675.

common to the offences of theft, deception and conspiracy to defraud, is the same in each case.[17] Our first task, then, is to examine the concept of criminal fraud developed in these and other cases with a view to isolating its essential features.

DISHONESTY

1.04 As we shall see, the types of conduct which may constitute fraud are many and various.[18] Often there will be an element of deception, but that is not essential. Usually there will be financial loss to the victim, but that too is not essential. The factor which lends this protean concept some semblance of unity is not so much what is actually done as the *character* of what is done, the element of disregard for the rights of others and for ordinary standards of conduct. This feature is commonly and conveniently referred to as "dishonesty", and in the case of several offences under the Theft Acts 1968 and 1978 is expressly so described. However, the use of this untechnical term should not be allowed to obscure the fact that the concept it represents is a highly complex one. It embraces at least two and arguably three distinct requirements, relating on the one hand to the defendant's legal rights (as he believes them to be, and arguably as they actually are) and on the other to the conformity of his conduct with generally accepted standards. We shall consider these different aspects in turn.

Dishonesty and legal rights

Supposed rights
1.05 A person who believes that he has a legal right to act as he does could hardly be described as acting "fraudulently" in the ordinary sense of the word, and the law has generally accepted "claim of right" as a defence to a charge of an offence involving fraud. As Stephen put it:

> "Fraud is inconsistent with a claim of right made in good faith to do the act complained of. A man who takes possession of property which he really believes to be his own does not take it fraudulently, however unfounded his claim may be."[19]

In the law of larceny the defence was not confined to a defendant who believed the property to be his own: it was sufficient if for any reason he thought he was entitled to take it,[20] and even if it must have been obvious

17 *Ghosh* [1982] Q.B. 1053.
18 *Infra*, para. 1.31ff.
19 *History of Criminal Law*, vol. 3, p. 124.
20 *Clayton* (1920) 15 Cr.App.R. 45.

to him that he was not entitled to take it in the way he did (*e.g.* by force).[21] There was no need for his belief to be correct or even reasonable.[22] The principle thus represented an exception to the rule that ignorance of the law is no defence. It was also applied in the law of false pretences,[23] but apparently not in forgery[24] (though the Forgery and Counterfeiting Act 1981 brings forgery into line on this point).[25] Presumably it also applies to other offences of fraud.

1.06 The defence of claim of right is preserved by the Theft Act 1968. Whereas in larceny the taking had to be "fraudulent", in theft the appropriation of the property must be "dishonest";[26] and although the Act does not define dishonesty it does prohibit certain cases from being so described. Section 2 provides:

"(1) A person's appropriation of property belonging to another is not to be regarded as dishonest—
　　(*a*) if he appropriates the property in the belief that he has in law the right to deprive the other of it, on behalf of himself or of a third person; or
　　(*b*) if he appropriates the property in the belief that he would have the other's consent if the other knew of the appropriation and the circumstances of it; or
　　(*c*) (except where the property came to him as trustee or personal representative) if he appropriates the property in the belief that the person to whom the property belongs cannot be discovered by taking reasonable steps.
　　(2) A person's appropriation of property belonging to another may be dishonest notwithstanding that he is willing to pay for the property."

Thus, for example, the rule that one does not steal by forcibly exacting payment of a debt[27] continues to apply.[28]

1.07 The intention is clear: a defendant whose state of mind falls within one of the three categories listed in section 2(1) is not dishonest, even if but for section 2(1) he might be so regarded. However, the courts have not been content to take the section at face value. In *Lawrence*[29] Megaw L.J. said that the "belief" referred to in section 2(1)(*b*) was "an *honest*

---

21 *Boden* (1844) 1 C. & K. 395; *Hemmings* (1864) 4 F. & F. 50; *Skivington* [1968] 1 Q.B. 166.
22 *Bernhard* [1938] 2 K.B. 264; *Hancock* [1963] Crim. L.R. 572.
23 *Williams* (1836) 7 C. & P. 354, as explained by Pollock C.B. in *Hamilton* (1845) 1 Cox 244 at p. 247; followed in *Strickland* (1850) 14 J.P. 784.
24 *Wilson* (1847) 1 Den. 284; *Parker* (1910) 74 J.P. 208; *Smith* (1919) 14 Cr.App.R. 101.
25 s. 10(2): *infra*, para. 6.26.
26 Theft Act 1968 s. 1(1): *infra*, para. 3.02.
27 *Supra* at n. 21.
28 *Robinson* [1977] Crim.L.R. 173.
29 [1971] 1 Q.B. 373, affirmed *sub. nom. Lawrence v. Metropolitan Police Commissioner* [1972] A.C. 626: *infra*, para. 3.23.

belief".[30] Probably his intention was merely to emphasise that section 2(1)(*b*) does not apply unless the defendant believes that the owner would consent *if he knew the circumstances*; a belief that the owner's consent could be obtained by deception (or, for that matter, that it has in fact been so obtained) does not in itself absolve the defendant from dishonesty.[31] But if that is what he believes, the reason why section 2(1)(*b*) does not apply is that the proposition which he believes to be true is not the proposition which section 2(1)(*b*) requires him to believe. It is not because his belief is not an honest one. In *Attorney-General's Reference (No. 2 of 1982)*[32] Kerr L.J., giving the opinion of the court, stated that the belief referred to must be "an honest belief" not only in section 2(1)(*b*)[33] but also in section 2(1)(*a*).[34] This statement appears to be open to two possible interpretations. One is that the word "honest" is synonymous with "genuine" and therefore adds nothing, since one cannot believe something without genuinely believing it. The other interpretation is that an additional requirement is being surreptitiously inserted into the section: that one may still be dishonest in spite of holding precisely the belief specified, if the belief is itself a dishonest one (*i.e.* if one is dishonest in holding it). This interpretation would be in direct conflict with the wording of the section and would indeed drain it of all content, since it would apply only to a person who is *ex hypothesi* not dishonest. This would have the effect of eroding the defence of claim of right, which traditionally has required only that the defendant should believe he is within his legal rights—however unattractive his conduct may be in other respects. Even Shylock had a claim of right.

1.08 Section 2 applies only to theft[35] and not to the deception offences or the others requiring dishonesty. It could be argued that this precludes any defence of claim of right in the case of those offences. But the reason for confining section 2 to theft is simply that it is drafted for the purposes of theft and most of it has no relevance to the other offences—though section 2(1)(*a*), the claim of right provision, could be applied to the offence of obtaining property by deception[36] if the word "obtains" were substituted for "appropriates". It is submitted that although section 2(1)(*a*) does not strictly apply to the deception offences, they should

---

30 At p. 377 (italics supplied).
31 But if the owner does consent, the defendant's act may not amount to an appropriation: *infra*, para. 3.23.
32 [1984] Q.B. 624.
33 His Lordship said, at p. 641, that it must be "an honest belief in a true consent, honestly obtained". But s. 2(1)(*b*) does not require the defendant to believe that the owner's consent *has* been obtained at all, only that it *would* be given if the owner knew the circumstances.
34 At p. 642.
35 s. 1(3).
36 s. 15(1); *infra*, para. 3.02.

nevertheless be construed in the light of it and by analogy with it—*i.e.* that it is not an offence to obtain by deception something to which one believes oneself legally entitled. An argument to this effect was put forward in *Woolven*.[37] The Court of Appeal apparently accepted that claim of right is a defence, but held that there is no need for the jury to be specifically directed on the point because a defendant with a claim of right will not be dishonest in the alternative sense of deliberately flouting accepted standards.[38] It is submitted with respect that it is unhelpful to merge the different aspects of dishonesty in this way. A belief that one is acting within one's legal rights should continue to be a defence in its own right, irrespective of the extra-legal standards currently accepted by society.

1.09 It should be noted that in the context of deception a claim of right may take two forms: the defendant may believe either that he is already entitled to the thing he obtains (as where he employs a deception to secure the payment of a debt), or that he is entitled to it by virtue of the very transaction which he effects by means of the deception—*e.g.* he misleads his victim into buying property, but believes that the deception does not invalidate the contract and that he is therefore legally entitled to the purchase price. Authority for this form of the defence is lacking, but it seems to fall within the concept of claim of right. A charge of theft would fall foul of section 2(1)(*a*), even apart from the factor of the owner's consent to the taking of the money,[39] and the analogy suggests that there is no dishonesty for the purposes of deception either. The point has implications for the situation where the defendant actually *is* within his legal rights, to which we now turn.

Actual rights
1.10 Claim of right is a defence based on what the defendant believes his legal rights to be. A question which has received far less attention is that of the relevance of his *actual* legal rights, whether or not he knows what they are. If his conduct is not unlawful as a matter of civil law, can it be fraudulent?[40] It would be very odd if it could. The function of the law of fraud is, in general, to provide criminal sanctions for certain infringements of other people's legal rights. If as far as the civil law is concerned there is no such infringement, it would seem inappropriate for the criminal law to intervene. It is of course true that not every criminal

---

37 (1983) 77 Cr.App.R. 231.
38 *Infra*, para. 1.16ff.
39 *Infra*, para. 3.23.
40 See generally Glanville Williams, "Theft, Consent and Illegality" [1977] Crim. L.R. 127, 205, 327; *cf.* J. C. Smith, "Civil Law Concepts in the Criminal Law" [1972B] C.L.J. 197.

offence involves civil liability: one may be guilty of careless driving although one causes no damage. But the function of the civil law of negligence is to provide compensation for the consequences of carelessness, whereas the offence of careless driving serves to deter people from driving carelessly in the first place. If the function of the law of fraud extended beyond the protection of legal rights to the deterrence of underhand conduct in general, there would be no reason why it should be restricted by the scope of the civil law. But it is doubtful whether this is really so.

1.11 Moreover it would be anomalous if the law were to accept a defence based on the defendant's legal rights as he supposes them to be, but not one based on his rights as they actually are. If he knows that he is legally entitled to act as he does, he is clearly not dishonest for legal purposes (though he may be dishonest in some less technical sense): in the context of theft this is expressly provided by section 2(1)(*a*) of the Theft Act 1968, and, as we have seen, this provision is merely a specific application of a wider principle running through the law of fraud in general. But if it is not dishonest to do what one knows one is entitled to do, how can it be dishonest to do what one wrongly supposes one is *not* entitled to do? Ignorance of the law may not be a defence, but it can hardly be a ground of criminal liability. It is even a defence that the defendant supposes he is entitled to do what he does when in fact, as any reasonably well-informed person would have known, he is not so entitled. Surely, then, it must be a defence that he *is* entitled to do it, even if he does not know that he is. To regard the former case as less blameworthy than the latter is to fall into the trap of regarding dishonesty as a purely subjective requirement, relating only to the defendant's state of mind. As we shall see, this is by no means so. To a large extent dishonesty depends on the objective character of the defendant's conduct as determined by the ordinary standards of society. If his conduct is not dishonest according to those standards, it matters not that he wrongly supposed it was.[41] But if it is a defence that his conduct is in accordance with extra-legal standards (whether or not he knows it), it must *a fortiori* be a defence that his conduct conforms to *legal* standards (whether or not he knows it).

1.12 There are admittedly certain authorities which, at first sight at least, appear to be against this view. In *Bonner*[42] several defendants were charged with theft. They claimed that the property alleged to have been stolen was the property of a partnership and that one of their number was

---

41 *Ghosh* [1982] Q.B. 1053; *infra,* para. 1.23.
42 [1970] 1 W.L.R. 838.

a member of that partnership. This fact, it was argued, would have provided a defence to a civil action for conversion;[43] and if their taking of the property was not a conversion it was not an "appropriation" and therefore was not theft. The argument was rejected by the Court of Appeal. It may be that the reasoning on this point was technically *obiter*, an "excursus . . . of an academic kind",[44] because the appeals were in fact allowed on other grounds. But the case is in any event of limited significance. The argument advanced by the defence was that what was done was not an appropriation, not that it was not dishonest. The court was clearly right to reject that argument: the Criminal Law Revision Committee, in proposing the use of the term "appropriation", may have supposed that it was synonymous with "conversion",[45] but the statutory definition[46] does not bear out that assumption. Moreover the defendant who was alleged to be a member of the partnership, by taking partnership property with the intention of permanently depriving his partner of it, was presumably committing a breach of the partnership agreement. His conduct may not have been tortious but it was still unlawful. Therefore the court's conclusion, that he could have been convicted of stealing the property, was not inconsistent with the argument advanced above.

1.13   In *Gilks*[47] a bookmaker inadvertently paid the defendant more than he had actually won. The defendant kept the money, and was charged with stealing it. It was argued that he had not appropriated "property belonging to another" because (a) the money became his when the bookmaker handed it over, and (b) he was not under a legal obligation to repay it (in which case, by virtue of section 5(4) of the Theft Act 1968,[48] it would have been deemed still to belong to the bookmaker) because that would involve taking an account of a gaming transaction which was void by statute.[49] The Court of Appeal accepted the second proposition but rejected the first. They held (probably wrongly) that title to the money had not passed and that it was therefore "property belonging to another" in the ordinary meaning of those words, without recourse to section 5(4). Therefore the defendant could be convicted of stealing the money by keeping it, even though he had no obligation to give it back. On the face of it this certainly suggests that conduct which is not otherwise unlawful may nevertheless be theft, and therefore by definition dishonest. But the court's reasoning is self-contradictory. If

---

43   But see now Torts (Interference with Goods) Act 1977 s. 10.
44   At p. 844, *per* Edmund Davies L.J.
45   Cmnd. 2977 at para. 35.
46   Theft Act 1968 s. 3(1); *infra,* para. 3.21.
47   [1972] 1 W.L.R. 1341.
48   *Infra,* para. 3.16.
49   Gaming Act 1845; *Morgan v. Ashcroft* [1938] 1 K.B. 49.

title to the money had passed, the defendant would have been legally
entitled to keep it and it would not have been property "belonging to
another" even in the extended sense laid down by section 5(4). But if (as
the court held) title did not pass, the defendant surely was *not* entitled to
keep the money: by doing so he was committing the tort of conversion.[50]
If his action had been otherwise lawful, he would not have been guilty of
theft; but since he was guilty of theft, his action must also have been
tortious. The case does not establish that conduct can be dishonest
although it involves no liability in civil law.

1.14 Possibly the strongest authority against the view here advanced is
Turner (No. 2).[51] The defendant, having arranged for a garage to carry
out repairs on his car, surreptitiously removed the car from outside the
garage without paying for the repairs. The Court of Appeal affirmed his
conviction of theft. The decision was clearly correct on the facts because
the garage proprietor had a lien on the car for the price of the repairs,
and the defendant's unauthorised retaking was therefore a conversion.
The difficulty is that the jury were directed not to consider the question of
the lien; and if there had been no lien the defendant would have been
legally entitled to take his car back. Nevertheless it was held that the
direction was correct. There was no need to show that the garage
proprietor was entitled to keep the car, only that it was in fact in his
possession or control.

> "The court . . . is quite satisfied that there is nothing in this point whatever.
> The whole test of dishonesty is the mental element of belief. No doubt,
> though the defendant may for certain purposes be presumed to know the
> law, he would not at the time have the vaguest idea whether he did have in
> law a right to take the car back again, and accordingly when one looks at
> his mental state, one looks at it in the light of what he believed. The jury
> were properly told that if he believed that he had a right, albeit there was
> none, he would nevertheless fall to be acquitted."[52]

Yet even if he *had* had a right to take the car back, he would apparently
still have been guilty—provided that he did not realise he had such a
right. The conclusion is absurd. The only thing that lends it any
semblance of logic is the assumption that "the whole test of dishonesty is
the mental element of belief". As we have already pointed out, this is
demonstrably not so. The mental element of belief is only *one* of the
factors which may preclude a finding of dishonesty. It is submitted with
respect that the court's reasoning is misconceived. If the decision is to be
justified it can only be on the basis that on the facts found by the jury

50 Glanville Williams [1977] C.L.J. 62 at p. 73.
51 [1971] 1 W.L.R. 901.
52 At p. 904f., *per* Lord Parker C.J.

there *was* a lien. That being a question of law, there was no need for the jury to be directed on it.

1.15 It is submitted that an appropriation of property which is not unlawful as a matter of civil law cannot constitute theft, because it cannot legitimately be categorised as dishonest. Similarly, it is not dishonest to obtain by deception something to which one is legally entitled; therefore it cannot constitute an offence of deception, or any offence requiring an intent to defraud. It will be recalled that in the context of deception the defence of claim of right could take two forms, *viz.* either a belief that the defendant was already entitled to the thing obtained even before the deception, or a belief that he was entitled to it by virtue of the transaction secured by the deception itself.[53] If there is a defence in the latter case as well as the former, it seems to follow that there must also be a defence where the transaction is indeed completely valid and does give the defendant a legal right to what he obtains, even though he does not realise it. The point could be significant if, as we argue in the following chapter, a contract may be secured by deception although there is no misrepresentation and the contract is therefore unimpeachable.[54] It is submitted that in spite of the deception it would not be dishonest to take advantage of such a contract, whether or not the defendant realised that he was merely enforcing his legal rights.

Dishonesty and extra-legal standards

1.16 Dishonesty is not simply a matter of legal rights, real or imagined: it has in addition a further dimension, that of the acceptability (or otherwise) of the defendant's conduct according to the standards of ordinary people with no special knowledge of the law. If these extra-legal standards are less stringent than those of the law, it follows that even conduct known to be unlawful is not necessarily dishonest. In the context of fraudulent trading Maugham J. expressed the view that

> ". . . the words 'defraud' and 'fraudulent purpose' . . . are words which connote actual dishonesty involving, according to current notions of fair trading among commercial men, real moral blame."[55]

The requirement of "moral blame" was recognised in *Wright*,[56] where the defendant obtained money from the Post Office on behalf of another person by means of a written authority signed by that person. The signature purported to have been witnessed by a third party, but the third

---

53 *Supra,* para. 1.09.
54 *Infra,* para. 2.06ff.
55 *Re Patrick & Lyon Ltd* [1933] Ch. 786 at p. 790.
56 [1960] Crim.L.R. 366.

party's signature had in fact been forged by the defendant. The Court of Criminal Appeal allowed his appeal against a conviction of obtaining the money by false pretences. The "intent to defraud" which had to be established was "really synonymous with dishonesty", and it was arguable that if the defendant intended to pay the money over to the person entitled to it he was not acting dishonestly. The issue should not have been withdrawn from the jury.

1.17   On the other hand the courts have sometimes appeared to assume that conduct which the defendant knows to be unlawful is by definition dishonest. In *Draper*[57] it was held that although forgery then required an intent to defraud, even a "perfectly honest motive" was no defence. This case followed *Welham v. D.P.P.*,[58] where the House of Lords had defined the requisite intent without reference to any requirement of dishonesty going beyond the disregard of legal rights. But it was in the context of larceny that the sharpest disagreement arose. The definition of larceny required that the property be taken "fraudulently and without a claim of right made in good faith",[59] which implied that a taking without a claim of right was not necessarily fraudulent. In *Williams*[60] the Court of Criminal Appeal denied that the word "fraudulently" was redundant, and proceeded to define it as meaning that the taking must be intentional, under no mistake, and with knowledge that the thing taken was the property of another person.[61] It might be objected that if that were all that were involved in a fraudulent taking the requirement of fraud *would* be redundant, because anyone falling outside the definition would in any event have a claim of right. But Lord Goddard C.J., speaking for the court, also said:

> "It is one thing if a person with good credit and with plenty of money uses somebody else's money which may be in his possession and which may have been entrusted to him or which he may have had the opportunity of taking, merely intending to use those coins instead of some of his own which he has only to go to his room or to his bank to obtain. No jury would then say that there was any intent to defraud or any fraudulent taking. It is quite another matter if the person who takes the money is not in a position to replace it at the time but only has a hope or expectation that he will be able to do so in the future . . ."[62]

1.18   This passage was relied upon in *Cockburn*,[63] where the manager of a shop was charged with stealing from the till. He claimed that he

---

57 [1962] Crim.L.R. 107.
58 [1961] A.C. 103.
59 Larceny Act 1916 s. 1(1).
60 [1953] 1 Q.B. 660.
61 At p. 666.
62 [1953] 2 W.L.R. 937 at p. 942.
63 [1968] 1 W.L.R. 281.

intended to replace the money before it was missed, and he apparently had good grounds for expecting to be in a position to do so. The Court of Appeal nevertheless affirmed his conviction. Winn L.J., giving the judgment of the court, pointed out that the passage quoted above did not appear in the official report of *Williams* and had probably been deleted by Lord Goddard himself when he came to revise the judgment. Winn L.J. described it as "an extremely dangerous and most misleading statement"[64] and expressed the court's hope that it would in future be disregarded. He went on to assert that even a taking which attracted no moral obloquy and did no harm at all might nevertheless be technically larcenous. However, this view was in turn criticised by a full Court of Appeal in *Feely*,[65] and the need for dishonesty in the ordinary sense of the word was reaffirmed. Lawton L.J., speaking for the court, said:

> "It is possible to imagine a case of taking by an employee in breach of instructions to which no one would, or could reasonably, attach moral obloquy; for example, that of a manager of a shop, who having been told that under no circumstances was he to take money from the till for his own purposes, took 40p from it, having no small change himself, to pay for a taxi hired by his wife who had arrived at the shop saying that she only had a £5 note which the cabby could not change. To hold that such a man was a thief and to say that his intention to put the money back in the till when he acquired some change was at the most a matter of mitigation would tend to bring the law into contempt. In our judgment a taking to which no moral obloquy can reasonably attach is not within the concept of stealing either at common law or under the Theft Act 1968."[66]

1.19 *Feely* was in fact concerned not with larceny but with the new offence of theft, the definition of which expressly requires dishonesty.[67] Following the decision of the House of Lords in *Brutus v. Cozens*,[68] to the effect that the meaning of an ordinary English word in a statutory provision is a question of fact, the Court of Appeal disapproved the practice of directing the jury that certain conduct is as a matter of law dishonest. They must be invited to decide the issue for themselves. Lawton L.J. said:

> "We do not agree that judges should define what 'dishonestly' means. This word is in common use whereas the word 'fraudulently' which was used in section 1(1) of the Larceny Act 1916 had acquired as a result of case law a special meaning. Jurors, when deciding whether an appropriation was dishonest, can be reasonably expected to, and should, apply the current standards of ordinary decent people. In their own lives they have to decide

---

64 At p. 284.
65 [1973] Q.B. 530.
66 At p. 539.
67 Theft Act 1968 s. 1(1); *infra*, para. 3.02.
68 [1972] A.C. 854.

what is and what is not dishonest. We can see no reason why, when in a jury box, they should require the help of a judge to tell them what amounts to dishonesty."[69]

This principle is equally applicable to the other offences under the Theft Acts 1968 and 1978 which expressly require dishonesty, such as those of deception. In view of the distinction drawn between the everyday term "dishonestly" and the technical term "fraudulently", it might be thought that the effect of *Feely* would be confined to the Theft Acts; but it has since been applied to conspiracy to defraud,[70] and there is little doubt that it now governs the element of dishonesty in any offence of fraud.

The ordinary meaning of dishonesty

1.20 The effect of *Feely* at first seemed clear enough: the jury were to be asked whether they thought the defendant's conduct dishonest according to their own standards of honesty, which could be taken as representative of "the current standards of ordinary decent people". In *Greenstein,*[71] a deception case, the Court of Appeal approved a direction that the jury should apply their own standards. But it began to be suggested that this "objective" test did not adequately represent the ordinary meaning of dishonesty, and that a more "subjective" test was required: in other words, that the standards to be applied by the jury were not their own standards but those of the defendant himself. In *Boggeln v. Williams*[72] (a case of dishonestly abstracting electricity, contrary to section 13 of the Theft Act 1968) Lloyd J. said that the defendant's own belief as to the honesty or dishonesty of his conduct was "not only relevant, but crucial",[73] and the other members of the court expressed agreement with his judgment. Similarly in *Landy,*[74] in the context of conspiracy to defraud, Lawton L.J. himself said, delivering the judgment of the court:

> "An assertion by a defendant that throughout a transaction he acted honestly does not have to be accepted but has to be weighed like any other piece of evidence. If that was the defendant's state of mind, or may have been, he is entitled to be acquitted. But if the jury, applying their own notions of what is honest and what is not, conclude that he could not have believed that he was acting honestly, then the element of dishonesty will have been established. What a jury must not do is to say to themselves: 'If we had been in his place we would have known we were acting dishonestly, so he must have known he was.' What they can say is: 'We are sure he was acting dishonestly because we can see no reason why a man of his intelligence and experience would not have appreciated, as right-minded

69 [1973] Q.B. 530 at p. 537f.
70 *Landy* [1981] 1 W.L.R. 355.
71 [1975] 1 W.L.R. 1353.
72 [1978] 1 W.L.R. 873.
73 At p. 877.
74 [1981] 1 W.L.R. 355.

people would have done, that what he was doing was dishonest.' In our judgment this is the way *R. v. Feely* should be applied in cases where the issue of dishonesty arises."[75]

1.21 In *McIvor*[76] Lawton L.J., again speaking for the Court of Appeal, attempted to reconcile these dicta with his own approach in *Feely*. *Boggeln v. Williams* was explained away on the grounds that it was not the defendant's *evidence* as to his own honesty which was crucial. The explanation, with respect, does not meet the point. The Divisional Court did not suggest that a defendant who claims to have acted honestly is automatically entitled to an acquittal. What Lloyd J. said, with the agreement of the other members of the court, was that the crucial factor was the magistrates' *finding* as to the defendant's belief in his own honesty—*i.e.* that a defendant who claims to have acted honestly is entitled to an acquittal *unless* the tribunal of fact is convinced that he did not in fact believe his conduct was honest. On this point Lawton L.J. made no comment. His own dictum in *Landy* he explained as follows:

> "The passage in my judgment in *Landy* to which we have referred should be read in relation to charges of conspiracy to defraud, and not in relation to charges of theft contrary to section 1 of the Theft Act 1968. Theft is in a different category from conspiracy to defraud, so that dishonesty can be established independently of the knowledge or belief of the defendant, subject to the special cases provided for in section 2 of the Act. Nevertheless, where a defendant has given evidence of his state of mind at the time of the alleged offence, the jury should be told to give that evidence such weight as they consider right, and they may also be directed that they should apply their own standards to the meaning of dishonesty."[77]

His Lordship had said in *Landy* that his remarks related to the way in which *Feely* should be applied "in cases where the issue of dishonesty arises". Since *Feely* was a case on theft, the assertion that the *Landy* test is confined to conspiracy cases would appear to be a departure from his Lordship's previous view rather than a clarification of it. Moreover the precise nature of the test suggested for theft cases is somewhat elusive. In this context (unlike conspiracy to defraud, it seems) the jury should apply their own standards of honesty, not the defendant's; indeed, dishonesty can be established independently of his knowledge or belief. Yet the jury may give such weight as they think fit to his evidence as to his own state of mind. How such evidence might be relevant is not explained.

1.22 The Court of Appeal tackled the problem again, this time led by Lord Lane C.J., in *Ghosh*.[78] The court rejected Lawton L.J.'s attempt to

75 At p. 365.
76 [1982] 1 W.L.R. 409.
77 At p. 417.
78 [1982] Q.B. 1053.

reconcile the authorities by applying an "objective" test of dishonesty to theft and a "subjective" one to conspiracy to defraud. It was pointed out that Viscount Dilhorne's reasoning in *Scott*[79] relied on the analogy between the two offences, and that the House of Lords do not appear to have envisaged any difference between the nature of the dishonesty required in each case. Lord Lane went on to discuss how the offences of deception (with which the appeal was in fact concerned) would fit into Lawton L.J.'s dichotomy. In the context of deception the requirement of dishonesty replaces the old element of "intent to defraud", which is the *mens rea* of conspiracy to defraud and must therefore fall on the subjective side of the line. The Criminal Law Revision Committee gave no indication that the use of the term "dishonestly" was intended to convert the subjective test into an objective one. But on Lawton L.J.'s view the test is objective in the case of theft. Section 2 aside, the word "dishonestly" can hardly be interpreted both objectively and subjectively in different sections of the same Act. In the light of these difficulties the court held that the test of dishonesty is the same whether the offence charged is theft or deception or conspiracy to defraud (or, presumably, any other offence requiring dishonesty). It was therefore necessary to consider afresh the question of what that test should be.

1.23 The solution adopted in *Ghosh* was a compromise between the totally objective approach, which Lawton L.J. appeared to be recommending in the case of theft ("dishonesty can be established independently of the knowledge or belief of the defendant"), and the totally subjective view apparently taken in *Boggeln v. Williams*[80] and *Landy*[81] (that the crucial question is whether the defendant himself thought his conduct was dishonest, according to his own scale of moral values). On the one hand it is obvious that a person's conduct cannot be stigmatised as dishonest in itself, without reference to his state of mind: *actus non facit reum nisi mens sit rea*. At the very least, his knowledge of the circumstances may be highly relevant. The example is given of a foreigner who travels on a bus without paying, because in his own country public transport is free and he has no idea that he is expected to pay. *Prima facie* his conduct is suggestive of dishonesty, but the inference is rebutted by his misapprehension. On the other hand it would be absurd to judge him not only by reference to his awareness of relevant circumstances but also according to his own moral standards, if any. It would follow from the extreme subjective view that a person who felt morally entitled to act as he did would be immune from liability, however much he might expect to

79   [1975] A.C. 819; *infra,* para. 1.38.
80   [1978] 1 W.L.R. 873.
81   [1981] 1 W.L.R. 355.

be punished if he were caught: "Robin Hood would be no robber". The test formulated by the court is objective in the sense that it is generally accepted standards which are to be applied, not the defendant's; but it is also subjective, in the sense that dishonesty according to ordinary standards is not enough—the defendant himself must realise that his conduct is dishonest on an objective test.

> "In determining whether the prosecution has proved that the defendant was acting dishonestly, a jury must first of all decide whether according to the ordinary standards of reasonable and honest people what was done was dishonest. If it was not dishonest by those standards, that is the end of the matter and the prosecution fails. If it was dishonest by those standards, then the jury must consider whether the defendant himself must have realised that what he was doing was by those standards dishonest. In most cases, where the actions are obviously dishonest by ordinary standards, there will be no doubt about it. It will be obvious that the defendant himself knew that he was acting dishonestly. It is dishonest for a defendant to act in a way which he knows ordinary people consider to be dishonest, even if he asserts or genuinely believes that he is morally justified in acting as he did. For example, Robin Hood or those ardent anti-vivisectionists who remove animals from vivisection laboratories are acting dishonestly, even though they may consider themselves to be morally justified in doing what they do, because they know that ordinary people would consider these actions to be dishonest."[82]

The application of ordinary standards

1.24 It must be emphasised that in most cases the defendant's awareness of how other people would regard his conduct will be a non-issue: it can usually be assumed that his moral standards are roughly the same as theirs, and the only question will be whether on the occasion in question he fell below those standards. If not, he was not dishonest, even if he knew that his conduct was unlawful. In theory the implications of this rule might be alarming. For example, a survey recently revealed that 44% of those questioned thought it would not be "bad" to conceal a small part of their income from the Revenue.[83] If the proportion were to reach 51%, would it follow that minor tax evasion was no longer dishonest? It might be argued that, although Lord Lane spoke mostly of "ordinary standards" and "ordinary people", he began the passage quoted above with a reference to "the ordinary standards of reasonable and honest people". Perhaps, then, the question is not to be determined on the basis of one person, one vote: only "reasonable and honest" people count. Presumably a person who thinks that tax evasion is morally permissible is neither a reasonable nor an honest person, even if most other people would agree with him. It is trite law that the reasonable man is not the

---

82 [1982] Q.B. 1053 at p. 1064.
83 Dean, Keenan and Kenney, "Taxpayers' Attitudes to Income Tax Evasion" [1980] B.T.R. 28.

same as the ordinary man: a practice commonly thought acceptable may nevertheless be negligent.[84] Similarly, perhaps, it may be dishonest. The difficulty with this argument is that the issue is one of fact. It would be improper to direct the jury that people who condone tax evasion are themselves dishonest and that their views are therefore to be disregarded: that would be a naked usurpation of what is, according to *Feely*,[85] the function of the jury. Even if the jury are to take account only of the views of reasonable and honest people, it must be for them to decide what constitutes such a person. Unless they are an unrepresentative sample, their view will coincide with the majority view: *i.e.*, if most people think that tax evasion is not dishonest, most juries will think so too. And therefore, according to *Ghosh*, it will not *be* dishonest.

1.25 However, the possibility of serious discrepancy between the dictates of the law and those of ordinary morality would seem to be largely academic. Juries have not on the whole been eager to find that unlawful conduct is not dishonest. Moreover it is immaterial whether most people would have done the same as the defendant, given the opportunity, or even that most people do in fact do the same: what matters is whether they think it dishonest to do it. In *Sinclair*[86] it was held to be fraudulent for a director to take dishonest risks with company assets, and a passage in the judgment suggested that the crucial factor in determining whether it was dishonest to take a given risk was whether it was a "normal" business risk. On an application for leave to appeal, it was argued that this was a novel proposition. Widgery L.J. said:

> "The court welcomes the opportunity to make it clear that no such test was intended, and, indeed, the normality of the transaction is not the test and was never intended so to be. The distinction is between honesty and dishonesty . . ."[87]

There is no reason to doubt that this still represents the law.

1.26 Claims of right apart, probably the only situation where there is any real possibility of unlawful conduct being found not to be dishonest is that which has given rise to most of the leading cases, *viz.* that of the person who obtains money which he intends to repay in due course. A typical example is the shop assistant who takes money from the till. Sometimes the defendant will be able to claim that he thought the owner would not object if he knew the circumstances, in which case dishonesty will be ruled out by section 2(1)(*b*) of the Theft Act 1968;[88] but in other

---

84 *Cavanagh v. Ulster Weaving Co. Ltd* [1960] A.C. 145.
85 [1973] Q.B. 530.
86 [1968] 1 W.L.R. 1246; *infra*, para. 1.39.
87 At p. 1251f.
88 *Supra*, para. 1.06.

cases it will be very clear to the defendant, either from the circumstances in which the money is entrusted to him or from his specific instructions, that the owner would not consent. It does not necessarily follow that the appropriation is dishonest, because it may be that there is no question of the owner suffering any real loss. In *Feely*[89] itself, for example, the defendant took £30 from the till in defiance of his employers' express instructions, but his employers owed him £70. When the deficiency came to light he put an I.O.U. in the till. If he really intended from the start that the £30 should be deducted from the £70, his employers would have lost nothing, and it would be arguable that he was not dishonest. Hence the judge was wrong to withdraw the issue from the jury. Similarly, to adapt the example given by Lord Goddard C.J. in the "missing passage" in *Williams*,[90] it might not be dishonest for an assistant to take money out of the till, even though he knew that his employer would not allow it, if he had the money with which to replace it in his jacket in the rest room and intended to substitute that money as soon as he had the chance; nor if he intended to go to the bank and cash a cheque during his lunch hour. He might, of course, be run over on the way to the bank, or the bank might collapse in the interim, but the risk is negligible. To all intents and purposes it is certain that the owner will suffer no loss, and in the absence of any financial detriment it is arguable that the law of fraud is out of place.

1.27   On the other hand it is arguable that strictly speaking even conduct such as this may be dishonest. In *Feely* the reason why the defendant's employers had forbidden the practice of borrowing from the till was no doubt to prevent the use of such borrowing as a cloak for dishonest embezzlement. To flout that prohibition could give rise to the very vice it was intended to avoid, and might for that reason be dishonest. Moreover there is a revealing analogy to be drawn with the obtaining of property by deception. If it is not dishonest simply to *take* someone else's money with the intention and expectation of paying it back, the same should in principle apply where the victim is deceived into handing the money over: the law would then recognise the popular notion of the "white lie". Yet few people would say that it is justifiable to obtain money by deception merely because the deceiver knows he can repay it. An entrepreneur who secures financial backing by misrepresenting the nature of his business is still dishonest even if he is certain that his victims are getting a good investment. And if an intent to repay does not prevent deception from being dishonest, arguably the same applies to theft. It can hardly make

---

89   [1973] Q.B. 530.
90   [1953] 2 W.L.R. 937 at p. 942; *supra,* para. 1.17.

any difference that the victim is exploited behind his back rather than to his face.

1.28 In any event the defendant who is genuinely certain that he can repay the money is a rare bird. Usually he will know that there is some risk that he will not be able to do so, even if he thinks he probably will; and as we shall see, exposing another person to financial risk is one of the established forms of criminal fraud. A defendant who takes even a slight risk with another's property, which he knows that the other would not allow him to take if he knew the true position, will invariably be dishonest. His ability to persuade himself that the risk will not materialise ought not to be a defence. Admittedly the Court of Appeal expressed the view in *Feely* that on the facts of that case the issue of dishonesty should have been left to the jury without explanation. But there would seem to be no reason why considerations such as those suggested above should not be explained to the jury, provided it is made clear that ultimately the decision is theirs.

Divergent standards

1.29 As we have seen, the issue of dishonesty typically arises where the defendant is guilty of a deception or an unauthorised taking, but claims that he intended to repay what he took. The question then is simply whether most people would regard his conduct as dishonest: there is no suggestion that his own standards of honesty are different from other people's, and the two-tiered concept of dishonesty developed in *Ghosh*[91] is unnecessary. The importance of *Ghosh* lies rather in its application to the less typical case where the defendant argues that his action was not dishonest even though most people might think it was, because he does not subscribe to the prevailing opinion of what constitutes dishonesty. The jury may of course simply disbelieve him, and probably will if there is no apparent reason why what to them is obviously dishonest should seem legitimate to him. But if it is possible that there is a genuine difference of opinion, the second limb of the *Ghosh* test comes into play: the defendant's conduct is dishonest not only if he knows it is, but also if most other people would think so and (though he thinks they would be wrong) he knows that they would think so. The effect is to rule out the "Robin Hood" defence. A defendant who knows that his conduct would be generally regarded as dishonest is not entitled to an acquittal merely because he personally sees nothing wrong in it. It would be absurd if the law were otherwise. The public ought not to be at risk from the huckster who constructs his own private standard of honesty and justifies himself by it. Commerce is conducted on the assumption that the person with

91 [1982] Q.B. 1053; *supra,* para. 1.23.

whom one is dealing operates according to ordinarily accepted standards, and it is the function of the law to curb the man who seeks to profit by flouting those standards. The defendant's personal opinion of his conduct cannot in itself be a defence.

1.30   On the other hand a person is not dishonest under the *Ghosh* test if he not only disagrees with the majority but is actually unaware that he disagrees with them—*i.e.* he is so cocooned from the views of ordinary people that he does not appreciate it is he who is out of step. To describe such a person as dishonest would not accord with the ordinary meaning of that word. But the scope of this defence is limited. Apart from morons and lunatics (who seldom engage in serious fraud), the only defendant likely to invoke it is the professional or commercial man who asserts that his activities are acceptable in the circles in which he moves: if outsiders disagree, that is because they are outsiders and therefore ill-informed. The point is not that businessmen have lower ethical standards than laymen, but that in some professional circles the way things are done is often regarded as by definition the right way to do them. It will be recalled that in the context of fraudulent trading Maugham J. laid down a requirement of "actual dishonesty involving, according to current notions of fair trading *among commercial men*, real moral blame".[92] But since *Ghosh* this appears too lenient. It is not a defence merely that commercial men regard what was done as acceptable, only that ordinary people would so regard it or that the defendant thought they would. Tampering with a car's odometer would still be dishonest even if all second-hand car dealers thought it was not. It is no doubt permissible to adduce evidence of the commercial background and of what is and is not common practice, in the hope of persuading the jury that their initial reaction is based on ignorance and enabling them to reach a more informed judgment. There is, moreover, a distinction between evidence of what was in fact done and opinions as to whether it was legitimate to do it. For example, the question whether certain accounts are misleading is a question of fact, and evidence of normal accounting practice will be highly relevant in determining what impression the accounts create.[93] But once the jury find that the accounts are in fact misleading, it is for them (not the accountancy profession) to decide whether it is dishonest to draw up accounts in that way. Professional opinion may be relevant if the jury choose to attach importance to it, or if it lends credibility to the defendant's assertion that he did not realise non-professionals might disapprove, and the more reputable the body of opinion the more likely it is to turn the scales; but it is not in itself decisive.

92   *Re Patrick & Lyon Ltd* [1933] Ch. 786 at p. 790 (italics supplied).
93   *Cf. infra*, para. 6.47.

FORMS OF FRAUD

1.31 It remains to consider what types of conduct will, subject to the requirement of dishonesty, constitute criminal fraud. The classic definition of fraud is Stephen's:

> "I shall not attempt to construct a definition which will meet every case which might be suggested, but there is little danger in saying that whenever the words 'fraud' or 'intent to defraud' or 'fraudulently' occur in the definition of a crime two elements at least are essential to the commission of the crime: namely, first, deceit or an intention to deceive or in some cases mere secrecy; and, secondly, either actual injury or possible injury or an intent to expose some person either to actual injury or to a risk of possible injury by means of that deceit or secrecy."[94]

The alternatives "deceit" and "mere secrecy" are well established in the modern law of fraud. It may be fraudulent either to obtain some economic benefit by deception or simply to take it for oneself. Strictly speaking fraud is not even confined to the economic sphere: as we shall see, the mere evasion of legal regulation (with or without deception) may be sufficient.

Deception causing loss

1.32 The element most obviously comprised in the notion of fraud is that of deception. The *Shorter Oxford English Dictionary* defines "fraud" as

> "Criminal deception; the using of false representations to obtain an unjust advantage or to injure the rights or interests of another."

Indeed, the word sometimes appears to be virtually synonymous with "deception", as in the offence (now repealed) of obtaining credit by fraud.[95] It is true that in this context "fraud" included certain kinds of conduct which did not amount to false pretences, since the definition referred to an obtaining of credit "under false pretences, or by means of any other fraud". In *Jones*,[96] for example, a man who ordered a meal without pointing out that he had no money was held to be guilty of obtaining credit by fraud but not of obtaining the meal by false pretences: his conduct, though fraudulent, did not amount to a false pretence. Similarly it has been suggested that a charge of conspiracy to defraud may be used where a "false front" has been presented to the public (*e.g.* a business appears to be reputable and creditworthy when in fact it is neither) but

---

94 *History of Criminal Law* vol. 2, p. 121f.
95 Debtors Act 1869 s. 13(1).
96 [1898] 1 Q.B. 119.

there has been nothing so concrete as a false pretence.[97] However, the concept of deception (as defined in the Theft Act 1968)[98] is broader than that of a false pretence in that (*inter alia*) it includes a misrepresentation as to the defendant's intentions;[99] both *Jones* and the "false front" could now be treated as cases of obtaining property by deception.[1] The concept of deception will be considered in the next chapter.

1.33 But even if the word "fraud" in a statutory definition can sometimes be read as roughly equivalent to "deception", it is clear that deception alone does not constitute fraud as that term is generally understood. What is required in addition is, broadly speaking, that the deception should cause the victim to suffer loss or at least induce him to alter his conduct in some way. The classic explanation of the distinction is that of Buckley J. in *Re London and Globe Finance Corporation Ltd.:*[2]

> "To deceive is, I apprehend, to induce a man to believe that a thing is true which is false, and which the person practising the deceit knows or believes to be false. To defraud is to deprive by deceit: it is by deceit to induce a man to act to his injury. More tersely it may be put, that to deceive is by falsehood to induce a state of mind; to defraud is by deceit to induce a course of action".[3]

Thus a person who pretends to be something which he is not, merely to win the esteem of others and with no thought of financial gain, commits deception but not fraud.[4]

1.34 We may, then, regard as a paradigm of fraud the case of a deception which induces the victim to act to his own detriment and to the deceiver's profit. Typically the victim will be induced to hand over money (as in the case of a straightforward investment fraud) or goods (as in the so-called "long firm fraud", which involves obtaining large quantities of goods on credit and absconding without paying for them). These cases will normally constitute the offence of obtaining property by deception,[5] and if a conspiracy is involved it must be charged as a conspiracy to commit that offence rather than as a conspiracy to defraud.[6] Alternatively, the victim may be induced to provide something of economic value other than property, such as accommodation or a service of some kind,

---

97 T. Hadden, "Conspiracy to Defraud" [1966] C.L.J. 248. Conspiracy to defraud would not now be available if any substantive offence were involved: *infra*, para. 12.34ff.
98 s. 15(4); *infra*, para. 2.03.
99 It is argued below that it does not require a misrepresentation at all: para. 2.06ff.
1 Theft Act 1968 s. 15(1); *infra*, para. 3.02ff.
2 [1903] 1 Ch. 728.
3 At p. 732f.
4 *Hodgson* (1856) Dears. & B. 3; *cf. Moon* [1967] 3 All E.R. 962.
5 Theft Act 1968 s. 15(1); *infra*, para. 3.02ff.
6 *Infra*, para. 12.34ff.

by the defendant's deception as to his own intention to pay for it. Frauds of this type will usually amount to the offence of obtaining services by deception,[7] or that of making off without payment,[8] or both. Finally it may be that, instead of transferring some benefit to the deceiver, the victim is induced to refrain from demanding that which is rightfully his, such as the payment of a debt. Tax evasion is an obvious example. A case of this type would probably fall within section 2 of the Theft Act 1978,[9] but would in any event amount to fraud at common law.[10]

1.35 A deception may be fraudulent even if there is no intention of leaving the victim financially worse off in the long run: it is sufficient that the deception induces him to take a risk which he would not otherwise have taken. As we have seen, conduct involving no risk at all is arguably not dishonest.[11] But no reasonable jury could regard it as acceptable to deceive another person into taking a real financial risk, and such conduct is not only dishonest but fraudulent. In *Allsop*[12] the defendant was a sub-broker for a hire-purchase company, and had inserted false particulars in application forms so as to induce the company to accept applications which it might otherwise have rejected. He was charged with conspiracy to defraud. His defence was that he expected all the transactions to be satisfactorily completed, and therefore did not intend to cause the company any loss. The corner-stone of this argument was the speech of Lord Diplock in *Scott v. Metropolitan Police Commissioner*,[13] where his Lordship stated that one does not intend to defraud a private individual unless it is one's purpose to cause him economic loss.[14] Shaw L.J., delivering the judgment of the Court of Appeal, rejected the argument:

> "Interests which are imperilled are less valuable in terms of money than those same interests when they are secure and protected. Where a person intends by deceit to induce a course of conduct in another which puts that other's economic interests in jeopardy he is guilty of fraud even though he does not intend or desire that actual loss should ultimately be suffered by that other in this context."[15]

1.36 This approach neatly sidesteps the effect of Lord Diplock's dictum: although the defendant must *intend* to cause the victim economic loss, he *does* cause such loss if he induces the victim to take a risk. A jury, however, might have difficulty in understanding how a person can be said

7   Theft Act 1978 s. 1; *infra*, para. 3.25ff.
8   Theft Act 1978 s. 3; *infra*, para. 9.42ff.
9   *Infra*, para. 3.29ff.
10 *Carlisle and Brown* (1854) 6 Cox 366.
11 *Supra*, para. 1.26.
12 (1976) 64 Cr.App.R. 29.
13 [1975] A.C. 819.
14 At p. 841; *infra*, para. 1.38.
15 (1976) 64 Cr.App.R. 29 at p. 32.

to suffer financial loss without in the long run being any worse off. It is submitted, with respect, that it would be preferable to abandon Lord Diplock's requirement and to admit that an intent to defraud may consist of something less than an intent to cause loss; in other words, that *foresight of the risk* of loss is sufficient. Shaw L.J. himself hinted at this possibility:

> "Generally the primary objective of fraudsmen is to advantage themselves. The detriment that results to their victims is secondary to that purpose and incidental. It is 'intended' only in the sense that it is a contemplated outcome of the fraud that is perpetrated."[16]

A defendant who knows that his plan will necessarily cause loss to his victim does of course intend that loss, notwithstanding that he has no malice towards the victim and desires the loss not for its own sake but only as a prerequisite of his own profit. But if he hopes to achieve his ends without actual loss to anyone else, and merely "contemplates" such loss as a possibility, it can hardly be said that he *intends* the loss. His state of mind is one of recklessness, in the "subjective" sense (*i.e.* the risk is not merely obvious but is in fact appreciated by the defendant himself);[17] and the law appears to be simply that recklessness as to a risk of actual loss is one form of intent to defraud.

Loss without deception

1.37   In some contexts a requirement of fraud seems inevitably to involve an element of deception. Forgery, for example, required an intent to defraud until the offence was recast by the Forgery and Counterfeiting Act 1981; but (with the exception of the special case where it is a machine which is "deceived")[18] it is hard to imagine how one might use a forged document to defraud another without any deception being committed. Admittedly the Court of Appeal in *Buono*[19] upheld a conviction of forging valuable securities although the persons with whom the defendant had dealt knew that the documents in question were forgeries, and therefore were not deceived.[20] But it seems improbable that the documents would have been forged in the first place if everybody who was likely to see them had known what was going on: presumably it was intended that the documents would be passed on to other people who *would* be deceived.

---

16   At p. 31.
17   *Cf. Caldwell* [1982] A.C. 341.
18   *Cf. infra*, para. 2.30.
19   [1970] Crim.L.R. 154.
20   *Infra*, para. 2.22.

1.38 It is, however, clear that the element of deception, though it may be necessarily present in certain types of fraud such as forgery, is not an essential ingredient of criminal fraud. Stephen's definition, it will be recalled, expressly allowed for "mere secrecy" as an alternative to "deceit" or an "intention to deceive".[21] It is true that Buckley J.'s dictum ("To defraud is to deprive by deceit")[22] appears to treat the element of deception as essential; but this can no longer be regarded as an exhaustive definition, whether or not it was so intended. The point is put beyond doubt by the House of Lords' decision in *Scott v. Metropolitan Police Commissioner*.[23] The defendant, who admitted bribing cinema employees to abstract films for the purpose of making illicit copies, was charged with conspiracy to defraud the owners of the copyright and distribution rights. Clearly he did not intend to deceive the owners, because he did not intend his conduct to come to their attention at all, and it was argued that he therefore did not have the necessary intent to defraud. The argument was rejected. Viscount Dilhorne, with whose speech the other Lords agreed, pointed out that until its repeal by the Theft Act 1968 the offence of larceny had expressly required the taking to be fraudulent; and deception was obviously not a necessary ingredient of that offence. Nor was it necessary in conspiracy to defraud:

> "One must not confuse the object of a conspiracy with the means by which it is intended to be carried out . . . I have not the temerity to attempt an exhaustive definition of the meaning of 'defraud'. As I have said, words take colour from the context in which they are used, but the words 'fraudulently' and 'defraud' must ordinarily have a very similar meaning. If, as I think, and as the Criminal Law Revision Committee appears to have thought, 'fraudulently' means 'dishonestly', then 'to defraud' ordinarily means, in my opinion, to deprive a person dishonestly of something which is his or of something to which he is or would or might but for the perpetration of the fraud be entitled."[24]

Lord Diplock added:

> "Where the intended victim of a 'conspiracy to defraud' is a private individual the purpose of the conspirators must be to cause the victim economic loss by depriving him of some property or right, corporeal or incorporeal, to which he is or would or might become entitled. The intended means by which the purpose is to be achieved must be dishonest. They need not involve fraudulent misrepresentation such as is needed to constitute the civil tort of deceit. Dishonesty of any kind is enough."[25]

These definitions are extremely wide. The obtaining of financial benefits which might otherwise have gone elsewhere is the objective of most

---

21 *Supra*, para. 1.31.
22 *Supra*, para. 1.33.
23 [1975] A.C. 819.
24 At p. 839.
25 At p. 841.

economic activity. What distinguishes fraud from legitimate competition is the crucial element of dishonesty; and that requirement, it is submitted, confines the concept of fraud to conduct which is unlawful as a matter of civil law.[26]

1.39   Furthermore, it will be recalled that one who deceives another into taking a financial risk is regarded as intending to defraud him.[27] A similar rule applies where the victim's interests are jeopardised not by deception but by the defendant's unilateral act. In *Sinclair*[28] a company director was a party to an agreement under which the company lent most of its funds to a third party in order to enable him to acquire a majority shareholding in the company. All it received in exchange was the third party's unsecured promise to transfer to it assets of equivalent value. The Court of Appeal held that this amounted to a conspiracy to defraud[29] even if the conspirators honestly believed that the third party would fulfil his promise, provided only that they knew it was a risk which they had no right to take. The difficulty lies in distinguishing between those risks which are legitimate and those which are not: it is after all one of the functions of directors to take risks with the company's assets. Since the element of deception is not essential, what is the hallmark of *fraudulent* risk-taking? It seems that the solution is to be found in the concept of the fiduciary duty owed by a director to his company. The Crown's argument in *Sinclair*, which was accepted by the Court of Appeal, was summed up by James J.:

> "The Crown . . . argue that there was a duty upon a director of a company owed to the company and its shareholders—and a corresponding right vested in the company and shareholders—the duty being to use the assets of the company in what is honestly believed to be the best interests of the company: if the assets are used in the honest belief that the best interests of the company are being served by that use there is no fraud and it is irrelevant that such use incidentally brings a personal benefit to the director. If on the other hand a risk is taken in using the assets which no director could honestly believe to be taken in the interests of the company and which is to the prejudice of the rights of others, that is taking a risk which there is no right to take and is fraudulent."[30]

Conduct in breach of a fiduciary duty is of course unlawful as a matter of civil law and therefore capable of being dishonest; but in the absence of any such breach, or any other breach of the civil law, it is submitted that the requirement of dishonesty could not be satisfied.[31]

---

26 *Cf. supra*, para. 1.10ff.
27 *Supra*, para. 1.35.
28 [1968] 1 W.L.R. 1246.
29 It would now have to be charged as a conspiracy to commit an offence under s. 151 of the Companies Act 1985: *infra*, para. 5.34ff., 12.34ff.
30 At p. 1249.
31 *Cf. supra*, para. 1.10ff.

Deception inducing conduct

1.40 The decision in *Scott*[32] demonstrates that, although a typical example of fraud may be the case of a deception which causes financial loss, the element of deception is not essential: any dishonest means of inflicting financial loss will do. Conversely, it is established by another line of authority that the element of financial loss is not essential either, and that the victim of a deception can sometimes be said to have been defrauded merely because he was deceived into acting (or refraining from acting) in a particular way. This is certainly the case where the victim is under some kind of public duty and is deceived into failing to carry it out, or at any rate failing to do what *would* have been his duty had he not been deceived. An early authority for this rule is *Toshack*,[33] where the defendant forged a testimonial in order to obtain a master's certificate from Trinity House. His conviction of forgery, an offence requiring an intent to defraud at common law, was upheld. Similarly it is fraud to use false documents for the purpose of being admitted as a student of one of the Inns of Court;[34] or to impersonate someone else in a driving test;[35] or to conceal from one's employer (at any rate where the employer is a public body) misconduct which might give rise to disciplinary proceedings;[36] or to display in a car the tax disc issued in respect of a different car, with a view to avoiding prosecution.[37] The case which confirmed the principle was *Welham v. D.P.P.*,[38] where forged documents were used for the purpose of evading statutory credit restrictions. The House of Lords held that the necessary intent to defraud was established because the appellant intended to deceive those responsible for enforcing the legislation into failing to do so.

1.41 The *Welham* principle, that a public officer is "defrauded" if he is deceived into not doing his duty, is one which applies not only to forgery[39] but also to offences of doing something "fraudulently"[40] and, it seems, to conspiracy to defraud. In *D.P.P. v. Withers*[41] the appellants obtained confidential information by deceiving both civil servants and employees of private concerns. They were charged with conspiracy to effect a public mischief. The House of Lords held that there was no such offence, but it was agreed that in the case of the public officials a charge

---

32 [1975] A.C. 819.
33 (1849) 4 Cox 38.
34 *Bassey* (1931) 22 Cr.App.R. 160.
35 *Potter* [1958] 1 W.L.R. 638.
36 *Garland* [1960] Crim.L.R. 129.
37 *Terry* [1984] A.C. 374.
38 [1961] A.C. 103.
39 See now Forgery and Counterfeiting Act 1981 s. 10(1)(*c*); *infra*, para. 6.25.
40 *Terry* [1984] A.C. 374.
41 [1975] A.C. 842.

of conspiracy to defraud might have succeeded.[42] And in *Scott*,[43] where there *was* an element of financial loss and it was the necessity for a deception which was in issue, Viscount Dilhorne was careful not to rule out the converse possibility:

> "In *Welham v. Director of Public Prosecutions* Lord Radcliffe referred to a special line of cases where the person deceived is a person holding public office or a public authority and where the person deceived was not caused any pecuniary or economic loss. Forgery whereby the deceit has been accomplished had, he pointed out, been in a number of cases treated as having been done with intent to defraud despite the absence of pecuniary or economic loss. In this case it is not necessary to decide that a conspiracy to defraud may exist even though its object was not to secure a financial advantage by inflicting an economic loss on the person at whom the conspiracy was directed. But for myself I see no reason why what was said by Lord Radcliffe in relation to forgery should not equally apply in relation to conspiracy to defraud."[44]

All their Lordships agreed with Viscount Dilhorne's speech. Lord Diplock added his own formulation of the principle:

> "Where the intended victim of a 'conspiracy to defraud' is a private individual the purpose of the conspirators must be to cause the victim economic loss . . . Where the intended victim . . . is a person performing public duties as distinct from a private individual it is sufficient if the purpose is to cause him to act contrary to his public duty, and the intended means of achieving this purpose are dishonest. The purpose need not involve causing economic loss to anyone."[45]

1.42 With respect, however, it is not clear that Lord Diplock's distinction between private individuals and public officers represents the law. What *Welham* decides (because the persons deceived in that case *were* public officers) is that it is fraud to deceive a public officer into failing to do his duty. It does not decide that this is the *only* form of fraud where financial loss is not essential; and indeed there are passages suggesting that the rule concerning public officers is but one application of a wider principle extending to private individuals too. Lord Radcliffe suggested that "defrauding" included "any deceiving of another to his injury, his detriment or his prejudice";[46] and although he referred to some of the authorities on the deception of public officials,[47] he appears to have regarded them as an example of this wide usage and not as the sole justification for it. Lord Denning was more explicit:

---

42 At p. 860 (*per* Viscount Dilhorne, with whom Lord Reid concurred), p. 862 (*per* Lord Diplock), p. 873 (*per* Lord Simon), p. 875 (*per* Lord Kilbrandon).
43 [1975] A.C. 819.
44 At p. 839.
45 At p. 841.
46 [1961] A.C. 103 at p. 128.
47 At p. 124f.

"Put shortly, 'with intent to defraud' means 'with intent to practise a fraud' on someone or other. It need not be anyone in particular. Someone in general will suffice. If anyone may be prejudiced in any way by the fraud, that is enough."[48]

1.43 The point may be illustrated by reference to *Withers*,[49] where some of those deceived were public officers (*e.g.* civil servants) and some were not (*e.g.* bank employees). No financial loss was sustained by them or their employers as a result of the confidential information being dishonestly obtained. In the case of the public officers it seems that a charge of conspiracy to defraud would have been successful.[50] Would such a charge have been possible in the case of the private individuals too? Lord Diplock[51] and Lord Kilbrandon[52] clearly thought not. Viscount Dilhorne, on the other hand, was not prepared to rule out the possibility;[53] and Lord Reid concurred with him. If the effect of *Welham* does extend beyond the deception of public officers, it is not clear how much further it goes. Lord Radcliffe conceded that "to defraud must involve something more than the mere inducing of a course of action by deceit",[54] and insisted that there be some "prejudice" to the victim; but if "prejudice" is not confined to economic loss on the one hand, and does not include every case of deception inducing a course of action on the other, it is hard to see what it does mean. Indeed, could it be said that the victims of the deception in *Withers* were prejudiced by it? If, however, Lord Diplock's distinction is correct, there is clearly scope for argument as to who is "a person performing public duties". Does the expression include, for example, an employee of a nationalised corporation?[55]

Evasion of prohibitions without deception

1.44 We have seen that although fraud typically involves both deception and financial loss, it may consist of loss without deception, or *vice versa*. This prompts the question: is it essential to establish one or the other? Or can a scheme be fraudulent even if no-one is deceived *and* no-one suffers loss? The element of financial loss appears to be central to the *Scott*[56] principle; and at first sight *Welham*[57] would seem to involve a

---

48 At p. 133.
49 [1975] A.C. 842.
50 *Supra,* n. 42.
   51 At p. 862; *cf.* his Lordship's speech in *Scott* [1975] A.C. 819 at p. 841, *supra,* para. 1.38.
52 At p. 877f.
53 At p. 860.
54 [1961] A.C. 103 at p. 127.
55 *Cf. infra,* para. 7.03.
56 [1975] A.C. 819: *supra,* para. 1.38.
57 [1961] A.C. 103: *supra,* para. 1.40.

requirement of deception. Thus in *Withers*,[58] where the information obtained from the Criminal Records Office was obtained by corruption rather than deception, Lord Kilbrandon thought that there was therefore no fraud "in the *Welham* sense".[59] But this interpretation of *Welham* may be too narrow. The essence of the fraud in that case lay in the evasion of statutory credit restrictions, and the gist of the decision was that that objective was fraudulent although nobody was intended to suffer loss. It might be argued that the deception was merely incidental, and that to regard it as crucial would be to "confuse the object of a conspiracy with the means by which it is intended to be carried out".[60] On this view the deliberate evasion of statutory restrictions is in itself fraudulent, whether it is effected by deception of the officials responsible or by clandestine means.

1.45 Support for this argument is to be found in *Attorney-General's Reference (No. 1 of 1981)*,[61] where it was held that a person who smuggles prohibited goods into the country without encountering a customs officer (and therefore without deceiving one) may nevertheless be convicted of the fraudulent evasion of a Customs and Excise prohibition.[62] Understandably, the court relied on *Scott* rather than *Welham*. But the case involved the evasion of a *prohibition,* not of customs *duty*: the objective was not to deprive the Customs of revenue but to make a profit on the black market. Perhaps, then, the case is closer to *Welham* than to *Scott.* In any event, it suggests that it is the nature of the defendant's objective which is crucial to a finding of fraud, rather than the method by which he seeks to achieve it. Fraudulent objectives include not only the infliction of financial loss but also the evasion of statutory prohibitions. At this point, however, a certain divergence is apparent between the technical and ordinary meanings of the word "fraud". To apply that description not only to tax evasion but also to (for example) the smuggling of drugs or pornography would, it is suggested, be out of line with ordinary usage. That is no criticism of the Court of Appeal's view that the latter activities are "fraudulent" for the purpose of criminal liability: the word is a term of art. But it should be emphasised that our objective in this book is to discuss the application of the criminal law to those activities which might naturally be described as frauds, rather than the whole range of offences involving "fraud" in the technical sense. In the vast majority of cases, such activities will involve the element of financial loss.

58   [1975] A.C. 842: *supra,* para. 1.41.
59   At p. 878.
60   *Per* Viscount Dilhorne in *Scott* [1975] A.C. 819 at p. 839: *supra,* para. 1.38.
61   [1982] Q.B. 848.
62   Customs and Excise Management Act 1979 s. 170(2): *infra,* para. 10.14.

CHAPTER 2

The Concept of Deception

2.01 We have seen that the element of deception, though not strictly essential to the concept of criminal fraud, is nevertheless one of its most important facets. In several of the offences of the most general application[1] there is an express requirement of deception rather than fraud in some wider sense. We must therefore examine this narrower concept, together with certain related elements which are common to all the deception offences. The additional requirements of the individual offences are considered in the following chapter.

DECEPTION AND FALSE PRETENCES

2.02 The word "deception" itself was not used in the legislation before 1968. Until then the central offence in this area was that of obtaining by false pretences,[2] and a false pretence was simply a misrepresentation, express or implied. In the Report which was implemented as the Theft Act 1968,[3] the Criminal Law Revision Committee proposed to replace the phrase "false pretence" with the term "deception". The change was not only in keeping with the Committee's aim of stating the law in simple, modern language, but was also intended to signify a change of emphasis:

> "The substitution of 'deception' for 'false pretence' is chiefly a matter of language. The word 'deception' seems to us (as to the framers of the American Law Institute's Model Penal Code) to have the advantage of directing attention to the effect that the offender deliberately produced on the mind of the person deceived, whereas 'false pretence' makes one think of what exactly the offender did in order to deceive. 'Deception' seems also more apt in relation to deception by conduct."[4]

The proposal was accepted, and the Theft Act 1968 created three offences of securing various objectives "by deception". Four more followed in the Theft Act 1978.

---

1 Theft Act 1968 ss. 15, 16, 20(2); Theft Act 1978 ss. 1, 2.
2 Larceny Act 1916 s. 32.
3 *Theft and Related Offences* (Cmnd. 2977).
4 At para. 87.

2.03   It is conventional to defer to the Committee's opinion that the use of the word "deception" was "chiefly a matter of language". But there is no reason to assume that this is so: a change of terminology may well involve a change of substance. The fact that the Committee may not have appreciated the full implications of their proposal is not in itself conclusive.[5] The only indication of the meaning of the word "deception" to be found in the Theft Acts is in section 15(4) of the 1968 Act, which provides:

> ". . . 'deception' means any deception (whether deliberate or reckless) by words or conduct as to fact or as to law, including a deception as to the present intentions of the person using the deception or any other person."

Clearly this is only a partial definition, intended to clarify certain specific points. It is concerned partly with the subject-matter of the deception and partly with the required mental element; it gives no indication of what is meant by "deception" itself. We must therefore enquire what is involved in the ordinary meaning of the word. The *Shorter Oxford English Dictionary* defines "deception" as "the action of deceiving", and "deceive" as "to cause to believe what is false". It will be recalled that Buckley J.'s definition (which was approved by two members of the House of Lords in the post-1968 case of *D.P.P. v. Ray*)[6] was in similar terms:

> "To deceive is, I apprehend, to induce a man to believe that a thing is true which is false, and which the person practising the deceit knows or believes to be false."[7]

These definitions suggest that the concept of deception, as generally understood, does in fact differ from that of a false pretence in two respects. On the one hand it would appear to be narrower, in that it requires the formation of some *belief* in the mind of the victim; but on the other hand it is arguably wider, in that it does not necessarily involve the making of any *representation*. These distinctions are central to our account of the concept of deception. They must therefore be explained at the outset and their implications considered.

Belief

2.04   Taken in isolation, the concept of a false pretence is clearly wider than that of deception, in the sense that it carries no connotation of success. If the intended victim sees through the pretence, there is still a

---

5   *Cf.* the House of Lords' disregard in *Caldwell* [1982] A.C. 341 of the intentions of the Law Commission with respect to the interpretation of the word "reckless" in the Criminal Damage Act 1971.
6   [1974] A.C. 370.
7   *Re London and Globe Finance Corporation Ltd* [1903] 1 Ch. 728 at p. 732.

false pretence; but there is no deception unless the pretence is believed. It may be objected that the distinction is academic, because the offence lies not in the false pretence or the deception itself, but in achieving a specified objective *by* false pretences or deception. A pretence which is not believed may still be a pretence, but its maker will not have achieved anything by making it. Therefore, it may be said, although there can be a false pretence without a deception, an obtaining *by* false pretences must necessarily be an obtaining by deception.

2.05 The flaw in this reasoning is that in certain circumstances a person's actions may be influenced by a false pretence although he does not positively believe it to be true. In such a case there might have been an obtaining by false pretences under the old law, but it is arguable that there is no deception. This possibility may arise where the victim gives no conscious thought to the matter at all, but simply makes an assumption: *e.g.* he buys goods on the assumption that the seller has the right to sell them. Alternatively, or (more likely) in addition, it may be of no concern to the "victim" (if indeed he can be so described) whether or not he is being misled: he does not regard the issue as material. An important example is that of cheque card or credit card fraud. The person accepting the card may not be interested in whether or not the user has a right to use it, because payment is in any event guaranteed. It has been pointed out that these attitudes of sub-conscious assumption, or indifference, or both, cannot necessarily be equated with belief, and that it is therefore debatable whether a person taking advantage of such attitudes can legitimately be described as having practised a deception.[8] In fact, as will be seen, the courts have declined to adopt such a restrictive interpretation.[9] But the fact that these difficulties have arisen at all is largely attributable to the use of the word "deception", since (unlike "false pretence") it implies the existence in the victim of a certain state of mind. It may be that this state of mind need not be one which might naturally be described as "belief", but a certain state of mind there must be (and "belief" seems as convenient a label as any). Our account of the concept of deception therefore begins with an attempt to define the essential characteristics of the state of mind required, before considering the question of how that state of mind may be induced. Central to our treatment of the latter issue is the question whether deception necessarily involves misrepresentation, to which we now turn.

Misrepresentation

2.06 Under the old law a false pretence always involved the making of a

---

8 A.T.H. Smith, "The Idea of Criminal Deception" [1982] Crim. L.R. 721.
9 *Infra,* para. 2–24 ff.

false representation, express or implied. It is commonly assumed that the same applies to deception.[10] This requirment does not in practice appear to be a serious limitation on the scope of the deception offences, because the courts have been very ready to find implied representations in the conduct of the dishonest. In *Thompson*,[11] for example, the defendant had programmed the computer of a bank in Kuwait to credit his accounts with sums to which he was not entitled. He then came to England and wrote to the bank requesting it to transfer these sums to his accounts in England. The Court of Appeal held that he had procured the transfer by deception. The "only proper construction" to be put on his letters was that they contained the implied representations alleged, *viz.* that the sums were genuine and accurate credits and that he was entitled to receive payment of those sums. The letters are not quoted in the report, but it seems unlikely that there was any direct reference to these matters. Presumably the mere act of requesting the transfer in itself constituted a representation that the defendant was entitled to the money. Similarly in *Williams (Jean-Jacques)*[12] a schoolboy bought obsolete Jugoslavian banknotes which were worthless except as collectors' items, took them to a bureau de change and said to the cashier either "Will you change these notes?" or "Can I cash these in?" The cashier paid him a total of over a hundred pounds for notes which had cost him only seven. The Court of Appeal, upholding a conviction of theft, criticised the recorder's ruling that there was no evidence of any false representation and that charges of obtaining property by deception could not be left to the jury. The defendant had in effect represented that he believed the notes to be valid currency in Jugoslavia. The court appears to have thought it self-evident that, if a dealer is known to accept only items of a certain description (*e.g.* valid currency), anyone who offers him items for sale is implicitly representing that the items are at least believed to be of that description.

2.07 This readiness to find implied representations seems particularly artificial where there have been no direct dealings between the parties, and the defendant's conduct is more naturally described as the creation of a false impression than as the making of a false statement. In *Scott v. Brown, Doering, McNab & Co.*[13] an agreement to buy shares at prices in excess of their real value, thus creating a false market, was held to be an indictable conspiracy; A. L. Smith L. J. expressed the view that a person induced to buy the shares would have had an action in deceit against the

---

10 J.C. Smith, *The Law of Theft* (5th ed.) at para. 166; E. Griew, *The Theft Acts 1968 and 1978* (4th ed.) at para. 6–15; *D.P.P. v. Ray* [1974] A.C. 370 at p. 388, *per* Lord Hodson; *D.P.P. v. Stonehouse* [1978] A.C. 55 at p. 65, *per* Lord Diplock.
11 [1984] 1 W.L.R. 962.
12 [1980] Crim.L.R. 589.
13 [1892] 2 Q.B. 724.

conspirators.[14] Presumably, therefore, the sham transactions constituted implied representations to potential investors that there was a genuine demand for the shares. But it seems odd to regard a person who buys shares as thereby making a statement to the rest of the market about his motives for buying them. A criminal case which stretches the idea of implied representation almost to breaking-point is *D.P.P. v. Stonehouse*,[15] where a prominent politician and businessman took elaborate steps to give the impression that he had drowned whilst swimming. His intention was to enable his wife (who was not a party to the fraud) to make a claim under his life assurance policy, but he was apprehended before she did so. The House of Lords dismissed his appeal against convictions of attempting to obtain property by deception. The alleged deception consisted of the false representation that he had drowned. But the only conduct on the defendant's part which could be said to imply such a representation was his conduct *after* the fake drowning (*e.g.* leaving the country with a false passport), conduct which was obviously unknown to the victims of the deception. Is it really possible to make a representation by means of conduct which never comes to the attention of the representee? In any event the notion of a representation that the representor is dead seems positively bizarre. It poses the curious paradox of a representation which can only be believed by someone who is unaware that it is being made.

2.08 It is not suggested that there was no deception in any of these cases. But it is submitted that the contortions involved in finding an implied representation are no longer necessary, because misrepresentation is not an essential element of deception. In its ordinary meaning, "deception" involves the creating of a false impression, but it is not confined to any particular *means* of doing so. Indeed this point was hinted at by the Criminal Law Revision Committee: the term "deception", it will be recalled, was preferred to "false pretence" on the ground that it directs attention to "the effect . . . produced on the mind of the person deceived" rather than "what exactly the offender did in order to deceive".[16]

2.09 This approach has the great advantage that it dispenses with the need for artificial reasoning. To say that Stonehouse falsely represented that he was dead is artificial to the point of unreality; to say that he committed a deception is entirely natural, because it means merely that he

---

14 At p. 734.
15 [1978] A.C. 55.
16 *Supra*, para. 2.02. *Cf.* N. McCormick, "What is Wrong with Deceit?" (1983) 10 Syd. L.R. 5 at p. 8.

created a false impression and says nothing about *how* he did so. Artificiality is admittedly not the most serious defect from which a legal rule can suffer. But the prosecution, at least, may have some incentive to avoid technicalities which are at best unnecessary and at worst liable to get between the jury and the realities of the case. Even law students have been known to find difficulty in understanding how statements of fact can be inferred from conduct. In this connection it is perhaps relevant to note the view expressed by the Court of Appeal in *Landy*,[17] in the context of indictments charging conspiracy to defraud, that "such terms as 'falsely representing' . . . are imprecise and likely to confuse juries".[18] This dictum is sharply criticised by the learned editors of Archbold,[19] who accordingly continue to recommend an allegation of false representation in counts of deception. It is submitted that although the imprecision of the term may be illusory, the risk of confusion is real; and that in an appropriate case it is both permissible and desirable simply to allege that the defendant, by certain specified conduct, "caused X to believe . . ." *etc.*

2.10 Whether the abandonment of the requirement of misrepresentation would have any *substantive* effect is another matter. The courts are so ready to find implied representations in dishonest conduct that there can be few cases of deception which could not, at a pinch, be analysed in those terms. Cases such as *Williams (Jean-Jacques)*[20] demonstrate that what appears at first sight to be the mere non-disclosure of a material fact can usually be treated as deception, even if misrepresentation is required. Nevertheless it is conceivable that even non-disclosure falling short of misrepresentation might qualify as deception. The crucial question is one of causation: can one *cause* another person to hold a mistaken belief merely by failing to point out the truth? The idea of causation by omission is a controversial one.[21] For the purposes of the law of homicide it is possible to cause death by an omission, at any rate where there is a duty to act.[22] Perhaps, then, one can deceive by silence if the law imposes a duty of disclosure? Such duties may be imposed by statute (*e.g.* the duty of a company director[23] or a member of a local authority[24] to disclose a financial interest in a proposed contract), by contract[25] (*e.g.* the obligation of an agent to make full disclosure of his dealings to his

17 [1981] 1 W.L.R. 355.
18 At p. 362.
19 *Pleading, Evidence and Practice in Criminal Cases,* 41st ed. at para. 28–25.
20 [1980] Crim.L.R. 589; *supra,* para. 2.06.
21 See J.C. Smith, "Liability for omissions in the criminal law" (1984) 4 Leg.Stud. 88.
22 *Pittwood* (1902) 19 T.L.R. 37; *Stone and Dobinson* [1977] Q.B. 354.
23 Companies Act 1985 s.317. Failure to comply with this requirement is an offence in itself, punishable on conviction on indictment with an unlimited fine: s. 317(7).
24 Local Government Act 1972 s. 94(1). Failure to comply is a summary offence: s. 94(2).
25 *Cf. Sybron Corporation v. Rochem Ltd* [1984] Ch. 112; *Stag Line Ltd v. Tyne Shiprepair Group Ltd* [1984] 2 Lloyd's Rep. 211.

principal)[26] or by equitable principles (*e.g.* that requiring a person in a fiduciary position to make full disclosure before entering into a contract with his beneficiary).[27] It would not necessarily be an abuse of language to describe the breach of such duties as deception.[28]

2.11 Problems of causation apart, there is a further reason why silence should not give rise to liability for deception in the absence of any duty of disclosure: *viz.* that it cannot legitimately be regarded as dishonest. It was suggested above that conduct which the civil law regards as entirely lawful should not be categorised as dishonest for the purposes of the criminal law.[29] A seller of goods, for example, is under no duty to disclose the fact that his price is exorbitant: *caveat emptor.* Even if he has induced the buyer to believe that the price approximates to the market price, in the absence of any representation to that effect the contract of sale is unimpeachable. Therefore, it is submitted, the seller may have obtained the price by deception but he has not done so dishonestly.[30] Similarly a commodity broker may well be deceiving his clients if he allows them to suppose that commodities are a safe investment; but on this view the deception would not be dishonest unless he either made some representation or was subject to a duty of disclosure by virtue of being in a fiduciary position.[31] It would be anomalous if the broker were guilty of an offence of deception when, in the eyes of the civil law, the client had only himself to blame.

2.12 This preliminary discussion suggests that on a charge of any deception offence the prosecution must prove the following (in addition to the specific requirements of the particular offence):

(1) that the alleged victim was in a certain state of mind, which may conveniently be referred to as "belief", with reference to a proposition which was in fact false;

(2) that this belief was induced, at least in part, by the defendant's words or conduct;

---

26 Possibly the practice of "churning" by a stockbroker (*i.e.* turning over the client's portfolio with excessive frequency so as to maximise the commission payable) could be treated as deception by failure to disclose the real reasons for the dealing.

27 *Gillett v. Peppercorne* (1840) 3 Beav. 78; *Bentley v. Craven* (1853) 18 Beav. 75; *Tate v. Williamson* (1866) L.R. 2 Ch. App. 55; *cf. Jenkins v. Livesey* [1985] 2 W.L.R. 47. On fiduciary relationships see *infra.* para. 4.14ff.

28 But *cf.R. v. Secretary of State for Home Department, ex p. Khawaja* [1984] A.C. 74, where the House of Lords apparently assumed that, even if a prospective immigrant owes a duty to disclose material facts to the immigration authority, a deliberate failure to do so would not amount to fraud or deception.

29 *Supra,* para. 1.10ff.

30 In *Williams (Jean-Jacques)* [1980] Crim.L.R. 589, *supra* para. 2.06, it was argued that the defendant had made no representation but conceded that he had been dishonest. The concession was perhaps unwarranted.

31 *Cf. infra,* para. 4.14ff.

(3) that the defendant obtained the benefit in question *by* the deception, *i.e.*

    (a) that the mistaken belief had some effect in inducing the victim to allow the defendant to obtain the benefit, and

    (b) that the obtaining of the benefit was not too remote a consequence of the victim's mistaken belief; and

(4) that the defendant acted in the necessary state of mind, *viz.*:

    (a) dishonestly,

    (b) intending to induce the belief (or being reckless whether he did so), and

    (c) knowing that the proposition believed by the victim was false (or being reckless whether it was).

These elements must now be considered in turn.

MISTAKEN BELIEF

The proposition believed

Fact and law

2.13 Since the essence of deception is the inducement of a mistaken belief in the victim's mind, the logical starting-point for the prosecution is to prove that the victim believed some proposition of fact to be true which was in fact false. It is not necessary for this purpose to observe the time-honoured distinction between propositions of fact and of law, since section 15(4) of the Theft Act 1968 expressly provides that the deception may be "as to fact or as to law". Thus a deception offence might be committed if a trader added 15% to a bill on the false pretext that VAT was payable, or if a seller of goods falsely assured the buyer that he had no redress in respect of defects. But it may be unwise to rely on a deception as to law unless there is no other way of framing the charge: the prosecution must be prepared to show both that the proposition of law is indeed incorrect and that the defendant realised it might be.

Intentions and promises

2.14 Probably the most important part of the statutory definition of "deception" is the provision that it includes "a deception as to the present intentions of the person using the deception or any other person".[32] The effect is to abolish the rule in *Dent*,[33] that it was not a false pretence to make a promise which one had no intention of keeping. There will now be a deception if a person who does not intend to do something

32 Theft Act 1968 s. 15(4).
33 [1955] 2 Q.B. 590.

leads another to believe that he does (or *vice versa*), whether he achieves this effect by promising to do it or in any other way. The prosecution need no longer attempt to disprove some implied proposition of concrete fact, *e.g.* that the defendant was *capable* of performing his promise, but can simply rely on the fact that he had no intention of doing so. Furthermore it is expressly provided that it is sufficient if one person deceives another as to the intentions of a third. It is, however, an essential element of deception that the proposition of fact which the victim is induced to believe must be false.[34] Therefore the prosecution must establish that the defendant (or the third party) did not in fact have the intention in question at the time when the victim was led to believe that he did—which may be either the time when the promise was made or some later stage. If the defendant originally intended to keep his promise (or it cannot be proved that he did not), his subsequent decision to break it, however dishonest, does not in itself constitute deception; but he may be guilty of deception if he fails to communicate his decision, particularly if he so conducts himself as to convey the impression that his intentions are unchanged.[35]

2.15 A less clear case is that of the defendant who *does* hope to carry out his promise if possible, but knows that he is unlikely to be in a position to do so: for example, the trader who is on the brink of insolvency but continues to order goods in the hope that something will turn up. There is no deception as to his intentions, since (like any honest debtor) he intends to pay if he can. The deception, if any, is as to the likelihood of his being *able* to pay. It will be necessary to establish that he deliberately induced his suppliers to over-estimate their prospects of being paid. An alternative approach is to rely on a deception as to the defendant's own estimate of the probabilities involved, rather than as to his actual financial position; but it comes to much the same thing, since in either case it will have to be proved that he knew he was creating a false impression. Whether his conduct was misleading at all will depend on the facts, but it is probably not sufficient merely to show that he was not supremely confident of his ability to pay: no-one expects a trader to go out of business as soon as he sees the slightest risk of insolvency.[36] Only if the risk is a serious one could it be said that the creditor is deceived.

Forecasts
2.16 Since a promise is not a statement and therefore cannot be true or false, it can only amount to a deception if it causes its recipient to believe

---

34 *Infra,* para. 2.20.
35 *Infra,* para. 2.44ff.
36 *Cf. infra,* para. 9.06ff.

some proposition to be true which is in fact false (*e.g.* that the maker of the promise intends to keep it). Indictments sometimes charge the defendant with the deception that he would do *x*, but this is strictly incorrect: the proper form is to allege the deception that he then intended to do *x*. The position is similar in the case of forecasts of future events. Admittedly a forecast is a statement of a sort and may be either true or false;[37] but (dicta to the contrary notwithstanding)[38] it is clear that for the purposes of the law of deception the victim's belief must relate to *existing* facts, past or present, and not to the future.[39] It does not follow that fraudulent forecasts cannot constitute deception. The making of a forecast, like that of a promise, will normally lead its recipient to draw certain inferences as to existing facts, and in particular as to its maker's state of mind. It is clearly a deception to make a forecast which one knows will not be fulfilled. As in the case of promises, the position is less clear if the person making the forecast is himself in doubt as to the outcome. A tipster is not expected to be certain that all of his tips will prove to be good ones. What he must not do is to give his customers the impression that he has inside knowledge which he does not in fact have,[40] or that for any other reason he is more confident of success than in fact he is.

Opinions
2.17 Propositions of fact must be distinguished from matters of opinion, which by definition cannot be shown to be true or false. The act of inducing another person to form an opinion cannot in itself amount to a deception, though there may be a deception if the victim is also misled on a point of fact (*e.g.* if he is led to believe that the defendant honestly holds the opinion in question, or that there are reasonable grounds for holding it). The distinction between fact and opinion is an issue verging on the philosophical, but for practical purposes it is essentially a matter of whether the belief in question can be *proved* to be false (or true). If it cannot, it is mere opinion, and it does not become fact merely because the consensus of informed opinion is all one way. In *Levine and Wood*[41] a tea and coffee service made of poor quality metal covered with a transparent film of silver was described as "the best silver plate"; this was held not to be a false pretence although no-one with any knowledge of plate would have agreed with the description. Clearly it is not deception merely to express a high opinion of poor merchandise. If, however, there is an

---

37 Even at the time when it is made, according to A.R. White (1974) 90 L.Q.R. 15.
38 *e.g. Metropolitan Police Commissioner v. Charles* [1977] A.C. 177 at p. 185 *per* Viscount Dilhorne.
39 *Gilmartin* [1983] Q.B. 953.
40 If he does have inside knowledge, he may be committing an offence for entirely different reasons: *infra,* para. 8.16ff.
41 (1876) 10 Cox 374.

accepted scale of quality, so that it can be objectively determined whether the goods merit the description they are given, the question is no longer one of opinion but of fact. Thus on the facts of *Levine and Wood* it would be sufficient if the expression "best silver plate" were commonly regarded as denoting a certain minimum content of silver.[42]

2.18 A similar problem arises where the defendant puts a specific and inflated value on his goods or services. He may do this either by way of comparison between his price and that charged by others (*e.g.* describing as "worth £10" goods which can be bought elsewhere for a fraction of that sum), or as an assessment of the amount due to him where no fixed price has been agreed. Ultimately the question is the same in each case, *viz.* was the statement intended to be understood as relating to the defendant's subjective opinion, or to the market value of what he was providing (which is a verifiable fact)? In most cases the latter interpretation will be the more natural one. In *Bassett and Jeff*[43] the defendants were charged with obtaining money by the false pretence that they had done necessary repairs on the victim's roof, that they had done the work in a proper and workmanlike manner and that £35 was a fair and reasonable sum to charge. The Court of Appeal rejected the argument that the last allegation related to a matter of opinion: it was

> "really part and parcel of the real false pretence alleged, which was that they had done necessary repairs to the roof and that those repairs could be measured by this sum of £35. In other words, it was all one false pretence. . ."[44]

It is not clear from the court's reasoning whether there would still have been a false pretence if the repairs *had* been necessary but the sum of £35 was an exorbitant charge for the work done. On principle this should have been sufficient, provided that the victim was led to believe that £35 was a rough approximation to the going rate for the job.

2.19 If it can be established that what was induced in the victim was a mistaken belief and not merely an opinion, the deception is (subject to the necessary mental element) made out. It is no defence that the statement which induced the belief was expressed as one of opinion rather than fact. On the orthodox view (*viz.* that deception always involves misrepresen-

---

42 At the time when the case was decided this would not have been sufficient, since the false pretence had to relate to the *type* of goods offered and not merely to their quality: *Bryan* (1857) Dears. & B. 265; *Lee* (1859) 8 Cox 233; *Williamson* (1869) 11 Cox 328. But in *Ardley* (1871) L.R. 1 C.C.R. 301 it was held a false pretence to describe 6-carat gold as 15-carat, because it was a misrepresentation as to an objective fact. It was immaterial that the item in question was of the *type* it was stated to be, *viz.* a gold chain. This decision clearly represents the law today.
43 (1966) 51 Cr.App. R. 28.
44 At p. 31, *per* Lord Parker C.J.

tation), the express statement of opinion carries an implied statement that there are reasonable grounds for it;[45] on the view here advanced, it is the inducement of the belief which constitutes the deception, and the manner in which that effect is achieved is immaterial. Nor is the deception nullified merely because it is a salesman's "puff" of a type which is often exaggerated. A *mere* puff is by definition a matter of opinion rather than fact; but a false statement of fact is no less a deception because such statements are commonly made. This factor may be relevant to the issue of dishonesty,[46] but not to that of deception.

Falsity

2.20   Clearly there is no deception if the proposition which the victim is induced to believe is in fact true; and this is so even if the defendant himself was convinced that it was false,[47] though in that case he could presumably be convicted of an attempt.[48] The falsity of the proposition is an element of the *actus reus* and must be proved by the prosecution.[49] Where the proposition is such that it would be easy for the defence to prove it if it were true, but difficult for the prosecution to disprove even if it were false, it has been said that the burden of proof is on the defence;[50] but the better view is that the burden remains on the prosecution throughout. In *Ng*[51] the defendant attempted to obtain money by claiming that she was in a position to influence a magistrate before whom the victim was due to appear; the Privy Council held that it was for the prosecution to prove that she was *not* in such a position, not for the defence to prove that she was. In *Mandry and Wooster*[52] the defendants were street traders who sold a certain scent at £1 for four bottles, claiming that it was on sale in the shops at two guineas a bottle. A police officer gave evidence that he had visited four local shops and that the scent was not on sale in any of them. In cross-examination he was asked whether he had been to Selfridges and he replied that he had not. The jury were directed that the question did not affect the prosecution's case because it was up to the defence to prove that the scent *was* on sale at Selfridges, and they had adduced no evidence to that effect. The Court of Appeal held that it was for the prosecution to disprove the statement and not for the defence to prove it, but dismissed the appeal on the ground that there was ample evidence of the statement's falsity in the absence of

45   *Smith v. Land and House Property Corp.* (1884) 28 Ch.D. 7.
46   *Supra,* para. 1.30.
47   *Deller* (1952) 36 Cr.App.R. 184.
48   Criminal Attempts Act 1981 s. 1(2); but *cf. Anderton v. Ryan* [1985] 2 All E.R. 355.
49   *Flint* (1821) Russ. & Ry. 460.
50   *Sampson* (1885) 52 L.T. 772 at p. 774, per Lord Coleridge C.J., *arguendo.*
51   [1958] A.C. 173.
52   [1973] 1 W.L.R. 1232.

any evidence of its truth. The question about Selfridges was, as the trial judge had indicated, of no evidential value.

> "Such a question with an unsatisfactory answer from the point of view of the person cross-examining constitutes no evidence at all to put into the scale against the evidence of the police officer. If the defence wished to prove anything about Selfridges, or even to suggest anything which the jury might accept, then they were, of course, at liberty to call evidence in relation thereto. . ."[53]

Belief

2.21 Before any deception can be said to have taken place it is essential that a certain state of mind be induced in the victim with reference to the false proposition in question. The required state of mind may conveniently be referred to as a belief that the proposition is true, although, as we have seen, the word "belief" is given a somewhat extended meaning in this context.[54] In any case the word does not appear in the statutory definition of "deception", and in a borderline case it is the scope of the latter word which is crucial. With this reservation, we now consider what a person's attitude to a given proposition must be before he can be said to believe it for the purposes of the law of deception.

Knowledge of falsity

2.22 In the first place, it is obviously not sufficient if the intended victim of the deception is fully aware that the proposition is false.[55] Formerly this would have been treated as a problem of causation: although there was a false pretence, the defendant did not obtain the property *by* false pretences because the pretence was unsuccessful. The new requirement of deception, however, is a "two-sided" concept,[56] involving not only deceptive conduct but also the intended effect on the victim's mind; if the victim knows the truth, there is no deception at all and the question of causation does not arise. It will therefore be impossible in these circumstances to obtain a conviction of one of the full offences of deception, even if the defendant hoped and expected that the victim would be taken in, and even if, in spite of knowing the truth, the victim allows him to get what he wanted (perhaps in order to trap him).[57] But a conviction of an attempt will be possible,[58] provided that the acts done

---

53 At p. 1238, *per* Mocatta J.
54 *Supra,* para. 2.05.
55 *Hickmott v. Curd* [1971] 1 W.L.R. 1221.
56 E.Griew, *op. cit.* at para. 6.42.
57 *Mills* (1857) D. & B. 205.
58 *Hensler* (1870) 11 Cox 570; *Light* (1915) 11 Cr.App.R. 111.

are "more than merely preparatory" to the obtaining of the benefit desired:[59] this was apparently so even after the House of Lords' ruling in *Haughton v, Smith*[60] that it is not an offence to attempt the impossible,[61] and the position is confirmed by the Criminal Attempts Act 1981.[62]

Awareness of risk of falsity
2.23   At the opposite extreme it is obviously sufficient if the victim is totally convinced that the proposition is true. Between the two extremes, however, the position is less clear. If, for example, the defendant offered goods for sale which were in fact stolen but which he claimed were his own property, the prospective purchaser might form various conclusions as to the truth of the statement. If he were certain that the goods belonged to the defendant, he would have been deceived; if he were certain that they were stolen, he would not. But he might not be sure either way. He might conclude that the goods were probably stolen, or that they probably were not. If, in either case, he agreed to buy them, could it be said that he believed they were not stolen? The converse question, *i.e.* whether he believed that they *were* stolen, would be crucial if the purchaser were himself charged with the offence of handling stolen goods: that offence may be committed by (*inter alia*) receiving stolen goods, "knowing or believing" them to be stolen.[63] In this context it has been held that a person does not "believe" goods to be stolen unless he realises that, in the light of the circumstances known to him, there can be no other reasonable conclusion:[64] it is not sufficient merely that he thinks they are more likely stolen than not.[65] It might be argued by analogy that a person who thinks a statement is probably true, but realises it may not be, does not *believe* it to be true and is therefore not deceived if it is false: he must be virtually certain that it is true. Such an interpretation would probably be unduly restrictive. It would mean, for example, that a person who accepted a bad cheque, unsupported by a cheque card, would not be deceived unless he failed to appreciate that there was a substantial risk of the cheque being dishonoured. This is perhaps a case where the ordinary meaning of the word "belief" may be misleading, since the definition of deception (unlike that of handling stolen goods) does not make express use of it. The concept of belief is a useful one for the purpose of exposition, but ultimately it is the meaning of "deception" which is crucial. It is submitted that a person should be regarded as deceived if he

59   Criminal Attempts Act 1981 s. 1(1).
60   [1975] A.C. 476.
61   *Cf. Edwards* [1978] Crim.L.R. 49.
62   s. 1(2).
63   Theft Act 1968 s. 22(1).
64   *Hall (Edward)* [1985] Crim.L.R. 377.
65   *Reader* (1977) 66 Cr.App.R. 33.

is led to believe that a proposition is probably true when in fact it is false, even if he appreciates that it may be false.

Subconscious assumptions

2.24 It is clearly unnecessary that the victim should have given conscious thought to the truth or falsity of the proposition in question. He may simply assume from the defendant's conduct that all is as it should be. A person who orders goods or services, for example, makes an implied representation that he intends to pay for them and expects to be in a position to do so. If the representee provides the goods or services requested without addressing his conscious mind to the question whether the representation is true, and in fact it is not, there is an obtaining by deception.[66] It has been objected that in this context the courts have paid insufficient attention to the requirement of belief which is implicit in the concept of deception, and that it is arguable that one is not deceived unless one consciously adverts to the matter in question.[67] Whatever the merits of this argument, its acceptance would drive a coach and horses through the legislation and must be regarded as highly unlikely. Whether or not a subconscious assumption is fairly described as a belief, it is sufficient for a charge of deception.

Indifference

2.25 A more controversial situation is that in which, whether or not he addresses his mind to the issue, the victim simply does not care whether the proposition in question is true or false. Usually this factor will be fatal to a deception charge because the element of causation will be lacking: the benefit in question will not have been obtained *by* the deception if the victim would still have co-operated even if he had known that the proposition was false.[68] But it may be that he is not concerned whether it is true or false, *provided he does not know it to be false*. This state of qualified indifference will in fact be the normal attitude of a person to whom a cheque card or credit card is presented by way of payment for goods or services. A person who accepts a cheque *not* backed by a cheque card does so on the assumption, induced by the drawer, that the cheque is good; if the drawer knows that it is bad, there is no difficulty in establishing an obtaining by deception. The position is quite different where a cheque card is used. There is still an implied representation that the cheque is good, in the sense that there is no reason to suppose it will not be honoured; but this representation is true, provided that the conditions set out on the card are fulfilled, because the effect is to create a

66 *Infra,* para. 2.39.
67 A.T.H. Smith, "The Idea of Criminal Deception" [1982] Crim.L.R. 721 at p. 723ff.
68 *Infra,* para. 2.49ff.

unilateral contract between the payee and the bank under which the bank is obliged to honour the cheque. However, there is in this case an additional representation to the effect that the drawer has the bank's authority to bind it in this way.[69] If the card is not his, or if there are insufficient funds in the account to meet the cheque and he has neither an overdraft facility nor any prospect of acquiring the necessary funds, this representation will be false. Thus far the position is clear. The difficulty is that it may be of no concern to the payee whether this latter representation is true or false: the cheque will be honoured anyway. Payment is guaranteed unless the stipulated conditions are not fulfilled (*e.g.* because the drawer's signature bears no resemblance to that on the card) or the payee actually *knows* that the drawer has no authority (in which case he would be a party to an attempted fraud on the bank). Can it then be said that the drawer has obtained goods or services by deception if in fact he has no authority to use the card? We must distinguish three issues:

(a) Did the payee *believe* that the drawer had the bank's authority?
(b) Did the drawer *induce* him to believe it? and
(c) Did the payee allow the drawer to obtain the benefit in question *because* he believed it?

It is the first of these issues with which we are concerned at this stage, and the others will be considered in due course.[70] But it will be apparent that all three are intimately connected.

2.26 In *Metropolitan Police Commissioner v. Charles*[71] the defendant drew 25 cheques for £30 each by way of payment for gaming chips, and backed each one with his cheque card. The effect was that his account became overdrawn to an extent greatly in excess of his agreed overdraft limit. He was convicted of obtaining a pecuniary advantage (*viz.* the increased overdraft) by deception (*viz.* the implied representation that he was authorised to use the card as he did), and the House of Lords dismissed his appeal. It was held to be immaterial that the manager of the gambling club was, as he made clear in his evidence, totally indifferent to the state of the defendant's account. The crucial point was that he would not have accepted the cheques if he had *known* that the defendant had no authority to back them with his cheque card. Lord Edmund-Davies put the matter thus:

---

69 Strictly speaking it is a question of fact whether this representation is implied in any given case: *Charles* [1977] A.C. 177 at p. 186, *per* Viscount Dilhorne. But in the normal case it clearly will be.
70 *Infra*, paras. 2.42, 2.53.
71 [1977] A.C. 177.

". . . the witness [*sc.* the manager] made clear that the accused's cheques were accepted *only* because he produced a cheque card, and he repeatedly stressed that, had he been aware that the accused was using his cheque book and cheque card 'in a way in which he was not allowed or entitled to use [them]' no cheque would have been accepted. The evidence of that witness, taken as a whole, points irresistibly to the conclusions (a) that by this dishonest conduct the accused deceived [the manager] in the manner averred in the particulars of the charges and (b) that [the manager] was thereby induced to accept the cheques because of his belief that the representations as to both cheque and card were true."[72]

Lord Diplock concluded similarly that the manager:

". . . would not have taken the accused's cheques had he not believed that the accused was authorised by the bank to use the cheque card to back them."[73]

2.27 Essentially their Lordships' reasoning was as follows: if the defendant makes a representation which he knows to be false, and he obtains a benefit which he would not have been allowed to obtain if the representee had known that the representation was false, he has obtained the benefit by deception. The weakness of this reasoning is that it skates over the essential element of belief. In so far as the decision recognises the requirement of belief at all, it is only in an attenuated form. Not only is there no need for the representee to address his mind to the truth of the representation, but it is sufficient if its truth or falsity is a matter of complete indifference to him as long as he does not know that it is false. To describe this frame of mind as a belief that the representation is true may be an odd use of language. It must be repeated, however, that the issue is not strictly whether this attitude constitutes a belief, but whether the inducement of it constitutes a deception; and *Charles* decides that it does.

2.28 Similar considerations apply where the defendant uses a credit card so as to impose on the issuing company an obligation to pay, but for some reason (*e.g.* because the card is stolen, or the transaction would take him over his credit limit) he does not have the company's authority to do so. In *Lambie*[74] the defendant used her card to buy goods in a Mothercare shop at a time when she had already substantially exceeded her credit limit. She was charged with obtaining a pecuniary advantage by deception.[75] The shop assistant who had sold her the goods gave evidence to the effect that she had made no assumption as to the state of

---

72 At p. 193.
73 At p. 183.
74 [1982] A.C. 449.
75 This charge would no longer be available since the repeal of Theft Act 1968 s. 16(2)(*a*): Theft Act 1978 s. 5(5).

the defendant's account and was concerned only to ensure that in due course Mothercare would be paid by the bank which had issued the card. The Court of Appeal quashed the conviction, distinguishing *Charles* on the ground that, where a shop has made arrangements with a bank for the acceptance of the bank's credit cards, it has bought from the bank the right to sell goods to card-holders without regard to the position as between each customer and the bank.[76] The House of Lords disapproved this reasoning and restored the conviction. Lord Roskill, giving the only reasoned speech, said:

> "My Lords, . . . the Court of Appeal . . . laid too much emphasis upon the undoubted, but to my mind irrelevant, fact that [the assistant] said she made no assumption about the respondent's credit standing with the bank. They reasoned from the absence of assumption that there was no evidence from which the jury could conclude that she was 'induced by a false representation that the defendant's credit standing at the bank gave her authority to use the card'. But . . . that is not the relevant question. Following the decision of this House in *R v. Charles,* it is in my view clear that the representation arising from the presentation of a credit card has nothing to do with the respondent's credit standing at the bank but is a representation of actual authority to make the contract with, in this case, Mothercare on the bank's behalf that the bank will honour the voucher upon presentation. Upon that view, the existence and terms of the agreement between the bank and Mothercare are irrelevant, as is the fact that Mothercare, because of that agreement, would look to the bank for payment."[77]

2.29 This reasoning is perhaps somewhat suspect in so far as it seeks to draw a distinction between an assumption as to the defedant's credit standing with the bank and an assumption as to her authority to use the credit card. Since she had authority to use the card only as long as she remained within her credit limit, the assistant could hardly make an assumption as to her authority without also making an assumption as to the state of her account. The distinction can perhaps be defended on the basis that by "credit standing" his Lordship was referring to the bank's view of the defendant's general creditworthiness, not to the state of the particular account; but it seems clear that this is not what the assistant meant by her evidence, nor what the Court of Appeal understood her to have meant. Nevertheless it is submitted with respect that the House was right to regard the case as being on all fours with *Charles.* The Mothercare assistant, like the manager of the gambling club, did not care whether the defendant had authority to use the card; but she would not have sold the goods had she known that no such authority existed. According to *Charles* this is equivalent to a belief that the defendant did have authority, and the assistant was therefore deceived.

76 [1981] 1 W.L.R. 78.
77 [1982] A.C. 449 at p. 459f.

Deception of a machine

2.30   Whatever the precise nature of the state of mind which must be induced, it presumably cannot exist unless there is a mind for it to exist in. It is no doubt possible to deceive a company, because the mental state of those who control the company can be imputed to it,[78] but the point is academic because it would be simpler to allege a deception of the controllers: the person deceived need not be the one from whom the benefit is obtained.[79] A more difficult problem is that of whether it is possible to deceive a machine. In *Davies v. Flackett*[80] Bridge J. doubted it, but the point was not decided; in *Clayman*[81] a trial judge ruled that it was not deception to jam a parking meter with a beer-can ring. The question is likely to be one of increasing importance in the context of computer fraud. If a person feeds inaccurate data into a computer, or gains access to confidential files by using someone else's password, can it be said that he is deceiving the computer? In *Moritz*[82] it was ruled by a trial judge that, since VAT returns are processed by computer, the submission of false returns does not involve an intent to deceive for the purposes of section 39(2)(*a*) of the Value Added Tax Act 1983;[83] and this is probably the prevalent view. One would hardly say (except metaphorically) that the computer *believes* the input to be accurate. On the other hand it might be argued that here again the notion of belief may be misleading, since it is not expressly used in the legislation: strictly speaking the question is not whether a computer can have beliefs but whether it can be deceived, and it is not self-evidently absurd to suggest that it can. The problem does not arise if the fraud depends on the generation of false output which will then be acted upon, because in that case the person reading the output will be deceived. It does not follow that every "deception" of a computer is also a deception of a person: it may be that the desired benefit (*e.g.* the printing of a cheque) will be conferred automatically without any human intervention. In that case it would be a transparent fiction to treat the computer as the agent of its human controllers.

INDUCEMENT OF THE BELIEF

Causation

2.31   The defendant cannot be held responsible for another's mis-apprehension unless it was induced by something which the defendant

---

78   *Cf. infra*, para. 4.26ff.
79   *Infra*, para. 2.60.
80   [1973] R.T.R. 8.
81   (1972) *The Times*, 1 July.
82   (1981), unreported.
83   *Infra*, para. 10.18.

said or did. If it was brought about by a third party, or by the stupidity or incompetence of the person mistaken, there is no deception by the defendant: the essential ingredient of causation is lacking.[84] In *Roebuck*[85] the defendant offered a chain to a pawnbroker, falsely claiming that it was silver; the pawnbroker tested it and accepted it as security for a loan. It was found that "he paid this money relying on his own examination and test of the chain, and without placing any reliance on the statement of the prisoner". It was held that there could be no conviction of the full offence but only of an attempt: the pawnbroker did believe that the chain was silver, as he was intended to, but on the basis of his own test and not the false pretence. The defendant tried to deceive him, but failed. The position would be otherwise if the pawnbroker had taken the statement into account in making his assessment. This is probably so even if he would have reached the same conclusion on the basis of the test alone. The defendant's conduct must be at least partly responsible for the misapprehension formed by the victim, but in principle there is no reason why it should be the *crucial* factor.[86]

2.32   Similar principles would apply if the defendant were to use a credit card without authority to do so, and the person to whom the card was tendered took the precaution of telephoning the issuing company for clearance. Normally such a check would of course reveal the fraud, and the attempt at deception would have failed. But if clearance were given (*e.g.* because the card had been stolen and its loss had not yet been reported) it might be argued that the payee's belief in the user's authority was induced entirely by the issuing company and not by the user himself. Similarly if the defendant tendered a bad cheque and the recipient consulted a "stop list" before accepting it, it might be argued that it was not the defendant's conduct which misled the recipient but the stop list. It is submitted that such a defence would be unsound. The element of causation is established if the belief is to some extent induced by the defendant, even if it is partly due to other factors for which he is not responsible. The telephone check and the stop list are safeguards but they are obviously not copper-bottomed guarantees of the customer's honesty; they may reassure the trader but they will not entirely displace the impression created by the defendant himself.

2.33   *A fortiori* there would be no difficulty in establishing the element of causation merely because the victim had the opportunity to discover the

---

84   But distinguish the requirement that the obtaining of the benefit be the result of the deception: *infra,* para. 2.49ff.
85   (1856) D. & B. 24.
86   *Cf. infra.* para. 2.56ff.

truth and omitted to do so, *e.g.* if a shop assistant accepted a credit card without telephoning the issuing company although the value of the transaction was in excess of the prescribed limit. There is no defence of "contributory negligence".[87] It might perhaps be argued in such a case that the assistant's failure to make the normal enquiries betrayed a state of total apathy with regard to the user's authority, and that such an attitude cannot fairly be treated as a belief that he *has* authority. Such an argument would be most unlikely to succeed. *Charles*[88] and *Lambie*[89] have established that the assistant is deceived if he does not know of the user's lack of authority, provided that he would not have accepted the card if he *had* known. His attitude may be one of total indifference. That being so, it seems immaterial whether his efforts to ascertain the truth have been assiduous or non-existent. Of course it may be that he would still have accepted the card even if he had known that the user was not authorised to use it, in which case (even if there is a deception at all) the benefit will not have been obtained *by* the deception.[90] But it cannot be assumed, merely because he fails to make proper enquiry, that he would still have co-operated even if the truth had been brought to his attention. Reluctance to prevent fraud is not the same as readiness to assist in it.

Means of inducement

Express statements

2.34 The indictment should give particulars of the means by which the defendant is alleged to have brought about the mistaken belief. The most obvious way of inducing someone to believe in the truth of a proposition is by expressly stating it to him, and an express statement should be relied upon whenever possible. It may be that the prosecution wish to allege not one false statement but several. Provided that all the statements are alleged to have been directed at the obtaining of the same benefit, they do not represent distinct offences but only different ways of committing the same one; therefore they may be included in a single count without thereby rendering it bad for duplicity or uncertainty.[91] For the same reason it is not necessary to prove more than one of the statements alleged.[92] In *Kevin Brown*,[93] in the context of the offence of procuring an investment by false statements,[94] the Court of Appeal set out the relevant principles as follows:

---

87 *Jessop* (1853) D. & B. 442.
88 [1977] A.C. 177; *supra,* para. 2.26.
89 [1982] A.C. 449; *supra,* para. 2.28.
90 *Infra,* para. 2.55.
91 *Linnell* [1969] 1 W.L.R. 1514.
92 *Lince* (1873) 12 Cox 451.
93 (1983) 79 Cr.App.R. 115.
94 Prevention of Fraud (Investments) Act 1958 s. 13(1); *infra,* para. 8.05ff.

"1. Each ingredient of the offence must be proved to the satisfaction of each and every member of the jury (subject to the majority direction). 2. However, where a number of matters are specified in the charge as together constituting one ingredient in the offence, and any one of them is capable of doing so, then it is enough to establish the ingredient that any one of them is proved; but (because of the first principle above) any such matter must be proved to the satisfaction of the whole jury. The jury should be directed accordingly, and it should be made clear to them as well that they should all be satisfied that the statement upon which they are agreed was an inducement as alleged."[95]

2.35 A decision which at first sight appears inconsistent with these principles is *Agbim*,[96] where it was alleged that the defendant had submitted an expenses claim which included various false statements as to the expenditure incurred. The Court of Appeal held that, provided the jury were satisfied that the claim as a whole was deceptive, there was no need for them to agree that any particular statement was false. The decision was subsequently explained in *Kevin Brown* on the basis that the false statement which had to be proved was the statement of the *total* expenditure claimed, not the individual items.

"The false statement was that £1,383.20 had been paid when it had not. The other false statements were the means by which the accused had sought to convince the . . . authorities of the truth of that statement. They were themselves statements, but not the statement relied upon as an ingredient in the offence. They were matters which on investigation would help to prove the falsity of the figure of £1,383.20, and also go to prove knowledge and the dishonesty of the accused. Different members of the jury may arrive at their conclusions by different routes. Far from invalidating their final conclusion, different approaches which lead to the same result may often be seen as strengthening the verdict. They may be able to say that, whichever way one looks at it, the case is proved."[97]

An alternative explanation is that, whereas *Kevin Brown* was concerned with an offence of making a false statement, *Agbim* was a case of deception; and it was suggested above that on a charge of a deception offence there is no need to prove a false statement at all.[98] In that case it follows that there is no need to prove any particular false statement. The deception in *Agbim* was not the *statement* that the defendant had paid out the amount claimed, but the inducement in the authorities of the *belief* that he had.

2.36 Even a statement which is literally true may constitute a deception if it is designed to give an impression which is false. The desired effect

95 At p. 119, *per* Eveleigh L.J.
96 [1979] Crim.L.R. 171.
97 (1983) 79 Cr.App.R. 115 at p. 118.
98 *Supra*, para. 2.06ff.

may be achieved by deliberately vague phraseology, as where an advertisement for sheet music was cunningly worded so as to suggest that what was being offered was some kind of musical contraption (although a careful reader would have realised that that could not be so).[99] Alternatively, it may be done by means of clear statements of fact which are true in themselves but are misleading by virtue of what is left out. As Lord Halsbury L.C. once pointed out:

> "If by a number of statements you intentionally give a false impression and induce a person to act upon it, it is not the less false, although if one takes each statement by itself there may be a difficulty in shewing that any specific statement is untrue."[1]

Thus in *Kylsant*[2] a prospectus saying (truthfully) that dividends had been regularly paid over a number of years was held to be "false in a material particular"[3] because it failed to point out that the dividends had not been paid out of current income. This type of case is greatly simplified if one accepts the argument that misrepresentation is not an essential element of deception:[4] it becomes unnecessary to explain to the jury how a statement can be literally true, yet at the same time false. It is not the statement that must be false, but the belief induced by the statement.

2.37   *A fortiori* it may be sufficient if the defendant's express statements are neither true nor false, but literally meaningless. In *Banaster*[5] a mini-cab driver picked up a foreign passenger at Heathrow Airport, claiming to be "an airport taxi", and told him that the "correct fare" for a ride to Ealing was £27.50. There was in fact no such thing as an airport taxi, nor was there any scale by which the "correct" fare might be determined. The driver's appeal against a conviction of obtaining by deception was dismissed by the Court of Appeal: even if he had said nothing which was positively false,[6] the jury had been properly directed that they might find in the defendant's statements the implication that it was "all official". If the decision is open to criticism it is not because the express statements made were not false, but because it was not made sufficiently clear exactly what was the false proposition which those statements might have induced the passenger to believe. Perhaps it was that the defendant was not merely entitled to pick up passengers at the airport but was also a member of a privileged class of taxi-drivers who were individually authorised to do so and were subject to supervision by the airport

99 *Lawrence* (1909) 2 Cr.App.R. 42.
1 *Aaron's Reefs Ltd v. Twiss* [1896] A.C. 273 at p. 281.
2 [1932] 1 K.B. 442.
3 Larceny Act 1861 s. 84.
4 *Supra*, para. 2.06ff.
5 (1978) 68 Cr.App.R. 272.
6 To say that one belongs to a class which does not in fact exist would seem to be a false statement: *cf. Barnard* (1837) 7 C. & P. 784.

authorities. Alternatively, it may have been simply that £27.50 was a reasonable approximation to the fare which most other taxi-drivers would charge.[7]

Words or conduct

2.38 The deception may be achieved "by words or conduct".[8] It is clear that words may be deceptive even if they do not amount to an express statement of fact (whether or not it is thought necessary to find an *implied* statement). A promise may give the impression that the maker intends to keep it, or has grounds for expecting to be able to do so. An expression of opinion may suggest that the speaker genuinely holds that opinion, or has grounds for doing so. A letter ordering goods may imply by its wording that the sender is carrying on a business requiring goods of that description.[9] A warning by a motor dealer that the reading on a car's odometer "may not be correct" can constitute a deception if it carries the false implication that the dealer does not *know* the reading is incorrect.[10] There is no reason to suppose that the categories of verbal deception are closed.

2.39 Nor is it necessary for a deception to be verbal. Perhaps nothing at all is written or said; even if words are used, the essence of the deception may lie rather in the nature of the transaction. There will probably be a deception where a person presents a money order or cheque which is not made out to him as if it were,[11] or purports to sell goods which he has no right to sell,[12] or conversely sells his own goods as if they were his employer's.[13] Where a person orders a meal in a restaurant,[14] takes a room in a hotel[15] or hails a taxi,[16] there is an implied representation that he has the money to pay,[17] or at least that he intends to pay[18] and expects to be able to do so when the time comes. In fact it seems that anyone who makes any contract is implicitly representing that he intends to perform at least the major obligations undertaken and has a reasonable prospect of being able to do so. The precise content of this representation in any given case will naturally depend on the terms of the contract, express or

---

7   *Cf. supra*, para. 2.18.
8   Theft Act 1968 s. 15(4).
9   *King* [1897] 1 Q.B. 214.
10   *King* [1979] Crim.L.R. 122.
11   *Story* (1805) Russ. & Ry. 81; *Davies (Arthur)* [1982] 1 All E.R. 513.
12   *Sampson* (1885) 52 L.T. 772.
13   *Rashid* [1977] 1 W.L.R. 298; *Doukas* [1978] 1 W.L.R. 372.
14   Conceded in *D.P.P. v. Ray* [1974] A.C. 370; but *cf. Jones* [1898] 1 Q.B. 119.
15   *Harris* (1975) 62 Cr.App.R. 28.
16   *Waterfall* [1970] 1 Q.B. 148.
17   *Ibid.*
18   In *Harris, supra* (n. 15), this was said to be a "more accurate description" of the deception.

implied, and therefore on what is expected in a particular commercial context.

2.40 The transaction which has given rise to the most discussion in the context of deception by conduct is that of writing a cheque. Several different representations have been suggested as being implicit in this action:

(1) That the drawer of the cheque has an account at the bank on which it is drawn. Admittedly this representation is incorporated in (4) below, but it certainly is implied[19] and it may be simpler to concentrate on it if it is in fact false: there will seldom be any difficulty in proving that the defendant knew he had no account there (unless he used to have an account and it is not clear whether he knew that it had been closed).[20]

(2) That there are sufficient funds in the account to cover the cheque. The suggestion that this representation is implied has been rejected,[21] since it would not normally be reasonable for the payee to infer that it is true. The drawer may have an overdraft facility, or he may have reason to expect that the bank will allow him to overdraw, or that sufficient money will be paid into the account before the cheque is presented.

(3) That the drawer has the bank's authority to draw a cheque on it for the amount in question.[22] This formulation was accepted until it was pointed out by Lord Diplock in *Charles*[23] that the customer is not the bank's agent for this purpose[24] and needs no authority to write cheques: it is the bank which needs the customer's authority to honour them.

(4) That the existing state of facts is such that in the ordinary course of events the cheque will be honoured. In various forms of words this representation has often been approved[25] and it should now be used instead of those above (with the possible exception of (1)). It is equally applicable to post-dated cheques, with the obvious qualification that the cheque will not be honoured if presented before the prescribed date.[26] The representation is not that the cheque *will* be honoured but that the existing circumstances are such that it is reasonable to *expect*

---

19 *Jackson* (1813) 3 Camp. 370; *Parker* (1837) 2 Mood. 1; *Maytum-White* (1957) 42 Cr.App.R. 165; *Page* [1971] 2 Q.B. 330.
20 *Walne* (1870) 11 Cox 647; *cf. Cosnett* (1901) 65 J.P. 472.
21 *Hazelton* (1874) L.R. 2 C.C.R. 134; *Page, supra* n. 19.
22 *Ibid.*
23 [1977] A.C. 177 at p. 182.
24 *Cf.* the position where he uses a cheque card: *supra,* para. 2.25.
25 *Hazelton, supra* n. 21; *Page, supra* n. 19; *Charles* [1977] A.C. 177; *Gilmartin* [1983] Q.B. 953.
26 *Gilmartin, supra* n. 25.

that it will be.[27] The traditional formulation, that the cheque is represented to be a "good and valid order" for the amount, has been criticised on the grounds that the validity of a cheque depends on the circumstances existing when it is presented, not when it is drawn;[28] it might alternatively be said that even a cheque which has no prospect of being honoured is "valid" if it satisfies the requirements of the Bills of Exchange Act.[29] Perhaps it is permissible, for the sake of brevity, to say simply that the cheque is represented to be a good cheque?

2.41 In particular circumstances there may be further representations implicit in the writing of a cheque, in addition to those referred to above. *Greenstein and Green*[30] concerned a variation on the practice (lawful in itself) of stagging, *i.e.* applying for new issues of shares with the intention of immediately selling at a profit. Knowing that the issues would probably be oversubscribed and that the shares would be allotted in proportion to the number applied for by each applicant, the defendants would apply for numbers of shares which were far in excess of the number they could afford to pay for. With each application they would enclose a cheque for the full amount; the issuing house would send a cheque (the "return cheque") for the difference between that amount and the price of the shares allotted; and the return cheque would generally be cleared in time for the original cheque to be honoured on first presentation. The defendants' convictions of obtaining property by deception were upheld by the Court of Appeal. Although the representation that each cheque would ordinarily be honoured on first presentation was in fact true (nearly 90% of them were), they were not "valid orders" because they could not be honoured unless the return cheques were cleared first. The court's reasoning emphasises that the defendants did not have the bank's authority to write the cheques, but since *Charles*[31] this argument appears to be suspect; and, that point aside, it is difficult to see how a cheque with a 90% chance of being honoured on first presentation can be said not to be a "valid order". In normal circumstances it will hardly be reasonable for the payee to assume that there is no risk whatsoever of the cheque's being dishonoured. It may or may not be *dishonest* to write a cheque without being absolutely certain that it will be honoured, but it is not necessarily a *deception*. It might have been preferable to treat *Greenstein* as a case where special circumstances (*e.g.* the expected level of demand for the shares) required the implication

27 *Ibid.*
28 Archbold (41st ed.) at para. 18–94.
29 Bills of Exchange Act 1882 s. 73.
30 [1975] 1 W.L.R. 1353.
31 [1977] A.C. 177.

of an additional representation, *viz.* that the cheques were likely to be honoured irrespective of any return cheque which might be forthcoming. The decision should not be taken as laying down a general rule that the drawer of a cheque is guilty of deception if the cheque can only be honoured when some repayment is received from the payee himself. In principle, and subject to special circumstances, it should depend whether the drawer expected to receive the repayment in time.

2.42   The cheque will often be backed by a cheque card, which operates as an undertaking on the part of the bank to honour the cheque if the prescribed conditions are fulfilled.[32] Even if the drawer of the cheque has no right to use the cheque card, it is impossible to convict on the basis of the representation that the cheque is likely to be honoured: it will be. Here too it is necessary to rely on a further representation, *viz.* that the drawer does have the bank's authority to use the card.[33] The same applies, *mutatis mutandis,* to the unauthorised use of a credit card.[34] It may be objected that a representation cannot legitimately be inferred as to a matter in which the representee has no interest; but the objection has less force if, as has been argued above, there is no need to find a representation at all.[35] The problem is whether a person can be said to have been deceived where the state of mind induced in him is one of indifference to the truth or falsity of the proposition in question. If (as the authorities suggest) he can,[36] it is immaterial whether the defendant induced that state of mind by means of a representation or by conduct alone.

2.43   In most cases of deception by conduct the victim will be aware of the conduct in question and will draw the appropriate inferences from the fact that the defendant is acting in that way; but this is not necessarily the case. The defendant may succeed in implanting a belief in the victim's mind without the victim ever realising that his belief is the defendant's doing, *e.g.* by altering a document in such a way that it does not appear to have been altered at all. There seems no reason why such conduct should not be regarded as deception. We have already suggested that it would be artificial to analyse the situation in terms of an implied representation,[37] but the difficulty disappears if there is no need to establish a representation at all. The defendant, by his conduct, has induced the victim to believe in the truth of a proposition which is in fact

---

32   *Supra,* para. 2.25.
33   *Charles* [1977] A.C. 177; *supra,* para. 2.26.
34   *Lambie* [1982] A.C. 449; *supra,* para. 2.28.
35   *Supra,* para. 2.06ff.
36   *Supra,* para. 2.25ff.
37   *Supra,* para. 2.07.

false. Whether the victim realises what the defendant has done in order to achieve that objective is beside the point.

Silence

2.44 A difficult problem is that of whether a deception may be effected by silence alone, *i.e.* by the failure to correct a misapprehension which was not brought about by deception in the first place. There are at least two variables which may be relevant, *viz.* (a) whether the uncorrected misapprehension has induced the victim to take some positive step in reliance on it, such as entering into a contract with the defendant, and (b) whether it was initially brought about (albeit innocently) by the defendant himself. If one party to a contract enters into it in reliance on a representation by the other party, which the other party at the time of making it believed to be true, but which he has since discovered to have been false at that time and has failed to correct, the latter party is guilty not merely of misrepresentation but of fraud (and presumably therefore of deception).[38] The original representation can be regarded as continuing up to the making of the contract, so that it is rendered fraudulent by knowledge subsequently acquired. The position appears to be the same if the representation was true when made but has ceased to be true, and the maker knew that it was no longer true but failed to correct it.[39]

2.45 In principle it should make no difference whether the representation which goes uncorrected relates to external facts or to the maker's own state of mind. In a fraud case it may well be the defendant's originally honest intentions which have altered, and the question may therefore arise whether he is committing a deception in failing to notify his change of heart to those with whom he is dealing. A possible obstacle to a finding of deception in this situation is the civil case of *Wales v. Wadham*.[40] Tudor Evans J. there refused to apply the principle of continuing representation to a woman who, having repeatedly told her estranged husband that she would never re-marry, subsequently agreed to settle her claim for maintenance without disclosing that she had changed her mind. Two reasons were given. First, the judge said:

> "A statement of intention is not a representation of existing fact, unless the person making it does not honestly hold the intention he is expressing, in

---

38 *Brownlie v. Campbell* (1880) 5 App. Cas. 925 at p. 950, *per* Lord Blackburn.
39 *Adamson v. Jarvis* (1827) 4 Bing. 66; *Denton v. Great Northern Railway Co.* (1856) 5 E. & B. 860. In *Arkwright v. Newbold* (1881) 17 Ch.D. 301 at p. 329, James L.J. appeared to suggest the contrary; but he gave no reasons for this view, and Cotton L.J. (with whom he purported to be in agreement) had expressly reserved his opinion on the point. See Spencer Bower and Turner, *The Law of Actionable Misrepresentation* (3rd ed.) at para. 104.
40 [1977] 1 W.L.R. 199; *cf. Jenkins v. Livesey* [1985] 2 W.L.R. 47.

which case there is a misrepresentation of fact in relation to the state of that person's mind."[41]

With respect, the fact that the person making the statement does have the intention he claims to have does not prevent the statement from being a representation of existing fact: it merely renders it true. The second reason was that the wife was not representing that she would never change her mind. This is true (indeed such an assurance would not be a representation at all), but irrelevant. The representation was that she intended not to re-marry, and her change of mind meant that that representation was no longer true. It is submitted that her failure to correct her earlier statements clearly amounted to misrepresentation, and indeed to deception.

2.46 If, however, a party to a contract enters into it under a misapprehension which was not induced by the other party at all, the other party's deliberate failure to point out the truth does not constitute misrepresentation. Whether it can ever amount to deception depends in part upon whether misrepresentation is an essential ingredient of deception. If so, mere silence is by definition insufficient (though what appears to be mere silence may on occasion be regarded as deception by conduct);[42] if not, the possibility of deception by silence remains open. The point is discussed above in connection with the implications of the view there advanced, that deception without misrepresentation is not a contradiction in terms.[43] It is there suggested that, even on this view, mere silence could not suffice unless the civil law imposed a positive duty of disclosure: in the absence of such a duty silence might or might not be deceptive, but it would not be dishonest.

2.47 Probably the position is much the same if the victim is not induced to enter into a contract but to act in reliance on his misapprehension in some other way, *e.g.* by providing services or handing over property: there will be a deception only if the misapprehension was originally brought about by the defendant himself. Duties of disclosure are unlikely to be applicable. If, however, the victim takes no positive steps at all, but merely refrains from taking steps which he would have taken if he had known the truth, it seems that silence does not constitute deception unless it can be treated as deception by conduct; but it may well be possible so to treat it. In *Borro and Abdullah*[44] airline passengers were held to have made a false representation, within the jurisdiction, by changing planes at Heathrow Airport without correcting their original representation to the

---

41 At p. 211.
42 *Supra,* para. 2.06; *infra,* para. 2.47.
43 *Supra,* para. 2.10f.
44 [1973] Crim.L.R. 513.

airline (outside the jurisdiction) that their baggage was for their own personal use and did not include prohibited goods. The misrepresentation was perceived in their conduct rather than in the mere failure to correct their earlier representation; but Lord Lane C.J. later observed that "the acts which were said to amount to deceit . . . were somewhat tenuous".[45] Similarly, in *D.P.P. v. Ray*[46] a bare majority of the House of Lords held that a diner in a restaurant had deceived the waiter by continuing to sit at his table after deciding to leave without paying the bill. But it was conceded by the Crown that there would have been no deception if the waiter had not been in the dining-room between the moment when the defendant changed his mind and the moment when he left. He deceived the waiter, not merely by failing to notify him of the position, but by continuing to present to him the appearance of an honest customer.[47] It is perhaps understandable that the courts should prefer to treat as deception by conduct what is in reality a mere failure to correct one's earlier representations, and the consequential restriction of the scope of deception is unlikely to be of practical significance. Where there is a continuing relationship between two parties (*e.g.* agent and principal), and one of them decides not to honour his obligations to the other (or even realises that he cannot do so), it seems that there will be a deception by conduct as soon as the defaulting party has any further dealings with the other and fails to make his position clear.

EFFECT OF THE BELIEF

2.48   One further element which is common to all the deception offences may conveniently be considered at this point, since, although not strictly part of the concept of deception itself, it is closely connected with that concept. This is the requirement that the benefit in question must be obtained *by* deception. This rule has two distinct aspects: first the obtaining of the benefit must be a *consequence* of the deception, and second it must not be *too remote* a consequence.

Causation

2.49   It must be proved that the benefit was obtained as a result of the deception. This obviously cannot be so if it was obtained before the deception took place. But it is not sufficient merely that the deception came first: it must have had some effect in inducing the victim to allow

---

45   *Attorney-General's Reference (No. 1 of 1981)* [1982] Q.B. 848 at p. 853.
46   [1974] A.C. 370.
47   But *cf. Nordeng* (1975) 62 Cr.App.R. 123 at p. 130, *per* Stephenson L.J.

the defendant to obtain the benefit. If this element of causation is absent, the full offence is not made out (though a charge of attempt may succeed if the defendant intended the deception to have that effect).[48] This requirement of a causal nexus between the deception and the obtaining should be distinguished from that of a nexus between the defendant's words or conduct and the victim's mistaken belief:[49] the latter is an essential ingredient of deception, the former is additional to it. Which of the two issues is raised by a given case may admittedly depend on how the deception is formulated. In *English*[50] a brickmaker agreed to take a lease of a brick field after inspecting it and being shown bricks which were falsely said to have been made from the earth of the field. It was argued (unsuccessfully) that the brickmaker relied on his own inspection rather than the false pretence. The argument might be put in either of two ways: (a) that the brickmaker believed it was a good and profitable brick field, but it was not the false pretence which induced him to believe it; or (b) that he believed that the defendant had been making good bricks from the field, but it was not that belief which induced him to take the lease.

2.50 Once it is established that the victim was in fact deceived, it must then be determined whether the defendant would still have obtained the benefit in question even if the victim had *not* been deceived. If not, he clearly obtained it *by* the deception.[51] In order to illustrate the operation of this rule it will be convenient to distinguish a number of situations.

2.51 (1) The point on which the victim is deceived may be one which in itself is important to him, such as the quality of goods which he is induced to buy. Normally it will be self-evident that the defendant would not have obtained the desired benefit (*e.g.* the purchase price) had the victim known the truth. But there may be exceptional cases where the victim has no choice in the matter, and would have had to co-operate (albeit reluctantly) even if he had known the truth. Thus if a creditor is obliged, under the terms of his contract with his debtor, to accept payment by cheque (unsupported by a cheque card), it cannot be said that he is induced to accept the debtor's cheque[52] by the debtor's implied representation that the cheque is good.[53] The truth or falsity of that representation is no doubt a matter of considerable importance to him, but he would not be entitled to refuse the cheque even if he knew that it was unlikely to be honoured: he would simply have to present it and see

---

48 *Edwards* [1978] Crim.L.R. 49.
49 *Supra,* para. 2.31.
50 (1872) 12 Cox 171.
51 Whether the converse is necessarily true, *i.e.* whether it is fatal to the prosecution's case that he *would* have obtained the benefit anyway, is considered *infra,* para. 2.56ff.
52 And therefore to wait for payment: Theft Act 1978 s. 2(3).
53 *Andrews and Hedges* [1981] Crim.L.R. 106.

what happened. The position would presumably be otherwise if he were not obliged to accept a cheque unless it was supported by a cheque card. If in that case he accepted a cheque which was not so supported, it might well be argued that he would not have accepted it had he known it was bad. And if the cheque were backed by a cheque card which the debtor was not authorised to use, and the use of which therefore amounted to a deception,[54] it could hardly be argued that the creditor would have accepted the cheque even if he had known of the debtor's lack of authority: it can normally be assumed that he would not knowingly have been a party to a fraud on the bank.[55] Although he is obliged to accept a cheque supported by a cheque card, he obviously need not do so if he knows that the debtor's use of the card is unauthorised. Similar considerations would no doubt apply if he were obliged to accept payment by credit card.

2.52   (2) The point on which the victim is deceived may be unimportant in itself, but may have important implications; therefore he would not necessarily refuse to co-operate if he knew the truth, but he would certainly refuse to do so in the absence of a satisfactory explanation. In *Laverty*[56] the defendant changed the number plates on a stolen car and sold it to an innocent purchaser. He was charged with obtaining the purchase price by means of a false implied representation that the car had originally been registered with the number it now bore. The conviction was quashed because there was no evidence that the representation as to the car's identity had any effect in inducing the purchaser to buy the car. This reasoning is hard to accept. No doubt the purchaser had no interest in the car's registration number as such,[57] and might still have bought the car even if he had known that the number had been changed. But one does not change a registration number without a reason, and some of the possible reasons would be highly unattractive to an honest purchaser. In the absence of special circumstances it will surely be permissible to infer that such a purchaser, if he knew that the number had been changed, would not buy the car *without further enquiry*. If he were given a false explanation which he accepted, the price would clearly have been obtained by deception. Does it make any difference that he is deceived into not demanding an explanation at all? It is submitted that it does not. The defendant cannot attain his objective without one deception or the other; it can hardly be crucial which of them he chooses to use. In either case it is the deception which enables him to obtain the price.

54   *Supra,* para. 2.26; but in this case the creditor would normally be indifferent whether he was being deceived (*cf. infra.* para. 2.53).
55   *Cf. Doukas* [1978] 1 W.L.R. 372.
56   [1970] 3 All E.R. 432.
57   He would of course be interested in the car's age, but the suffix of the new number was the same as that of the old one.

2.53   (3) The subject-matter of the deception may be of no interest to the victim at all, except that he would not co-operate if he *knew* the truth. This will normally be the case where a cheque card or credit card is used without authority: the user's implied representation that he has authority may be of no concern to the payee (because he will be paid anyway), *provided* that he does not actually know it to be false (because in that case he would be a party to the user's fraud and would not be entitled to payment). The main difficulty in this situation is that of whether the payee can be said to have been deceived at all; but as we have seen, the House of Lords has held that he can.[58] Ignorance of the user's lack of authority, coupled with indifference whether he has it or not, is treated as a "belief" that he has it. If this "belief" is in fact mistaken, and it was induced by the user's conduct, the payee will have been deceived. That being so, there seems little further difficulty in concluding that the benefit in question is obtained *by* the deception: if it were not for the payee's "belief" that the user has authority (*i.e.* if he knew that the user does not) he would not accept the card and would not allow the user to have the benefit.

2.54   (4) It may be that the victim is quite unconcerned as to the truth or falsity of the proposition which he is led to believe, in the sense that he would still have co-operated if the defendant had admitted the truth in the first place, but that he might be disinclined to co-operate if he knew that the defendant was trying to deceive him. This possibility may be illustrated by reference to the facts of *Sullivan*,[59] where the defendant obtained money from a number of people by advertising dartboards for sale. The false pretence alleged was that he made the dartboards himself—a pretence which, in the court's view, must have influenced the customers. It may be questioned whether this inference was inevitable, since none of the customers gave evidence that they were anxious to buy dartboards from the manufacturer rather than anyone else. It would seem equally plausible to infer that as long as they received the dartboards they did not care a scrap who the manufacturer was. But even on this view it would not necessarily follow that the defendant had not obtained the money *by* the deception. The customers might have been willing to buy dartboards from someone who was not the manufacturer *and did not claim to be*; but they might have been more chary of parting with their money if they had known that one of the statements in the advertisement was a downright lie. Could it then be said that the defendant did obtain their money by deception, since they would not have sent it to him if they had known that his statement was false? The point is not free from doubt,

58   *Supra,* para. 2.25ff.
59   (1945) 30 Cr.App.R. 132.

but it is submitted that it would be a misuse of language to describe this situation as an obtaining *by* deception. It was suggested above that if the defendant can obtain a benefit in either of two ways, but either way involves a deception, he is obtaining the benefit by deception whichever way he chooses.[60] It does not follow that he is still obtaining by deception if one way involves a deception and the other does not, and he chooses the one which does. It cannot properly be said that a person has obtained a benefit by deception if the deception played no part in enabling him to obtain it. On this view it is not conclusive that the victim would not have co-operated if he had known that the statement was false: the question is whether he would have done so if the defendant had not tried to deceive him at all. Normally, of course, the reason for employing the deception will be the expectation that it will have some effect; and in that case, even if the expectation proves unfounded, there will in any event be an attempt to obtain by deception.[61]

2.55   (5) The last possibility is that the point on which the victim is deceived is of no concern to him whatsoever: not only could the defendant have obtained the benefit without resorting to deception, but he would still have obtained it even if the victim had realised that he was lying. In this case it is clear that the essential element of causation is missing. In *Rashid*[62] a British Rail steward was charged with the possession of articles for use in the course of a cheat (*i.e.* an obtaining of property by deception).[63] The articles in question were two loaves of sliced bread and a bag of tomatoes; the cheat was to consist in selling the defendant's own tomato sandwiches to the passengers instead of British Rail's sandwiches, and pocketing the proceeds. The prosecution had to establish that if the defendant had carried out his scheme he would have obtained the proceeds *by* the deception that the sandwiches were British Rail's. The Court of Appeal held that it was impossible to draw any such inference:

> "The immediate reaction of all three members of this court was that in the ordinary case it would be a matter of complete indifference to a railway passenger whether the materials used in making a sandwich were materials belonging to British Rail or materials belonging to the steward employed by British Rail, so long as the sandwich was palatably fresh and sold at a reasonable price. Who knows but that the steward's sandwiches might have been fresher than British Rail's?"[64]

In more recent cases the Court of Appeal has preferred to assume that the

60   *Supra,* para. 2.52.
61   *Edwards* [1978] Crim.L.R. 49.
62   [1977] 1 W.L.R. 298.
63   Theft Act 1968 s. 25(1).
64   At p. 300, *per* Bridge L.J.

intended victims of the deception would not have been willing to participate in the fraud if they had known of it.[65] But it is only where the charge is one of going equipped (or possibly of an inchoate offence) that the law can legitimately make assumptions as to what the victims' reaction would have been: on a charge of the full offence there will be an identifiable victim, and whether that person would still have co-operated if he had known the truth will be a question of fact. If he would, then (subject to a problem now to be considered) the benefit was not obtained *by* the deception.

2.56 The deception must be *a* reason for the victim's action, but it need not be the only reason or even the main reason.[66] It is less clear whether it must be a decisive factor, *i.e.* whether it is necessary to prove that the defendant would not have obtained the benefit but for the deception. If he would have obtained the benefit anyway, the deception is not a *causa sine qua non,* and it is arguable that nothing less will do. But this test is probably too strict. It is certainly *sufficient* that the defendant would not have obtained the benefit if the victim had known the truth; whether it is *necessary* is another matter. In the civil law of misrepresentation it appears that this is not so. According to Spencer Bower:

> "Whether, if a full disclosure of the truth had been made, the representee would or would not have altered his position in the manner in which he did, is a question to which the law does not require an answer. It is enough if a full and exact revelation of the material facts *might* have prevented him from doing so—if it would have 'given him pause'. As against the wrong-doer, when once it is proved that the representation had an influence upon the mind and conduct of the representee, no burden is placed upon the latter, or right conferred upon the former, of conjecturing what would have happened if certain things had been said which, in fact, have not been."[67]

2.57 The point is illustrated by the civil case of *JEB Fasteners Ltd. v. Marks Bloom & Co.*[68] It was alleged that the plaintiffs had been induced to take over a company by accounts which the defendants had negligently prepared. At first instance Woolf J. held that the plaintiffs had "relied on" the accounts (in the sense that the accounts encouraged them to make the takeover) but that the defendants' negligence did not "cause" the loss because the plaintiffs would still have taken over the company even if they had known the true position.[69] In the Court of Appeal Donaldson L.J. (as he then was) approved this reasoning; but the

---

65 *Doukas* [1978] 1 W.L.R. 372; *Corboz* [1984] Crim.L.R. 629.
66 *English* (1872) 12 Cox 171; *Lince* (1873) 12 Cox 451.
67 Spencer Bower and Turner, *The Law of Actionable Misrepresentation* (3rd ed.) at para. 120.
68 [1983] 1 All E.R. 583 (CA).
69 [1981] 3 All E.R. 289.

majority rejected Woolf J.'s distinction between reliance and causation and apparently thought it unnecessary to enquire what would have happened if the representee had known the truth. Stephenson L.J. said:

> ". . . as long as a misrepresentation plays a real and substantial part, though not by itself a decisive part, in inducing a plaintiff to act, it is a cause of his loss and he relies on it, no matter how strong or how many are the other matters which play their part in inducing him to act."[70]

And later he went on:

> ". . . if the plaintiffs' directors were motivated or influenced by the accounts to any substantial extent, there would be the necessary reliance on the misrepresentation they contained to make a case [*sic*] of the kind which the law takes into account, and sometimes describes in Latin as a *causa causans,* and the judge should have found for the plaintiffs. Nor would it necessarily follow from his finding that the plaintiffs would have taken over the company without having false accounts to consider, that the judge's conclusion was right: he had to decide what in fact caused the plaintiffs to take over the company when they did have the false accounts before them."[71]

2.58 Oddly enough the plaintiffs' appeal was dismissed, on the grounds (questionable, in the light of Woolf J.'s clear reasoning) that they had *not* been influenced by the accounts to any substantial extent. Nevertheless the case appears to support Spencer Bower's view that it is immaterial whether the representee would still have suffered the loss if he had known the truth: it is sufficient that the misrepresentation was one of the factors which encouraged him to act as he did. A similar approach was adopted in the criminal case of *English*,[72] where the jury found that the victim "was not influenced solely by means of the pretences". Cockburn C.J. replied:

> "That finding is not sufficient. Was he partly influenced by them? that is, did they materially affect his judgment?"[73]

2.59 The victim should normally be called to give evidence that it was the deception which induced him to act.[74] Where, for example, the defendant has obtained money in advance for goods or services which he has failed to provide, the victim should be asked why he parted with his money;[75] the obvious reply, that he paid because he wanted the goods or the service, will normally be quite adequate if the gist of the deception

---

70 At p. 589.
71 *Ibid.*
72 (1872) 12 Cox 171; *Supra,* para. 2.49.
73 At p. 173.
74 *Laverty* [1970] 3 All E.R. 432.
75 *Grail* (1944) 30 Cr.App.R. 81.

alleged is that the defendant never intended to supply them. But evidence to this effect is not always essential, *e.g.* if the victim cannot attend,[76] if he cannot be expected to remember the transaction in question,[77] or if it is obvious that the deception must have influenced him.[78]

2.60 In most cases it will be the victim of the deception who is induced to confer on the defendant the benefit which he is charged with obtaining, but this is not necessarily so. It would obviously be sufficient if the benefit were conferred by someone who acted on the instructions of the person deceived but was not himself deceived, provided that the benefit was conferred *because* of the deception. It may not matter even that the person conferring the benefit is well aware of the deception, provided that he would not have done so if the deception had never been committed. Thus if a person obtains goods by using a cheque card when he has insufficient funds to meet the cheque and no agreed overdraft facility, he may be charged either with obtaining the goods by deception[79] or with obtaining a pecuniary advantage (*viz.* the overdraft).[80] The bank confers the pecuniary advantage on him by honouring the cheque and thus creating the overdraft; it matters not that the bank is not deceived, because it has no choice. It creates the overdraft because it has a legal obligation to do so, and it has an obligation to do so because the payee was deceived into accepting the cheque card.[81] Therefore the defendant has obtained the overdraft by deception. Nor is it essential that there should be a legal obligation to confer the benefit. In *Beck*[82] the defendant cashed forged traveller's cheques which were subsequently honoured by the bank which had issued them; he was charged with procuring the execution of valuable securities (*i.e.* the honouring of the traveller's cheques) by deception.[83] It was argued that the execution was not procured by the deception, because the bank was under no legal obligation to pay and voluntarily chose to do so in the knowledge that the traveller's cheques were forgeries. The argument was rejected by the Court of Appeal. In legal theory the bank may have acted voluntarily; in commercial terms it had no choice. Had it not been for the deception the bank would not have been put in that position. Therefore the defendant had procured the execution of valuable securities by deception.

---

76 *Tirado* (1974) 59 Cr.App.R. 80.
77 *Lambie* [1982] A.C. 449; *Etim v. Hatfield* [1975] Crim.L.R. 234.
78 *Rosenson* (1917) 12 Cr.App.R. 235; *Sullivan* (1945) 30 Cr.App.R. 132; *Etim v. Hatfield, supra* n. 77.
79 Theft Act 1968 s. 15; *infra,* para. 3.02ff.
80 Theft Act 1968 s. 16(2)(*b*), *infra* para. 3.37; see *Waites* [1982] Crim.L.R. 369.
81 *Supra,* para. 2.25.
82 [1985] 1 W.L.R. 22.
83 Theft Act 1968 s. 20(2); *infra,* para. 3.40ff.

Remoteness

2.61 Even if the deception did have some effect on the chain of events leading up to the obtaining of the benefit, the benefit will not have been obtained *by* the deception if the intervening events were such a predominant factor that the deception can be treated as merely part of the background. As a matter of *fact* the deception is one of the causes of the obtaining; as a matter of law it is not so regarded. In *Gardner*[84] a lady was induced by the defendant's false pretences to accept him as a lodger, and twelve days later agreed (for an additional consideration) to provide him with board as well. The food was not paid for. In a sense the deception contributed towards the obtaining of the food: had it not been for the deception the defendant probably would not have been accepted as a lodger, and had he not already become known to the victim as a lodger, she probably would not have agreed to provide him with food on credit. Nevertheless it was held that the obtaining of the food was "too remotely the result of the false pretence". In terms of the modern metaphor, the intervention of the defendant's spell as a lodger had broken the chain of causation.

2.62 Where the deception has not directly led to the obtaining of the benefit, but has merely given the defendant the opportunity to obtain it later, the eventual obtaining cannot necessarily be regarded as a consequence of the original deception. It may be arguable that the reason for the obtaining of the benefit is simply that the conditions to which it is subject have been fulfilled. In *Clucas*[85] the defendants induced a bookmaker to accept large bets by pretending to be acting as commission agents. It was held that they did not obtain their winnings by false pretences, but by backing the right horse.

> "No doubt the bookmaker might never have opened an account with these men if he had known the true facts, but we must distinguish in this case between one contributing cause and the effective cause which led the bookmaker to pay the money."[86]

In *Button*,[87] on the other hand, it was held that where an athlete's false pretences secure him a handicap in a race, he obtains the prize money by the false pretences and not merely by running fast enough to win. It is as if the punters' deception in *Clucas* had not only enabled them to place the bet but had improved their chances of winning. And it has long been settled that one who deceives another into making a contract with him may be obtaining the proceeds of the contract by deception even though

84 (1856) D. & B. 40.
85 [1949] 2 K.B. 226.
86 At p. 229f., *per* Lord Goddard C.J.
87 [1900] 2 Q.B. 597.

the immediate cause of the obtaining is his performance of the contract.[88] Presumably, therefore, a rogue who falsely assures a householder that certain repairs are necessary, and on the strength of that assurance is engaged to carry out those repairs, obtains the contract price by deception even if he has performed the contract in accordance with its terms.

2.63   These authorities are not easy to reconcile. It has been suggested that the test is whether the deception is still influencing the victim at the time of the obtaining,[89] and this is no doubt a useful guide in some cases; but it is not clear how such a restriction can be extracted from the wording of the legislation. The victim may perform his contract because he has undertaken to do so, and not because he is still labouring under the misapprehension which induced him to make the contract in the first place; it does not follow that his performance is not obtained "by . . . deception". It may be that no general rule will cover every case, and that one is compelled to resort to the metaphorical language of remoteness. Fortunately the difficulty is rendered largely academic by section 16 of the Theft Act 1968, which treats certain types of opportunities to obtain money as "pecuniary advantages" in themselves: the offence may be committed where a deception enables the deceiver to secure a job, an insurance policy or the acceptance of a bet, and there is no need to trace a causal link between the deception and the obtaining of the proceeds.[90] Thus the defendants in *Clucas* could now be charged with obtaining not their winnings but the bet itself by deception. It is not clear why these particular types of opportunity should be singled out for special treatment, but they are certainly among the most important; and the effect will be to render the problem of remoteness comparatively insignificant.

THE MENTAL ELEMENT

Dishonesty

2.64   Although all the offences of deception require an element of dishonesty, this requirement is separate from that of deception. The two are often confused.[91] Indeed it is sometimes suggested that deception is *per se* dishonest,[92] but this view must now be regarded as mistaken: the word "dishonestly" is not redundant and the jury should be directed on

---

88   *Abbott* (1847) 1 Den. 273; *Burgon* (1856) D. & B. 11; *Roebuck* (1856) D. & B. 24.
89   E. Griew, *op. cit.* at para. 6–38. Professor Griew suggests that it is also necessary for the defendant to be still making the representation, but clearly this cannot be so if there is no need for any representation at all: *cf. supra*, para. 2.06ff.
90   *Infra*, para. 3.39.
91   *Waterfall* [1970] 1 Q.B. 148; *Royle* [1971] 1 W.L.R. 1764; *Halstead v. Patel* [1972] 1 W.L.R. 661; *Lewis* (1975) 62 Cr.App.R. 206.
92   *e.g. Page* [1971] 2 Q.B. 330 at p. 333, *per* Phillimore L.J.

the issue, not only where the deception may not have been deliberate[93] but also where it clearly was.[94] Indeed it is not the deception which must be dishonest but the obtaining of the benefit (though it need not be the person from whom the benefit is obtained who suffers loss).[95] The requirement of dishonesty has already been examined.[96]

"Deliberate or reckless"

2.65 Inherent in the concept of deception itself, however, is the requirement that the deception be "deliberate or reckless".[97] This elliptical phrase embraces two separate requirements. On the orthodox view, according to which there must be a false representation, the phrase signifies both (1) that the defendant must know that the representation is false (or be reckless whether it is), and (2) that he must intend the victim to be deceived by it (or be reckless whether he is). On the view here advanced (*i.e.* that deception consists of inducing a mistaken belief, with or without a false representation),[98] it means both (1) that the defendant must intend to induce the victim to believe that a particular proposition is true (or be reckless whether he does), and (2) that he must know that that proposition is false (or be reckless whether it is). Clearly the crucial element on either view is that of recklessness, whether as to consequences (*i.e.* the inducement of the belief) or as to circumstances (*i.e.* the falsity of the representation or of the proposition believed). On the latter point, at least, there is authority that the test of recklessness is subjective—*i.e.* the defendant must actually realise that the proposition may be false.[99] It might perhaps be argued that the term "reckless" must now be given the extended interpretation laid down by the House of Lords in *Caldwell*,[1] in which case it would be sufficient if there were an obvious risk that the proposition might be untrue (or that the victim might be induced to believe it) and the defendant gave no thought to that possibility. But the meaning of a word must depend upon its context, and it is submitted that an objective interpretation of recklessness would be inconsistent with the ordinary meaning of "deception". To describe the inadvertent (albeit careless) creation of a false impression as "deception" would be a misuse of language. In any event the point seems academic: a defendant who had no idea that his words or conduct might be misleading could hardly be described as dishonest.

93 *Potger* (1970) 55 Cr.App.R. 42.
94 *Greenstein* [1975] 1 W.L.R. 1353; *supra,* para. 2.41.
95 *Charles* [1977] A.C. 177; *Lambie* [1982] A.C. 449; *supra, para.* 2.25ff.
96 *Supra,* para. 1.04ff.
97 Theft Act 1968 s. 15(4).
98 *Supra,* para. 2.06ff.
99 *Waterfall* [1970] 1 Q.B. 148; *Royle* [1971] 1 W.L.R. 1764; *Staines* (1974) 60 Cr.App.R. 160.
1 [1982] A.C. 341.

CHAPTER 3

Theft and Offences of Deception

3.01 Having examined the nature of deception, and the implications of a requirement that some benefit be obtained *by* the deception, we now turn to the individual offences under the Theft Acts 1968 and 1978 which are defined in terms of these two elements. The most important, for present purposes, is that of obtaining property be deception; this offence has several features in common with that of theft, and it will therefore be convenient to consider both offences together. It should be emphasised, however, that we are concerned with theft only in its application to fraud. We therefore make no attempt to provide an exhaustive exposition, but confine ourselves to pointing out some problems which are particularly likely to arise in a fraud case. The other deception offences concern the obtaining of various benefits other than property, *viz.* services, the evasion of liability, certain other types of pecuniary advantage, and the execution of a valuable security.

THEFT AND OBTAINING PROPERTY BY DECEPTION

3.02 We have seen that criminal fraud generally consists in the dishonest obtaining of financial benefits at the expense of others, either surreptitiously or by means of deception.[1] Financial benefits come in various forms, and the appropriate head of criminal liability (if any) may depend on the type of benefit obtained as well as on the means employed to obtain it. The chief distinction to be drawn is between those benefits which are capable of being owned (*i.e.* property) and those which are not. The obtaining of property may involve either of two main offences, theft and obtaining property by deception, and the choice between them will normally depend on *how* the property was obtained—*i.e.* whether the owner (or someone acting on his behalf) was deceived into parting with it or did not consent at all. With this exception, the ingredients of the two offences are essentially identical. Section 1(1) of the Theft Act 1968 provides:

"A person is guilty of theft if he dishonestly appropriates property

1 *Supra*, para. 1.31ff.

belonging to another with the intention of permanently depriving the other of it; and 'thief' and 'steal' shall be construed accordingly."

Theft is punishable on conviction on indictment with ten years' imprisonment.[2] Section 15(1) provides:

"A person who by any deception dishonestly obtains property belonging to another, with the intention of permanently depriving the other of it, shall on conviction on indictment be liable to imprisonment for a term not exceeding ten years."

Both offences are triable either way.[3] We consider in turn the concept of property, the requirement that the property belong to someone other than the defendant, and the requirement of an intention permanently to deprive that person of it; we then compare the concept of appropriation in theft with that of obtaining by deception (discussed in the previous chapter). The concept of dishonesty, common to both offences and indeed to all the offences discussed in this chapter, has already been examined.[4]

Property

3.03   The distinction between property and other benefits is important for two reasons. In the first place, it may determine whether the offence committed in a particular case is that of obtaining property by deception or one of the other deception offences examined later in this chapter. If, however, no deception is involved, the question whether the benefit obtained is a form of property may determine whether *any* offence is committed: the obtaining of property without deception may constitute theft, but the obtaining of benefits other than property cannot be charged as theft and indeed may not involve any criminal liability at all (though the possibility of conspiracy to defraud must be borne in mind).[5] "Property" is defined, partially at least, by section 4(1) of the Theft Act 1968:

" 'Property' includes money and all other property, real or personal, including things in action and other intangible property."

We must consider what is and is not covered by this definition.

Land

3.04   Real property is expressly included in the term "property". Land can therefore be the subject of both theft and obtaining property by deception. Section 4(2), however, provides that a person cannot *steal* land

2   s. 7.
3   Magistrates' Courts Act 1980 s. 17(1), Sch. 1.
4   *Supra*, para. 1.04ff.
5   *Cf. infra*, para. 12.34ff.

(as against obtaining it by deception) except in certain cases, of which only the first is of importance for the law of fraud:

> ". . . when he is a trustee or personal representative, or is authorised by power of attorney, or as liquidator of a company, or otherwise, to sell or dispose of land belonging to another, and he appropriates the land or anything forming part of it by dealing with it in breach of the confidence reposed in him. . . ."

This provision is wide enough to cover not only the persons specified but also other agents such as company directors: a disposal which is effected in the interests of the agent himself, *e.g.* to an associate at an undervalue, will constitute a breach of his fiduciary obligations to his principal and will probably amount to theft. However, it is not sufficient that the defendant is in a fiduciary position: he must be *authorised to dispose of* the land in question. Thus a solicitor who arranged for the sale of his client's land to his own nominee would be guilty of a breach of duty but not (unless he actually sold the land on the client's behalf) of stealing the land. He might, however, be guilty of obtaining the land by deception. The question of criminal liability for breaches of fiduciary obligations is considered further in chapter 4.

Intangible property
3.05 "Property" also includes "things in action and other intangible property", *e.g.* debts, company shares and intellectual property such as copyrights and patents. To deceive the owner of such an asset into assigning it might therefore amount to an offence of obtaining property by deception. The *theft* of intangible property is more difficult to envisage. Even if the property is "appropriated" by the defendant, he will not normally have any expectation of depriving its owner of it, permanently or otherwise: since intangible property consists solely of legal rights, one can hardly be deprived of it without one's consent. The problem might arise in the type of case where a bank's computer system is programmed to transfer small amounts from numerous accounts into one controlled by the programmer. He is unlikely to suppose that his conduct will have the effect of *depriving* the customers of their rights against the bank (though he may well hope that they will not notice the discrepancy and will therefore not attempt to *enforce* those rights).[6] In *Thompson*[7] the question arose whether a fraud of this type amounted to an "obtaining" of the customers' balances within the meaning of section 15. The Court of Appeal held that it did not, partly because the defendant himself acquired

---

6 s. 6(1) (*infra,* para. 3.17) does not appear to assist: it can hardly be said that the programmer intends to treat the customers' rights as his own to dispose of regardless of those rights. He is not disposing of them at all, but simply hoping that their exact value will be overlooked.

7 [1984] 3 All E.R. 565.

no chose in action against the bank, but partly also because the customers did not lose theirs:

> "In so far as the customers whose accounts had been fraudulently debited and who had to be reimbursed by the bank, as counsel for the appellant[8] submitted, are concerned, we prefer the approach of counsel for the Crown. He submitted that properly considered it was not a question of reimbursement: it was merely a question of correcting forged documents, forged records, to the condition in which they ought to have been but for the fraud."[9]

By the same token, presumably, the defendant did not *steal* the customers' rights. The appropriate charge would be one of false accounting.[10]

3.06 The requirement of an intention permanently to deprive thus renders it difficult to establish a charge of stealing intangible property against a person who was totally unauthorised to deal with the property. As in the case of land, however, it is possible that the defendant may have authority to assign the property on behalf of its owner; it is then arguable (though not beyond dispute)[11] that a fraudulent assignment can constitute theft although it is in a sense effected with the owner's consent. Thus in *Kohn*[12] a company director wrote cheques on the company's bank account for his own purposes. The Court of Appeal held that this amounted to theft of the thing in action represented by the credit balance in the account. The defendant's position as the authorised agent of the company empowered him to deprive the company of that balance, and he clearly intended to do so. It was as if he had fraudulently, but effectively, disposed of any other asset belonging to the company.

3.07 It is important to appreciate exactly what is involved in the contention that a person has stolen (or obtained by deception) intangible property such as the balance of a bank account. First, the property in question must belong to a person other than the defendant before he appropriates or obtains it.[13] Therefore these charges cannot normally be brought in respect of the defendant's own bank account (though in certain circumstances part of his credit balance may be deemed to belong to another).[14] This difficulty arose in *Thompson*,[15] and was not

---

8 Due to the manner in which the issue arose, it was the appellant who argued that he *had* obtained the balances: see *infra,* para. 3.07.
9 At p. 569f., *per* May L.J., delivering the judgment of the court.
10 *Infra,* para. 6.41ff.
11 *Cf. infra,* para. 4.19ff.
12 (1979) 69 Cr.App.R. 395.
13 *Infra,* para. 3.13ff.
14 *e.g. Attorney-General's Reference (No. 1 of 1983)* [1984] 3 W.L.R. 686.
15 [1984] 3 All E.R. 565; *supra,* para. 3.05.

satisfactorily resolved. The computer fraud had been effected in Kuwait, outside the jurisdiction. The prosecution therefore relied on the fact that the defendant had subsequently arranged for the resulting credit balance to be transferred to an account in England: this, it was argued, amounted to an obtaining by deception, within the jurisdiction, of money belonging to the bank in Kuwait. The Court of Appeal rejected the defence's argument that the obtaining had already taken place in Kuwait, and dismissed the appeal. But insufficient attention appears to have been paid to the question of *what* property was obtained when the balance was transferred. The bank in Kuwait did not literally send any money to England: there was merely an exchange of telex messages, with the effect that the English bank undertook a liability to the defendant corresponding to that supposedly owed to him by the Kuwait bank. What the defendant obtained by his deception was not money but, at most,[16] a chose in action; and that chose in action had never belonged to anyone but him. The conviction can perhaps be justified on the basis that, as a result of the defendant's deception, the English bank would eventually receive a sum of money from the Kuwait bank by way of reimbursement for the transfer. A defendant whose deception enables another person to obtain property belonging to another is deemed for the purposes of section 15 to have obtained that property himself.[17] Strictly speaking an argument along these lines would need to be supported by evidence of the banking procedures involved. It might have been simpler to rely on the defendant's withdrawal of the money from the English bank; but was there a deception at this stage? It could hardly be said that the defendant deceived the bank cashier merely by failing to disclose that the balance of the account represented the proceeds of fraud.[18]

3.08   The second point to bear in mind in this context is that the credit balance of a bank account is the property of the account-holder because it represents a debt owed to him by the bank. This is not so if, at the time of the alleged appropriation or obtaining,[19] the account was not in credit but overdrawn: in that case the debt is owed by the account-holder to the bank and is therefore the property of the bank. Further drawings on the account will not deprive the bank of that property but on the contrary

---

16   The Court of Appeal denied that the original fraud gave him a chose in action against the Kuwait bank; could it not be argued that he acquired no valid rights against the English bank either?
17   s. 15(2).
18   *Cf.* ch. 2. The same point could perhaps be made in relation to the obtaining from the Kuwait bank of which the defendant was in fact convicted: the issue of deception turned on the construction of the defendant's letters to the bank (p. 570), which are not quoted in the report.
19   *i.e.* when the cheque is honoured, not when it is drawn: *Kohn* (1979) 69 Cr. App.R. 395 at p. 407.

will increase the size of the debt. It may be, however, that the bank has agreed to allow the account-holder to overdraw up to a certain amount, in which case he has a contractual right[20] to have his cheques honoured until the agreed limit is reached. This right is another form of intangible property; if its value is eroded or extinguished as a result of another person dishonestly drawing on the account, that person can be said to have stolen it.[21] It is only where there is no overdraft facility, or the agreed limit has already been exceeded, that the account-holder has no rights left to steal.[22]

3.09   Irrespective of the state of the account, however, a person other than the account-holder who fraudulently writes cheques on it may be charged with theft of the cheques themselves. One way of justifying such a charge would be to treat the cheques (or rather the cheque forms) simply as pieces of paper: they belong to the account-holder and they are appropriated when another person uses them to write cheques for his own purposes. It is true that the account-holder may eventually be able to retrieve them from his bank, and it might therefore be argued that the defendant has no intention of permanently depriving him of them; but since they will no longer retain their original character as blank cheque forms which may be converted into valid cheques,[23] the necessary intention will probably be deemed to exist.[24] In *Kohn*,[25] however, the court appears to have treated the cheques not as mere pieces of paper but as intangible property:

> ". . . when the writing gets on to the cheque, it becomes a bill of exchange and becomes a necessary demand upon the bank to honour the bank's obligations to the customer. . .[26] But that is being done for the defendant's own purposes, and when he sends it on to [his associates] it has come to the point where he has made the cheque his own. For the purposes of the Theft Act he has appropriated the cheque. . ."[27]

The difficulty with this approach is that the intangible property represented by the cheque (as against the balance of the account on which it is drawn) belongs not to the account-holder but to the payee; and the defendant's objective is not to deprive him of that property but on the contrary to confer it on him. It is submitted that, if it is thought necessary

---

20   Though probably one which is revocable on reasonable notice by the bank: *Rouse v. Bradford Banking Co. Ltd.* [1894] A.C. 586 at p. 595 *per* Lord Herschell L.C.
21   *Kohn* (1979) 69 Cr. App. R. 395.
22   *Ibid.*
23   In theory a valid cheque could no doubt be written on a used cheque form, but this is hardly a practical possibility.
24   *Cf. Duru* [1974] 1 W.L.R. 2; *infra*, para. 3.19.
25   (1979) 69 Cr. App. R. 395.
26   But in *Kohn* itself the argument was held to apply even if the account is overdrawn and the bank has no further obligations to the customer.
27   At p. 410, *per* Geoffrey Lane L.J., delivering the judgment of the court.

to charge theft of the cheques rather than of the account-holder's rights against the bank (*e.g.* because the account is overdrawn beyond any agreed overdraft facility), the prosecution must be prepared to argue that the property stolen is the paper on which the cheques are written and not any rights which they may themselves confer. Such an artificial charge should clearly be a last resort.

3.10   The fact that intangible property can be stolen does not, however, mean that *anything* intangible can be stolen. The subject of a theft charge must be *property:* what cannot be owned cannot be stolen. For example, the mere use of an asset (however valuable) is not a form of property known to English law. Therefore it is not theft for a director to use the services of company employees for his own purposes, or for an employee to "steal" computer time.[28] A more controversial question is that of whether secret information can constitute property. Industrial espionage, and the illicit obtaining of secret information generally, pose difficult problems for the criminal law. There may of course be copyright in a trade secret such as a technical drawing, a flow-chart[29] or (probably) a computer program or data base,[30] and copyright certainly is a form of intangible property.[31] As we have seen, however, a person infringing a copyright does not intend to deprive the owner of the copyright itself and therefore cannot be charged with stealing it.[32] Nor does he steal the infringing copy, since (notwithstanding section 18(1) of the Copyright Act 1956, which gives the copyright owner certain civil remedies *as if* he were the owner of the infringing copy) it does not belong to another.[33] Section 21 of the Copyright Act creates summary offences, punishable with two months' imprisonment,[34] of selling, hiring or distributing

---

28   Unless it constituted theft of the proceeds: *infra,* para. 4.03ff. It would probably amount to the offence of dishonestly using electricity: Theft Act 1968 s. 13.
29   Diagrams and other drawings are "artistic works" for the purposes of the Copyright Act 1956: s. 3(1), s. 48(1).
30   There is no reason why the nature of the *content* of a computer program should disqualify it from being a "literary work" for the purposes of the Copyright Act: *e.g.* a telegraphic code consisting of meaningless "words" constitutes such a work (*D.P. Anderson & Co. Ltd v. Lieber Code Co.* [1917] 2 K.B. 469). The difficulty lies rather in the program's form, *e.g.* if it does not exist in writing but only on a tape or disc or even in the computer's memory. But s. 49(4) of the Act provides that a work is "made" when it is first reduced to writing *or* some other material form. It is now generally agreed that copyright can exist in software irrespective of how it is recorded: Laddie, Prescott and Vitoria, *The Modern Law of Copyright,* para. 2.14ff.; Copinger and Skone James (12th ed.), para. 154. See also Copyright (Computer Software) Amendment Bill 1985.
31   The statement by Lord Denning M.R. in *Rank Film Distributors Ltd v. Video Information Centre* [1982] A.C. 380 at p. 409, that copyright is not "property" within the meaning of the Theft Act, is clearly incorrect.
32   *Supra,* para. 3.05.
33   *Storrow and Poole* [1983] Crim.L.R. 332.
34   Heavier penalties are available in the case of copies of sound recordings and cinematograph films: Copyright (Amendment) Act 1983 s. 1.

infringing copies, and of making, or having in one's possession, a plate,[35] knowing that it is to be used for making infringing copies; but there is no offence of simply making a copy for one's own use.

3.11   Hence a prosecutor may be tempted simply to charge theft of the information itself, or perhaps obtaining it by deception contrary to section 15 of the Theft Act 1968 (although the "deception" of a computer, so as to gain access to software or data, is probably not sufficient).[36] In either case it would be necessary to argue that secret information is not merely an interest capable of protection by injunction (which it clearly is)[37] but a form of property, something which can be owned in the strict sense of the word. There is some authority for this view. It has been held, for example, that a secret formula can be held on trust[38] and passes to a trustee in bankruptcy.[39] In *Exchange Telegraph Co. Ltd. v. Howard*,[40] where the plaintiffs complained that their news of the latest cricket scores was being poached, Buckley J. said:

> "The knowledge of a fact which is unknown to many people may be the property of a person in that others will pay the person who knows it for information as to that fact. In unpublished matter there is at common law a right of property, or there may be in the circumstances of the case. The plaintiffs here sue, not in copyright at all, but in respect of that common law right of property in information which they had collected and which they were in a position to sell. Their case is that the defendant has stolen their property. . ."[41]

These cases were not referred to in *Oxford v. Moss*,[42] where a university student was charged with stealing the information contained in an examination paper by obtaining a proof of it before the date of the examination. The Divisional Court held that information is not "property" for the purposes of the Theft Act and that the charge was therefore misconceived. It is submitted that the correctness of this view is not as self-evident as the court appears to have supposed, and that the issue warrants further consideration by a higher court.

3.12   There are in any event various alternatives to a charge of stealing information as such. It has been suggested, for example, that the defendant in *Oxford v. Moss* should have been charged with stealing not

---

35 Including any stereotype, stone, block, mould, matrix, transfer, negative or other appliance: s. 18(3).
36 *Supra,* para. 2.30.
37 *e.g. Lion Laboratories Ltd v. Evans* [1984] 3 W.L.R. 539.
38 *Green v. Folgham* (1823) 1 Sim. & Stu. 398.
39 *Re Keene* [1922] 2 Ch. 475.
40 (1906) 22 T.L.R. 375.
41 At p. 375. *Cf.* also *Boardman v. Phipps* [1967] 2 A.C. 46, at p. 107 (*per* Lord Hodson) and p. 115 (*per* Lord Guest).
42 (1978) 68 Cr.App.R. 183.

the contents of the examination paper but the paper itself, since an examination paper which has been read in advance by one of the candidates is useless; the borrowing was equivalent to an "outright taking" of the paper, and the requisite intention permanently to deprive the university could therefore have been imputed to the defendant under section 6(1) of the Theft Act 1968.[43] It may perhaps be doubted whether this would have been a legitimate application of the subsection.[44] In any event the reasoning presupposes that the effect of the borrowing is to render the document valueless, and this would not normally be the case where secret information is obtained without authority. Thus in *Lloyd (Sidney)*[45] the Court of Appeal held that one does not steal a film by borrowing it for the purpose of making "pirate" copies: the economic interests of the copyright owner are damaged, but the film itself is still a thing of value. Presumably the same reasoning would apply to the illicit acquisition of secret formulae or software. In certain circumstances a charge of obtaining *services* by deception[46] might be possible, but only if it was understood that the information was to be paid for: this would exclude, for example, the device of tricking employees into revealing confidential information in the course of interviews for non-existent jobs. And the notion of deceiving a computer might again present difficulties.[47] The unauthorised use of a computer to obtain data or software would presumably constitute the offence of dishonestly using electricity,[48] but such a charge would not be possible if the defendant simply borrowed a tape or disc containing the information and copied it. If an employee is induced to divulge the information, an offence of corruption may be committed;[49] if he uses it for his own profit he might conceivably be guilty of theft of the proceeds.[50] A civil servant might be charged under section 2 of the Official Secrets Act 1911. Finally, an *agreement to* obtain secret information, thus depriving its possessor of some of its value, would seem to amount to a conspiracy to defraud at common law.[51] However, it could only be charged as such if it did not involve any substantive offence: otherwise it would have to be charged as a statutory conspiracy to commit the offence in question.[52] Thus an agreement to *make* an illicit copy of a document, tape or disc is probably a conspiracy at common

---

43 J.C. Smith [1979] Crim. L.R. 120. For s. 6(1) see *infra*. para. 3.17.
44 An examination is not rendered completely futile by the fact that one of the candidates cheats. No doubt a new paper will be set if the breach of security is discovered, but the candidate presumably hopes it will not be.
45 *The Times*, 29 April 1985.
46 *Infra*, para. 3.25ff.
47 *Supra*, para. 2.30.
48 Theft Act 1968 s. 13.
49 *Infra*, ch. 7.
50 *Infra*, para. 4.03ff.
51 *Supra*, ch. 1. *Cf. D.P.P. v. Withers* [1975] A.C. 842, para. 1.41.
52 *Infra*, para. 12.34ff.

law, punishable at large; an agreement to *sell* it is a statutory conspiracy to contravene section 21 of the Copyright Act, punishable with two months' imprisonment.

Belonging to another

3.13   On a charge of either theft or obtaining by deception it must be proved that the property appropriated or obtained was property "belonging to another" at the time of the appropriation or obtaining. The implications of this requirement are sometimes overlooked, particularly in the context of intangible property. It is not sufficient that the defendant acquires property from his victim: the property must have belonged to the victim (or at any rate to someone other than the defendant) before the defendant acquired it. Clearly this cannot be so if it belonged solely to the defendant as soon as it came into existence. Therefore a person who procures the creation of a new chose in action in his own favour is not guilty of stealing it or of obtaining it by deception contrary to section 15. Probably the most important example is that of a fraudsman who by deception induces his victim to write him a cheque. In *Duru*[53] it was held that in this situation the obtaining of the chose in action represented by the cheque amounts to the offence under section 15; but this is clearly not so, because that chose in action does not exist until the cheque is drawn, and as soon as it is drawn the chose in action belongs to the payee (*i.e.* the defendant). The decision in *Duru* can only be defended on the alternative ground relied upon, *viz.* that it is the piece of paper on which the cheque is written that is obtained by deception. That piece of paper does belong to the victim (or possibly his bank) before the defendant obtains it. If the cheque drawn by the victim were backed by a cheque card, so that the defendant acquired a legal right to receive payment from the bank,[54] it might perhaps be arguable that he was obtaining part of the victim's credit balance (*i.e.* his rights against the bank).[55] Alternatively he might be charged with procuring the execution of a valuable security by deception.[56] Another example of the same problem is that of the person who by deception procures the allotment of company shares, *e.g.* by making multiple applications in various names for an issue which is expected to be oversubscribed. If the shares are allotted directly by the company, there is no offence of obtaining them contrary to section 15, because they do not belong to the company before they are allotted: they do not exist until then. But there might be an

---

53   [1974] 1 W.L.R. 2.
54   *Cf. supra*, para. 2.25.
55   *Infra*, para. 3.20.
56   *Infra*, para. 3.40ff.

offence of obtaining the share certificate or letter of acceptance,[57] or of procuring the execution of a valuable security,[58] or (since the shares are to be paid for) of obtaining services by deception.[59] If, however, the shares are issued by means of an offer for sale (*i.e.* through an issuing house), the problem does not arise: the shares belong to the issuing house before the applicants obtain them.

3.14   Section 5(1) of the Theft Act 1968 provides:

> "Property shall be regarded as belonging to any person having possession or control of it, or having in it any proprietary right or interest (not being an equitable interest arising only from an agreement to transfer or grant an interest)."

This basic definition applies to both theft and obtaining by deception,[60] although for the purposes of theft it is extended in various ways by the remainder of section 5.[61] The rule that property "belongs" to anyone with possession or control of it appears at first sight to mean that even the owner of the property can be convicted of stealing it, or obtaining it by deception, from someone with no title at all and no right to retain possession or control[62]—*e.g.* where he discovers property which has previously been stolen from him and surreptitiously takes it back with the intention of making a fraudulent claim on his insurance policy. But theft and obtaining by deception both require the element of dishonesty, and it was argued above that conduct cannot legitimately be described as dishonest for the purpose of criminal offences against property unless it is unlawful as a matter of civil law.[63] On this view it could not be theft or obtaining by deception for the owner of property to retrieve it from someone with no right to keep it, irrespective of the owner's motives.[64] More important for present purposes is the straightforward case in which some person other than the defendant has a proprietary interest in the property. Whether the defendant also has such an interest is immaterial: the requirement is not that the property must not belong to the defendant, but that it must belong to somebody else. Thus a partner who misappropriates the firm's assets may be convicted of stealing them from his partner or partners.[65]

57   *Greenstein* [1975] 1 W.L.R. 1353.
58   *Infra,* para. 3.40ff.
59   *Infra,* para. 3.25ff.
60   s. 34(1).
61   *Infra,* para. 3.15.
62   *Turner (No.2)* [1971] 1 W.L.R. 901.
63   Para. 1.10ff.
64   *Cf. Meredith* [1973] Crim.L.R. 253.
65   *Bonner* [1970] 1 W.L.R. 838. Like *Turner* (*No.* 2), *supra* n. 62, this decision is questionable in so far as it suggests that conduct which gives rise to no civil remedy may nevertheless constitute theft; but in any event the misappropriation of assets by a partner is now actionable at the suit of the other partners: Torts (Interference with Goods) Act 1977 s. 10(1).

3.15   In the case of theft, but not of obtaining by deception, the basic definition of "belonging to another" is extended in various ways by the remainder of section 5, which provides:

> "(2) Where property is subject to a trust, the persons to whom it belongs shall be regarded as including any person having a right to enforce the trust, and an intention to defeat the trust shall be regarded accordingly as an intention to deprive of the property any person having that right.
>
> (3) Where a person receives property from or on account of another, and is under an obligation to the other to retain and deal with that property or its proceeds in a particular way, the property or proceeds shall be regarded (as against him) as belonging to the other.
>
> (4) Where a person gets property by another's mistake, and is under an obligation to make restoration (in whole or in part) of the property or its proceeds or of the value thereof, then to the extent of that obligation the property or proceeds shall be regarded (as against him) as belonging to the person entitled to restoration, and an intention not to make restoration shall be regarded accordingly as an intention to deprive that person of the property or proceeds.
>
> (5) Property of a corporation sole shall be regarded as belonging to the corporation notwithstanding a vacancy in the corporation."

By far the most important of these provisions is subsection (3), which means in effect that an agent or other fiduciary who misappropriates property entrusted to him may be convicted of theft even if he had acquired full ownership of the property before appropriating it. This form of fraud will be considered in the next chapter, and discussion of section 5(3) is postponed until then.[66]

3.16   Of the rest of section 5, the only provision which warrants mention is subsection (4). This provision is directed at persons who obtain property as a result of someone else's mistake and dishonestly decide to keep it, the standard case being that of the employee who is inadvertently overpaid.[67] Its application in the context of fraud is limited. If the beneficiary of the mistake is not merely taking advantage of an unexpected windfall but is a party to a fraudulent enterprise, such as the manipulation of an accounting system so as to extract unearned wages, there will in any event be either an obtaining by deception or (if it is only a computer which is "deceived" into paying the money)[68] a theft of the victim's money. There is no need to argue that by virtue of section 5(4) the money is deemed still to belong to the victim even after it is obtained. Indeed such an argument would pose difficulties of its own. If there were a deception, it would be arguable that the payment was merely voidable

---

66   *Infra,* para. 4.07ff.
67   *Attorney-General's Reference (No. 1 of 1983)* [1984] 3 All E.R. 369; *cf. Moynes v. Coopper* [1956] 1 Q.B. 439.
68   *Cf. supra,* para. 2.30.

and that the recipient was not therefore under an obligation to make restoration, but only under a *potential* obligation.[69] And if there was no deception because the fraud was effected by interfering with a computer system, could it be said that the money was obtained "by another's mistake"?

Intention permanently to deprive

3.17 On a charge of either theft or obtaining property by deception it must be proved that at the time of the appropriation or obtaining the defendant intended permanently to deprive the victim[70] of the property. The mere unauthorised use of an asset, such as the "theft" of computer time, will not normally amount to theft of that asset; the obtaining of such use by deception might in some circumstances constitute the offence of obtaining services by deception,[71] but not normally that of obtaining property. We have seen that a charge of stealing intangible property (as against obtaining it by deception) may be difficult to establish because the victim cannot be deprived of his rights without his consent.[72] With these exceptions, however, it will be unusual for the defence in a fraud case to derive much assistance from the requirement of an intention permanently to deprive. In the first place, the objective of the typical fraudsman is to obtain someone else's money; and even if he hopes to repay an equivalent sum at a later date,[73] he will hardly expect to return the *same* money. Moreover, even a defendant who does intend to return the very thing he obtains or appropriates must reckon with the notorious convolutions of section 6(1) of the Theft Act 1968:[74]

> "A person appropriating property belonging to another without meaning the other permanently to lose the thing itself is nevertheless to be regarded as having the intention of permanently depriving the other of it if his intention is to treat the thing as his own to dispose of regardless of the other's rights; and a borrowing or lending of it may amount to so treating it if, but only if, the borrowing or lending is for a period and in circumstances making it equivalent to an outright taking or disposal."

With the substitution of "obtaining" for "appropriating", the section applies for the purposes of obtaining property by deception as well as theft.[75]

---

69 It is also arguable that in the light of *Morris* [1984] A.C. 320 property obtained by deception is not "appropriated" and is therefore not stolen: *infra*, para. 3.24.
70 *i.e.* the person to whom the property "belongs".
71 *Infra*, para. 3.25ff.
72 *Supra*, para. 3.05.
73 A factor which *may* negative dishonesty: *supra*, para. 1.26ff.
74 s. 6(2) appears to be concerned solely with the unauthorised pawning of one person's property by another, and does not require consideration here.
75 s. 15(3).

3.18   Although Edmund Davies L.J. stated in *Warner*[76] that section 6 merely gives "illustrations, as it were" of the required intention, and that "it is a misconception to interpret it as watering down section 1",[77] it is quite clear that the section has the effect of deeming the necessary intention to exist in certain cases where in fact it does not—*i.e.* where the defendant appropriates or obtains the property "without meaning the other permanently to lose the thing itself". What is less clear is *when* it has this effect. Two main possibilities have received general support.[78] The first is the case where the defendant intends the victim to get the property back only if he pays for it: in effect, and whether or not the victim realises it, the property is being "held to ransom". This principle would apply, for example, if the defendant intended to sell the property back to the victim without revealing that it belonged to him in the first place.[79] In this case there would be an obtaining of the price by deception, but the property would already have been stolen when it was first appropriated. The second principle which section 6(1) appears to implement is that there is an intention permanently to deprive the victim if he is intended to get the property back only when it no longer has any value, or only when it has undergone some fundamental alteration. In *Downes*[80] a defendant who improperly disposed of Inland Revenue sub-contractor vouchers,[81] knowing that they would be used to defraud the Revenue, was held to have stolen them although the fraud would necessarily involve returning them to the Inland Revenue. A used voucher was something essentially different from an unused one, and the intention to return them in such an altered state was therefore, by virtue of this principle, an intention permanently to deprive. Indeed, the court apparently thought that the vouchers lost their essential character as soon as they fell into unauthorised hands, even before they were used.

3.19   Either or both of these principles may assist the prosecution in the case of a defendant who by deception induces his victim to draw a cheque in the defendant's favour,[82] or himself draws a cheque on the victim's account. If the offence is presented as consisting in the obtaining or appropriation of the piece of paper itself, it may be objected that there is no intention permanently to deprive the victim of that piece of paper

---

76   (1970) 55 Cr. App. R. 93.
77   At p. 97.
78   *e.g.* J. R. Spencer, "The Metamorphosis of Section 6 of the Theft Act" [1977] Crim. L.R. 653; J. C. Smith, *The Law of Theft* (5th ed.) paras. 127, 133; E. Griew, *The Theft Acts 1968 and 1978* (4th ed.) para. 2.74.
79   *Cf. Hall* (1849) 1 Den. 381.
80   (1983) 77 Cr. App. R. 260.
81   See *infra*, para. 10.05ff.
82   In this case the difficulties can be avoided by framing the charge under s. 20(2) of the Theft Act 1968: *infra*, para. 3.40ff.

because he will eventually be able to retrieve it from his bank. But the argument is unsound: the defendant is deemed to have the required intention, either because a cancelled cheque is something fundamentally different from a valid cheque[83] or a blank cheque form,[84] or because the victim will only get the cheque back once the bank has, as it were, paid for it on his behalf by honouring it. Thus the defendant may be convicted of obtaining the cheque by deception or (subject to any difficulties arising out of his fiduciary position)[85] of stealing it, as the case may be. A charge framed in this way would of course appear somewhat technical, and it might be thought preferable to allege a theft or obtaining of the intangible property which the cheque represents. The flaw in this approach is that although the defendant acquires (or bestows on an associate) the right to the sum for which the cheque is drawn—a right which is a thing in action and a form of intangible property—he cannot be charged with stealing that right, or obtaining it by deception, because it is created by the execution of the cheque itself. It is not property "belonging to another" before the defendant obtains or appropriates the cheque, because it does not exist until then.[86] The intangible property which does belong to the victim[87] is that consisting in his rights against his bank, and the defendant who abuses his authority to draw on the account may be guilty of stealing those rights.[88] Similarly it is no doubt possible to obtain them by deception.[89]

Obtaining and appropriation

Obtaining
3.20 Apart from minor differences relating to the type of property which can be the subject-matter of the charge,[90] and the meaning of "belonging to another",[91] the feature which distinguishes theft from obtaining property by deception is the nature of the act required on the defendant's part. In obtaining by deception he must, obviously, *obtain* the property. Section 15(2) of the Theft Act 1968 provides:

> "For purposes of this section a person is to be treated as obtaining property if he obtains ownership, possession or control of it, and 'obtain' includes obtaining for another or enabling another to obtain or to retain."

---

83 *Duru* [1974] 1 W.L.R. 2, where the court thought it unnecessary to invoke s. 6(1).
84 *Cf. Kohn* (1979) 69 Cr.App.R. 395; *supra*, para. 3.06.
85 *Infra*, ch. 4.
86 *Supra*, para. 3.13.
87 Assuming that his account is in credit, or he has an overdraft facility which has not been exceeded: *Supra*, para. 3.08.
88 *Kohn* (1979) 69 Cr.App.R. 395; *supra*, para. 3.06.
89 *Infra*, para. 3.20.
90 *e.g.* in the case of land: *supra*, para. 3.04.
91 *Supra*, para. 3.15.

Clearly this definition is wide enough to cover the defendant who enables some other (possibly innocent) person to reap the fruits of his deception, *e.g.* by faking his own death so that his spouse can claim on a life assurance policy.[92] It is also sufficient if the defendant already has possession or control and by deception obtains title to the property in question, or *vice versa*.[93] But there must be some property which initially belongs to another and of which the defendant or his associate, by means of the deception,[94] obtains ownership, possession or control. It is not sufficient if the property did not exist until the defendant acquired it (*e.g.* where he induces the victim to create a new right in his favour, perhaps by writing him a cheque),[95] nor if the property which the defendant acquires is not the property of which the victim is deprived. Thus if the victim is deceived into drawing a cheque which the defendant pays into his own account, and which is honoured, the victim has lost part of his credit balance (*i.e.* his rights against his bank) but the defendant has not obtained it. He may have acquired fresh rights against his own bank, but there is no assignment of the victim's rights against his.[96] It might be otherwise if the cheque were backed by a cheque card: in that case the diminishing of the victim's rights would be matched by the simultaneous conferment on the defendant of an equivalent right against the same bank.[97] In effect the defendant would have obtained the victim's property.

Appropriation

3.21 Theft, on the other hand, requires neither a deception nor an obtaining, but only an "appropriation" of the property. The Criminal Law Revision Committee preferred this term to the old "conversion" for much the same reason as that invoked to justify replacing "fraudulently" with "dishonestly", *viz.* that it means the same, but is more intelligible to the layman.[98] Whether it does mean the same is doubtful. Probably there can be an appropriation which does not involve civil liability for conversion;[99] but it is argued above that conduct which involves no civil liability at all should not be treated as theft, not because there is no appropriation but because there is no dishonesty.[1] Section 3(1) of the Theft Act 1968 provides:

---

92 *D.P.P. v. Stonehouse* [1978] A.C. 55. *Cf.* the suggested explanation of *Thompson* [1984] 3 All E.R. 565, *supra*, at para. 3.07.
93 *Cf. Collis-Smith* [1971] Crim.L.R. 716.
94 *Supra*, para. 2.48ff.
95 *Supra*, para. 3.13.
96 Bills of Exchange Act 1882 s. 53; *Schroeder v. Central Bank of London* (1876) 34 L.T. 735.
97 *Supra*, para. 2.25.
98 Cmnd. 2977 at para. 34.
99 *Bonner* [1970] 1 W.L.R. 838.
 1 *Supra*, para. 1.10ff.

"Any assumption by a person of the rights of an owner amounts to an appropriation, and this includes, where he has come by the property (innocently or not) without stealing it, any later assumption of a right to it by keeping or dealing with it as owner."

This definition covers not only a wrongful taking of possession (as in larceny) but also wrongful dealings with property of which the defendant is already in possession (as in fraudulent conversion),[2] provided always that it still "belongs to another".

3.22   The question of what constitutes an "assumption of the rights of an owner" was considered by the House of Lords in *Morris*.[3] The decision was that a person who switched the price labels on goods in a self-service store, with a view to buying the more expensive item for the price of the cheaper, was thereby guilty of theft even if he was apprehended before he reached the check-out. It was argued by the defence that there was no appropriation at this stage because the defendant had not assumed *all* the rights of an owner; but it was held to be sufficient if he assumed *any* of the rights of an owner, provided always that he did so with the intention of permanently depriving the owner of the property.

3.23   That was sufficient to dispose of the appeals before the House. Lord Roskill, however (with whom all their Lordships agreed), felt it necessary to deal with a further argument put forward by the prosecution, to the effect that even an honest customer is appropriating the goods which he removes from the shelf—*i.e.* that any act which would be unlawful if done without the owner's consent is an appropriation, even if it is in fact done *with* the owner's consent. Lord Roskill rejected the argument:

"In the context of section 3(1), the concept of appropriation in my view involves not an act expressly or impliedly authorised by the owner but an act by way of adverse interference with or usurpation of [his] rights."[4]

This statement was *obiter* and should be treated with caution. Admittedly it is in line with several earlier decisions of the Court of Appeal.[5] On the other hand it is hard to reconcile with the House of Lords' own decision in *Lawrence v. Metropolitan Police Commissioner*,[6] where a taxi-driver was held to have committed theft by extracting from a foreign passenger's

---

2   *Cf.* ch. 4.
3   [1984] A.C. 320.
4   At p. 332.
5   *Meech* [1974] Q.B. 549; *Skipp* [1975] Crim.L.R. 114; *Hircock* (1978) 67 Cr.App.R. 278.
6   [1972] A.C. 626.

wallet a sum far in excess of the correct fare. The passenger consented to the taking of the money, because he assumed that the sum taken was the correct amount. Yet in *Morris* their Lordships thought it "beyond question" that there was an appropriation in *Lawrence*. If this is so, it follows that the owner's consent to what is done is not necessarily and in all circumstances a defence to a charge of theft. It may be that Lord Roskill's view reads more into the wording of the Act than is really there. The word "appropriate" is defined by the *Shorter Oxford English Dictionary*[7] as "to take for one's own, or to oneself", with no qualification that the taking must be unauthorised. The more recent *Concise Oxford Dictionary*[8] gives "take possession of; take to oneself, [especially] without authority", which provides some support for the argument, but is a slender peg on which to hang it. If Parliament really intended that the owner's consent should be a defence it would have been easy to say so, either in the definition of theft itself or in that of appropriation. Moreover, such a restriction would leave the express requirement of dishonesty largely redundant.

3.24   Lord Roskill's view, if correct, would have at least two important implications for the law of fraud. In the first place it would follow that a person who is authorised by the owner of property to dispose of it on the owner's behalf is not stealing the property if he disposes of it within the scope of his authority, albeit dishonestly. This possibility is examined in the following chapter.[9] The second point is that the owner's consent will often have been obtained by deception; if the consent is a defence to a theft charge, there will be hardly any overlap between the offences of theft and obtaining property by deception, and it will be essential to charge the right one. The moral for prosecutors is clear: the deception offences should be employed in preference to theft if at all possible. Only if no deception can be proved is it advisable to resort to a charge of theft; and even then *Morris* may present difficulties if the fraud consists in the abuse of a fiduciary position, since it may be argued that the defendant had authority to act as he did. A straightforward misappropriation of money belonging to other people (or deemed to do so by virtue of section 5(3))[10] can certainly be treated as theft, and must be so treated if it cannot be proved that the defendant intended to misappropriate the money at the time when he accepted it. But in most fraud cases it will be the deception offences which the prosecutor should first consider.

7   3rd ed. 1944.
8   7th ed. 1982.
9   *Infra*. para. 4.19ff.
10   *Infra,* para. 4.07ff.

OBTAINING SERVICES BY DECEPTION

3.25　Where the benefit obtained by the fraud is not "property" within the meaning of the Theft Act 1968,[11] a charge of theft or of obtaining property by deception will fail. Provided that the benefit is obtained by deception, however, it may be possible to invoke certain other deception offences under the Theft Acts. The offence of the most general application is that created by section 1 of the Theft Act 1978, which provides:

> "(1) A person who by any deception dishonestly obtains services from another shall be guilty of an offence.
> (2) It is an obtaining of services where the other is induced to confer a benefit by doing some act, or causing or permitting some act to be done, on the understanding that the benefit has been or will be paid for."

The offence is punishable on conviction on indictment with five years' imprisonment.[12]

Benefit

3.26　The effect of subsection (2) is that the offence is not confined to the obtaining of services in the ordinary sense, but extends to the obtaining of virtually[13] any form of benefit whatsoever—provided that the element of dishonesty is established[14], that the benefit is obtained by deception,[15] and that it is conferred on the understanding that it has been or will be paid for. Indeed this last requirement appears to render the element of "benefit" redundant, since people do not pay for things they do not want.[16] In *Halai*[17] the defendant opened a building society savings account with a cheque which he knew would not be honoured, thus inducing the society's employees by deception to do certain acts. The Court of Appeal held that he had not obtained a service. O'Connor L.J. said:

11　*Supra*, para. 3.03ff.
12　s. 4(2). The offence is triable either way and on summary conviction carries six months' imprisonment or a fine of the prescribed sum or both: s. 4(1), (3).
13　*Quaere* whether it is ever possible to obtain a benefit by deception without inducing someone to do an act or to cause or permit an act to be done.
14　*Supra*, para. 1.04ff.
15　*Supra*, ch. 2.
16　Professor J.C. Smith suggests (*The Law of Theft* (5th ed.) at para. 227ff) that certain acts which are illegal or contrary to public policy might not be regarded as benefits even if some people think them worth paying for. But this may be to attach undue significance to the word "benefit", which is perhaps employed for the sake of brevity rather than content. If the legislature had intended to exclude the incurring of liabilities which are unenforceable due to the illegal nature of the "benefit" constituting the consideration, would it not have done so expressly as it did in s. 2(2) and s. 3(3) (*infra*, n. 24, para. 9.42, n.87)?
17　[1983] Crim. L.R. 624.

"Where a customer pays £500 into a bank, by no stretch of the use of ordinary English can anyone suggest that the bank is conferring a benefit on the customer. . ."

This would no doubt be so in the unlikely event of the customer making the bank a gift of the £500. However, the mere fact of recording the credit as a debt owed to the customer (plus, in the case of the opening of an account, the issue of a cheque book or building society pass book) would seem to constitute a benefit: it is, after all, what the customer wants. It is submitted that the true reason for the decision in *Halai* was the alternative ground relied on by the Court of Appeal, that even if the defendant did obtain a benefit, there was no expectation that it was to be paid for. Building societies do not charge for the privilege of opening an account.[18] The real criminality of Halai's conduct lay in his subsequent withdrawal of money to which he was not entitled, and a conviction of obtaining *property* by deception was upheld.

3.27 This extended sense of the term "services" in section 1(1) is clearly wide enough to include the transfer of property as well as the conferring of non-proprietary benefits. It seems that an offence of obtaining property by deception will inevitably constitute that of obtaining services by deception unless the transfer of the property is intended to be gratuitous (in which case the benefit is not conferred on the understanding that it has been or will be paid for). The charge should nevertheless be laid under section 15 of the 1968 Act if possible: not only does that offence better represent the nature of the conduct alleged, but the maximum penalty is ten years' imprisonment as against five. The offence under the 1978 Act might however be a useful alternative if there is any doubt as to the intention permanently to deprive.[19] Thus a person who hires a car with a bad cheque or a stolen credit card may not be guilty of obtaining property by deception if he intends to let the owner have the car back, but he is clearly guilty of obtaining services by deception.[20]

Expectation of payment

3.28 Even the requirement that the benefit be conferred on the understanding that it has been or will be paid for does not appear to be a serious limitation on the scope of the offence. It excludes the obtaining of benefits which are intended by the person conferring them to be

---

18 The position might be otherwise in the case of a current account with one of the banks which charge for this service: *cf.* J. C. Smith [1983] Crim. L.R. at p. 625.
19 Or as to whether the property belonged to another.
20 He would not be guilty of taking a conveyance without the owner's consent: *Whittaker v. Campbell* [1984] Q.B. 318.

gratuitous, even if payment would normally be expected and it is only as a result of the defendant's deception that an exception is made; but such cases are unlikely to be of significance.[21] It is possible, but unlikely, that a benefit is not expected to be "paid for" unless the payment is to be in money rather than money's worth. What is clearly *not* required is that the expectation of payment should be unfounded. Normally the deception will relate to the victim's prospect of being paid for the benefit conferred, but it need not do so, and the offence may be committed even if the defendant fully intends the victim to receive payment and is confident that he will. A person who obtains services by using a cheque card or credit card without authority, for example, is deceiving the person from whom he obtains the services into believing that the defendant is authorised to use the card;[22] the fact that that person will nevertheless be paid by the bank or credit card company does not mean that the defendant is not obtaining the services *by* the deception,[23] and the benefit is conferred on the understanding that it will be paid for even though that understanding is quite correct. Subject to the issue of dishonesty, the offence is therefore made out.

EVASION OF LIABILITY BY DECEPTION

3.29 Section 1 of the 1978 Act is confined to the case where the defendant obtains by deception something which he is expected to pay for. Where his deception does not enable him to incur a fresh liability, but only to avoid the necessity of meeting an existing one, the appropriate charge will be under section 2(1) of the 1978 Act:

". . . where a person by any deception—
  (*a*) dishonestly secures the remission of the whole or part of any existing liability[24] to make a payment, whether his own liability or another's; or
  (*b*) with intent to make permanent default in whole or in part on any existing liability to make a payment, or with intent to let another do so, dishonestly induces the creditor or any person claiming payment on behalf of the creditor to wait for payment (whether or not the due date for payment is deferred) or to forgo payment; or
  (*c*) dishonestly obtains[25] any exemption from or abatement of liability to make a payment;
  he shall be guilty of an offence."

---

21 In any event there would seem to be an offence of obtaining an exemption from liability, contrary to s. 2(1)(*c*) of the 1978 Act: *infra,* para. 3.29.
22 *Supra,* para. 2.42.
23 *Supra,* para. 2.53.
24 "Liability" in this section means "legally enforceable liability", and does not extend to a liability that has not been accepted or established to pay compensation for a wrongful act or omission: s. 2(2).
25 "Obtains" includes obtaining for another or enabling another to obtain: s. 2(4).

A person convicted on indictment of an offence under section 2 is liable to five years' imprisonment.[26]

3.30   Section 2(1) appears to create three offences.[27] Clearly there is some overlap between them,[28] but it seems reasonable to assume that each one applies in certain circumstances where the others (and section 1) do not. Unfortunately it is not clear precisely how they differ from one another. In *Holt*[29] Lawson J., speaking for the Court of Appeal, said:

> ". . . we are not sure whether the choice of expressions describing the consequences of deception employed in each of [section 2(1)'s] paragraphs, namely in paragraph (*a*) 'secures the remission of any existing liability', in paragraph (*b*) 'induces the creditor to forgo payment' and in paragraph (*c*) 'obtains any exemption from liability', are simply different ways of describing the same end result or represent conceptual differences. Whilst it is plain that there are substantial differences in the elements of the three offences defined in section 2(1), they show these common features: first, the use of deception to a creditor in relation to a liability, second, dishonesty in the use of deception, and third, the use of deception to gain some advantage in time or money. Thus the differences between the offences relate principally to the different situations in which the debtor-creditor relationship has arisen."[30]

3.31   The last sentence of this passage appears to be something of a *non sequitur*. Section 2(1) makes no mention of the circumstances in which the liability arises, but distinguishes between several different *effects* which the deception may achieve (*viz.* remission and abatement of the liability, exemption from it, and the creditor's waiting for payment or forgoing it). Possibly the court was referring to the fact that paragraph (*c*), unlike paragraphs (*a*) and (*b*), is not confined to the evasion of an *existing* liability: it also extends to the case where the deception enables the defendant to incur a fresh liability. Indeed, its chief significance probably lies in the way it complements section 1 in this situation. Section 1 would not apply if the victim of the deception believed neither that the defendant would pay nor that he had already done so, because the benefit would not be conferred on the understanding that it had been or would be paid for.[31] But if it is obtaining an "exemption" from a liability to escape payment by pretending that one has already paid,[32] the obtaining of a benefit by means of such a deception would fall under both section 1

---

26   s. 4(2). The offences are triable either way (s. 4(1)) and on summary conviction carry six months' imprisonment or a fine of the prescribed sum or both: s. 4(3).
27   *Holt* [1981] 1 W.L.R. 1000.
28   *Sibartie* [1983] Crim. L.R. 470, *Jackson* [1983] Crim. L.R. 617.
29   [1981] 1 W.L.R. 1000.
30   At p. 1002f.
31   *Supra,* para. 3.28.
32   *Cf. Sibartie* [1983] Crim. L.R. 470, *infra,* para. 3.32.

and section 2(1)(c). Obtaining the *abatement* of a fresh liability by deception (*i.e.* obtaining the benefit at a reduced price) would also constitute the offence under section 1: in that case there clearly *is* an understanding that the benefit is to be paid for.

Exemption

3.32 Where the liability evaded is already in existence, however, it is hard to see what paragraph (*c*) adds to paragraph (*a*). Unlike paragraph (*b*), it does not require an intent to make permanent default; but nor does paragraph (*a*). Is it possible to obtain an exemption from an existing liability, or an abatement of it, without securing the remission of the liability in whole or in part? In *Sibartie*[33] the defendant passed a ticket inspector while changing trains on the London Underground and "flashed" a season ticket at her which did not in fact cover the journey he was making. The Court of Appeal held that this was an attempt to obtain an exemption from liability by deception. But it is doubtful whether the defendant would in fact have obtained exemption from his obligation to pay the fare if he had successfully deceived the inspector. The obligation itself would not have been affected, since the defendant would still have been liable for the fare; indeed, the inspector would not even have *intended* to exempt him from liability, because she would have been under the impression that he had already paid and that there was no liability to exempt him from. Inducing a creditor to refrain from demanding payment by pretending to have already paid is more naturally described as inducing him to forgo payment, contrary to paragraph (*b*)[34]—but that paragraph requires an intent to make permanent default. Perhaps the explanation of *Sibartie* is that the defendant was trying to give the impression not merely that he had paid for the particular journey he was making but that he had bought a season ticket: season ticket holders are "exempt" from the requirement to pay for individual journeys because they have already paid. But even on this view there seems to be no requirement that the liability itself be affected, nor that the person deceived should realise that there is an existing liability at all.

Remission

3.33 The concept of the *remission* of a liability, an essential element of the offence under paragraph (*a*), is arguably somewhat narrower than that of an exemption. The word "remission" is ambiguous. It might refer either to the *release* of a debt, or to the mere abstention from exacting

---

33   [1983] Crim. L.R. 470.
34   *Cf. Holt* [1981] 1 W.L.R. 1000.

payment. In a penal provision the narrower sense (*i.e.* the former) should in principle be preferred. Moreover, this construction derives support from a comparison with paragraph (*b*). That offence can be committed in two ways, by inducing the creditor either to wait for payment or to forgo payment. Both forms of the offence require an intent to make permanent default, and in that respect are narrower than the offence under paragraph (*a*). Therefore they must both be wider than the paragraph (*a*) offence in some way: otherwise they would be redundant. Clearly a creditor can wait for payment without remitting the liability; but can he *forgo* payment without doing so? This is a possibility if remission necessarily involves the discharge of the obligation, but apparently not if it means no more than refraining from demanding payment: the latter seems to be precisely the same thing as forgoing payment. Therefore the only way to save this form of the paragraph (*b*) offence from redundancy is to construe "remission" in the former, narrower sense.

3.34 A possible objection to this narrow interpretation of "remission" is that it leaves the paragraph (*a*) offence with little content, since the liability will not be extinguished (though it may be waived) unless there is consideration for the release. But it is not necessarily exceptional for consideration to be present. In *Jackson*[35] the Court of Appeal held that a person who pays a debt with a stolen credit card is securing the remission of the debt by deception; and this is quite consistent with the narrow view of what constitutes a remission, since the use of the credit card so as to confer on the creditor a claim against the issuing company[36] can be regarded as sufficient consideration for the discharge of the original debt.[37] Even if credit card fraud were the only case to which paragraph (*a*) applied, it could hardly be said to be of excessively narrow scope. Admittedly it is confined to the evasion of *existing* liabilities, but the liability may be incurred only a matter of seconds before the credit card is used—*e.g.* where (as in *Jackson*) the card is used to pay for petrol which has already been pumped into the defendant's tank.[38]

---

35 [1983] Crim. L.R. 617.
36 Provided that the defendant produces a signature which is a reasonable approximation to that on the credit card, the fact that he is not authorised to use the card will not prevent the creditor acquiring such a claim.
37 Professor J. C. Smith suggests (*The Law of Theft* (5th ed.) paras. 234, 249) that the original obligation is not discharged, because if the issuing company failed to pay the creditor, for whatever reason, he would be able to recover the price from the defendant. This would certainly be so if the conditions necessary for the imposition of liability on the issuing company had not been complied with, *e.g.* if the defendant's signature were nothing like the one on the card; but is the holder of a credit card really still liable for the price even after he has successfully rendered the issuing company liable for it? Is it not a term of his contract with the creditor that the creation of a valid claim against the issuing company is all he is required to do?
38 A charge of obtaining the petrol by deception might present difficulties, since the obtaining may precede the deception: *cf. Edwards v. Ddin* [1976] 3 All E.R. 705.

Cheques

3.35 The position would seem to be much the same where an existing debt is paid by cheque, backed with a cheque card which the defendant is not authorised to use. The creditor accepts a fresh claim against the defendant's bank by way of substitution for his original claim against the defendant, and this too can be regarded as a remission (even in the narrow sense) of the original liability.[39] If the cheque is not backed with a cheque card, however, the creditor clearly retains his rights against the defendant in the event of the cheque being dishonoured. The liability is suspended but not remitted in the strict sense. Provided that the intent to make permanent default can be established, the payment of a debt with a bad cheque unsupported by a cheque card should be charged under paragraph (*b*) rather than paragraph (*a*). A possible argument to the effect that the creditor is not induced to wait for or forgo payment, but on the contrary is being paid (albeit conditionally) when he accepts the cheque, is anticipated by section 2(3):

> "For purposes of subsection (1)(*b*) a person induced to take in payment a cheque or other security for money by way of conditional satisfaction of a pre-existing liability is to be treated not as being paid but as being induced to wait for payment."

It is doubtful whether paragraph (*b*), even as buttressed by section 2(3), can properly be invoked where a cheque card or credit card is used. Does the creditor forgo payment of the original debt by accepting a claim against a third party in lieu? He can hardly be said to be waiting for payment of the original debt; and section 2(3) does not apply if, as argued above, the use of the card constitutes full and not merely conditional satisfaction of the liability. It is submitted that this type of case should be charged under paragraph (*a*), which has the additional advantage of not requiring an intent to make permanent default.

3.36 Where the debt is paid with a bad cheque unsupported by a cheque card, there is no offence unless it is the deception which induces the creditor to accept the cheque instead of insisting on cash or on the use of a cheque card.[40] If the terms of the defendant's contract are such that he is entitled to pay by cheque, it cannot be said that he is inducing the creditor to accept the cheque *by* the deception that the cheque is good.[41]

39　If the reason why the defendant is not authorised to use the cheque card is that his account is not sufficiently in credit, the use of the card may also constitute the offence of obtaining a pecuniary advantage by deception contrary to s. 16(2)(*b*) of the Theft Act 1968: *Waites* [1982] Crim. L.R. 369; *infra*, para. 3.38.
40　*Cf. supra*, para. 2.51.
41　*Andrews and Hedges* [1981] Crim. L.R. 106.

The creditor is not entitled to reject a valid[42] cheque tendered in payment, even if he has good reason to suspect that it will not be honoured: it is open to the drawer to ensure that by the time the cheque is presented the account is sufficiently in credit, or to arrange for an overdraft facility. The problem does not arise in the case of cheque cards and credit cards. Even if the creditor is obliged to accept payment by credit card, or by cheque provided it is supported by a cheque card, he clearly need not do so if the use of the card is unauthorised.[43] Therefore it is the defendant's deception as to his authority to use the card which induces the creditor to accept it.

OBTAINING A PECUNIARY ADVANTAGE BY DECEPTION

3.37 Sections 1 and 2 of the Theft Act 1978 cover most of the cases which formerly would have constituted the offence of obtaining a pecuniary advantage by deception, contrary to section 16 of the Theft Act 1968. The 1978 Act drastically restricted the scope of section 16 by repealing the notoriously obscure paragraph (*a*) of subsection (2), which set out a variety of circumstances in which a pecuniary advantage was deemed to be obtained; but the rest of the section is still in force, and in the relatively few situations specified in the remainder of subsection (2) it may prove a useful alternative to the other deception offences. It provides:

"(1) A person who by any deception dishonestly obtains for himself or another any pecuniary advantage shall on conviction on indictment be liable to imprisonment for a term not exceeding five years.[44]

(2) The cases in which a pecuniary advantage within the meaning of this section is to be regarded as obtained for a person are cases where—

. . .

(*b*) he is allowed to borrow by way of overdraft, or to take out any policy of insurance[45] or annuity contract, or obtains an improvement of the terms on which he is allowed to do so; or

(*c*) he is given the opportunity to earn remuneration or greater remuneration in an office or employment, or to win money by betting."

The section creates one offence which may be committed in various ways.[46]

---

42   "Valid" in the strict sense, *i.e.* complying with the requirements of the Bills of Exchange Act 1882. Obviously he need not accept a forged cheque.

43   His right to reject the card in these circumstances underlies the reasoning in *Metropolitan Police Commissioner v. Charles* [1977] A.C. 177 and *Lambie* [1982] A.C. 449: *supra,* para. 2.25ff.

44   The offence is triable either way and on summary conviction carries six months' imprisonment or a fine of the prescribed sum or both: Magistrates' Courts Act 1980 s. 17, Sch. 1, s. 32(1).

45   The offence may be committed even though the policy is void due to a mistake of identity: *Alexander* [1981] Crim. L.R. 183.

46   *Bale v. Rosier* [1977] 1 W.L.R. 263.

Overdrafts

3.38 A person "is allowed to borrow by way of overdraft" not only when he induces a bank to give him permission to overdraw (whether or not he actually does so),[47] but also when he succeeds in overdrawing *without* the bank's permission—which will be the effect if his cheques are honoured only because they were backed with a cheque card.[48] In this case it can hardly be said that the deception involved in the use of the card induces the bank to allow him to overdraw: the bank has no choice. Perhaps the rule can be justified on the ground that it is not the bank which "allows" the defendant to overdraw, but the recipient of the cheque. In any event it is doubtful whether a person who uses a *stolen* cheque book and cheque card can be said to be "borrowing" at all; and a person who simply induces a bank to lend him money is not borrowing it *by way of overdraft*. These cases should be charged as obtaining property or services by deception,[49] or in the former case possibly as the evasion of an existing liability.[50]

Other advantages

3.39 The remaining situations mentioned in subsection (2) were thought to require special treatment because, although the defendant hopes eventually to obtain money by means of the transaction which the deception enables him to procure, it may be that the obtaining will be too remote a consequence of the deception to justify a charge of obtaining property by deception:[51] *e.g.* a punter who by deception induces a bookmaker to accept bets on credit does not obtain his winnings by deception but by backing the right horse.[52] The difficulty can be avoided by charging an obtaining of a pecuniary advantage, *viz.* the *opportunity* to obtain the money. With the exception of the obtaining of an office or employment (where there is no understanding that the opportunity to earn money is to be paid for), these cases would in any event appear to fall within section 1 of the 1978 Act.[53] There is some doubt whether the

---

47 *Watkins* [1976] 1 All E.R. 578. If the bank charges a fee for granting the overdraft facility there will in any case be an offence of obtaining services by deception: *supra*, para. 3.25ff.
48 *Waites* [1982] Crim. L.R. 369.
49 If the bank loan is made by crediting an account in the defendant's name, he is obtaining property (*viz.* the chose in action represented by the credit), but that property never belonged to another: *cf. supra*, para. 3.13. There will, however, be an obtaining of services, unless the loan is interest-free and incurs no bank charges (in which case there is no understanding that it is to be paid for—one can hardly be said to pay for a loan merely by repaying it).
50 *Supra*, para. 3.35.
51 *Cf. supra*, para. 2.61ff.
52 *Clucas* [1949] 2 K.B. 226.
53 *Supra*, para. 3.25.

term "employment" in paragraph (*c*) is intended to include any form of paid work or is confined to contracts of employment in the strict sense. If, for example, a rogue obtains the job of carrying out house repairs by falsely telling the householder that they appear to be necessary, is he obtaining the opportunity to earn remuneration in an employment? It is submitted that the term should in principle be read in its narrower sense, though this may leave a small lacuna in the law. The difficulty arises only if the rogue does the work as agreed before claiming payment, in which case it is arguable that he is not obtaining the money by the original deception but by doing the job. If he asks for payment in advance, or pretends to have done work which he has not done, he clearly will be attempting to obtain money by deception.

PROCURING THE EXECUTION OF A VALUABLE SECURITY BY DECEPTION

3.40   Section 20(2) of the Theft Act 1968 provides:

> "A person who dishonestly, with a view to gain for himself or another or with intent to cause loss to another, by any deception procures the execution of a valuable security shall on conviction on indictment be liable to imprisonment for a term not exceeding seven years. . ."

The offence is triable either way.[54] It clearly overlaps with some of the other offences of deception discussed above: a defendant who deceived his victim into indorsing a cheque in the defendant's favour, for example, could be charged either with obtaining property (*viz.* the chose in action) by deception or with the offence under section 20(2). But the subsection also serves to stop up what might otherwise be unfortunate loopholes. If the victim is induced to draw a *fresh* cheque in the defendant's favour, there will be no chose in action belonging to the victim which the defendant can be charged with obtaining;[55] and a charge of obtaining the cheque itself would be artificial. The appropriate course is to proceed under section 20(2). Similarly, a person who makes out a bill of lading in respect of non-existent goods is probably guilty of forgery if he knows that the goods do not exist.[56] If he induced another person to make out the bill of lading, by leading that other to believe that the goods did exist, a forgery charge might be technically possible;[57] but it would be preferable, if only to avoid confusing the jury, to charge him with procuring the execution of the bill of lading by deception.

---

54   Magistrates' Courts Act 1980 s. 17, Sch. 1.
55   *Supra,* para. 3.13.
56   *Cf. Donnelly* [1984] 1 W.L.R. 1017; *infra,* para. 6.17.
57   *Infra,* para. 6.21.

Valuable security

3.41   The expression "valuable security" is defined by section 20(3). It includes any document which

(a) creates, transfers, surrenders or releases any right to, in or over property,

(b) authorises the payment of money or the delivery of any property, or

(c) evidences

(i) the creation, transfer, surrender or release of any such right,

(ii) the payment of money or the delivery of any property, or

(iii) the satisfaction of any obligation.

This definition clearly covers such commercial documents as cheques, traveller's cheques, bills of lading, share certificates *etc.*—even if they are forged and therefore invalid.[58] In *Benstead and Taylor*[59] it was held to include an irrevocable letter of credit, because such a document confers on its beneficiary a right to payment and is therefore a document creating a right to property (*i.e.* money). This is, with respect, a surprising interpretation: on a natural reading the phrase "any right to, in or over property" refers to a proprietary right, not a personal one. The reference to the payment of money in clause (b) above is conspicuously absent from clause (a), yet it seems that a document creating a right to the payment of money is within clause (a). In that case virtually any written contract must be a valuable security. But the definition clearly does not extend to a document which has none of the functions referred to and which serves merely as a record (*e.g.* a set of accounts). For that reason alone, a computer file would not normally qualify. If such a file did have one of the specified functions (*e.g.* authorising the payment of money) the question would arise whether it was a "document" at all. It is arguable that an article is not a document unless it can be read by the human eye. But a microfiche is clearly a document although it cannot be read without the assistance of a machine; and it has been held in another context that a tape recording is a document.[60] It must in any event be remembered that the computer itself probably cannot be the victim of the deception which is an essential ingredient of the offence.[61]

Execution

3.42   The benefit which must be obtained by means of the deception is referred to as the "execution" of a valuable security; but that expression

---

58 *Beck* [1985] 1 W.L.R. 22; *infra,* para. 3.42.
59 (1982) 75 Cr.App.R. 276.
60 *Grant v. Southwestern and County Properties Ltd* [1975] Ch. 185.
61 *Supra,* para. 2.30.

is deemed to include the "making, acceptance, indorsement, alteration, cancellation or destruction in whole or in part" of the valuable security.[62] In *Beck*[63] the defendant obtained money and goods in France by means of forged traveller's cheques and a stolen Diners Club card, issued by an English bank and by Diners Club Ltd respectively. The prosecution case was that the traveller's cheques and the credit card bills were "executed" when they were honoured by the bank and Diners Club, and that the offence under section 20(2) was therefore committed within the jurisdiction;[64] "execution", it was argued, meant no more than "giving effect to". The defence contended that all the acts of execution had taken place in France. The appeal was dismissed. Watkins L.J., delivering the judgment of the Court of Appeal, said:

> "In our view, having regard only to the facts of this case, execution bears one of the extended meanings given to it in section 20(2). Thus it is clear that, for example, the alteration, cancellation or destruction of a valuable security can amount to an execution of it. So may an acceptance of it. To attribute to the word the very restricted meaning [counsel for the appellant] would have us accept and even to [*sic*] the somewhat more expansive definition provided by [counsel for the Crown] would be, in our judgment, to fail to recognise the plain indication of its meaning in the subsection itself. Thus, when a traveller's cheque is accepted as genuine by a payer who pays the monetary value of it to the holder, he executes it. Likewise, when Diners Club (France) accepts a bill for payment signed by the actual or ostensible holder of a club card and pays it, execution takes place."[65]

Since the credit card bills were paid not by Diners Club (France) but by Diners Club Ltd in England, they were "accepted" (and therefore "executed") in England. Similarly the traveller's cheques, having first been accepted by the bank's agents in France, were subsequently accepted when they were honoured by the bank in England. Therefore the defendant had procured their execution in England, and the offences were made out. It is submitted with respect that this decision is questionable. Given the definition of a "valuable security", and in the context of the phrase "making, acceptance, indorsement, alteration, cancellation or destruction", the term "acceptance" was surely intended to be read not in its ordinary sense (*i.e.* treating the valuable security as if it were valid) but in its technical sense, *i.e.* the acceptance of a bill of exchange by the drawee so as to render himself liable upon it. Acceptance in this sense requires the drawee's signature on the bill.[66] This interpretation is therefore consonant with the other actions deemed to constitute "execution", all of which involve bringing about some change

62 s. 20(2).
63 [1985] 1 W.L.R. 22.
64 *Cf. infra,* para. 11.03ff.
65 At p. 26f.
66 Bills of Exchange Act 1882 s. 17(2)(*a*).

in the security's legal effect by either writing on it or destroying it. The Court of Appeal's interpretation ignores this common feature and creates a degree of overlap with the other deception offences which is unlikely to have been envisaged by the legislature.

3.43 A valuable security is also deemed to have been executed, even if there is no valuable security in existence, if any paper or other material is signed or sealed in order that it may be made or converted into, or used or dealt with as, a valuable security.[67] The phrasing suggests that the intention referred to must be that of the person signing or sealing the paper or material, not merely that of the defendant; in other words it would seem that the offence would not be committed if the defendant, intending to use a document as a valuable security, induced his victim to sign it under the impression that the signature was required for some purpose which would not involve such use. But if the victim knew that the document would be used as a valuable security, it would presumably be immaterial that he did not appreciate the use to which it would be put or even the type of valuable security into which it would be converted.

Procuring

3.44 The execution of the valuable security must be "procured" by the deception. In *Beck*[68] it was argued that one procures an objective only if one obtains it by endeavour, by "setting out to see that it happens and taking the appropriate steps to produce that happening".[69] It could hardly be said that Beck had set out to see that the cost of his fraudulent activities should be borne by Diners Club and the English bank rather than by his victims in France. This argument too was rejected.

> "It [*sc.* "procure"] is a word in common usage which, in our view, a jury can be relied upon safely to understand. The most common meaning attached to it in our experience is to cause or to bring about. It has no special meaning for the purpose of section 20(2) and none, in our view, should be attributed to it by reference to its use in other enactments."[70]

Beck had brought about the execution of the valuable securities in England because he had put Diners Club and the bank in a position where for legal or commercial reasons they were obliged to pay up. Furthermore he had achieved this result by deception, because if it had not been for the deceptions in France Diners Club and the bank would not have been put in that position. It was immaterial that they knew of

---

67 s.20(2).
68 [1985] 1 W.L.R. 22: *supra*, para. 3.42.
69 *Attorney-General's Reference (No. 1 of 1975)* [1975] Q.B. 773 at p. 779, *per* Lord Widgery C.J., with reference to s. 8 of the Accessories and Abettors Act 1861.
70 At p. 28, *per* Watkins L.J.

the deception by the time they accepted the bills and the traveller's cheques, and therefore were not themselves deceived: the valuable security need not be executed by the person deceived, provided that its execution is a consequence of the deception.[71]

Gain and loss

3.45 The *mens rea* of the offence consists of (i) dishonesty and (ii) a view to gain *or* intent to cause loss. The concept of dishonesty has already been discussed.[72] "Gain" and "loss" are defined by section 34(2)(*a*):

> " 'gain' and 'loss' are to be construed as extending only to gain or loss in money or other property, but as extending to any such gain or loss whether temporary or permanent; and
> (i)   'gain' includes a gain by keeping what one has, as well as a gain by getting what one has not; and
> (ii)   'loss' includes a loss by not getting what one might get as well as a loss by parting with what one has. . . ."

The reference to temporary gain brings within the scope of the offence a person who has no intention of making permanent default but finds it necessary to resort to deception in order to prevent the discovery of previous misconduct. In *Eden*[73] a sub-postmaster had submitted accounts showing payments in excess of the value of the corresponding vouchers. He was charged, *inter alia*, with false accounting contrary to section 17 of the Theft Act[74] (an offence which, like section 20(2), requires a view to gain or intent to cause loss). His defence was that he had, incompetently but not dishonestly, got into a muddle and had falsified the returns in order to conceal the position. The Court of Appeal expressed the view that, if the jury had been properly directed, a conviction of false accounting would have been in order: an intention to make a temporary gain was sufficient, and, as Sachs L.J. put it:

> "Such a gain could be constituted by putting off the evil day of having to sort out the muddle and pay up what may have been in error kept within the sub-post office when it ought to have been sent to head office."[75]

LIABILITY OF COMPANY OFFICERS FOR OFFENCES OF DECEPTION

3.46 Where an offence is committed by a person whose position within a company is such as to justify regarding his actions and intentions as

71 *Supra*, para. 2.60.
72 *Supra*, para. 1.04ff.
73 (1971) 55 Cr.App.R. 193; *cf. Wines* [1954] 1 W.L.R. 64.
74 *Infra*, para. 6.41ff.
75 (1971) 55 Cr.App.R. 193 at p. 197.

those of the company itself, the company will also be guilty of the offence;[76] and in that case liability may be imposed on other officers of the company who have allowed the offence to be committed. Section 18 of the Theft Act 1968 provides:

> "(1) Where an offence committed by a body corporate under section 15, 16 or 17 of this Act is proved to have been committed with the consent or connivance of any director, manager, secretary or other similar officer of the body corporate, or any person who was purporting to act in any such capacity, he as well as the body corporate shall be guilty of that offence, and shall be liable to be proceeded against and punished accordingly.
>
> (2) Where the affairs of a body corporate are managed by its members, this section shall apply in relation to the acts and defaults of a member in connection with his functions of management as if he were a director of the body corporate."

The section applies not only to the deception offences under sections 15 and 16 of the 1968 Act[77] but also to those created by the 1978 Act.[78] It probably adds little to the position at common law. An officer who positively encouraged or assisted in the commission of the offence would in any event be guilty as an accessory. It is arguable that the same would apply to a director, at least, who simply acquiesced in the fraud, on the ground that a person who has the authority to prevent an offence being committed may be implicated by the mere failure to exercise that authority.[79] But section 18 renders such possibilities academic. A director, manager, secretary "or other similar officer" need only be proved to have consented to or connived at the commission of the offence. Mere neglect of duty is clearly not enough: one cannot consent to something, or connive at it, without knowing about it. But once knowledge is established, passive acquiescence would seem to be all that is required.

---

76 *Tesco Supermarkets Ltd v. Nattrass* [1972] A.C. 153.
77 But not s. 20(2).
78 Theft Act 1978 s. 5(1).
79 *Tuck v. Robson* [1970] 1 W.L.R. 741.

CHAPTER 4

Theft by Fiduciaries

4.01 Strictly speaking, any theft is by definition within the legal concept of fraud;[1] but the connotations of the term "fraud" in common parlance are perhaps best exemplified by a particular type of theft, *viz.* the misappropriation of money or other property which has been *entrusted* to the thief or which for some other reason he holds in a fiduciary capacity. In this chapter we consider the application of the law of theft to this situation. Apart from those elements of the offence which present no more difficulty in this context than elsewhere, such as the extra-legal aspects of dishonesty[2] and the intention permanently to deprive,[3] two main issues require examination: firstly, whether the property in question "belongs to another" for the purposes of a theft charge; and secondly, whether the defendant's fiduciary status can, paradoxically, redound to his advantage by enabling him to claim that he was acting with the consent of the person to whom the property belonged.

PROPERTY BELONGING TO ANOTHER

Property subject to a trust

4.02 Where property is entrusted to a person for some purpose, or for any reason he is not free to use it as he likes, it is likely that the property will "belong to another" for the purposes of the law of theft. In the first place, the person entrusted with it may well be constituted a trustee in the strict sense: *i.e.* the beneficial interest may be retained by someone else even if the fiduciary acquires the legal title. Since property "belongs" to anyone with a proprietary interest in it, legal or equitable,[4] the misappropriation by a trustee of trust property can certainly amount to theft.[5] Whether the defendant does hold the property on trust will

---

1 *Cf.* ch. 1.
2 *Supra,* para. 1.16ff.
3 *Supra,* para. 3.17ff.
4 *Supra,* para. 3.14.
5 For the purposes of theft, property held on trust is deemed to belong to any person with a right to enforce the trust, even if he has no proprietary interest in it: Theft Act 1968 s. 5(2).

normally depend on the intention of the person who transferred it to him, but in certain circumstances a "constructive" trust may be imposed by operation of law: for example, a person who receives trust assets with actual or constructive notice that they have been misapplied in breach of trust will himself be treated as a constructive trustee.[6] The same applies to property extracted from a company by its directors in breach of their fiduciary duty,[7] and although such a breach can normally be ratified by a majority of the shareholders, this is not so in the case of fraud;[8] indeed it is unlikely that fraud can be ratified by even a unanimous vote.[9] Thus the constructive trust will be imposed even if the directors responsible for the fraud are the only shareholders. A subsequent dishonest appropriation, either by the directors themselves or by a third party, could therefore constitute theft. It would of course be less artificial to charge the directors with stealing the property by extracting it from the company in the first place, rather than by dealing with it *after* extracting it; but, as we shall see, it might be difficult to establish that the original transaction involved an appropriation on the directors' part.[10] On the other hand it would be odd if the original extraction did not amount to theft but subsequent dealings with the property did.

4.03 A somewhat more dubious application of the constructive trust is the case where a person in a fiduciary position makes a secret profit by acting in his own interests rather than those of his beneficiary, and is in consequence accountable for that profit. Those regarded as fiduciaries for this purpose include not only trustees, receivers and liquidators but also company directors,[11] partners[12] and even employees (provided at any rate that the employee is enabled to make the profit by virtue of a position of authority).[13] Agents in the strict sense are normally fiduciaries:[14] thus, for

---

6 *Barnes v. Addy* (1874) L.R. 9 Ch.App. 244 at p. 251f., *per* Lord Selborne L.C.
7 *Russell v. Wakefield Waterworks Co.* (1875) L.R. 20 Eq. 474 at p. 479, *per* Jessel M.R.; *Re Canadian Oil Works Corp. (Hay's Case)* (1875) L.R. 10 Ch.App. 593; *Selangor United Rubber Estates Ltd v. Cradock (No. 3)* [1968] 1 W.L.R. 1555; *Belmont Finance Corp. v. Williams Furniture Ltd (No. 2)* [1980] 1 All E.R. 393; *International Sales and Agencies Ltd v. Marcus* [1982] 3 All E.R. 551.
8 *Atwool v. Merryweather* (1876) L.R. 5 Eq. 464n.; *Mason v. Harris* (1879) 11 Ch.D. 97.
9 *Re George Newman & Co.* [1895] 1 Ch. 674 at p. 685f., *per* Lindley L.J.; *Re Horsley & Weight Ltd* [1982] Ch. 442 at p. 455 (*per* Cumming-Bruce L.J.) and p. 456 (*per* Templeman L.J.). Comments on these dicta in *Multinational Gas and Petrochemical Co. v. Multinational Gas and Petrochemical Services Ltd* [1983] Ch. 258 do not appear to be relevant to the context of fraud: *cf. Attorney-General's Reference (No. 2 of 1982)* [1984] Q.B. 624.
10 *Cf. infra.* para. 4.19ff.
11 *Cook v. Deeks* [1916] 1 A.C. 554.
12 *Thompson's trustee in bankruptcy v. Heaton* [1974] 1 W.L.R. 605.
13 *A.-G. v. Goddard* (1929) 98 L.J.K.B. 743; *Reading v. A.-G.* [1951] A.C. 507.
14 In *Limako B.V. v. Hentz & Co. Inc.* [1979] 2 Lloyd's Rep. 23 the court was prepared to envisage the possibility of an agent who by custom is not subject to the normal fiduciary duties of an agent. But such a custom would probably be unreasonable and therefore not binding on a client without notice of it: *cf. infra.* para. 4.17.

example, a Lloyd's underwriter who in his own interests accepted obviously bad risks,[15] or deliberately channelled the most lucrative business to a "baby" syndicate whose membership was jealously restricted, would be in breach of duty and would be accountable to his syndicate for the resulting profit. Moreover, an intermediary who is not an agent in the strict sense, such as an estate agent engaged merely to advertise a property,[16] may nevertheless be in a fiduciary position for this purpose:[17] the categories of fiduciary obligation are never closed[18] and the nature of the intermediary's duty to his client is ultimately a matter of the construction of the contract between them. An investment consultant, for example, is clearly under an implied duty to give objective advice uninfluenced by any consideration of the effect on his own dealings.

4.04   It is commonly stated that a fiduciary who makes a secret profit by abusing his position in this way will be treated as a constructive trustee of the profit. If this is so, the defrauded beneficiary will have an equitable interest in the proceeds and they will literally belong to him. It would follow that any subsequent dealings with them might amount to theft, even if the actual making of the profit was not in itself an offence.[19] But there are certain difficulties involved in the application of the law of theft to this situation. In the first place it is not every secret profit which is subject to a constructive trust. A clear case where this is not so is that of an agent who accepts a bribe: he is personally liable to his principal for the sum received but is not a trustee of the bribe itself.[20] As to other types of secret profit the authorities are inconclusive, because generally the issue is whether the fiduciary is liable at all rather than whether he is a trustee.[21] Thus there are two extreme views, *viz.* (a) that all secret profits except bribes are held on trust, and (b) that no secret profits are held on trust.[22] The orthodox view is a compromise: there is a trust if, and only if, the profit is obtained through the misuse of either property or confidential information which has been entrusted to the fiduciary.[23] In

---

15   *Cf. Hambro v. Burnand* [1904] 2 K.B. 10; *infra.* para. 4.23.
16   *Regier v. Campbell-Stuart* [1939] Ch. 766.
17   *Cf. Ireland v. Livingston* (1872) L.R. 5 H.L. 395; *infra,* para. 4–14 at n. 71.
18   *English v. Dedham Vale Properties* [1978] 1 W.L.R. 93.
19   A.T.H. Smith, "Constructive Trusts in the Law of Theft" [1977] Crim. L.R. 395.
20   *Lister v. Stubbs* (1890) 45 Ch.D. 1; *cf. Powell v. MacRae* [1977] Crim.L.R. 571. An agent who accepts a bribe will normally be guilty of an offence under the Prevention of Corruption Acts 1889–1916; *infra.* ch. 7.
21   *e.g. Parker v. McKenna* (1874) L.R. 10 Ch.App. 96; *Cook v. Deeks* [1916] 1 A.C. 554; *Boardman v. Phipps* [1967] 2 A.C. 46.
22   J.C. Smith [1979] Crim.L.R. 220 at p. 225f.
23   Goff & Jones, *The Law of Restitution* (2nd ed.) at p. 509f. A trust may of course be imposed by statute: *e.g.* a company director who, without the approval of the general meeting, accepts compensation for loss of office in connection with a take-over is deemed to hold the sum received on trust for his company (Companies Act 1985 s. 313(2)).

the case of the Lloyd's underwriter who keeps the best business for a baby syndicate, or the investment consultant who advises the purchase of securities which he himself is planning to sell, this is not so; therefore, on the orthodox view, there is no question of a charge of stealing the proceeds.

4.05 In any event it is not clear that a constructive trust imposed on these grounds would be sufficient to justify a charge of theft. It is true that English law (unlike American law)[24] regards the constructive trust as a substantive proprietary concept and not merely a remedial device,[25] and that property subject to such a trust is therefore literally property "belonging to another". There is nevertheless a real distinction between a fiduciary who misappropriates property entrusted to him and one who merely obtains a profit which as a matter of law is deemed to belong to his beneficiary. For the purposes of restitution it is no doubt convenient to treat the two cases alike: in particular, the imposition of a trust will give the beneficiary preferential status in the event of the fiduciary's insolvency. But such considerations have little relevance to the purposes served by the criminal law. Moreover the law should not be allowed to diverge too far from the layman's notion of what theft is. As Lord Lane C.J. has said in a different context:

> "It seems to me that the court should not be astute to find that a theft has taken place where it would be straining the language so to hold, or where the ordinary person would not regard the defendant's acts, though possibly morally reprehensible, as theft."[26]

In *Tarling (No. 1) v. Government of the Republic of Singapore,*[27] where a company chairman was alleged to have made secret profits at his company's expense, Lord Wilberforce expressed the view that this in itself would not constitute theft or indeed any other offence:

> "Breach of fiduciary duty, exorbitant profit making, secrecy . . . are one thing: theft and fraud are others . . . The highest . . . that the evidence can be put is that the participants made a secret profit . . . and that they kept it secret: it would not otherwise be a secret profit. This by itself is no criminal offence, whatever other epithet may be appropriate."[28]

Lord Salmon[29] and Lord Keith[30] agreed. It must however be said that, even if the dishonest making of a secret profit does not amount to theft, the view that it does not amount to *fraud* is surprisingly generous. The

---

24 R. H. Maudsley (1959) 75 L.Q.R. 234 at p. 237.
25 *e.g. Re Sharpe* [1980] 1 W.L.R. 219 at p. 225f.
26 *Kaur v. Chief Constable for Hampshire* [1981] 1 W.L.R. 578 at p. 583.
27 (1978) 70 Cr.App.R. 77.
28 At p. 110f.
29 At p. 130.
30 At p. 137.

conduct alleged in *Tarling* clearly fell within the definition of fraud laid down in *Scott v. Metropolitan Police Commissioner.*[31] The House's rejection of charges of conspiracy to defraud would seem to have been heavily influenced by the convoluted drafting of those charges.[32] It is submitted that an agreement for the dishonest making of a secret profit by a fiduciary, if it is not an agreement to commit any substantive offence,[33] will normally amount to a conspiracy to defraud.

Property belonging to a company

4.06 Another situation where it may be arguable that property should not be treated as belonging to another for the purposes of theft, although another person is the owner not only in equity but also at common law, is that of property vested in a company which is itself wholly owned by those charged. In theory the company is of course a legal person in its own right, distinct from the shareholders, and from their point of view its property does literally belong to another person. It might however be objected that in reality the company's property is the property of the shareholders themselves, and that it is the reality which should be reflected in the criminal law. In *Squire,*[34] for example, it was conceded at the trial that it would not be theft for the only two shareholders to co-operate in siphoning off the company's funds. In *Arthur*[35] most of the shares were held by the directors responsible for the fraud, but a few were held by their wives. The Court of Appeal dismissed an appeal against conviction of fraudulent conversion on the ground that

"... there was fraud on the company because it was a separate entity consisting of more shareholders than [the parties to the fraud]."[36]

The implication was that if there were no other shareholders the company would not be defrauded. This may be the explanation for the ruling in *Pearlberg and O'Brien*[37] that there was no case to answer on a charge of theft where the directors and sole shareholders of a company wrote company cheques for their own purposes. But when the ruling was referred to the Court of Appeal,[38] it was apparently assumed that the money did belong to another for the purposes of a theft charge, and the argument was confined to the issue of dishonesty. The Court of Appeal's decision that a conviction would have been legitimate is therefore no

---

31 [1975] A.C. 819, *supra* para. 1.38.
32 *Cf. infra,* para. 11.20.
33 *Infra,* para. 12.34ff.
34 [1963] Crim.L.R. 700.
35 (1967) 111 S.J. 435.
36 *per* Sellers L.J.
37 [1982] Crim. L.R. 829.
38 *Attorney-General's Reference (No. 2 of 1982)* [1984] Q.B. 624; *infra,* para. 4.26.

more than an authority *sub silentio* on this point. Nevertheless, there is no obvious justification in this context for "lifting the veil" of corporate personality and deeming the company's property to belong to the shareholders. There might be a grain of robust common sense in such a rule, but it would essentially be a distortion of the reality. Company capital cannot simply be returned to the shareholders on demand. In a sense it belongs to the company's creditors too.

Obligation to deal with property in a particular way

4.07   Even property of which the defendant is the sole owner, both at law and in equity, may nevertheless be deemed to belong to another by virtue of section 5(3) of the Theft Act 1968. Section 5(3) provides:

> "Where a person receives property from or on account of another, and is under an obligation to the other to retain and deal with that property or its proceeds in a particular way, the property or proceeds shall be regarded (as against him) as belonging to the other."

In effect, this provision means that property held in a fiduciary capacity is virtually always property belonging to another. In many cases a person holding property subject to the obligation described will in fact be a trustee, so that the property will belong to another by virtue of section 5(1) and it will be unnecessary to resort to section 5(3). But this is not invariably so: one may have a personal right that certain property be dealt with in a particular way without necessarily having a proprietary interest in it. In *Palmer v. Carey*,[39] for example, a contractual obligation to put certain receipts into a particular bank account was held not to constitute a trust of the money. The effect of section 5(3) is that the absence of a trust would not in itself be fatal to a charge of stealing the money by misappropriating it. This possibility is important in the type of fraud where a trader or professional person is paid money for one purpose and dishonestly uses it for another, knowing that he has little or no prospect of providing the consideration for which the money was paid. If it cannot be proved that he intended to misapply the money at the time when he received it, a charge of obtaining it by deception will fail. If the money became his to use as he liked, a charge of theft will also fail.[40] But if he incurs an obligation to deal with the money in a particular way (whether or not the client retains an equitable interest in it), a misappropriation of the money may constitute theft.

Nature of the obligation required

4.08   The "obligation" referred to in section 5(3) must clearly be a *legal* obligation, and the defendant's rights and obligations in civil law must

39   [1926] A.C. 703.
40   *Hall* [1973] Q.B. 126, *infra*, para. 4.13.

therefore be determined when the subsection is relied upon. Notwithstanding earlier dicta suggesting that it is for the jury to decide what amounts to an obligation for this purpose,[41] the correct procedure was laid down by Lawton L.J. (speaking for the Court of Appeal) in *Mainwaring and Madders:*[42]

> "Whether or not an obligation arises is a matter of law, because an obligation must be a legal obligation. But a legal obligation arises only in certain circumstances, and in many cases the circumstances cannot be known until the facts have been established. It is for the jury, not the judge, to establish the facts, if they are in dispute. What, in our judgment, a judge ought to do is this: if the facts relied upon by the prosecution are in dispute he should direct the jury to make their findings on the facts, and then say to them: 'If you find the facts to be such-and-such, then I direct you as a matter of law that a legal obligation arose to which section 5(3) applies.' "[43]

Thus it is not sufficient that the defendant does in fact keep certain funds separate, even if the person from whom or on whose account he receives them requests him to do so,[44] unless he has an obligation to do so as a matter of civil law. If there is no such obligation, section 5(3) cannot apply.[45]

4.09 Logically the result should be the same if the "obligation" undertaken is vitiated by illegality and could not therefore be enforced by the person to whom it is apparently owed.[46] In *Meech,*[47] however, the Court of Appeal held that this is not necessarily so, at any rate if the person subject to the supposed obligation is unaware of the illegality. Meech was charged with stealing the proceeds of a cheque which had been entrusted to him by one McCord. McCord had obtained the cheque by means of a forged instrument; but Meech did not know this when he accepted the cheque, and it was held that he was therefore under an obligation to McCord to deal with the proceeds as requested, although an attempt by McCord to enforce that obligation would presumably have been met with a plea of *ex turpi causa.* Roskill L.J., delivering the judgment of the court, said:

---

41   *Ibid.; Hayes* (1977) 64 Cr.App.R. 82.
42   (1981) 74 Cr.App.R. 99.
43   At p. 107.
44   *Cf. Cuffin* (1922) 127 L.T. 564.
45   *Cullen* (unreported, 1974), referred to in J.C. Smith, *The Law of Theft* (5th ed.) at para. 71, is probably wrong in holding that a man's mistress is under a legal obligation to use a housekeeping allowance for the purpose for which it is given to her: *cf. Balfour v. Balfour* [1919] 2 K.B. 571. In *Davidge v. Bunnett* [1984] Crim.L.R. 297, on the other hand, the parties were not cohabitants but merely flat-mates, and a legal obligation probably did exist.
46   *Cf. Gilks* [1972] 1 W.L.R. 1341, *supra,* para. 1.13.
47   [1974] Q.B. 549.

"The question has to be looked at from Meech's point of view, not McCord's. Meech plainly assumed an 'obligation' to McCord which, on the facts then known to him, he remained obliged to fulfil and, on the facts as found, he must be taken at that time honestly to have intended to fulfil. The fact that on the true facts if known McCord might not and indeed would not subsequently have been permitted to enforce that obligation in a civil court does not prevent that 'obligation' on Meech having arisen. The argument confuses the creation of the obligation with the subsequent discharge of that obligation either by performance or otherwise. That the obligation might have become impossible of performance by Meech or of enforcement by McCord on grounds of illegality or for reasons of public policy is irrelevant."[48]

With respect, the confusion appears to lie in the court's own reasoning. Even if the obligation was not at first "impossible . . . of enforcement" but only became so when Meech discovered the illegality (because he could hardly plead the illegality until he knew about it), it does not follow that he was ever under an obligation as a matter of law. Unless we are to accept the somewhat metaphysical concept of a legal obligation which is legally unenforceable, Meech never did have any legal obligation to deal with the cheque according to McCord's instructions. If the decision is right, section 5(3) must be read as if it did not require the defendant to *be* under an obligation but only to *believe* that he is under one.

4.10 Even if the Court of Appeal's reasoning is correct, and Meech was initially under an obligation to McCord within the meaning of section 5(3) because he did not then know of the circumstances in which the cheque had been obtained, there is the further difficulty that he discovered the truth before he appropriated the proceeds. Whether or not he was originally under a legal obligation, he was no longer under one at the time of the alleged theft: indeed, performance of the alleged obligation might well have constituted an offence. But this was held to be irrelevant.

"... Meech being under the initial obligation already mentioned, the proceeds of the cheque continued as between him and McCord to be deemed to be McCord's property so that if Meech dishonestly misappropriated those proceeds he was, by reason of section 5(3), guilty of theft even though McCord could not have enforced performance of that obligation against Meech in a civil action."[49]

In other words, if a legal obligation is once created, the fact that it is subsequently discharged before the time of the appropriation does not prevent the application of section 5(3). As his Lordship said in connection with the argument that Meech was never under a legal obligation at all (where the remark does not appear to be relevant):

48 At p. 554f.
49 At p. 556.

"The opening words of section 5(3) clearly look to the time of the creation of or the acceptance of the obligation by the bailee and not to the time of performance by him of the obligation so created and accepted by him."[50]

But this is not the only possible interpretation. Section 5(3) could equally be construed as requiring that the defendant must be under the obligation at the time when the property is alleged to belong to another, *i.e.* (because it is the only time at which that question is relevant) at the moment of appropriation; and it is submitted that this is the more natural reading.

4.11 If *Meech* is correct on this point, and section 5(3) does not cease to apply merely because the obligation which originally existed has been discharged by illegality, the position is presumably the same where the obligation is discharged for some other reason such as the agreement of the parties. In *Wilsons and Furness-Leyland Line Ltd v. British and Continental Shipping Co. Ltd*[51] the defendant company collected freight on behalf of the plaintiff company but paid the money into its own general trading account instead of segregating it. The plaintiff company consented to this procedure. Walton J. held that, even if the defendant company was originally a fiduciary of the money, the relationship had by mutual consent been converted into one of debtor and creditor. Even if the defendant company's fiduciary obligations were indeed discharged and not merely waived,[52] the reasoning in *Meech* suggests that for the purposes of the law of theft the money might still be deemed to belong to the plaintiff company under section 5(3). However, the point may be academic. The House of Lords has stated that something done with the consent of the person to whom the property belongs is not an "appropriation" of the property;[53] and if the person entitled to the money consents to the defendant treating it as his own, it would seem to follow that even a dishonest use of the money by the defendant could not constitute theft.

Identity of the parties
4.12 Section 5(3) requires not only that the defendant be under a legal obligation to deal with the property or its proceeds in a particular way, but that that obligation be owed to the person from whom or on whose account he receives the property. It is not sufficient if the obligation is owed to some other person. If, for example, a professional association requires its members to keep client accounts separate from their general trading accounts, this does not in itself confer on members' clients any

---

50 At p. 555.
51 (1907) 23 T.L.R. 397.
52 *Cf. Brewster* (1979) 69 Cr.App.R. 375.
53 *Morris* [1984] A.C. 320; *cf. infra,* para. 4.19ff.

legal right that their money be segregated: the obligation imposed on the members may be owed only to the association or to each other. But if it is the usual practice in a particular trade or profession to keep client accounts, the contract with a client will readily be construed as including an implied term that that practice must be followed; and in that case section 5(3) will apply. Similarly, professional people who are required by statute to keep client accounts (*e.g.* solicitors,[54] estate agents[55] and licensed dealers in securities[56]) are no doubt under an implied contractual obligation to their clients to comply with the legislation. The corollary of this point is that the subsection operates only against the person who receives the property and incurs the obligation to deal with it in a particular way, not against a third party. If, for example, money were paid to a company in such circumstances that the company acquired the beneficial interest in it, but incurred a personal obligation to use it for a particular purpose, the money would be deemed to belong to the transferor as against the company but not as against the directors. The fact that the company is in a fiduciary position with regard to a client does not mean that its directors are too.[57] If a director misappropriated the money he would not therefore be stealing from the client (though the company might be). He might be stealing from the company, but such a charge might involve certain difficulties arising from his status as the company's agent.[58]

Content of the obligation

4.13   The obligation which must exist, before section 5(3) can come into play, is an obligation to retain and deal with the property or its proceeds in a particular way—as it has been paraphrased by a trial judge, "an obligation to keep in existence a separate fund".[59] It is not sufficient that the defendant has an obligation to provide the agreed consideration for the property he receives if he is under no obligation to preserve the property as a fund for that purpose. Thus in *Hall*[60] it was held that the subsection did not apply to a travel agent who accepted payment from customers for the purpose of buying air tickets but failed either to provide the tickets or to refund the money: he was of course under an obligation to provide the tickets, but not to keep the customers' money separate for that purpose. Subject to the provisions of the bankruptcy legislation,[61] he was entitled to use the money in any way he wished. On

54   Solicitors' Accounts Rules 1975.
55   Estate Agents (Accounts) Regulations 1981.
56   Licensed Dealers (Conduct of Business) Rules 1983.
57   *Bath v. Standard Land Co. Ltd* [1911] 1 Ch. 618; *cf. Grubb* [1915] 2 K.B. 683.
58   *Infra*, para. 4.19ff.
59   *Robertson* [1977] Crim.L.R. 629, *per* Judge Rubin Q.C.
60   [1973] Q.B. 126.
61   *Infra*, para. 9.16ff.

the other hand it is clear, if only from the reference to an obligation to deal with the *proceeds* in a particular way, that he need not be under an obligation to preserve the property *in specie*.[62] The subsection may apply to a sum of money even though the recipient is expected to put it in a bank account. Nor does it matter that he is entitled to put it in his *own* account rather than a separate one. Under the old law a professional person who misappropriated client money could be convicted of fraudulent conversion even if he was entitled or required to pay the money into his general account.[63] In *Davidge v. Bunnett*[64] the defendant was charged with stealing money entrusted to her by her flat-mates for the purpose of paying the gas bill. It was held that the money belonged to the others by virtue of section 5(3), although the defendant would have been entitled to pay it into her own bank account (had she had one) and to pay the bill with her own cheque. Presumably her obligation would then have been to ensure that the bill was paid within a reasonable time and that until then the account remained in credit at least to the extent of her flat-mates' contributions—thus keeping the fund in existence, albeit as an unidentifiable part of the larger fund represented by the credit balance. If (like Hall) she had been entitled to draw on the account for her own purposes so as to reduce the balance below the sum contributed by the others, or to pay that sum into an account which was already overdrawn (so that the fund would be automatically depleted), it would seem that section 5(3) could not have applied.

Fiduciary relationships

4.14 Whether a particular asset in the defendant's possession does in fact belong to another within the meaning of section 5 may be a difficult question, and one which (the occasional judicial denial notwith-standing)[65] will require an analysis of the position in civil law. Normally the most important factor will be the relationship between the defendant and the person to whom the property is alleged to belong. If they are dealing at arm's length, *e.g.* where the property in question is simply an advance payment for goods or services to be provided by the defendant, it is likely that the defendant will become the beneficial owner and will not be a fiduciary of the property so as to bring section 5(3) into play;[66]

---

62 *Légaré* (1977) 78 D.L.R. (3d.) 645 at p. 651, *per* Pigeon J.; *cf. Re Bellencontre* [1891] 2 Q.B. 122 at p. 142, *per* Wills J.
63 *Banyard and Lacey* [1958] Crim.L.R. 49 (stockbroker); *Yule* [1964] 1 Q.B. 5 (solicitor).
64 [1984] Crim.L.R. 297.
65 *e.g.* Lord Roskill's suggestion in *Morris* [1984] A.C. 320 that the law of theft is not concerned with questions of whether contracts are vitiated by fraud or mistake. But *cf. Walker* [1984] Crim.L.R. 112, where the Court of Appeal thought it crucial whether a contract of sale had been rescinded for breach of condition.
66 *Hotine* (1904) 68 J.P. 143; *Jones* (1948) 33 Cr.App.R. 11; *cf. Foley v. Hill* (1848) 2 H.L.C. 28 (bank deposit). If the defendant never intended to provide the expected consideration, he will of course have obtained the property by deception.

but it must be added that the criminal courts have occasionally appeared to give this presumption less weight than its due.[67] If, on the other hand, the defendant receives the property by virtue of an existing fiduciary relationship, *e.g.* as a trustee or personal representative, he will almost certainly hold the property in a fiduciary capacity if not as a trustee. This will be so whether he receives it from his beneficiary or from a third party.[68] Similarly if the defendant is an intermediary arranging for the sale or purchase of goods on his client's account, the question whether property in the defendant's hands belongs to the client will depend primarily on whether the relationship between them is one of agency or whether the defendant is dealing as a principal in his own right. If he is acting as a principal he is unlikely to be a trustee or even a fiduciary of property in his hands, although it is possible that under the terms of their contract the client may retain a proprietary interest in goods delivered to the intermediary: *e.g.* the goods may be delivered on a "sale or return" basis,[69] or subject to a *Romalpa*[70] clause which prevents the buyer from acquiring title until the price is paid. If the defendant is acting as his client's agent, he will normally be a trustee (or at least a fiduciary) of property received from the client for the purpose of dealings with third parties and of property received from third parties in the course of such dealings.[71] But if the relationship is a continuing one and the agent is expected merely to keep a running account, remitting the balance due at periodic intervals, this principle may be overridden by commercial convenience[72] and the agent treated not as a trustee but only as a debtor.[73] It is ultimately a question turning on the construction of the contract.[74]

4.15 These considerations may in turn raise the question of whether a particular defendant *was* acting as an agent or as a principal. Again this is

67 *Smith* [1924] 2 K.B. 194; *Bryce* [1956] Crim.L.R. 122; *Hughes* [1956] Crim.L.R. 835.
68 *Cuffin* (1922) 127 L.T. 564; *Messer* [1913] 2 K.B. 421; but *cf. South* (1907) 71 J.P. 191.
69 *John Towle & Co. v. White* (1873) 29 L.T. 78.
70 *Aluminium Industrie Vaassen B.V. v. Romalpa Aluminium Ltd* [1976] 1 W.L.R. 676.
71 *Burdick v. Garrick* (1870) L.R. 5 Ch.App. 233; *Re Strachan, ex p. Cooke* (1876) 4 Ch.D. 123; *Re Cotton, ex p. Cooke* (1913) 108 L.T. 310; but *cf. Henry v. Hammond* [1913] 2 K.B. 515. In *Ireland v. Livingston* (1872) L.R. 5 H.L. 395 at p. 408f. Blackburn J. suggested that an agent engaged to purchase goods might nevertheless be a vendor of the goods *vis-à-vis* his principal. But his Lordship was presumably using the word "agent" in a somewhat unusual sense, since it normally denotes an intermediary who does not contract in his own right but brings his principal into privity with a third party: see F.M.B. Reynolds, "Agency: Theory and Practice" (1978) 94 L.Q.R. 224. Perhaps he meant only that an intermediary who is not an agent in the strict sense may nevertheless owe fiduciary duties to his client, which is clearly true.
72 *New Zealand & Australian Land Co. v. Watson* (1881) 7 Q.B.D. 374 at p. 382, *per* Bramwell L.J.
73 *Kirkham v. Peel* (1880) 43 L.T. 171; *King v. Hutton* [1900] 2 Q.B. 504; *cf. Robertson* [1977] Crim.L.R. 629.
74 *Kirkham v. Peel* (1880) 43 L.T. 171 at p. 197, *per* Cotton L.J.

essentially a matter of the construction of the contract between the defendant and his client. The fact that he is described as an agent is not conclusive.[75] More important are the terms of the contract, such as those which determine the mode of accounting required. If, for example, the intermediary accounts to his client only for goods *delivered* to him, he is probably a purchaser in his own right;[76] if he accounts for the goods *as sold* he is probably an agent, even if his commission depends on the price he manages to obtain.[77] As Jessel M.R. put it:

> "If a gentleman sent his groom with a horse to a fair to sell it for £80 and said to him, 'Whatever you get over £80 you shall have for yourself', would that make the groom the purchaser of the horse?"[78]

Relevance of market practice

4.16 The question whether the defendant is an agent or a principal may also be affected by the established practices of the particular trade or market in which he operates:

> "A person who deals in a particular market must be taken to deal according to the custom of that market, and he who directs another to make a contract at a particular place, must be taken as intending, that the contract may be made according to the usage of that place."[79]

Subject to an important qualification referred to below, this is so whether or not the client is aware of the practice in question.[80] It would seem to follow that a client who engages an intermediary to act for him, assuming that the intermediary will be acting as his agent and will be subject to the fiduciary obligations inherent in that position, may subsequently find that his intention is overridden by an accepted practice which allows intermediaries of that class to deal with their clients as principals and at arm's length. In *Limako B.V. v. H. Hentz & Co. Inc.*[81] such a practice was found to exist in relation to commodity brokers, and was held to preclude a relationship of agent and principal between broker and client. Earlier authority to the contrary[82] was not referred to. In the light of this

---

75   *John Towle & Co. v. White* (1873) 29 L.T. 78; *W.T.Lamb & Sons v. Goring Brick Co. Ltd* [1932] 1 K.B. 710; *Press and General Publicity Services v. Percy Bilton* [1979] C.L.Y. 26; *Potter v. Commissioners of Customs and Excise* [1985] S.T.C. 45.
76   *John Towle & Co. v. White* (1873) 29 L.T. 78 at p. 79, *per* Lord Selborne L.C.
77   *Re Smith, ex p. Bright* (1879) 10 Ch.D. 566.
78   *Ibid.* at p. 570.
79   *Bayliffe v. Butterworth* (1847) 1 Ex. 425 at p. 429, *per* Alderson B.
80   *Sutton v. Tatham* (1839) 10 Ad. & El. 27; *Pollock v. Stables* (1848) 12 Q.B. 765. *Bartlett v. Pentland* (1830) 10 B. & C. 760 appears to be authority to the contrary, but is explicable on the ground that the custom was unreasonable: *cf. Sweeting v. Pearce* (1861) 9 C.B.(N.S.) 534.
81   [1979] 2 Lloyd's Rep. 23.
82   *Woodward v. Wolfe* [1936] 3 All E.R. 529; *E.Bailey & Co. Ltd v. Balholm Securities Ltd* [1973] 2 Lloyd's Rep. 404.

decision a prosecution of commodity brokers for deception and conspiracy to defraud was halted by the judge on the ground that the brokers owed their clients no duty of disclosure;[83] and presumably it would follow that such a broker is not a fiduciary of money received from his clients[84] and may therefore use it as he likes with impunity.

4.17 It is submitted, however, that *Limako v. Hentz* is not such a rogues' charter as it may appear. There is a major exception to the rule that a contracting party may be bound by a custom of which he is unaware, *viz.* that this is so only if the custom is reasonable.[85] Moreover there is high authority for the proposition that a custom which allows a broker to act as a principal *vis-à-vis* his client is not a reasonable one. In *Robinson v. Mollett*[86] brokers were engaged to purchase tallow, but (in accordance with the usual practice of the London market) bought in their own names and offered the client the required quantity out of their own purchases. The client lived in Liverpool and knew nothing of this practice. The House of Lords held that he was under no obligation to accept the tallow, because the custom was inconsistent with the relationship of broker and client and was therefore unreasonable and not binding on a party without notice of it. *Limako v. Hentz* is not inconsistent with this decision, since the client in that case was a dealer with experience of the market and was therefore assumed to have known of the practice in question; in any event it was not the broker who was relying on the practice but the client. But in the light of *Robinson v. Mollett* it seems that the relationship between broker and client is one of agency unless there is an established usage to the contrary *and* the client can be taken to know of that usage, whether through previous dealings on the market in question or from information provided by the broker. In the absence of such experience or information, a small investor on the commodity markets may after all be able to invoke the law of agency against his broker; and a broker who misappropriates funds received from such a client may after all be guilty of theft.

Conclusions

4.18 We may summarise our conclusions as follows:

(1) Property held in a fiduciary capacity will almost invariably be property belonging to another for the purposes of a theft charge. This will be so for one of two reasons:

---

83 Trial of Sir Bruce Tuck and others, reported in *The Times*, 15 January 1983.
84 Unless, perhaps, he belongs to a professional association which requires client accounts to be kept: *supra,* para. 4.12.
85 *Sweeting v. Pearce* (1861) 9 C.B.(N.S.) 534; *Pearson v. Scott* (1878) 9 Ch.D. 198
86 (1874) L.R. 7 H.L. 802.

(a) because the person for whom the property is held is technically the owner, at law or in equity or both (but *quaere* whether it is sufficient if the holder of the property is a constructive trustee by virtue only of the property being the proceeds of a breach of fiduciary duty; on the other hand it probably makes no difference on this point that the owner is a company wholly owned by the defendant), or

(b) because the fiduciary, even if he is the sole owner, will be under an obligation to his beneficiary to deal with the property in a particular way; it will therefore be deemed to belong to the beneficiary by virtue of section 5(3) of the Theft Act 1968.

(2) Whether property is held in a fiduciary capacity will depend on the relationship between the parties and the terms of any contract between them. An agent is normally a fiduciary, a principal usually is not. The practice of a particular profession or market may be relevant, but will not be decisive if it decrees that a person whom his client reasonably expects to act in a fiduciary capacity need not do so.

It must however be emphasised that by establishing the defendant's fiduciary position the prosecution will have made out only one element of the offence. They must also prove that he appropriated some or all of the property, that he intended to deprive the other person permanently of the property appropriated, and that he was acting dishonestly in doing so. The fact that he subsequently decided not to replace the property, or found himself unable to do so, is not in itself sufficient. In *Hall*[87] Edmund Davies L.J. said:

> ". . . it is . . . essential . . . that dishonesty should be present at the time of appropriation. We are alive to the fact that to establish this could present great (and maybe insuperable) difficulties when sums are on different dates drawn from a general account. Nevertheless, they must be overcome if the Crown is to succeed."[88]

EFFECT OF OWNER'S AUTHORITY

4.19 We have seen that property held in a fiduciary capacity will normally "belong to another" and can therefore be stolen by the fiduciary. But there is a more serious difficulty which may arise if the defendant is not merely entrusted with the property but is also authorised to dispose of it. The existence of such authority may enable him to argue either that his appropriation was not dishonest or alternatively that there was no appropriation at all. For the sake of simplicity it will be assumed in what follows that the defendant is an agent with authority to dispose

87 [1973] Q.B. 126.
88 At p. 131; applied in *Hayes* (1977) 64 Cr.App.R. 82.

of property on the owner's behalf, rather than an owner of property which is deemed to belong to another by virtue of section 5(3) of the Theft Act 1968; but much of the argument will be equally applicable, *mutatis mutandis,* in the latter case too. It will, however, be convenient to distinguish between those considerations which apply to agents in general (including the agents of natural persons) and those applying specifically to the agents of companies.

Agents in general

4.20   An agent, authorised to dispose of his principal's property, does so in a fraudulent manner (*e.g.* to an accomplice at an undervalue). Is he guilty of theft? Clearly the property belongs to another, and we may assume that there is an intention permanently to deprive the owner of it. Nor does the requirement of dishonesty present any particular difficulty here: the agent is not legally entitled to act in breach of duty and is unlikely to suppose that he is.[89] It is the element of appropriation which may prove harder to establish. The stumbling-block is Lord Roskill's statement in *Morris*,[90] with the agreement of the rest of their Lordships, that

> ". . . the concept of appropriation . . . involves not an act expressly or impliedly authorised by the owner but an act by way of adverse interference with or usurpation of [his] rights."[91]

A disposal of property by an agent with authority to dispose of it is, arguably, by definition an act expressly or impliedly authorised by the owner. It is of course improbable that the owner will be asked for, or if asked will give, his specific consent to the individual transaction in question. But if he has given the agent general authority to carry out transactions of a particular description, it would seem to follow that any individual transaction of that description carried out by the agent must necessarily be authorised. And according to *Morris* an act authorised by the owner is not theft.

4.21   It was suggested above that Lord Roskill's dictum may be unduly restrictive and not entirely borne out by the wording of the Theft Act 1968.[92] It seems unlikely that the legislature had any intention of exonerating an agent who fraudulently disposes of his principal's property. Section 4(2)(*a*), for example, provides that land can be stolen by a person who is authorised to dispose of it and who appropriates it by dealing with it in

---

89   *Cf. supra*, para. 1.05ff.
90   [1984] A.C. 320.
91   At p. 332.
92   *Supra*, para. 3.23.

breach of the confidence reposed in him—the implication being that even an authorised disposal, if carried out in breach of confidence, would amount to an appropriation. Yet it seems to follow inexorably from Lord Roskill's dictum that such a disposal would not be an appropriation and therefore would not be theft. If this is indeed the logical conclusion to be drawn from his Lordship's view, it may perhaps suggest, with respect, that that view requires some qualification. But until it becomes clear what qualifications (if any) are necessary, it will be arguable that *Morris* must be applied as it stands, and that a fiduciary whose conduct is in some sense authorised cannot therefore be convicted of theft. We shall suggest some possible objections to this reasoning, and some possible counters to those objections. Our conclusion is that if *Morris* is correct it may in certain circumstances provide the dishonest fiduciary with a defence. But it must be emphasised at the outset that if the views stated in *Morris* were eventually held to be wrong, or even in need of substantial qualification, most of the possibilities adverted to would disappear and the dishonest fiduciary would have no defence to a charge of theft.

Authority and fraud

4.22   The most fundamental objection to a defence based on *Morris* is that it is logically impossible for a fraudulent agent to rely on it, because the agent's actual authority (as distinct from apparent or usual authority, which may exist irrespective of the principal's intentions) can never extend to fraud. In *Kohn*,[93] for example, a director who had authority to write company cheques, but dishonestly used one for his own purposes, was said to be "dealing with the cheque not as the agent of the company duly authorised";[94] but the point does not appear to have been raised by the defence. A similar argument has been advanced by Professor J.C. Smith. Commenting on the view expressed by Lord Salmon in *Tarling (No. 1) v. Government of the Republic of Singapore*[95] that the sale of company assets at an undervalue would not amount to theft, he objects:

> "The crucial question here is that of authority . . . However wide an express authority, there must be some implied limitations. If a particular transaction is in breach of a fiduciary duty, . . . does the agent really have authority to carry it out?"[96]

4.23   It is submitted, however, that there is no contradiction in the idea of a transaction which constitutes a breach of duty on the agent's part but is nevertheless within the scope of his authority. Whether he acts

93   (1979) 69 Cr.App.R. 395.
94   At p. 410, *per* Geoffrey Lane L.J.
95   (1978) 70 Cr.App.R. 77.
96   "Theft, Conspiracy and Jurisdiction: Tarling's Case" [1979] Crim.L.R. 220 at p. 224.

within his authority depends on what he does; whether he acts in breach of duty may depend in addition on his motives for doing it. In *Hambro v. Burnand*[97] a Lloyd's underwriter, acting on behalf of his syndicate, underwrote a policy guaranteeing the repayment of certain advances made to a company by the plaintiffs. He knew that the company was insolvent, but he had a personal interest in it and was anxious to keep it afloat. The Court of Appeal held that the syndicate was liable on the policy in spite of the fraud. The decision was not, as has sometimes been suggested,[98] based on an agency by estoppel: estoppel was not relied on and indeed (as Bigham J. pointed out at first instance)[99] could not have been, since there was no holding out or representation of authority on the part of the other members of the syndicate. The Court of Appeal's decision (reversing Bigham J. on this point) was that the transaction in question was within the underwriter's actual authority, because it was precisely the sort of transaction which he was expressly authorised to make; and the fact that he made it with a fraudulent motive did not take it outside the scope of that authority. As Lord Hailsham L.C. explained in a later case:

> ". . . the Court of Appeal held that the act done by [the underwriter] was within the actual authority conferred upon him, although his motive in doing the act was to benefit himself and not his principals."[1]

It would seem to follow that a Lloyd's underwriter who fraudulently arranged reinsurance at excessive premiums with companies in which he had an interest would not (according to *Morris*) be guilty of stealing his syndicate's money.

4.24   This view of *Hambro v. Burnand* is supported by the criminal case of *Moore v. I. Bresler Ltd*,[2] where a company was held liable for offences committed by its agents in fraud of the company. The reason advanced for this somewhat paradoxical decision was that the fraudulent transactions entered into by the company's agents were effected within their authority on the company's behalf. Viscount Caldecote C.J. said:

> "It seems to me that if [the respondent company's agents] sold goods which were the property of the respondents and intended for sale, they were acting within the scope of their authority . . . The sales undoubtedly were fraudulent, but they were sales made with the authority of the respondent company by these two men as agents for the respondent company."[3]

97   [1904] 2 K.B. 10.
98   *e.g.* G.H. Fridman, *The Law of Agency* (5th ed.) at p. 109f.
99   [1903] 2 K.B. 399 at p. 413f.
  1   *Reckitt v. Barnett, Pembroke & Slater Ltd* [1929] A.C. 176 at p. 183.
  2   [1944] 2 All E.R. 515.
  3   At p. 516.

Humphreys J. agreed:

> "I think . . . it is perfectly obvious that in fact and in law those sales of the company's goods were made by those persons as agents of and with the authority of the respondents, and the sale is not less made with the authority of the master because the employee means to put into his own pocket the proceeds of the sale when he receives them."[4]

If the sale is made with the authority of the master, the employee is presumably not guilty of stealing the goods. He might however be guilty of stealing the *proceeds,* on the ground that they too belong to the master (if only by virtue of section 5(3))[5] and he has no authority to keep them.

4.25 Of course it may be that in order to carry out the fraud the agent must deal with the principal's property in a way which, irrespective of his motives, is simply not what he is authorised to do; and in that case the problem of the principal's consent does not arise. Thus a supermarket cashier has no authority to sell the stock at less than the marked price.[6] Other agents may have more discretion as to the terms of the contracts which they are authorised to make. The line between an unauthorised transaction and one which is authorised but fraudulent may be a fine one. In *Reckitt v. Barnett, Pembroke & Slater Ltd,*[7] for example, the holder of a power of attorney was authorised to draw cheques on the plaintiff's account, and drew one in payment of a debt owed by himself to the defendants. The House of Lords held that this was outside his authority and that *Hambro v. Burnand* was therefore distinguishable. There was no legitimate reason for the agent to pay his principal's money to the defendants at all. Had such a reason existed, *e.g.* if the plaintiff had owed money to the defendants, the payment would presumably have been within the agent's authority irrespective of his motives for making it; the case would have been on all fours with *Hambro v. Burnand.* But this is a question of fact. What *Hambro v. Burnand* establishes is that there is no general rule restricting an agent's actual authority to acts done *bona fide* in the interests of his principal.

Agents of companies

Dishonesty
4.26 The difficulties are multiplied when the defendant is the agent not of a natural person but of a company.[8] A director who uses his

---

4   At p. 517.
5   *Supra,* para. 4.07ff.
6   *Bhachu* (1976) 65 Cr.App.R. 261; *cf. Pilgram v. Rice-Smith* [1977] 1 W.L.R. 671.
7   [1929] A.C. 176.
8   See generally G.R. Sullivan, "Company Controllers, Company Cheques and Theft" [1983] Crim.L.R. 512; Janet Dine, "Another View" [1984] Crim.L.R. 397; Sullivan, "A Reply" *ibid.* at p. 405.

company's assets for his own purposes may be able to claim, not only that there was no appropriation, but even that his conduct was legally incapable of being "dishonest". This somewhat startling argument was put forward in *Attorney-General's Reference (No. 2 of 1982)*[9] and was based on section 2(1) of the Theft Act 1968, which provides:

> "A person's appropriation of property belonging to another is not to be regarded as dishonest—
> . . .
> (b) if he appropriates the property in the belief that he would have the other's consent if the other knew of the appropriation and the circumstances of it . . .""

The defendants in the trial which gave rise to the reference were alleged to have fraudulently disposed of assets belonging to a company of which they were the directors. It was argued on their behalf that they were "the sole will and directing mind" of the company and were therefore to be identified with it; in other words, that their actions were the company's actions.[10] They did therefore believe that the company would consent to their defalcations, because everything they did was automatically done with the company's consent.

4.27 The Court of Appeal rejected the argument, for several reasons. First they denied that an act in fraud of a company could be regarded as the act of the company itself at all. This point is equally relevant to the issue of appropriation and is discussed below.[11] More specifically, it was held that section 2(1)(b) did not apply. This was partly on the ground that the "belief" referred to must be an *honest* belief (a totally unwarranted gloss on the plain wording of the section),[12] and partly because the defence position was in any event self-contradictory.

> "The essence of the defendants' argument is the alleged identity, in all respects, and for every purpose, between the defendants and the company. It is said, in effect, that their acts are necessarily the company's acts; that their will, knowledge and belief are those of the company, and that their consent necessarily implies consent by the company. But how then can the company be regarded as 'the other' for the purposes of *this* provision [*sc.* section 2(1)(b)]? One merely has to read its wording to see that it cannot be given any sensible meaning in a context such as the present, where the mind and will of the defendants are also treated in law as the mind and will of 'the other'."[13]

The defence's position was certainly an awkward one to maintain. But it is not clear why the corollary of this Catch-22 did not work against the

---

9 [1984] Q.B. 624.
10 *Cf. Tesco Supermarkets Ltd v. Nattrass* [1972] A.C. 153.
11 Para. 4.30ff.
12 *Supra,* para. 1.07.
13 At p. 642.

prosecution. Was it not equally inconsistent to argue both that the company's property belonged to another *and* that the company was not another person for the purposes of section 2(1)(*b*)?

4.28 A more straightforward reason for rejecting the argument would have been that the wording of section 2(1)(*b*) simply did not square with the alleged facts. The defendants did not believe that the company *would* have consented *if* it had known the circumstances: they believed (rightly or wrongly) that, through them, it *did* know the circumstances and it *did* consent. It might of course seem reasonable that, if a belief that the owner *would* consent is a defence, *a fortiori* so must be a belief that he does in fact consent. But the appropriate defence in the latter case is based not on section 2(1)(*b*) but on section 2(1)(*a*), which provides that it is not dishonest to appropriate property belonging to another in the belief that one has in law the right to deprive the other of it. Normally a belief that one has the owner's consent will be a claim of right within section 2(1)(*a*); but in the situation which arose in *Attorney-General's Reference (No. 2 of 1982)* this was not so. It was arguable that the defendants believed they had the company's consent to what they did, but hardly that they believed they were legally entitled to do it. Hence the decision to rely on section 2(1)(*b*). The court's reaction, understandably enough, was that the difficulty could not be evaded in this way: it was section 2(1)(*a*) or nothing. But the result is paradoxical, to say the least. A defendant who believes that the owner *would* have consented to the appropriation had he known the circumstances is not dishonest, whether or not he believes that that consent would have given him a legal right to deprive the owner of the property. But a defendant who believes (rightly or wrongly) that the owner does in fact consent may still be dishonest unless he believes that this consent gives him a legal right to act as he does.

Appropriation
4.29 It is arguable that the solution to this paradox is to be found in *Morris*,[14] which was decided shortly after the argument in *Attorney-General's Reference (No. 2 of 1982)* and was not referred to in the judgment. In the *Attorney-General's Reference* it was conceded by the defence that on the facts alleged there would have been an appropriation, and the only issue was that of dishonesty. This concession was perhaps a trifle generous even on the authorities as they then stood,[15] and with the hindsight conferred by *Morris* it now seems all the more so. Lord Roskill stated in *Morris* that an act done with the owner's consent is not an

---

14 [1984] A.C. 320.
15 *e.g. Meech* [1974] Q.B. 549; *Skipp* [1975] Crim.L.R. 114; *Hircock* (1978) 67 Cr.App.R. 278.

appropriation; it follows that it cannot be theft, even if the defendant falls between the two stools of section 2(1)(*a*) and (*b*) and is therefore accounted dishonest. In the context of company fraud a defence based on this proposition might take either of two forms. In the first place it might simply be argued, as in the case of an agent of a natural person, that what is done is within the scope of the agent's authority and is therefore done with the company's consent. It has been suggested that this is not so unless the agent is not merely acting on the company's behalf but is himself its "directing mind", its *alter ego*.[16] But it is not obvious why this should be so. It may be that the actions of an agent who is not an *alter ego* cannot be *attributed* to the company, in the sense of being treated as the actions of the company itself; but it does not follow that they are not consented to by the company. Obviously a company cannot consent, or do anything else, except vicariously through its agents and ultimately through an *alter ego*. But once it is established that an agent has been validly[17] authorised on the company's behalf to carry out a given transaction, or transactions of that type, precisely the same considerations apply as in the case of an agent of a natural person. As we have seen, there are certain difficulties in regarding a fraudulent disposal by such an agent as within the scope of his authority, but these difficulties are not necessarily insuperable.[18] And on the assumption that Lord Roskill's dictum in *Morris* is correct as it stands, a disposal within the scope of an agent's authority cannot be theft.

4.30 The alternative line of defence based on the need for an appropriation is peculiar to the context of company fraud. It is essentially the same as the argument put forward in *Attorney-General's Reference (No. 2 of 1982)*,[19] *viz.* that the actions of a company's *alter ego* are not merely authorised by the company but are in law the actions of the company itself. The difference is that in that case the argument was directed at the issue of dishonesty rather than that of appropriation. According to *Morris,* however, an act done with the owner's consent is not an appropriation even if it is dishonest; and an act done by the owner himself can hardly be done without his consent. The difficulty with this argument (even on the assumption that Lord Roskill's dictum is correct) is again the *Attorney-General's Reference,* where the Court of Appeal held that it is impossible to attribute to a company the actions of its *alter ego* when those actions are a fraud on the company itself. This reasoning cannot be sidestepped merely by pointing out that the court was

16 G.R. Sullivan [1984] Crim.L.R. 405 at p. 410 n. 45.
17 *i.e.* assuming that the transaction is *intra vires: infra,* para. 4.34ff.
18 *Supra,* para. 4.20ff.
19 [1984] Q.B. 624; *supra,* para. 4.26ff.

concerned with dishonesty and not appropriation: it is equally applicable to both.

4.31 On the other hand the Court of Appeal's conclusion may be open to a more direct attack. The only authority adduced for it was the civil case of *Belmont Finance Corporation Ltd v. Williams Furniture Ltd*,[20] where an action was brought in a company's name in respect of allegedly fraudulent misuse of the company's funds by its shareholders and directors. At first instance the action was dismissed on the ground that on the facts alleged the company must itself have been a party to the conspiracy. This decision was reversed by the Court of Appeal. With the agreement of the other members of the court, Buckley L.J. said:

> "The plaintiff company was the party at which the conspiracy was aimed. It seems to me that it would be very strange that it should also be one of the conspirators. . . It may emerge at a trial that the facts are not as alleged in the statement of claim, but if the allegations in the statement of claim are made good, the directors of the plaintiff must . . . have known that the transaction was an illegal transaction. But in my view such knowledge should not be imputed to the company, for the essence of the arrangement was to deprive the company improperly of a large part of its assets. As I have said, the company was a victim of the conspiracy. I think it would be irrational to treat the directors, who were allegedly parties to the conspiracy, notionally as having transmitted this knowledge to the company; and indeed it is a well-recognised exception from the general rule that a principal is affected by notice received by his agent that, if the agent is acting in fraud of his principal and the matter of which he has notice is relevant to the fraud, that knowledge is not to be imputed to the principal. So in my opinion the plaintiff company should not be regarded as a party to the conspiracy, on the ground of lack of the necessary guilty knowledge."[21]

In the *Attorney-General's Reference* the court added:

> "There can be no reason, in our view, why the position in the criminal law should be any different."[22]

4.32 It is worth noticing that in *Moore v. I. Bresler Ltd*,[23] which was not referred to in the *Belmont* case, a company was in fact held criminally liable for a fraud of which it was itself the victim (though such an outcome is admittedly somewhat bizarre). Moreover, Buckley L.J.'s analogy with the law of agency is unhelpful, since the agent of a natural person is not regarded as his *alter ego*. Assuming, however, that the *Belmont* case was correctly decided, it is submitted with respect that its

20 [1979] Ch. 250.
21 At p. 261f.
22 [1984] Q.B. 624 at p. 641.
23 [1944] 2 All E.R. 515; *supra*, para. 4.24.

relevance to the point at issue is limited. The decision was that the company was not a party to the alleged conspiracy because it lacked *mens rea:* the directors' fraudulent intentions could not be attributed to it because on the facts alleged it was the victim of the fraud. This proposition is not inconsistent with the argument advanced by the defence in the *Attorney-General's Reference, viz.* that the disposal of a company's assets by its directors is in law a disposal by the company itself. It was no part of the defendants' case that the company had fraudulent intentions or was itself a guilty party, only that it had (through their agency) applied its own assets to their purposes; and that proposition was correct on the law as it had previously been understood.

4.33 A further objection to the decision in the *Attorney-General's Reference* is that the court omitted to explain how its reasoning was to be reconciled with that of a majority of the House of Lords in *Tarling (No. 1) v. Government of the Republic of Singapore.*[24] In that case a company chairman was alleged to have purchased certain shares from his company at a considerable undervalue. Three of their Lordships expressed the view that on those facts a charge of theft would not have been made out. Lord Wilberforce said:

> ". . . there was no evidence of any appropriation of property belonging to another so as to satisfy the Theft Act 1968, section 1. There were, putting it briefly, transfers of property, passing the property, possibly for inadequate consideration, but nothing approaching theft."[25]

Lord Salmon said:

> "If a vendor transfers shares to a purchaser under a contract of sale and is paid the agreed price for them, I do not understand how the purchaser can be said to be appropriating the property belonging to another within the meaning of the word 'appropriate' in section 1 of the Theft Act 1968."[26]

Lord Keith agreed.[27] These statements certainly suggest that an extraction of company property by the company's *alter ego* is not an appropriation. Moreover it is arguable that they constitute part of the *ratio*: although there was in any event a lack of jurisdiction, none of the three expressly based his conclusion on this ground rather than the appropriation point. On the other hand it would be easy to explain the decision as turning on the question of jurisdiction and to dismiss their Lordships' remarks on appropriation as *obiter*. The man on the Clapham omnibus might well say that a director who sells himself company property at an undervalue is appropriating it. Even if Lord Roskill was

24   (1978) 70 Cr.App.R. 77.
25   At p. 110.
26   At p. 131.
27   At p. 137.

right in *Morris* and the owner's consent is normally a defence, it does not follow that this is so where the owner is a fictitious person whose "consent" is given by the defendant himself. *Morris* should not be allowed to become a rogues' charter.

Validity of transaction

4.34 Even if it is a defence that the transaction in question was authorised on the company's behalf, or that it was in law the company's own act, such a defence will hardly be arguable unless the transaction is at least valid. Certain transactions may not lawfully be entered into by a company unless approved in advance by the general meeting, *e.g.* the payment to directors of compensation for loss of office;[28] a payment in breach of such a requirement could hardly be regarded either as authorised by the company or as effected by it. The same would seem to apply *a fortiori* if the transaction is one which the company has no power to enter into at all, with or without the approval of the general meeting. It is true that for the purposes of criminal liability even *ultra vires* transactions may be attributed to a company[29]—indeed any other rule would render corporate liability a contradiction in terms, since it can hardly be *intra vires* for a legal person to break the law—but it would be bizarre if a rule designed to impose liability on the company had the effect of exculpating its controllers. And a company can hardly give a valid consent to a transaction entered into on its behalf which the company itself has no power to enter into. It is therefore submitted that the company's consent to, or participation in, the suspect transaction cannot be a defence unless the transaction is at least *intra vires* the company. This was conceded in *Attorney-General's Reference (No. 2 of 1982)*[30] in relation to the issue of dishonesty, and the court expressed the view that the concession was correct; but since it was held that the company's consent even to an *intra vires* transaction would not prevent that transaction from being dishonest, the point did not call for decision, If the company's consent *is* a defence after all, because it precludes the element of appropriation rather than that of dishonesty, it must at least be necessary that the transaction should be one which the company has power to make. In a fraud case it will almost inevitably be arguable that the company had no such power, and we must therefore consider how this issue falls to be determined.

4.35 In determining whether a particular transaction is *intra vires* the company, the first question to be considered is whether it falls within the

28 Companies Act 1985 s. 312, replacing Companies Act 1948 s. 191 with effect from 1 July 1985.
29 Janet Dine [1984] Crim.L.R. 397 at p. 403f.
30 [1984] Q.B. 624.

category of transactions which the company is, in general terms, empowered to make. This category includes not only the activities expressly set out in the company's memorandum of association but also, by implication, any activity which is reasonably incidental to the pursuit of the company's objects.[31] If the transaction falls outside this category it is on any view *ultra vires*. Moreover it is not sufficient merely that on its face it presents the appearance of an authorised transaction, if that appearance does not reflect the substance of what is done. Thus the payment of substantial remuneration to a director who was taking no active part in the running of the company has been held to be in substance a gift out of capital.[32] The same conclusion was reached in the case of an issue of debentures at a totally disproportionate rate of interest.[33] In another case payments purporting to be loans by a company were held to have been made in reality by way of repayment of a personal loan to the majority shareholder.[34] In *Re W. & M. Roith Ltd*[35] a company entered into a service agreement with a director (who was also the controlling shareholder) under which his wife would be entitled to a pension on his death. Plowman J. held that the widow was not entitled to the pension because the objective was to benefit her rather than the company; and the decision was subsequently explained by the Court of Appeal on the basis that the service agreement was a mere facade.[36]

4.36 Even if the defence can establish that the transaction in question was in substance the kind of transaction which the company had power to effect, they may still be met with the argument that this particular instance must necessarily have been *ultra vires* because it was in fact fraudulent. This is a formidable argument which, if sound, would demolish a defence based on *Morris*.[37] The defence is that something done with the company's consent is not an appropriation of the company's property, however dishonest it may be; the reasoning collapses if the dishonesty of what is done automatically renders it *ultra vires* and therefore invalidates the company's consent. The best-known exposition of this view is a passage in the judgment of Eve J. in *Re Lee, Behrens & Co. Ltd*,[38] which concerned an annuity granted by a company to the widow of a former director:

---

31   *A.-G. v. Great Eastern Railway Co.* (1880) 5 App.Cas. 473; *Deuchar v. Gas, Light & Coke Co.* [1925] A.C. 691; *A.-G. v. Smethwick Corp.* [1932] 1 Ch. 562.
32   *Re Halt Garage (1964) Ltd* [1982] 3 All E.R. 1016.
33   *Ridge Securities v. I.R.C.* [1964] 1 W.L.R. 479.
34   *International Sales and Agencies Ltd v. Marcus* [1982] 3 All E.R. 551.
35   [1967] 1 W.L.R. 432.
36   *Re Horsley & Weight Ltd* [1982] Ch. 442 at p. 451f., *per* Buckley L.J.
37   [1984] A.C. 320.
38   [1932] 2 Ch. 46.

" . . . whether they be made under an express or implied power, all such grants involve an expenditure of the company's money, and that money can only be spent for purposes reasonably incidental to the carrying on of the company's business, and the validity of such grants is to be tested, as is shown in all the authorities, by the answers to three pertinent questions: (i) Is the transaction reasonably incidental to the carrying on of the company's business? (ii) Is it a *bona fide* transaction? and (iii) Is it done for the benefit and to promote the prosperity of the company?"[39]

The obvious answer to the *Morris* defence is that a fraudulent disposal of the company's property satisfies neither the second test nor the third; but it will be argued below that, *pace* Eve J., this does not necessarily render the disposal *ultra vires*. We shall then consider whether, even if this is so, the prosecution might still fall back on Eve J.'s first test.

4.37 If Eve J.'s second and third tests are indeed crucial to the issue of corporate capacity, it follows that fraud on the company is by definition *ultra vires:* a fraudulent dealing with the company's property is neither a *bona fide* transaction nor (in so far as there is any difference) one done for the benefit and to promote the prosperity of the company. In *Mainwaring and Madders*[40] the controllers of an estate agency company were charged with stealing advance payments made to the company for houses in France and Spain. Some of the money was used for the purpose of promoting a pop singer, a purpose which was argued by the prosecution to be unrelated to the company's objects and therefore *ultra vires*. According to the defence, however, the venture fell within the terms of the company's memorandum of association and was therefore *intra vires* by virtue of the liberal approach established by the Court of Appeal's decision in *Bell Houses Ltd v. City Wall Properties Ltd.*[41] Lawton L.J., giving the judgment of the court, said:

" . . . a good deal depends upon the state of mind of the directors of the company when they decide to conduct a separate activity. Clearly if they do so honestly the decision cited above [*sc. Bell Houses*] protects them from the suggestion that they acted *ultra vires* but if their decision to conduct some other activity is not made honestly the criminal law intervenes."[42]

The clear implication is that an activity engaged in on a company's behalf is necessarily *ultra vires* unless the decision to engage in it is at least honest. In *Attorney-General's Reference (No. 2 of 1982)*[43] this passage was referred to by the court with apparent approval.

---

39 At p. 51f.
40 (1981) 74 Cr.App.R. 99.
41 [1966] 2 Q.B. 656.
42 At p. 108.
43 [1984] Q.B. 624.

4.38   However, a closer examination of the civil authorities reveals that the view taken in *Mainwaring and Madders* is, with respect, something of an over-simplification. The landmark decision was *Charterbridge Corporation Ltd v. Lloyds Bank Ltd*,[44] where Pennycuick J. held that a transaction expressly authorised by the company's memorandum was *intra vires* whether or not it was intended to benefit the company. He said:

> "Apart from authority, I should feel little doubt that where a company is carrying out the purposes expressed in its memorandum, and does an act within the scope of a power expressed in its memorandum, that act is an act within the powers of the company. The memorandum of a company sets out its objects and proclaims them to persons dealing with the company and it would be contrary to the whole function of a memorandum that objects unequivocally set out in it should be subject to some implied limitation by reference to the state of mind of the parties concerned. Where directors misapply the assets of their company, that may give rise to a claim based on breach of duty. Again, a claim may arise against the other party to the transaction, if he has notice that the transaction was effected in breach of duty. Further, in a proper case, the company concerned may be entitled to have the transaction set aside. But all that results from the ordinary law of agency and has not of itself anything to do with the corporate powers of the company."[45]

He went on to express the view that Eve J.'s three tests were not necessarily relevant to the issue of *vires,* at least in the case of a power expressly conferred by the memorandum, but rather to the distinct issue (which also arose in *Re Lee, Behrens & Co. Ltd*) of whether the transaction amounted to a breach of duty on the part of the directors which could only be authorised by a general meeting.

> "It seems to me, on the best consideration I can give to this passage, that the learned judge must have been directing his mind to both the issues raised by the liquidator, without differentiating them. In truth (i), the first of the three pertinent questions which he raises, is probably appropriate to the scope of the implied powers of a company where there is no express power. Question (ii) is appropriate in part again to the scope of implied powers, and in part, and perhaps principally, to the duty of directors. Question (iii) is, I think, quite inappropriate to the scope of express powers, and notwithstanding the words 'whether they be made under an express or implied power' at the beginning of the paragraph, I doubt very much whether the judge really intended to apply this last question to express powers. None of the cases cited by him . . . would support such an application. If he did so intend, his statement is obiter, and with great diffidence I do not feel bound to follow it. Finally, I would observe that the whole passage proceeds on the footing that the transaction might have been ratified, which would not be possible if it had been *ultra vires* the company."[46]

44   [1970] Ch. 62.
45   At p. 69.
46   At p. 70.

4.39 In *Re Halt Garage (1964) Ltd*[47] Oliver J. agreed that Eve J.'s dictum was misleading in its failure to differentiate between *vires* and fiduciary duty:

> "Part of the difficulty, I think, arises from the fact that Eve J. in *Re Lee, Behrens & Co. Ltd* combined together, in the context of an inquiry as to the effective exercise of directors' powers, two different concepts which have since been regarded as a single composite test of the corporate entity's capacity. In fact, however, as it seems to me at any rate, only one of the three tests postulated in *Lee, Behrens & Co.* is truly applicable to that question. The court will clearly not imply a power, even if potentially beneficial to the company, if it is not reasonably incidental to the company's business . . . and express powers are to be construed as if they were subject to that limitation . . . But the test of *bona fides* and benefit to the company seems to me to be appropriate, and really only appropriate, to the question of the propriety of an exercise of a power rather than the capacity to exercise it."[48]

In *Re Horsley & Weight Ltd*[49] the Court of Appeal held, approving the view expressed by Pennycuick J. in the *Charterbridge* case, that the test of benefit to the company had no application to the question whether the exercise of an express power was *intra vires*. It was unnecessary to decide whether that test, and the test of good faith, would be relevant to the validity of an exercise of an *implied* power. *Charterbridge* had confined these tests to the sphere of implied powers rather than denying their relevance to the issue of *vires* altogether; but in *Rolled Steel Products (Holdings) Ltd. v. British Steel Corporation*[50] the Court of Appeal confirmed that a transaction *prima facie* within a company's express or implied powers is not *ultra vires* merely because it is not arranged in good faith in the interests of the company.

4.40 If Eve J.'s second and third tests do not rule out the possibility of fraud being *intra vires,* because they do not relate to the issue of *vires* at all, it remains to consider whether this is nevertheless the effect of the first test—*viz.* whether the transaction is reasonably incidental to the carrying on of the company's business.[51] The dishonest abstraction of the company's assets can hardly be so described. There are, however, two possible difficulties involved in this line of attack. It might first be argued that, like the other two tests, the question whether the transaction is reasonably incidental to the company's business is not strictly a matter of *vires* at all. Secondly, it may be possible to show that the test is simply

47 [1982] 3 All E.R. 1016.
48 At p. 1034.
49 [1982] Ch. 442.
50 [1984] B.C.L.C. 466.
51 *Supra*, para. 4.36.

inapplicable, because the transaction in question is the kind of thing which the company exists to do; that, in other words, it is actually *part* of the company's business.

4.41   The former argument, *viz.* that Eve J.'s first test is no more relevant to the question of *vires* than are the other two, would be difficult to maintain on the present state of the authorities. Admittedly Pennycuick J. suggested in the *Charterbridge* case[52] that the first test is "probably appropriate to the scope of the implied powers of a company where there is no express power",[53] in which case the exercise of an express power could not be impugned on the ground that it was not reasonably incidental to the company's business. But it seems that the limitation represented by Eve J.'s first test applies to express as well as implied powers. Thus in *Re Introductions Ltd*[54] a company carrying on an *ultra vires* pig-breeding business issued debentures in favour of a bank by way of security for its overdraft. The Court of Appeal held that the debentures were void in spite of an express clause in the company's memorandum authorising it to borrow money and to issue debentures, because it was implicit that the power could only be exercised for the purpose of an *intra vires* business. In *Re Halt Garage (1964) Ltd*[55] Oliver J. pointed out that the decision in *Re Introductions Ltd* was not strictly an application of the *Lee, Behrens & Co.* principles, but nevertheless went on to cite it as authority for the proposition that express powers must be construed as being subject to the limitation represented by Eve J.'s first test. Similarly in *Re Horsley & Weight Ltd*[56] Buckley L.J. stated that an exercise of an express power can only be *intra vires* if it is in fact ancillary or incidental to the pursuit of one of the company's main objects.[57]

4.42   A considerably more promising basis for the argument that a transaction unrelated to the company's objects is not necessarily *ultra vires* is the judgment of Vinelott J. in *Rolled Steel Products (Holdings) Ltd v. British Steel Corporation*,[58] where he pointed out that the phrase "*ultra vires*" is used in two distinct senses:

> "It is used in a narrow sense to describe a transaction which is outside the scope of the powers expressed in the memorandum of association of a company or which can be implied as reasonably incidental to the furtherance of the objects thereby authorised. . . The phrase . . . is also

52   [1970] Ch. 62.
53   At p. 71.
54   [1970] Ch. 199.
55   [1982] 3 All E.R. 1016.
56   [1982] Ch. 442.
57   At p. 449.
58   [1982] Ch. 478; affirmed in part [1984] B.C.L.C. 466.

used to describe a transaction which, although it falls within the scope of
the powers of a company, express or implied, is entered into in furtherance
of some purpose which is not an authorised purpose."[59]

It should be emphasised that what his Lordship meant by "some purpose
which is not an authorised purpose" was not a *dishonest* purpose, or one
which does not further the interests of the company; in essence he was
referring to a transaction which fails the first of the *Lee, Behrens & Co.*
tests, not the second or the third. This is clear from the fact that the
example given is that of a company which, as in *Re Introductions Ltd,*[60]
borrows money for the purpose of an unauthorised business. Such a
transaction is sometimes described as *"ultra vires"* (*sc.* in Vinelott J.'s
wider sense),[61] sometimes not.[62]

4.43   In the light of Vinelott J.'s distinction it might perhaps be argued
that the narrower sense of the phrase *"ultra vires"* is the one which is
strictly correct, and that a transaction effected in furtherance of an
unauthorised purpose is not *ultra vires* in this strict sense, although it may
conveniently be described as *ultra vires* in a loose sense. Indeed, the Court
of Appeal was of the opinion that the phrase ought not to be used in this
loose sense at all, since a transaction of this type is not inevitably void and
is therefore not literally beyond the company's capacity. With respect,
this view seems somewhat dogmatic: the wider sense is too well-
established and too useful to be simply abolished overnight. Moreover,
it is the wider sense which in the present context is arguably more
relevant. Vinelott J. went on to explain that the significance of the
distinction relates only to the rights of third parties:

> "The difference between a transaction which is *ultra vires* in the narrow
> sense and one which is *ultra vires* in the wider sense is, of course, that a
> transaction which is *ultra vires* in the narrow sense is altogether void and
> cannot confer rights on third parties, whereas a transaction which is *ultra
> vires* in the wider sense may confer rights on a third party who can show
> that he dealt with the company in good faith and for valuable consideration
> and did not have notice of the fact that the transaction, while ostensibly
> within the powers, express or implied, of the company, was entered into in
> furtherance of a purpose which was not an authorised purpose."[63]

Whether the transaction may be enforced by a third party, acting in good

---

59   At p. 497.
60   [1970] Ch. 199; *supra,* para. 4.41.
61   *e.g. Re David Payne & Co. Ltd* [1904] 2 Ch. 608 at p. 612, *per* Buckley J.; *Re Jon
      Beauforte (London) Ltd* [1953] Ch. 131 at p. 135, *per* Roxburgh J.; *Re Introductions Ltd*
      [1968] 2 All E.R. 1221 at p. 1225, *per* Buckley J.; *Re Horsley & Weight Ltd* [1982] Ch.
      442 at p. 448f., *per* Buckley L.J.
62   *Re David Payne & Co. Ltd, supra,* at p. 613 *per* Buckley J.
63   At p. 499.

faith or bad, is hardly of central importance for present purposes.[64] What we are here concerned with is the scope of the company's legal capacity— *i.e.* ultimately, the powers of the general meeting. And as Vinelott J. pointed out, even a transaction which is *ultra vires* only in the wider sense cannot validly be authorised by the general meeting. It is therefore submitted that for present purposes it is the wider sense which is crucial; and in that sense a transaction which fails Eve J.'s first test is necessarily *ultra vires*.

4.44 However, to say that a transaction must not fail Eve J.'s first test is not to say that it must *pass* it: it may be that the test is literally inapplicable. This brings us to the second difficulty which may be encountered if the prosecution seek to argue that a fraudulent transaction must necessarily be *ultra vires* because it will not be reasonably incidental to the pursuit of the company's objects. The defence may simply reply that the transaction in question need not be *incidental* to the company's objects because it *is* one of those objects. In *Re Horsley & Weight Ltd*[65] Buckley L.J. pointed out:

> "The objects of a company do not need to be commercial; they can be charitable or philanthropic; indeed, they can be whatever the original incorporators wish, provided that they are legal. Nor is there any reason why a company should not part with its funds gratuitously or for non-commercial reasons if to do so is within its declared objects."[66]

Moreover it is now commonplace for the company's memorandum to include not only a comprehensive and wide-ranging list of objects but also a clause to the effect that each of the objects mentioned is independent and is not to be construed as ancillary to any of the others. It is true that here again the substance is more important than the form. Purposes which are stated to be objects, but which in reality are merely incidental to the company's main objects, will be construed as ancillary powers which may only be exercised in pursuit of the substantive objects.[67] Such an interpretation is not necessarily ruled out by the existence of a "separate objects" clause. According to Buckley L.J., such a clause may be disregarded in the case of a stated object which is by its nature incapable of taking effect as a substantive object: for example, a company can hardly exist for the purpose of borrowing money or of advertising its own services.[68] But in *Horsley & Weight* itself it was held

---

64 Hence the question is not affected by s. 9 of the European Communities Act 1972, which provides that *in favour of a person dealing with a company in good faith* any transaction decided on by the directors is deemed to be *intra vires*.
65 [1982] Ch. 442.
66 At p. 450.
67 *Re German Date Coffee Co.* (1882) 20 Ch.D. 169.
68 [1982] Ch. 442 at p. 448, citing *Re Introductions Ltd* [1970] Ch. 199.

that the granting of pensions to employees was capable of being, and was, a substantive object. With a little forethought it should be possible for a fraudulent director to argue plausibly that his depredations fell not merely within the company's powers but within its objects.

4.45 If it can be established that the transaction in question fell within the company's substantive objects, it becomes meaningless to enquire whether the transaction was reasonably incidental to the carrying on of the company's business: its objects *are* its business. As Buckley L.J. put it in *Re Horsley & Weight Ltd:*

> ". . . the doing of an act which is expressed to be, and is capable of being, an independent object of the company cannot be *ultra vires,* for it is by definition something which the company is formed to do and so must be *intra vires.*"[69]

Since in that case it was one of the company's substantive objects to grant pensions to employees, the granting of such a pension was held to be necessarily *intra vires* in spite of the company's impending insolvency. Had it been done in bad faith, which was not the case, it would have amounted to a breach of duty on the part of the directors; but it would still have been *intra vires*, because it was one of the things which the company existed to do. *Re W. & M. Roith Ltd,*[70] where the granting of a pension was held to be *ultra vires* although falling within the company's express objects, was explained as a decision which could only be justified on the basis that the granting of pensions was not in truth a substantive object but only an ancillary power. Had it been a substantive object, Eve J.'s first test would have been irrelevant.

Conclusions

4.46 The conclusions suggested by this discussion may be summarised as follows:

(1) On the assumption that Lord Roskill's dictum in *Morris*[71] is correct, *i.e.* that a dealing with property in a manner authorised by the owner is not an appropriation, an agent or other fiduciary may in certain circumstances have an arguable defence to a charge of stealing property entrusted to him even if his conduct was in fact fraudulent.

(2) This defence may rest on the assertion that the agent (or fiduciary) had the actual authority of his principal (or beneficiary) to enter into transactions of the kind in question. Whether he did have such authority is a question of fact. A dishonest motive does not in itself take an

69 At p. 449.
70 [1967] 1 W.L.R. 432.
71 [1984] A.C. 320.

otherwise authorised transaction outside the scope of his authority, but an express authority will often be subject to implied qualifications which exclude the circumstances in which the transaction was in fact entered into.

(3) Where the owner of the property in question is a company, both the defence and the prosecution may have additional arguments at their disposal.

(a) Instead of (or as well as) simply arguing that the transaction in question was authorised by the company, the defence may claim that it was entered into by a person who is in law identified with the company and that it was therefore the act of the company itself. This reasoning does not rule out the element of dishonesty, but it is arguable in the light of *Morris* that it rules out that of appropriation. The argument collapses if, as the Court of Appeal has held,[72] an act in fraud of a company can never be attributed to the company; but this view is not borne out by the authorities.

(b) Whichever form the defence takes, the prosecution may attack it by arguing that the transaction in question was not a lawful one for the company to enter into and cannot therefore be regarded either as authorised by the company or as the company's own act. It will usually be arguable that a fraudulent transaction was *ultra vires* and was therefore invalid even if approved by all the shareholders. A transaction is *ultra vires* (i) if it does not fall within the category of transactions which the company has in general terms the power to make, whether that power be expressly conferred by the memorandum or implied as reasonably incidental to the pursuit of the company's objects, or (ii) if the power to enter into such transactions is on its true construction not one of the company's substantive objects but only ancillary to those objects, and the particular transaction in question is not reasonably incidental to the pursuit of those objects, but *not* (iii) merely because the transaction is not entered into in good faith in the interests of the company.

(4) It should finally be emphasised that we are here concerned only with the possibility of a charge of theft. Other charges may well be available and may be more appropriate. In particular, a dishonest agreement by an agent or fiduciary to cause loss to his principal or beneficiary by acting in breach of duty will, if it is not an agreement to commit a substantive offence,[73] almost certainly be a conspiracy to defraud.[74] And in a case of company fraud, there may be available one or more of the specific offences considered in the following chapter.

72 *Attorney-General's Reference (No. 2 of 1982)* [1984] Q.B. 624.
73 *Infra*, para. 12.34ff.
74 *Cf. supra*, para. 4.05.

CHAPTER 5

Offences of Company Fraud

5.01 Undoubtedly the most generous concession made by the law to those of a fraudulent disposition is the doctrine of corporate personality. Not only may a fraudulent enterprise be concealed behind a corporate facade, but in addition the company itself is a potential victim. Those in control may seek to abuse their position by entering into transactions which further their own interests rather than the company's. In the previous chapter we saw that the making of such transactions may sometimes be charged as theft of the company's assets, but that a theft charge may present difficulties if it can be argued that the transaction was consented to, or was actually made, by the company itself.[1] In this chapter we turn to offences of a much more specific character, all of them directed at particular types of transaction which are thought to involve an unacceptable risk of fraud on the company's shareholders or creditors, or both. It is a curious paradox that these specific offences exist only for the more subtle forms of company fraud. A director who arranges for his company to make him a loan, for example, can be prosecuted under section 342 of the Companies Act 1985,[2] whereas if he dispenses with formality and simply uses the company's money for his own purposes, the prosecution must fall back on the law of theft. Another defect in the legislation considered here is that it is directed primarily at frauds involving *public* companies; the fraudulent controller of a private company will find it comparatively easy to ensure that any liability he may incur is confined to the civil sphere.

LOANS TO DIRECTORS AND CONNECTED PERSONS

5.02 The practice of directors obtaining loans and similar benefits from their companies was formerly rendered unlawful (but not, apparently, criminal) by section 190 of the Companies Act 1948. This rather toothless rule has been replaced by some highly complex provisions which now appear in Part X of the Companies Act 1985.[3] The prohibitions are to be

---

1   *Supra,* para. 4.26ff.
2   *Infra,* para. 5.02ff.
3   Replacing Part IV of the Companies Act 1980 with effect from 1 July 1985.

found in section 330. Section 342 provides that an offence, punishable on conviction on indictment with two years' imprisonment or a fine or both,[4] is committed by the following:

(1) A director of a "relevant company"[5] who authorises or permits the company to enter into a transaction or arrangement, knowing or having reasonable cause to believe[6] that the company is thereby contravening section 330.[7]

(2) A relevant company which enters into a transaction or arrangement for one of its directors, or for a director of its holding company (but not a person connected with such a director), in contravention of section 330;[8] but it is a defence for the company to show that, at the time the transaction was entered into, it did not know the relevant circumstances.[9]

(3) Any person who procures a relevant company to enter into a transaction or arrangement, knowing or having reasonable cause to believe that the company is thereby contravening section 330.[10]

The term "director" in sections 330 to 346 includes a "shadow director",[11] *i.e.* a person in accordance with whose directions or instructions the directors are accustomed to act (unless they do so only on advice given by him in a professional capacity).[12] A relevant company is defined, in effect, as a company which is a public company or which belongs to a group including a public company.[13] Some of the prohibitions in section 330 apply equally to companies other than relevant companies, but criminal liability under section 342 arises only in the case of relevant companies. For present purposes, therefore, the position of non-relevant companies may be ignored, and in this section the term "company" will be used to denote a relevant company.

Prohibited borrowers

5.03 The prohibitions in section 330 apply to certain transactions made by a company with, or for the benefit of, certain persons. It will be convenient to refer to these persons as "prohibited borrowers", though

---

4   s. 342(4), Sch. 24. On summary conviction the offences carry up to six months' imprisonment or a fine of the statutory maximum or both.
5   Defined *infra*.
6   *Mens rea* is not therefore required.
7   s. 342(1).
8   s. 342(2).
9   s. 342(5).
10   s. 342(3).
11   s. 330(5).
12   s. 741(2). But a company is not a shadow director of its subsidiary merely because the subsidiary's directors act in accordance with its directions or instructions: s. 741(3).
13   s. 331(6).

that expression is not used in the legislation. They include not only the directors[14] of the company but also the directors of its holding company,[15] as well as persons "connected" with a director of either company. The definition of a connected person appears in section 346. There is an overriding rule that a person is not connected with a director if he is himself a director of the company in question.[16] In that case, of course, he will still be a prohibited borrower by virtue of being a director; but in a number of cases the transactions regulated by section 330 are permitted up to a maximum figure for each director and his connected persons, taken together.[17] This maximum can therefore be multiplied by arranging for a person who would otherwise be connected with a director to be appointed a director himself. This can even be done where the connected person is not a natural person but a company associated with the director. Subject to this exception, the following are regarded as connected with a director:

(a) The director's spouse or child[18] (including a step-child and an illegitimate child, but excluding a person aged 18 or over—a remarkably generous concession).[19]

(b) A body corporate with which the director is associated (unless the context requires otherwise).[20] He is associated with a body corporate if he and the persons connected with him,[21] together,

    (i) are interested in shares[22] comprised in the equity share capital[23] of that body corporate of a nominal value equal to at least one-fifth of that share capital, or

    (ii) are entitled to exercise (or control the exercise of) more than one-fifth of the voting power at any general meeting of that body.[24] A director (but not apparently a connected person) is taken to control the exercise of voting power if he controls a body corporate which controls the exercise of that voting power (section 346(8)); and he controls a body corporate if he or a person connected with him is interested in any part of the equity

---

14   Including shadow directors: *supra*, para. 5.02.
15   As defined by s. 736.
16   s. 346(2).
17   *Infra*, para. 5.07.
18   s. 346(2)(*a*).
19   s. 346(3)(*a*).
20   s. 346(2)(*b*). But most transactions between members of the same group will not be prohibited merely because a director of one is associated with the other: *infra*, para. 5.10.
21   For this purpose the category of connected persons is more narrowly defined: a person is not connected with a director merely by virtue of being:
    (i) a body corporate with which the director is associated, or
    (ii) a trustee of a trust the beneficiaries of which include or may include such a body corporate: s. 346(6).
22   See Sch. 13 Part I.
23   See s. 744.
24   s. 346(4).

share capital of that body *or* is entitled to exercise (or control the exercise of) any part of the voting power at any general meeting of that body, *and* he, the persons connected with him and the other directors of his own company, together, are interested in more than half of that share capital *or* are entitled to exercise (or control the exercise of) more than half of that voting power: section 346(5).

(c) A person acting in his capacity as the trustee[25] of any trust the beneficiaries of which include the director or a person falling within category (a) or (b) above (whether or not that person is connected with the director). For this purpose a person for whose benefit a power conferred on the trustees may be exercised is regarded as a beneficiary.[26]

(d) A person acting in his capacity as partner of the director or of any person who is connected with the director by virtue of falling within categories (a) to (c) above. Thus if a married couple are both directors of the same company, the husband's business partner is connected with the husband but not with the wife: although the husband falls within category (a), he is not thereby connected with the wife because he is himself a director.[27]

Prohibited transactions

5.04 In the case of a relevant company section 330 prohibits six types of transactions, subject to certain exceptions considered below. The prohibited transactions involve not only the giving of various kinds of credit by a company to a prohibited borrower but also certain indirect ways of achieving a similar result. They are as follows:

(1) A *loan* to a prohibited borrower.[28]

(2) A *"quasi-loan"* to a prohibited borrower.[29] A quasi-loan is a transaction under which one party (the "creditor") agrees to pay (or pays otherwise than in pursuance of an agreement) for another (the "borrower"), or agrees to reimburse (or reimburses otherwise than in pursuance of an agreement) expenditure incurred for another (the borrower) by a third party, either on terms that the borrower (or a person on his behalf) will reimburse the creditor, or in circumstances giving rise to a liability on the borrower to reimburse the creditor.[30] A

---

25 Other than as trustee under an employees' share scheme or a pension scheme: s. 346(3)(*b*).
26 s. 346(2)(*c*).
27 s. 346(2), *supra.*
28 s. 330(2)(*a*), (3)(*b*).
29 s. 330(3)(*a*), (*b*).
30 s. 331(3).

reference to the person to whom a quasi-loan is made is a reference to the borrower, and a reference to the borrower's liabilities includes the liabilities of any person who has agreed to reimburse the creditor on the borrower's behalf.[31]

(3) A *credit transaction* for a prohibited borrower.[32] A credit transaction is a transaction under which one party (the creditor)

    (a) supplies any goods or sells any land under a hire-purchase agreement or a conditional sale agreement,[33]

    (b) leases or hires any land or goods in return for periodical payments, or

    (c) otherwise disposes of land, or supplies goods or services,[34] on the understanding that payment (whether in a lump sum or instalments or by way of periodical payments or otherwise) is to be deferred.[35]

The person "for" whom a credit transaction is made is the person to whom the goods or services are supplied, or the land sold or otherwise disposed of.[36]

(4) A *guarantee*,[37] or the provision of a *security*, in connection with a transaction of types (1) to (3) above made for a prohibited borrower by a third party.[38]

(5) An arrangement for the *assignment* to the company, or the assumption by it, of any rights, obligations or liabilities under a transaction which would have been prohibited by virtue of falling within types (1) to (4) above if it had itself been entered into by the company on the date of the arrangement.[39]

(6) A *"back-to-back"* arrangement, *i.e.* one whereby another person enters into a transaction which would have been prohibited by virtue of falling within types (1) to (5) above if it had been entered into by the company, and that person obtains some benefit from the company or from another company in the same group.[40] But the person obtaining the benefit must be the same person as the one entering into the transaction. Hence, it seems, the definition does not cover an arrangement under which each of two companies makes loans to the directors of the other: in each case it is not the company but the directors who obtain the benefit.

---

31 s. 331(4).
32 s. 330(4)(*a*).
33 See the Consumer Credit Act 1974; 1985 Act s. 331(10).
34 Defined as anything other than goods or land: s. 331(8).
35 s. 331(7).
36 s. 331(9)(*b*).
37 Including an indemnity: s. 331(2).
38 s. 330(2)(*b*), (3)(*c*), (4)(*b*).
39 s. 330(6). For the purposes of sections 330 to 347 the transaction is deemed to have been entered into on the date of the arrangement: *ibid.*
40 s. 330(7).

Financial limits

5.05 The prohibitions in section 330 are subject to a number of exceptions, some of which permit transactions only up to specified financial limits.[41] Sometimes the limit is set simply according to the "amount" provided or guaranteed; but often it is determined by reference to the concept of "relevant amounts", which is in turn defined in terms of the "value" of the transaction or arrangement in question. Before turning to the exceptions themselves we must therefore examine the definitions of these two terms.

Value

5.06 The *value* of a transaction or arrangement depends on the type of transaction or arrangement in question:

(1) The value of a *loan* is the amount of the principal.[42]

(2) The value of a *quasi-loan* is the amount, or maximum amount, which the borrower is liable to reimburse the creditor.[43]

(3) The value of a *credit transaction* is the price which the goods, land or services in question could reasonably have been expected to fetch if they had been supplied at the time of the transaction and on the same terms (apart from price) but in the ordinary course of business.[44]

(4) The value of a *guarantee* or *security* is the amount guaranteed or secured.[45]

(5) The value of an arrangement of type (5) or (6) in 5.04 above (*i.e.* an arrangement for the *assignment* to the company of a prohibited transaction, or a *back-to-back* arrangement) is the value of the transaction to which it relates *minus* any amount by which the borrower's liabilities have been reduced.[46] In other words, in the case of a transaction previously entered into it is only the amount outstanding which is taken into account in determining the value of an arrangement relating to that transaction.[47]

If for any reason the value of the transaction or arrangement cannot be expressed as a specific sum of money, it is deemed to exceed £50,000 (whether or not the borrower's liability has been reduced).[48]

---

41 These limits may be increased by order of the Secretary of State: s. 345.
42 s. 340(2).
43 s. 340(3).
44 s. 340(6).
45 s. 340(4).
46 s. 340(5).
47 *Cf.* s. 339, which refers not to the "value" of any existing arrangement of types (5) or (6) but to the "amount outstanding" under any other relevant transaction (*infra,* para. 5.07). Since the value of an existing arrangement is defined, in effect, as the amount outstanding under the transaction to which it relates, the difference is only apparent: in both cases it is only the amount outstanding which is relevant.
48 s. 340(7).

Relevant amounts

5.07 For the purpose of determining whether the proposed transaction or arrangement falls within one of the exceptions below, the "relevant amounts" are:

(a) the value[49] of the proposed transaction or arrangement;[50]
(b) the amount outstanding[51] under any previous transaction which was made
    (i) by the company or one of its subsidiaries[52] (or, where the proposed transaction or arrangement is to be made for a director of its holding company or a person connected with such a director, by that holding company or any of its subsidiaries),
    (ii) for the director for whom (or for a person connected with whom) the proposed transaction or arrangement is to be made, or[53] for any person connected with him,[54] and
    (iii) by virtue of the exception now relied upon;[55] and
(c) the value[56] of any existing arrangement of type (5) or (6) in 5.04 above (*i.e.* an arrangement for the assignment to the company of a prohibited transaction, or a back-to-back arrangement) which was entered into
    (i) by one of the companies specified in (b)(i) above,[57]
    (ii) in relation to a transaction made for one of the persons specified in (b)(ii) above,[58] and
    (iii) by virtue of the exception now relied upon.[59]

Exceptions

5.08 Sections 332 to 338 create eight exceptions to the prohibitions in section 330. The order in which they appear in the Act appears to be almost totally random, but they can be roughly classified into three groups as follows:

(a) Transactions between members of the same group of companies.
(b) Transactions entered into in the ordinary course of the company's

49 *Supra*, para. 5.06.
50 s. 339(2)(*a*).
51 *i.e.* the initial value of the transaction less any amount by which that value has been reduced: s. 339(6).
52 Provided that that subsidiary is still a subsidiary of the company in question: s. 339(5).
53 Except in the case of the exception under s. 334, *infra* para. 5.14: s. 339(1).
54 s. 339(3).
55 s. 339(2)(*c*). Previous transactions may therefore be disregarded if they were permissible under some other exception. Where more than one exception is applicable to a transaction the company may presumably select the one on which to justify it.
56 *i.e.* the amount outstanding: *supra*, para. 5.06.
57 s. 339(5), *supra* n. 52, is expressed to apply only to transactions and not to arrangements. It is submitted that it must be read as applying to arrangements as well.
58 s. 339(3).
59 s. 339(2)(*b*).

business or for the company's own purposes.

(c) Other transactions permitted up to specified financial limits.

It should be noted that if an exception refers to transactions of one of the first four types listed in paragraph 5.04 above, it must also cover an arrangement of type (5) or (6) which indirectly achieves the same effect as the transaction thus exempted: *e.g.* if a loan by the company would be exempt, so would be a back-to-back arrangement for a loan by a third party.

Transactions within a group

5.09   (1) Section 336 permits a company to make a *loan, quasi-loan* or *credit transaction* for its holding company, or to provide a *guarantee* or *security* in connection with such a transaction made for its holding company by any other person. This is so whether the holding company is "associated" with a director, and therefore a connected person, or is itself a director of the lending company.

5.10   (2) By virtue of section 333, section 330 does not prohibit a *loan* or *quasi-loan* by one member of a group of companies to another (nor the provision by one member of a *guarantee* or *security* in connection with a loan or quasi-loan made by any person to another member of the group) merely because the borrowing company is associated with a director of the lending company (or of its holding company) and is therefore a connected person. This exception does not apply to credit transactions: such a transaction is exempt if the borrowing company is the holding company of the lending company,[60] but not merely because they are members of the same group. Nor does the exception apply where the borrowing company is itself a director of the lending company rather than merely being associated with such a director.

Transactions in the ordinary course of business etc.

5.11   (3) Section 338 permits a money-lending company[61] to make a *loan* or *quasi-loan* to any person, or to enter into a guarantee (but not to provide a security) in connection with any other loan or quasi-loan, provided that

---

60   *Supra,* para. 5.09.
61   Defined as a company whose ordinary business includes the making of loans or quasi-loans, or the giving of guarantees in connection with loans or quasi-loans: s. 338(2). Since these are the only transactions permitted by this exception, and it is expressly required that the transaction in question be entered into in the ordinary course of the company's business, it would seem that a company which enters into a transaction fulfilling the other requirements of this exception must by definition be a money-lending company.

(a) it does so in the ordinary course of its business,[62]

(b) the amount of the loan or quasi-loan (or the amount guaranteed, as the case may be) is no greater, and the terms no more favourable, than the company might reasonably be expected to offer to a person of the same financial standing who was unconnected with the company,[63] and

(c) (unless the company is a recognised bank)[64] the aggregate of the relevant amounts does not exceed £50,000.[65] In determining the relevant amounts for this purpose, a company is not regarded as being connected with a director unless he controls it.[66]

5.12 (4) Section 335(2) permits a company to enter into a *credit transaction,* or to provide a *guarantee* or *security* in connection with such a transaction, provided that

(a) it does so in the ordinary course of business, and

(b) the value[67] of the transaction is not greater, and the terms no more favourable, than the company might reasonably be expected to offer to a person of the same financial standing who was unconnected with the company.

5.13 (5) By virtue of section 337, section 330 does not prohibit anything done by a company to enable any of its directors to meet expenditure incurred or to be incurred by him for the purposes of the company, or for the purpose of enabling him properly to perform his duties as an officer of the company, or to enable him to avoid incurring such expenditure, provided that

(a) *either*

    (i) the thing in question is done with the prior approval of a general meeting, which has been informed of the purpose of the expenditure in question, the amount of the funds to be provided by the company and the extent of the company's liability under this and any connected transaction, *or*

    (ii) it is done on condition that, if it is not so approved at or before

---

62 s. 338(3)(*a*).

63 s. 338(3)(*b*). By s. 338(6), this condition does not apply to a housing or house-improvement loan made to a director of the company or of its holding company, provided that:

    (i) the company ordinarily makes such loans to its employees on terms no less favourable, and

    (ii) the aggregate of the relevant amounts does not exceed £50,000. Where the company is a registered bank, previous loans (*etc.*) are ignored for this purpose unless they too were made by virtue of s. 338(6): s. 339(4).

64 Defined as a company which is recognised as a bank for the purposes of the Banking Act 1979: s. 744.

65 s. 338(4).

66 s. 338(5). For "control" of a company, see *supra* n. 24.

67 *Supra,* para. 5.06.

the next annual general meeting, the loan shall be repaid (or any other liability discharged) within six months of that meeting, *and*

(b) the aggregate of the relevant amounts does not exceed £10,000.

Other transactions permitted up to specified limits

5.14   (6) Section 334 permits a company to make a *loan* to a director of the company or of its holding company, provided that the aggregate of the relevant amounts does not exceed £2,500. This exception covers only loans made to directors themselves and not to persons connected with them; hence it is only previous transactions with the director in question, not with his connected persons, which are taken into account in determining the relevant amounts.[68]

5.15   (7) Section 332 permits a company to make a *quasi-loan* to a director of the company or of its holding company (but not to a connected person) provided that

(a) the quasi-loan contains a term requiring reimbursement of the company's expenditure within two months of its being incurred, and

(b) the total amount outstanding under this and previous quasi-loans does not exceed £1,000. For this purpose previous quasi-loans are taken into account if they were made to the director concerned, by virtue of section 332, by the company or a subsidiary of the company[69] or (where the quasi-loan in question is made to a director of the company's holding company) by any other subsidiary of the holding company.

5.16   (8) Section 335(1) permits a company to enter into a *credit transaction,* or to provide a *guarantee* or *security* for such a transaction, provided that the aggregate of the relevant amounts does not exceed £5,000.

TRANSACTIONS BETWEEN NEW PUBLIC COMPANIES AND SUBSCRIBERS OR MEMBERS

5.17   Section 104 of the Companies Act 1985[70] prohibits a new public company (*i.e.* either a company newly formed as a public company, or a joint-stock or private company newly registered or re-registered as a

---

68   s. 339(1).
69   Even, it would seem, if it is no longer a subsidiary: s. 339(5), *supra* n. 52, does not appear to apply.
70   Replacing s. 26 of the Companies Act 1980 with effect from 1 July 1985.

public company) from making certain agreements with certain persons unless a stipulated procedure is followed. Failure to comply with this procedure is an offence on the part of the company and any officer in default, punishable on conviction on indictment with an unlimited fine.[71] The persons caught by this rule are, in the case of a newly formed company, the subscribers to the memorandum,[72] and in the case of a newly registered or re-registered company, the members of the company at the date of registration or re-registration.[73] Section 104 applies to an agreement between the company and such a person for the transfer by him to the company or another (within an "initial period" of two years)[74] of one or more non-cash assets,[75] for a consideration[76] from the company worth at least 10% of the nominal value of the company's issued share capital at the time of the agreement. But it does not apply to an agreement in the ordinary course of a company's business for the acquisition of an asset, where it is part of the company's ordinary business to acquire assets of that description.[77]

5.18 The procedure which must be adopted before an agreement falling within section 104 can lawfully be made is as follows:

(1) The consideration to be received by the company,[78] together with any non-cash consideration to be given by the company, must be valued by an "independent person", *i.e.* a person qualified to be the company's auditor.[79] If, however, he thinks it reasonable to do so, he may delegate the task of valuation to (or accept a valuation made by) another person who appears to him to have the requisite knowledge and experience, provided that the delegate is not an officer or servant[80] of the company or of another company in the same group, nor a partner or employee of such an officer or servant.[81]

---

71 s. 114. On summary conviction the offence carries a fine of the statutory maximum: Sch. 24.
72 s. 104(1)(*a*).
73 s. 104(3)(*a*).
74 *i.e.* two years from the issue of the trading certificate under section 117 or its predecessor, in the case of a newly formed public company (s. 104(2)); in the case of a newly registered or re-registered company, two years from the date of registration or re-registration (s. 104(3)(*b*)).
75 *i.e.* any property or interest in property other than cash: s. 739(1). "Cash" includes foreign currency.
76 Including the appropriate proportion of a consideration given partly for the transfer: s. 109(3).
77 s. 104(6)(*a*). Nor does it apply to an agreement entered into under the supervision of the court or of an officer authorised by the court for the purpose: s. 104(6)(*b*).
78 *i.e.* the asset to be transferred to the company, or the advantage to the company of its transfer to a third party.
79 s.104(4)(*a*), s. 109(1).
80 An auditor is not an officer for this purpose: s. 108(3).
81 s. 108(2)

(2) The independent person must make a report to the company within the six months preceding the date of the agreement.[82] The report must state the following matters:

(a) the consideration to be received by the company (with a description of the assets in question and a statement of the amount to be received in cash);

(b) the consideration to be given by the company (with a statement of the amount to be given in cash); and

(c) the method and date of valuation.[83]

A note to the report must state:

(d) that the method of valuation was reasonable in all the circumstances;

(e) that it appears to the independent person that there has been no material change in the value of the consideration in question since the valuation; and

(f) that on the basis of the valuation the value of the consideration to be received by the company is not less than the value of the consideration to be given by it.[84]

(3) The terms of the agreement must be approved by an ordinary resolution of the company.[85]

(4) Not later than the giving of the notice of the meeting at which the resolution is proposed, copies of the resolution and of the report must have been circulated to the members of the company entitled to receive that notice and (even if he is not such a member) to the person with whom the proposed agreement is to be made.[86]

5.19 A person carrying out a valuation or making a report under section 104 may require from the officers of the company such information and explanation as he thinks necessary to enable him to do so.[87] It is an offence under section 110(2) (punishable on conviction on indictment with two years' imprisonment or a fine, or both)[88] knowingly or recklessly to make to such a person an oral or written statement which is misleading, false or deceptive in a material particular and which conveys (or purports to convey) any information or explanation which he

---

82 s. 104(4)(*b*).
83 s. 109(2)(*a*), (*b*).
84 s. 109(2)(*c*), (*d*). Where the valuation has been delegated, the report must give details of the delegate's name, knowledge and experience, of the consideration valued by him and of the method and date of the valuation; and the independent person must state in a note to the report that it appeared to him reasonable to arrange for the valuation to be made by the delegate or to accept a valuation made by him: s. 108(5), (6)(*a*).
85 s. 104(4)(*c*).
86 s. 104(4)(*d*).
87 s. 110(1).
88 Sch. 24. On summary conviction the offence carries six months' imprisonment or a fine of the statutory maximum or both.

requires or is entitled to require.[89] It is submitted that a statement is misleading or deceptive if it is likely to induce another person to believe in the truth of a proposition which is in fact false.[90] A statement is probably reckless not only if its maker does not believe it to be true but also if he has no possible grounds for such a belief.[91]

CONSIDERATION FOR ALLOTMENT OF SHARES

5.20 Another way in which directors can in effect siphon off the company's assets is by allotting shares to themselves or their associates without obtaining for the company the full value of the shares in exchange. The Companies Act 1985[92] lays down rules as to the consideration which a company (and in particular a public company) may accept by way of payment for its shares. Breach of these rules constitutes an offence on the part of the company and of any officer in default, punishable on conviction on indictment with an unlimited fine.[93]

Allotment of shares at a discount

5.21 Section 100(1) of the Companies Act 1985 prohibits a company from allotting its shares at a discount, *i.e.* for a cash consideration of less than the shares' nominal value. The prohibition would presumably apply if the same effect were achieved indirectly, *e.g.* if debentures issued at a discount (lawfully) were converted into paid-up shares.[94] But it does not apply merely because the shares are allotted for less than their *market* value (though this would no doubt constitute a breach of duty on the part of the directors).[95] Nor does it apply merely because some or all of the consideration received is not in the form of cash, and the shares are credited as paid up to an extent in excess of the value of the consideration received (except in the unlikely event of the consideration's value being agreed at less than the credit given); but in the case of a public company the consideration would have to be valued, and it would be an offence to give greater credit than the valuation.[96]

---

89 s. 110(3).
90 *Supra.* ch. 2.
91 *Cf. Bates* (1952) 36 Cr.App.R. 175, *Grunwald* [1963] 1 Q.B. 935 (*infra,* para. 8.07); *Caldwell* [1982] A.C. 341.
92 Replacing ss. 20 to 30 of the Companies Act 1980 with effect from 1 July 1985.
93 s. 114, Sch.24. On summary conviction the offence carries a fine of the statutory maximum.
94 *Cf. Mosely v. Koffyfontein Mines Ltd* [1904] 2 Ch. 108.
95 *Shaw v. Holland* [1900] 2 Ch. 305.
96 s. 103; *infra,* para. 5.24.

Payment for shares in public company

5.22 Section 101(1) requires shares allotted by a *public* company (except for shares allotted in pursuance of an employees' share scheme)[97] to be paid up as to at least a quarter of the nominal value, plus the whole of any premium. The required proportion need not be paid up in cash, but any consideration other than cash must be valued in accordance with the rules discussed below.

Non-cash consideration for shares in public company

5.23 The general rule is that shares may be paid up, as to both nominal value and any premium, in either money or money's worth (including goodwill and know-how).[98] In the case of a public company, however, there are three situations where an allotment of shares for a consideration other than cash[99] may constitute an offence under section 114:

(1) A subscriber to the memorandum of a public company who undertakes in the memorandum to take shares in the company must pay for the shares (including any premium) in cash.[1]

(2) A public company must not accept, by way of payment for shares, an undertaking to do work or perform services.[2]

(3) Nor may a public company accept an undertaking of any kind which may be performed more than five years after the date of the allotment.[3]

5.24 Even if the proposed non-cash consideration is permissible at all, a public company may not accept it in payment for shares without first having it valued by an independent person under the provisions of section 108. The procedure is essentially similar to that required by section 104:[4] the rules as to who may carry out the valuation are the same. The valuation report must state the following matters:

(a) the nominal value of the shares to be wholly or partly paid for by the consideration in question;

---

97 s. 101(2).
98 s. 99(1).
99 Payment in cash includes payment in foreign currency, payment by a cheque received by the company in good faith which the directors have no reason for suspecting will not be paid, the release of a liability of the company for a liquidated sum, and an undertaking to pay cash to the company at a future date, but not the payment of cash to a third party: s. 738.
1 s. 106.
2 s. 99(2).
3 s. 102(1). A contract for the allotment of shares which is initially lawful may not be varied so as to contravene this rule, even if it was made before the company was re-registered as a public company: s. 102(3), (4).
4 *Supra*, para. 5.18.

F–M

(b) the amount of any premium payable;

(c) the description of the consideration;

(d) the method and date of valuation; and

(e) the extent to which the nominal value of the shares and any premium are to be treated as paid up

   (i) by the consideration, and

   (ii) in cash.[5]

A note to the report must state:

(f) that the method of valuation was reasonable in all the circumstances;

(g) that it appears to the independent person that there has been no material change in the value of the consideration in question since the valuation; and

(h) that on the basis of the valuation the value of the consideration, together with any cash by which the nominal value of the shares or any premium payable on them is to be paid up, is at least the amount which is being treated as paid up.[6]

The report must be made to the company during the six months before the allotment, and a copy sent to the prospective allottee.[7] As in the case of a valuation under section 104, the valuer may require information from the officers of the company and it is an offence knowingly or recklessly to give false or deceptive information.[8]

5.25 The valuation procedure is not required in two cases:

(1) Where a take-over bid involves the offer of shares in the offeror company in exchange for shares in the target company, provided that the offer is open to all the shareholders of the target company (or, where it relates only to shares of a particular class, to all the holders of shares of that class.)[9]

(2) Where the shares are allotted in connection with a proposed merger of the company with another company.[10]

---

5 s. 108(4).

6 s. 108(6). Where the valuation has been made by another person further details must be given: *supra* n. 84. Where the consideration is accepted partly in payment for shares and partly for some other consideration given by the company, the independent person must determine what proportion of it is attributable to the shares, and must give details in his report of any other valuations carried out for this purpose: s. 108(7).

7 s. 103(1).

8 s. 110, *supra* para. 5.19.

9 s. 103(3),(4). For this purpose, shares in the target company held by (or by a nominee of) the offeror company or another company in the same group as the offeror company may be disregarded.

10 s. 103(5). There is a proposed merger where one company proposes to acquire all the assets and liabilities of the other in exchange for the issue of shares or other securities of that one to shareholders of the other.

ACQUISITION BY A COMPANY OF ITS OWN SHARES

5.26 It was until recently a basic principle of English company law that a company could not purchase shares in itself,[11] a principle usually defended on the grounds that this would involve a reduction of capital. The argument did not entirely justify the rule, since a mere transfer of ownership in shares (even a transfer to the company itself) cannot affect the company's issued share capital. It is the company's *assets* that are reduced, to the extent of the purchase price, and the transaction may therefore be objectionable either if the price is excessive (*i.e.* the purchase is a device for looting the company) or if there are no distributable profits (in which case it will amount to an unauthorised return of capital to the shareholders and may therefore constitute a fraud on the company's creditors). In either case a charge of theft might succeed, subject to the difficulties adverted to in the preceding chapter. But section 143(1) of the Companies Act 1985 provides that:

> ". . . a company limited by shares or limited by guarantee and having a share capital shall not acquire its own shares, whether by purchase, subscription or otherwise"

and a purported acquisition in breach of this provision is an offence on the part of the company and every officer in default, punishable (in the case of an officer) with two years' imprisonment or a fine or both.[12] There are a number of exceptions designed to permit such acquisitions where the risk of fraud is less serious, *e.g.* where the company has distributable profits available and the purchase is approved by the shareholders.

5.27 The prohibition in section 143 does not apply to the following transactions:[13]

(1) The acquisition by a company limited by shares of its own fully paid shares otherwise than for valuable consideration. This case had been recognised as an exception to the rule at common law.[14] As suggested above, it is not the acquisition of the shares which offers scope for fraud but the payment for them.

(2) The acquisition of shares in a reduction of capital duly made.

(3) The purchase of shares in pursuance of an order of the court (on application by dissentient shareholders) under sections 5 or 54 or Part XVII of the 1985 Act.

---

11   *Trevor v. Whitworth* (1887) 12 App. Cas. 409.
12   s. 143(2), Sch. 24, replacing s. 35(3) of the Companies Act 1980 with effect from 1 July 1985. On summary conviction the offence carries six months' imprisonment or a fine of the statutory maximum or both.
13   s. 143(3).
14   *Kirby v. Wilkins* [1929] 2 Ch. 444; *Re Castiglione's Will Trusts* [1958] Ch. 549.

(4) The forfeiture of shares, or the acceptance of shares surrendered in lieu, in pursuance of the company's articles, for failure to pay any sum payable in respect of the shares.

(5) The redemption or purchase of shares in accordance with Chapter VII of Part V of the 1985 Act. This exception constitutes a major inroad into the old rule, and requires further examination.

Redemption and purchase under Companies Act 1985 Part V

5.28   Chapter VII of Part V of the Companies Act 1985[15] permits a company either to redeem shares issued as redeemable[16] or to purchase its own shares (whether or not issued as redeemable),[17] provided that its articles authorise it to do so, and subject to stringent safeguards in both cases. These safeguards are concerned partly with the funds which must be available to finance the transaction and partly with the procedure which must be followed; the two aspects interrelate in that additional procedural steps are required when the transaction is to be financed out of capital. Failure to comply with the rules prescribed, in either respect, will render the transaction unlawful and the offence under section 143(2) will be committed.

Financing of the transaction
5.29   The rules as to the funds which must be available for the redemption or purchase are stricter in the case of public companies than in the case of private ones. A private company may, subject to additional procedural requirements, finance the transaction out of capital.[18] A public company, on the other hand (and a private company which does not follow the stipulated procedure), must ensure that its capital is preserved. Hence the price must come out of either distributable profits[19] or the proceeds of a fresh issue made for the purpose;[20] and in so far as the lost share capital is not replaced by a fresh issue it must be "topped up" by a transfer of an equivalent sum to the capital redemption reserve.[21] Certain payments other than the purchase price itself must be

---

15   Replacing Part III of the Companies Act 1981 with effect from 1 July 1985.
16   s. 159.
17   s. 162. A company may not purchase its own shares if the result would be that no member held any shares other than redeemable ones: s. 162(3).
18   *Infra*, para. 5.31.
19   *i.e.* in relation to the making of a payment, those profits out of which a distribution equal in value to the payment could lawfully be made: s. 181(*a*).
20   s. 160(1)(*a*), s. 162(2). Any premium paid may come out of the proceeds of a fresh issue only up to the aggregate of the premiums originally received on the shares, or the current amount of the share premium account (including any sum transferred to that account in respect of premiums on the new shares), whichever is the less: s. 160(2), s. 162(2).
21   s. 170.

made out of distributable profits, whether the company is a public or a private one: they include the consideration for a "contingent purchase contract" (*e.g.* an option)[22] and the consideration for the variation of such a contract or of a contract for an "off-market" purchase.[23] If these payments are made otherwise than out of distributable profits, the purchase of the shares under the contract in question will not be lawful by virtue of Part V of the Act.[24]

Procedure

5.30   The procedure for the *redemption* of shares is that prescribed by the company's articles.[25] For a *purchase* of the company's shares, however, the Act requires prior authorisation by the general meeting. In the case of a "market purchase"[26] an ordinary resolution is sufficient, and the authority conferred by the resolution may be limited or general, conditional or unconditional;[27] but it must specify the maximum number of shares which may be acquired, the maximum and minimum prices which may be paid,[28] and the date on which it is to expire[29] (not more than 18 months after the passing of the resolution).[30] In the case of an "off-market purchase"[31] or a "contingent purchase contract",[32] however, the terms of the proposed contract must be *specifically* approved in advance by a *special* resolution of the company.[33] Where the company is

---

22   A contingent purchase contract is a contract relating to any of a company's shares which does not amount to a contract to purchase them but under which the company may (subject to any conditions) become entitled or obliged to purchase them: s. 165(1).

23   s. 168. A purchase of shares is an off-market purchase if it is not made on a recognised stock exchange, or if it is so made but the shares are not subject to a marketing arrangement on that stock exchange: s. 163(1). A recognised stock exchange is one recognised for the purposes of the Prevention of Fraud (Investments) Act 1958, *i.e.* the Stock Exchange of the U.K. and Ireland: s. 744. Shares of a company are subject to a marketing arrangement if they are listed on the stock exchange in question, or if the company has been accorded facilities for dealings in those shares to take place on that stock exchange without prior permission for individual transactions from the authority governing that stock exchange and without limit as to the time during which those facilities are to be available: s. 163(2). Therefore a purchase on the Stock Exchange is a market purchase if the shares are listed or are traded on the Unlisted Securities Market, but an off-market purchase if it is made with the permission of the Stock Exchange under rule 163(2). A purchase on the "over-the-counter" markets operated by certain licensed dealers is also an off-market purchase.

24   s. 168(2)(*a*), (*b*).

25   s. 160(3).

26   *i.e.* one to be made on a recognised stock exchange where the shares are subject to a marketing arrangement: s. 163(3). See *supra* n. 23.

27   s. 166(1), (2).

28   Or a formula for calculating them without reference to any person's discretion or opinion: s. 166(6).

29   s. 166(3).

30   s. 166(4). The company may overstep the time limit if the contract of purchase was concluded before the authority expired and the terms of the authority permitted the company to make a contract which would or might be executed wholly or partly after the authority expired: s. 166(5).

31   *Supra* n. 23.

32   *Supra* n. 22.

33   s. 164(2), s. 165(2).

a public company, the authority conferred must specify a date (not later than 18 months after the passing of the resolution) on which it is to expire.[34] The resolution is ineffective if it is passed as a result of the exercise of voting rights carried by the shares in question,[35] or if a copy of the proposed contract[36] is not available for inspection at the company's registered office for at least 15 days before the meeting and also at the meeting itself.[37] If the resolution appropriate to the proposed contract is not passed, or the resolution passed does not conform to the Act's requirements, the effect is presumably to render the purchase of the shares unlawful and an offence under section 143(2). The company is also required, in every case, to keep a copy of the contract[36] available for inspection at its registered office for ten years,[38] and to make a return to the registrar of companies within 28 days of the delivery of the shares.[39] Breach of either requirement is a specific offence, summary in the former case,[40] and triable either way (but punishable with only a fine) in the latter:[41] presumably, therefore, it does not render the purchase itself illegal under section 143.

5.31   By way of exception to the rule that the redemption or purchase of a company's shares must be financed either out of distributable profits or out of the proceeds of a fresh issue, section 171 permits a *private* company to make payments for this purpose out of capital, provided certain steps are taken in addition to those referred to above. The directors must first make a statutory declaration that in their opinion there will be no ground on which the company could be found to be unable to pay its debts immediately after the payment out of capital, and that it will be able to continue to carry on business as a going concern (and will accordingly be able to pay its debts as they fall due) throughout the following year.[42] The declaration must be supported by an auditors' report.[43] It is an offence punishable on conviction on indictment with two years' imprisonment or a fine, or both, for a director to make the declaration without having reasonable grounds for the opinion expressed in it:[44] *mens rea* does not appear to be necessary. Within a week of the

---

34   s. 164(4).
35   s. 164(5). R.R. Pennington, in *The Companies Acts 1980 and 1981: A Practitioners' Manual* at p. 98, points out that this rule does not apply to a resolution authorising a market purchase, even if the purchase authorised is so large that it must necessarily include some of the shares held by those voting on the resolution.
36   Or a written memorandum of its terms if it is not in writing.
37   s. 164(6).
38   s. 169(4), (5).
39   s. 169(1).
40   s. 169(7), Sch. 24.
41   s. 169(6), Sch. 24..
42   s. 173(3).
43   s. 173(5).
44   s. 173(6), Sch. 24. On summary conviction the offence carries six months' imprisonment or a fine of the statutory maximum or both.

making of the declaration,[45] the company must pass a special resolution approving the payment out of capital.[46] The resolution is ineffective if it is passed as a result of the exercise of voting rights carried by the shares in question,[47] or if the statutory declaration and the auditors' report are not available for inspection at the meeting.[48]

5.32   Within a week of the resolution the company must give notice, in the *London Gazette* and *either* in an appropriate national newspaper[49] *or* in writing to each of its creditors, that the statutory declaration and auditors' report are available for inspection and that any creditor may apply for an order prohibiting the payment out of capital.[50] Not later than the date on which the first of these notices is given, the company must deliver a copy of the statutory declaration and the auditors' report to the Registrar of Companies.[51] The originals must be kept available for inspection at the company's registered office by members or creditors from that date until five weeks after the passing of the resolution.[52] A creditor, or a member who did not consent to the resolution or vote in favour of it, may apply to the court within five weeks of the date of the resolution to have it cancelled.[53] If no such application is made, or if the court confirms the resolution, the payment out of capital must be made between five and seven weeks after the date of the resolution[54] (unless the court orders otherwise).[55]

5.33   It is expressly provided that, subject to any order of the court on an application for cancellation of the resolution, a payment out of capital is not lawful unless the requirements summarised above are satisfied.[56] It follows that the exception under section 143(3)(*a*) (for transactions "in accordance with Chapter VII") will not apply, and the offence under section 143(2) will be committed.

FINANCIAL ASSISTANCE FOR PURCHASE OF COMPANY SHARES

5.34   Since 1929 it has been unlawful for a company to give financial assistance in the purchase by any person of shares in that company. The

---

45   s. 174(1).
46   s. 173(2).
47   s. 174(2).
48   s. 174(4).
49   *i.e.* one circulating throughout England and Wales in the case of a company registered in England and Wales, or one circulating throughout Scotland in the case of a company registered in Scotland: s. 175(3).
50   s. 175(1), (2).
51   s. 175(5).
52   s. 175(6). Refusal to allow inspection is a summary offence: s. 175(7).
53   s. 176(1).
54   s. 174(1).
55   s. 177(2).
56   s. 173(1).

rule is partially directed at the purchasing of shares by a nominee of the company or by an associated company, thus evading the prohibition on the purchase of shares by the company itself, but more particularly at the practice of taking over a cash company with the aid of the company's own money. This practice was described by Lord Greene M.R. in *Re V.G.M. Holdings Ltd:*[57]

> "Those whose memories enable them to recall what had been happening for several years after the last war will remember that a very common form of transaction in connection with companies was one by which persons— call them financiers, speculators, or what you will—finding a company with a substantial cash balance or easily realisable assets, such as War Loan, bought up the whole, or the greater part, of the shares of the company for cash, and so arranged matters that the purchase money which they then became bound to provide was advanced to them by the company whose shares they were acquiring, either out of its cash balance or by realisation of its liquid investments. That type of transaction was a common one, and it gave rise to great dissatisfaction and, in some cases, great scandals."[58]

The relevant provision of the Companies Act 1948, section 54, has been replaced by what is now Chapter VI of Part V of the Companies Act 1985.[59] Section 151 creates two offences, both punishable on conviction on indictment with a fine in the case of the company and with two years' imprisonment (or a fine, or both) in the case of any officer in default.[60]

The offences

5.35　Section 54 of the 1948 Act prohibited the giving of financial assistance by a company "for the purpose of or in connection with" a purchase of shares in the company. Clearly assistance can only be given for the purpose of the purchase if it is given before the purchase is made, whereas it would still be given in connection with the purchase in the common case where the purchaser first acquires the shares with the aid of a loan and then extracts from the company the money to repay the loan. Section 151 of the 1985 Act draws a sharper distinction between the two situations by creating two separate offences:

> "(1) Subject to the following provisions of this Chapter, where a person is acquiring or is proposing to acquire shares in a company, it is not lawful for the company or any of its subsidiaries to give financial assistance directly or indirectly for the purpose of that acquisition before or at the same time as the acquisition takes place.

57　[1942] Ch. 235.
58　At p. 239. See, *e.g., Selangor United Rubber Estates Ltd v. Cradock (No. 3)* [1968] 1 W.L.R. 1555, *Wallersteiner v. Moir* [1974] 1 W.L.R. 991. For a graphic illustration, see Finer, "Company Fraud" [1966] *The Accountant* 583 at p.585.
59　Replacing ss. 42 to 44 of the Companies Act 1981 with effect from 1 July 1985.
60　s. 151(3), Sch. 24. On summary conviction the offences carry six months' imprisonment or a fine of the statutory maximum or both.

(2) Subject to those provisions, where a person has acquired shares in a company and any liability has been incurred (by that or any other person), for the purpose of that acquisition, it is not lawful for the company or any of its subsidiaries to give financial assistance directly or indirectly for the purpose of reducing or discharging the liability so incurred."

5.36   "Financial assistance" is defined by section 152(1)(*a*) as:

"(i) financial assistance given by way of gift;
(ii) financial assistance given by way of guarantee, security or indemnity, other than an indemnity in respect of the indemnifier's own neglect or default, or by way of release or waiver;
(iii) financial assistance given by way of a loan or any other agreement under which any of the obligations of the person giving the assistance are to be fulfilled at a time when in accordance with the agreement any obligation of another party to the agreement remains unfulfilled, or by way of the novation of, or the assignment of rights arising under, a loan or such other agreement; or
(iv) any other financial assistance given by a company the net assets[61] of which are thereby reduced to a material extent or which has no net assets. . ."

This appears to be an exhaustive definition. The assistance may be given either "directly or indirectly",[62] *e.g. via* a chain of interlinking loans; and the prohibition extends to assistance given not only by the company whose shares are acquired but also by a subsidiary of that company.

5.37   For the purposes of subsection (2) a person incurs a liability if he changes his financial position by making an agreement or arrangement (whether enforceable or unenforceable, and whether made on his own account or with any other person) or by any other means.[63] A liability presumably cannot be incurred "for the purpose of" the acquisition unless it is incurred *before* (or at any rate at the same time as)[64] the acquisition. Hence the assistance is not prohibited unless *either* it is given before (or at the same time as) the acquisition *or* it is given for the purpose of reducing or discharging a liability which was incurred before (or at the same time as) the acquisition. At first sight there appears to be a lacuna in the case where the shares are acquired with the help of a loan, the loan is repaid by means of a second loan, and the company then provides assistance in the repayment of the second loan. The company's

---

61   *i.e.* the aggregate of assets minus the aggregate of liabilities: s. 152(2).
62   Ralph Instone suggests ("Illegal Assistance Updated" (1982) 132 N.L.J. 727) that these words might be interpreted as qualifying the words "for the purpose of" rather than the verb "to give"; but he prefers the latter interpretation (rightly, it is submitted) because (a) in the old s. 54 it was clearly the giving of the financial assistance which might be direct or indirect, (b) this is the more natural reading, and (c) the prohibition does not apply if the acquisition of the shares is not the company's *principal* purpose: *infra,* para. 5.39.
63   s. 152(3)(*a*).
64   *Cf.* s. 151(1).

purpose is not to reduce or discharge the first loan, because that has already been discharged: its purpose *is* to reduce or discharge the second loan, but that loan was incurred for the purpose of discharging the first loan, not for the purpose of the acquisition. Section 152(3)(*b*) is apparently an attempt to meet the difficulty:

"... a reference to a company giving financial assistance for the purpose of reducing or discharging a liability incurred by a person for the purpose of the acquisition of shares includes its giving such assistance for the purpose of wholly or partly restoring his financial position to what it was before the acquisition took place."

This provision is not happily expressed. In the first place, the financial position of the person acquiring the shares surely includes his ownership of those shares; so there is no question of restoring it to what it was before he acquired them. Presumably it is sufficient if, apart from the fact that he now owns the shares, his position is being restored to what it was. But even this presents difficulties. Immediately before acquiring the shares, he has assets consisting of the price of the shares and a corresponding liability to repay it to the lender. There is no question of restoring that position either. Perhaps the reference to his financial position "before the acquisition took place" must be taken to mean his position before he incurred any liability for the purpose of the acquisition. That position may be restored (still disregarding the shares themselves) if he comes under no obligation to reimburse the company for its assistance, but not if the assistance is by way of a loan: in that case the only change is in the identity of his creditor. The reference to a *partial* restoration of his position does not appear to meet the difficulty.

Exceptions

5.38   The prohibitions in section 151 are subject to a number of exceptions, which fall into four groups:

(1) exceptions relating to the company's purposes in giving the financial assistance (section 153(1) and (2));
(2) transactions permissible as a matter of general company law (section 153(3));
(3) exceptions retained from section 54, 1948 Act (section 153(4)); and
(4) a procedure whereby *private* companies may obtain exemption from section 151 (sections 155 to 158).

Exceptions relating to the company's purposes
5.39   Under the old section 54 the question had arisen whether it was lawful for a company to enter into a transaction which was commercially

justifiable in itself, but which would also have the effect of providing some other person with funds which he would use to purchase shares in the company. The point was discussed but not decided in *Belmont Finance Corporation v. Williams Furniture Ltd (No 2).*[65] The financial assistance must now be given for the *purpose* of the acquisition (or of reducing or discharging a liability incurred for that purpose) and not merely "in connection with" it. But the new provisions seek to restrict the scope of the offence still further by means of a pair of exceptions, one applying to each of the two offences. Under section 153(1) and (2), the assistance is not prohibited by section 151(1) or (2) respectively if the acquisition (or the reduction or discharge of the liability) is not the company's *principal* purpose in giving it, or (even if it *is* the company's principal purpose) it is "but an incidental part of some larger purpose of the company"—provided, in either case, that it is given in good faith in the interests of the company. How something can be both the principal purpose and an incidental part of some larger purpose is not explained. In any event the requirement of good faith renders these exceptions of limited importance for present purposes.

Generally permissible transactions

5.40   The following transactions are permissible as a matter of general company law and are expressly excluded by section 153(3) from the prohibitions in section 151:

"(*a*) a distribution of a company's assets by way of dividend lawfully made or a distribution made in the course of the company's winding up,
(*b*) the allotment of bonus shares,
(*c*) a reduction of capital confirmed by order of the court under section 137,
(*d*) a redemption or purchase of shares made in accordance with Chapter VII of [Part V],[66]
(*e*) anything done in pursuance of an order of the court under section 425 (compromises and arrangements with creditors and members),
(*f*) anything done under an arrangement made in pursuance of section 582 (acceptance of shares by liquidator in winding up as consideration for sale of property), or
(*g*) anything done under an arrangement made between a company and its creditors which is binding on the creditors by virtue of section 601 (winding up imminent or in progress)."

Old exceptions retained

5.41   Three exceptions which formerly appeared in section 54 of the 1948 Act are retained, with amendments, in the new provisions. Section 153(4) provides that the following transactions are not prohibited by section 151(1) and (2):

---

65   [1980] 1 All E.R. 393.
66   *Supra,* para. 5.28 ff.

> "(a)   where the lending of money is part of the ordinary business of the company, the lending of money by the company in the ordinary course of its business. . ."

For this exception to apply the company's ordinary business must include the lending of money "in general", in the sense that the money lent is normally at the free disposition of the borrower and not restricted to particular purposes. Moreover, the loan in question must be made in the ordinary course of the company's business, *i.e.* on a scale and for a purpose similar to the loans which the company regularly makes.[67] If these requirements are satisfied it seems likely that the case would in any event fall within the new exceptions created by section 153(1) and (2).

> "(b)   the provision by a company in accordance with an employees' share scheme of money for the acquisition of fully paid shares in the company or its holding company,
>
> (c)   the making by a company of loans to persons (other than directors) employed in good faith by the company with a view to enabling those persons to acquire fully paid shares in the company or its holding company to be held by them by way of beneficial ownership."

None of these three exceptions applies to financial assistance by a *public* company unless the company has net assets[68] which are not thereby reduced, or, to the extent that they are thereby reduced, the assistance is provided out of distributable profits.[69]

Exemption for private companies

5.42   Subject to a procedure laid down in sections 155 to 158, a *private* company may obtain exemption from the prohibitions in section 151. Not only must the company giving the assistance be a private company, but, if the shares being acquired are shares in that company's holding company, the holding company must also be a private company.[70] So too must any subsidiary of that holding company which is itself a holding company of the company giving the assistance[71] (hereafter referred to as an intermediate holding company). The company giving the assistance must have net assets which are not thereby reduced, or, to the extent that they are thereby reduced, the assistance must be provided out of distributable profits.[72]

---

67   *Steen v. Law* [1964] A.C. 287; *Fowlie v. Slater* (1979) 129 N.L.J. 465. See also Keith Walmsley, "Lending in the 'Ordinary Course of Business' " (1979) 129 N.L.J. 801; R.C.B. Hopkins, "Section 54: The Slater Case and Proviso (a)" (1979) 129 N.L.J. 1089.

68   Defined as the amount by which the company's aggregate assets exceed its aggregate liabilities, taking the amounts in both cases to be as stated in the company's accounting records immediately before the assistance is given: s. 154(2)(a).

69   s. 154(1).

70   s. 155(1).

71   s. 155(3).

72   s. 155(2).

5.43 The required procedure is as follows. The directors of the company proposing to give the financial assistance (and, where the shares being acquired are shares in its holding company, the directors of that company and of any intermediate holding company) must make a statutory declaration of solvency.[73] This declaration must include details of the proposed assistance,[74] and must state that in the directors' opinion the company will be able to pay its debts as they fall due during the next year after the giving of the proposed assistance (or, if it is intended to commence the winding up of the company within that period, that it will be able to pay its debts in full within a year of the commencement of the winding up).[75] Making the statutory declaration without reasonable grounds for the opinion expressed in it is an offence, punishable on conviction on indictment with two years' imprisonment or a fine, or both.[76] The declaration must be supported by an auditors' report.[77]

5.44 Within a week of the making of the statutory declaration,[78] the company giving the assistance (unless it is a wholly owned subsidiary) and, where the shares being acquired are shares in its holding company, that company and any intermediate holding company (except for wholly owned subsidiaries), must by special resolution approve the giving of the assistance.[79] The statutory declaration and the auditors' report must be available for inspection at the meeting.[80] Copies of the declaration, the report and the resolution must be delivered to the Registrar of Companies:[81] failure to do so is a summary offence[82] and therefore arguably does not invalidate a defence based on the private company exception to section 151. The assistance may not be given until four weeks after the passing of the special resolution (or the last of them) unless (in the case of each resolution) every member entitled to vote did in fact vote in favour of the resolution.[83] This delay enables objecting shareholders to apply to the court for cancellation of the resolution,[84] in which case the assistance may not be given before the application is finally determined

---

73 s. 155(6).
74 s. 156(1).
75 s. 156(2).
76 s. 156(7), Sch. 24. On summary conviction the offence carries six months' imprisonment or a fine of the statutory maximum or both.
77 s. 156(4).
78 s. 157(1).
79 s. 155(4), (5).
80 s. 157(4)(*a*).
81 s. 156(5).
82 s. 156(6).
83 s. 158(2).
84 s. 157(2).

(unless the court orders otherwise),[85] nor of course if the court cancels the resolution.[86] If no application is made, the assistance must be given within eight weeks of the statutory declaration (or the earliest of them).[87]

85   s. 158(3).
86   s. 157(4)(*b*).
87   s. 158(4).

CHAPTER 6

Documents, Records and Accounts

6.01 This chapter sets out to consider the offences which may be committed by a person who adopts one of the commonest fraudulent devices, *viz.* the falsification of documents or records. It should be emphasised at the outset that, although there is substantial overlap between these two categories (*i.e.* many records are in documentary form), neither category is wholly included in the other: in other words, some documents are not records and some records (*e.g.* computer-based accounting systems) are not documents—not, at any rate, in the ordinary sense of the word. Hence it is possible to draw a broad distinction between two types of fraudulent activity: the falsification of records, documentary or otherwise, and the falsification of documents which are not (or not primarily) records. The former type is self-explanatory—records are deliberately made up incorrectly, or altered so as to give a false impression of what has occurred. This may be done either for the purpose of facilitating fraud or simply to cover it up afterwards. The latter type, which may be loosely described as "documentary fraud", involves the use of commercial documents which have been fabricated or altered with a view to misleading another party to the transaction. It will almost invariably involve the commission of one of the offences of deception discussed above,[1] but the element of false documentation may bring other offences such as forgery into play. The offences to be considered may therefore be divided into two groups, *viz.* those concerned primarily with documentary fraud and those concerned primarily with the falsification of accounts and other records. It must be added that this division is made for convenience only and is far from watertight. Forgery, for example, is the paradigm offence of documentary fraud; but it is arguable that it may also be committed by falsifying records.[2] Conversely, the offence of false accounting has been given such a wide interpretation that it might be committed in the course of a documentary fraud.[3]

---

1 *Supra,* ch. 3.
2 *Infra,* para. 6.04 ff.
3 *Infra,* para. 6.43.

DOCUMENTARY FRAUD

6.02 "Wealth, in a commercial age, is made up largely of promises",[4] and commercial promises are frequently to be found in documentary form. In modern business the trust placed in documents is immense, and the opportunities for fraud correspondingly great. Cheque cards and credit cards can be stolen and used by unauthorised persons; they can even be forged, though the technology required is becoming ever more advanced. Fake share certificates can be used as security for loans. Spurious invoices can be submitted in respect of goods which have not been supplied; an accomplice within the "purchasing" firm will then authorise payment. Alternatively, such invoices may be presented to a finance house for discounting. Perhaps the most fertile ground for documentary fraud is the export trade, where shipping documents are commonly treated as actually representing the goods; thus payment can be obtained in respect of inferior or non-existent goods by means of a forged certificate of quality or bill of lading. Apart from offences of deception and theft, the main offences relevant to this type of fraud are those created by Part I of the Forgery and Counterfeiting Act 1981. Consideration will also be given to section 20(1) of the Theft Act 1968.

Forgery

6.03 The complex provisions of the Forgery Act 1913, together with the offence of forgery at common law, have now been replaced by the eight comparatively simple offences to be found in sections 1 to 5 of the Forgery and Counterfeiting Act 1981.[5] The offence of forgery itself is created by section 1, which provides:

> "A person is guilty of forgery if he makes a false instrument, with the intention that he or another shall use it to induce somebody to accept it as genuine, and by reason of so accepting it to do or not to do some act to his own or any other person's prejudice."

The offence is punishable on conviction on indictment with ten years' imprisonment.[6] Its elements will be considered under the following headings:

(1) Instruments
(2) False instruments
(3) Making a false instrument
(4) Acceptance of the instrument as genuine
(5) Prejudice
(6) Causation.

---

4   R. Pound, *Introduction to the Philosophy of Law*, p.236.
5   The Act came into force on 27 October 1981.
6   s. 6(2).

Instruments

6.04　Section 8(1) defines the word "instrument":

> ". . . in this Part of this Act 'instrument' means—
>
> (a) any document, whether of a formal or informal character;[7]
> (b) any stamp issued or sold by the Post Office;[8]
> (c) any Inland Revenue stamp;[9] and
> (d) any disc, tape, sound track or other device on or in which information is recorded or stored by mechanical, electronic or other means."

This definition presents certain difficulties. The old offence of forgery, which was replaced by the new section 1, was one of making a false *document*.[10] The Law Commission, in the report which was eventually implemented as the Forgery and Counterfeiting Act 1981, expressed the view that there was no need to include all types of document within the scope of the offence:

> "In the straightforward case [*sc.* of forgery] a document usually contains messages of two distinct kinds—first a message about the document itself (such as the message that the document is a cheque or a will) and secondly a message to be found in the words of the document that is to be accepted and acted upon (such as the message that a banker is to pay a specified sum or that property is to be distributed in a particular way). In our view it is only documents which convey not only the first type of message but also the second type that need to be protected by the law of forgery."[11]

The word "instrument" was intended to denote a document conveying *both* types of message. There is some authority for confining the term to documents of this kind. In *Attorney-General of Hong Kong v. Pat Chiuk-Wah*,[12] Lord Diplock, delivering the advice of the Privy Council, said:

> ". . . the expression 'instrument' in the context of the Forgery Ordinance [*sc.* of Hong Kong] is not confined to a formal document, but includes any document intended to have some effect, as evidence of, or in connection with, a transaction which is capable of giving rise to legal rights or obligations."[13]

6.05　On the other hand the word "instrument" was in fact used, without definition, in earlier forgery legislation, and was sometimes given a much wider interpretation. In *Riley*[14] the defendant placed a bet by

---

7　But not a currency note as defined by s. 27(1): s. 8(2).
8　Including a mark denoting payment of postage which the Post Office authorise to be used instead of an adhesive stamp: s. 8(3).
9　Including a stamp impressed by means of a die as well as an adhesive stamp for denoting any duty or fee: s. 8(4), applying Stamp Duties Management Act 1891 s. 27.
10　Forgery Act 1913 s. 1(1).
11　Law Com. No. 55, at para. 22.
12　[1971] A.C. 835.
13　*Ibid.* at p. 840.
14　[1896] 1 Q.B. 309.

means of a telegram which purported to have been sent before the race in question but which was not in fact sent until the result was known. His conviction of obtaining money by means of a forged instrument was upheld by the Court for Crown Cases Reserved. Hawkins J. thought that the word "instrument" was sufficiently wide to cover

> "an infinite variety of writings, whether penned for the purpose of creating binding obligations or as records of business or other transactions."[15]

Wills J. took a similar view:

> ". . . I think it [*sc.* 'instrument'] is meant to include writings of every description if false and known to be false . . ."[16]

In *Howse,*[17] on essentially similar facts, this view was adopted by the Court of Criminal Appeal. But neither decision is inconsistent with Lord Diplock's narrow sense of the word, because in each case the communication in question was one which effected a legal transaction (albeit a transaction invalidated by section 18 of the Gaming Act 1845). Hawkins J. described the telegram in *Riley* as an "instrument of contract",[18] *i.e.* an acceptance of an offer made to all the world. Wills J., after indicating his preference for a broad interpretation, went on:

> "I think further that, even if the true construction of the word 'instrument' required a more restricted meaning, the telegram in the present case would fall within it. It was a writing which, if accepted and acted upon, would establish a business relation and lead directly to business dealings with another person . . ."[19]

And in *Cade,*[20] where the document in question was a letter purporting to be signed by the victim's employee and requesting money for the hire of equipment, the Court of Criminal Appeal upheld a conviction under section 7 of the Forgery Act 1913 (the successor to the offence charged in *Riley*) on the grounds that the letter was a "business document" and fell within Wills J.'s alternative, narrower interpretation.

6.06 The Law Commission's intention was to use the term "instrument" in a similarly narrow sense, so that not every document would qualify as an instrument for the purposes of the new offence. But this intention appears to have been thwarted by Parliament's decision to define "instrument" as including "any document". On a literal reading it would seem that any document is by definition an "instrument", whether or not

---

15 *Ibid.* at p. 314.
16 *Ibid.* at p. 321.
17 (1912) 107 L.T. 239.
18 [1896] 1 Q.B. 309 at p. 315.
19 *Ibid.* at p. 322.
20 [1914] 2 K.B. 209.

it conveys "a message . . . that is to be accepted and acted upon". A set of accounts, for example, could on this view be the subject of forgery as well as the less serious offence of false accounting. It might perhaps be argued that such an interpretation should be rejected as running directly counter to the intentions of the Law Commission; but it may be that by inserting the reference to "any document" Parliament was deliberately departing from those intentions. Alternatively it is arguable that, appearances notwithstanding, it is the word "document" which is governed by the word "instrument" and not *vice versa*—in other words, that it is not *every* document which qualifies as an instrument, but only those documents which would have done so if the word "instrument" had been left undefined and had been interpreted in some narrower sense.

6.07 There is, however, a powerful argument against this narrow interpretation of section 8(1)(*a*)—even apart from the fact that at first sight its meaning is plain. Any attempt to confine the scope of the word "instrument" to documents which are themselves used in the course of business transactions must come to terms with section 8(1)(*d*), which provides that the word includes "any . . . device on or in which information is recorded or stored . . ." Clearly the intention is to include computer files and other forms of information technology as well as more traditional media. But the reference to the recording and storing of information would seem to rule out any argument that section 8(1)(*d*) only applies where the computer system is serving as an "instrument" in the narrow sense, *e.g.* where instructions for the payment of money are transmitted. Presumably it applies equally to all forms of databases and accounting systems. And if electronic accounting systems are included, it would be anomalous to exclude accounts kept in documentary form. It is submitted, therefore, that section 8(1)(*a*) should be construed according to its natural meaning and that any document may be the subject of forgery. But if it is debatable whether a particular article qualifies even as a document, it will no doubt be permissible to construe the word "document" in the light of the word "instrument", and hence to confine it to articles whose primary function lies in the writing which they bear. A signed painting may conceivably be a document,[21] but it can hardly be described as an instrument.

False instruments
6.08 At common law it was necessary to prove that the document was not merely misleading but "false", *i.e.* that it purported to be that which

---

21 *Douce* [1972] Crim. L.R. 105; *cf. Closs* (1858) Dears. & B. 460, *Smith* (1858) Dears. & B. 566.

it was not.[22] In Kenny's phrase,[23] it must not only tell a lie: it must tell a lie *about itself.* The Law Commission's intention was that this requirement of "automendacity"[24] should be retained in the new legislation. Their report stated:

> ". . . the primary reason for retaining a law of forgery is to penalise the making of documents which, because of the spurious air of authenticity given to them, are likely to lead to their acceptance as true statements of the facts related in them. We do not think that there is any need for the extension of forgery to cover falsehoods that are reduced to writing, and we do not propose any change in the law in this regard."[25]

Section 1 of the Forgery and Counterfeiting Act 1981 refers to the making of a "false instrument", and section 9(1) provides:

> "An instrument is false for the purposes of this Part of this Act—
>   (*a*) if it purports to have been made in the form in which it is made by a person who did not in fact make it in that form; or
>   (*b*) if it purports to have been made in the form in which it is made on the authority of a person who did not in fact authorise its making in that form; or
>   (*c*) if it purports to have been made in the terms in which it is made by a person who did not in fact make it in those terms; or
>   (*d*) if it purports to have been made in the terms in which it is made on the authority of a person who did not in fact authorise its making in those terms; or
>   (*e*) if it purports to have been altered in any respect by a person who did not in fact alter it in that respect; or
>   (*f*) if it purports to have been altered in any respect on the authority of a person who did not in fact authorise the alteration in that respect; or
>   (*g*) if it purports to have been made or altered on a date on which, or at a place at which, or otherwise in circumstances in which, it was not in fact made or altered; or
>   (*h*) if it purports to have been made or altered by an existing person but he did not in fact exist."

This definition appears to be exhaustive. Section 35 of the Criminal Justice Act 1925, which provided in effect that the statutory definition of falsity was merely illustrative, has been repealed.[26]

6.09 In each of the cases set out in section 9(1), the instrument "purports" to have been made or altered by (or on the authority of) a certain person, or in particular circumstances. The word "purports" is not defined. It is debatable whether the requirements of section 9(1) would be satisfied if the instrument were designed to create a false

---

22   *Per* Blackburn J. in *re Windsor* (1865) 10 Cox 118 at p. 123.
23   *Outlines of Criminal Law* (3rd ed.), para. 387.
24   An expression attributed to Professor E. Griew.
25   Law Com. No. 55, at para. 42.
26   Forgery and Counterfeiting Act 1981 s. 30 and Schedule.

impression as to one of the matters specified, without making any express reference to it; if, for example, the handwriting resembled that of a person other than the true author, but that other person's name were neither signed nor otherwise mentioned. Would the document purport to have been written by him? In *Keith*[27] it was said by Coleridge J. that

> ". . . an instrument purports to be that which on the face of the instrument it more or less accurately resembles."[28]

But the offence under discussion was that of engraving a promissory note purporting to be that of a banking company,[29] and Crompton J. pointed out:

> ". . . one must give the word 'purporting' a larger meaning than it ordinarily bears, or the statute would be ineffectual in many cases."[30]

Certainly a document which is signed purports to have been made by the person in whose name it is signed, whether or not the signature bears any resemblance to his.[31] It is submitted that Coleridge J.'s dictum is to be confined to its context, and that the ordinary meaning of the word was better summed up by Buller J. in *Gilchrist:*[32]

> ". . . the purport of an instrument . . . is that alone which appears on the face of it."[33]

On this view, an instrument does not purport to have been made by a particular person unless it is signed in his name or otherwise refers to him as its author.

6.10   It may be argued that this restrictive interpretation is inconsistent with a number of authorities on the old law, which established that it was forgery to sign one's own name with the intention that the signature should be taken for that of another person with a similar name.[34] In this situation it could hardly be said that the document told a lie about itself;[35] but the rule was enacted as section 1(2)(*c*) of the Forgery Act 1913, which provided that a document was false if it was made in the name of its maker but with the intention that it should pass as having been made by some other person. The 1981 Act contains no corres-

---

27   (1855) 24 L.J.M.C. 110.
28   *Ibid.* at p. 112.
29   Forgery Act 1830 s. 18.
30   (1855) 24 L.J.M.C. 110 at p. 112.
31   *Hare v. Copland* (1862) 13 I.C.L.R. 426.
32   (1795) 2 Leach 657, following *Reading* (1794) 2 Leach 590.
33   *Ibid.* at p. 662.
34   *Mead v. Young* (1790) 4 T.R. 28 (approved by Parke B., Patteson J. and Pollock C.B. in the course of the argument in *White* (1847) 2 Cox 210 at p.215), *Hudson* [1943] 1 All E.R. 642, *Abdullah* [1982] Crim.L.R. 122; *cf. Mitchell* (1844) 1 Den. 282, *Nisbett* (1853) 6 Cox 320, *Mahony* (1854) 6 Cox 487.
35   See R.N. Gooderson "When is a document false in the law of forgery?" (1952) 15 M.L.R. 11.

ponding provision. An instrument signed by a person in his own name is not false unless it "purports" to have been signed by somebody else: does it so purport merely[36] because it is intended to give that impression? Buller J.'s definition would suggest not. It may be significant that it was thought necessary to include section 1(2)(c) in the 1913 Act: this fact suggests that the situation would not have been covered by the preceding provisions of section 1(2), which referred to a document purporting to have been made by a person who did not in fact make it. And in that case section 9(1) of the 1981 Act would not now apply.

6.11   A variation on this theme is the case of a person who signs his own name in an unusual manner, with the intention of subsequently denying that the signature is his. Thus in *Brittain v. Bank of London*[37] the drawer of a cheque altered it, after it was returned to him by his bank, so as to disguise his handwriting. He then alleged that the payee had forged it. According to Cockburn C.J., the drawer was not guilty of forgery;[38] and this view seems consistent with principle. A similar decision was reached in *Macer*,[39] where the defendant wrote a cheque in his own name but with an unusual signature. This too was held not to be forgery: the cheque did not "tell a lie on its face" because it did not purport to be signed by anybody other than the defendant himself. If it had been proved that the defendant intended the signature to be taken as that of some other person, the case would no doubt have fallen within section 1(2)(c) of the 1913 Act. Since no equivalent of section 1(2)(c) appears in the 1981 Act, it is submitted that Macer would not now be guilty of forgery even if such intention could be proved: the cheque would still purport, truthfully, to have been written by him.

6.12   Section 9(1) sets out various matters on which an instrument may "tell a lie about itself". Broadly speaking these matters may be grouped into four categories:

(*a*) the identity of the person making the instrument;
(*b*) the identity of the person authorising its making;
(*c*) the date, place or circumstances of its making; and
(*d*) the circumstances of any alteration to it.

These possibilities will be considered in turn.

---

36   In *Abdullah* [1982] Crim.L.R. 122, where the defendant signed his own name on a credit card issued to his wife, it was said that the signature did purport to be his wife's. But before a credit card is issued it is stamped with the prospective holder's name. Clearly, therefore, the signature purports to be that of the person to whom the card is issued—at any rate if, as in this case, the signature could reasonably be taken for that person's name.
37   (1863) 3 F. & F. 465.
38   *Ibid.* at p. 473.
39   [1979] Crim. L.R. 659.

6.13 *(a) Identity of maker of instrument.* Where an instrument purports to have been made (in its present form and its present terms) by a particular person, it will be false within section 9(1)(*a*) or (*c*) if that person either

  (i) did not make it at all, or

  (ii) did make it, but not in that form or in those terms (*i.e.* it has been unobtrusively altered).

The corresponding provision in the 1913 Act[40] was construed so as not to apply where a document was made with the authority of the person in question, although it purported to have been made by him in person;[41] such a document would clearly fall within section 9(1). More debatable is the case where the purported maker of the instrument did in fact make it, but he did so under some misapprehension (perhaps fraudulently induced) as to its nature or contents; for example, a blind or illiterate testator is induced to execute a will which does not correspond with his wishes. It seems that this would not formerly have been regarded as forgery,[42] and it would be difficult to bring within the wording of section 9(1). Even if the circumstances were such as to bring the doctrine of *non est factum*[43] into play, it is submitted that that maxim cannot be taken literally: the maker of an instrument is still its maker even if he did not know what it was. But if the mistake is deliberately induced, the offence of procuring the execution of a valuable security by deception[44] might be made out.

6.14 Section 9(1)(*h*) provides for a specific example of an instrument which purports to have been made by a person who did not in fact make it: *viz.*, one which purports to have been made by a person who did not in fact exist. At common law it was sufficient not only if the document purported to have been executed by some totally fictitious person,[45] but also if the defendant himself (while admitting that the document was his own handiwork) pretended to be some other person who did not exist.[46] In the latter case it is arguable that the document does not purport to have been made by any non-existent person but by the defendant himself, who is merely claiming certain attributes which he does not in fact have;[47] but the courts have come to the conclusion that it is forgery to execute a

40 s. 1(2).
41 *Vincent* (1972) 56 Cr.App.R. 281. *Cf. Potter* [1958] 1 W.L.R. 638, where the difficulty was evaded by invoking s. 35 of the Criminal Justice Act 1925.
42 *Collins* (1843) 2 M. & Rob. 461, *Chadwick* (1844) 2 M. & Rob. 545.
43 See *Saunders v. Anglia Building Society* [1971] A.C. 1004.
44 Theft Act 1968 s. 20(2); *supra,* para. 3.40ff.
45 *Lewis* (1754) Fost. 116.
46 *Dunn* (1765) 1 Leach 57.
47 See G. Williams, "Forgery and Falsity" [1974] Crim. L.R. 71.

document in an assumed name[48] (unless the other party to the transaction knows the defendant by his real name),[49] because the document purports to have been executed by the person (real or fictitious) whose name is used. Presumably section 9(1)(*h*) is intended to preserve this bizarre doctrine. It must, however, be remembered that a person's name is merely what other people call him. It is not forgery to change one's name informally and to sign documents in the new name,[50] nor to use an alias by which one is commonly known. Only if the name used in the document is one by which the maker has not previously been known does the document purport to have been made by somebody else. A person who finds it convenient to undergo frequent changes of identity is safe from a charge of forgery provided that he uses each name for a while before signing anything with it.

6.15   *(b) Identity of person authorising making of instrument.* Under section 9(1)(*b*) and (*d*), an instrument is also false if it purports to have been made (in its present form and its present terms) *on the authority* of a particular person, and that person either

  (i) did not authorise its making at all, or
  (ii) did authorise its making, but not in that form or in those terms.

There appears to be a lacuna in the (admittedly somewhat unlikely) case where the instrument purports to have been made on the authority of a person who did not in fact exist—for example, the holder of some impressive-sounding but non-existent post in an organisation. Section 9(1)(*h*) applies only where the instrument purports to have been made by the fictitious person himself. It could be argued that the case falls within section 9(1)(*b*) or (*d*), or both: *i.e.* the instrument purports to have been made on the authority of a person who did not authorise its making because he did not exist. This argument would have more force if section 9(1)(*h*) had been omitted. The fact that it was thought necessary to include it suggests that a fictitious person is not "a person" within the meaning of section 9(1)(*a*) and (*c*), in which case he presumably does not count as one for the purposes of section 9(1)(*b*) or (*d*) either. But it is arguable that section 9(1)(*h*) was included *ex abundanti cautela* and is to be read without prejudice to the generality of the preceding paragraphs.

6.16   *(c) Date, place or circumstances of making of instrument.* By virtue of section 9(1)(*g*), an instrument is false if it falsely purports to have been made on a certain date, or at a certain place, or otherwise in certain circumstances. Thus it would be forgery to make out a bill of lading with

---

48   *Hassard and Devereux* [1970] 2 All E.R. 647, *Gambling* [1975] Q.B. 207.
49   *Martin* (1879) 5 Q.B.D. 34.
50   *Cf. Hadjimitsis* [1964] Crim.L.R. 128.

a date earlier (or later) than that on which the goods were in fact shipped, or to ante-date a deed with a view to tax evasion.[51] It would probably not be sufficient that the defendant merely mis-dated a cheque, since a cheque does not necessarily purport to have been written on the date which it bears: the post-dated cheque is a common device for the payment of a debt at or after some future date, and is clearly legitimate provided that the payee accepts the cheque in the knowledge that it is post-dated. If he were given the impression that the cheque would be honoured on immediate presentation the drawer might well be guilty of an offence of deception, but not (it is submitted) of forgery.

6.17   The wording of section 9(1)(g) makes it clear that the "circumstances" in which the instrument purports to have been made may include matters other than the date and the place of its making. An instrument would obviously be false if, for example, it purported to have been made on the date on which it was in fact made, but at a different time of day. But the possible implications of section 9(1)(g) are far-reaching. In *Donnelly (Ian)*[52] the manager of a jeweller's shop, for the purpose of an insurance fraud, made out a valuation certificate describing six items of jewellery which did not in fact exist. It was conceded by the Crown that this document would not have been a forgery either at common law or under the Forgery Act 1913, and the concession was clearly correct: in *Dodge and Harris,*[53] for example, bonds were executed in respect of a non-existent debt for the sole purpose of inducing a third party to believe that the debt was in fact owed. The bonds were held not to be forgeries because they were precisely what they purported to be, *viz.* bonds executed by the person named in them: they did not tell a lie about themselves but only about the existence of the debt. Yet in *Donnelly* the valuation certificate was held by the Court of Appeal to be a false instrument by virtue of section 9(1)(g). Lawton L.J., giving the judgement of the court, said:

> "There can be no doubt that in 1981 Parliament intended to make new law. The long title of the Act starts with these words: 'An Act to make fresh provision . . . with respect to forgery and kindred offences.' . . . In our judgment the words coming at the end of paragraph (g) 'otherwise in circumstances . . .' expand its ambit beyond dates and places to *any* case in which an instrument purports to be made when it was not in fact made. This valuation purported to be made *after* the appellant had examined the items of jewellery set out in the schedule. He did not make it after examining these items because they did not exist. That which purported to be a valuation after examination of items was nothing of the kind: it was a

---

51   *Cf. Wells* [1939] 2 All E.R. 169.
52   [1984] 1 W.L.R. 1017.
53   [1972] 1 Q.B. 416.

worthless piece of paper. In our judgment the trial judge's direction was correct. This purported valuation was a forgery."[54]

6.18   Carried to its logical conclusion this decision would sweep away the traditional distinction between a document which is not what it purports to be and one which merely contains a false statement. If a document makes a statement which is false it literally purports to have been made in certain circumstances (*viz.* circumstances in which the statement would be true) in which it was not in fact made. It would follow that any false statement in writing would be capable of constituting forgery. This would be a remarkable extension of the offence: making a document which is not what it purports to be is distinguishable from, and more serious than, the mere writing of falsehoods. The latter can be adequately dealt with as deception or attempted deception. It is true that the Act does make new law in some respects, but it would need very plain words indeed to effect such a radical change. Far from dispensing with the old distinction, section 9(1) is clearly a careful attempt to spell out its implications. The phrase "in circumstances in which it was not in fact made" must surely have been intended to be construed *ejusdem generis* with the rest of the subsection. It is therefore submitted that *Donnelly* should not be interpreted in such a way as to obliterate the distinction between forgery and deception. The actual decision may perhaps be justified on the grounds that the valuation certificate had what the Law Commission called a "spurious air of authenticity":[55] it was nothing but a sham. "That which purported to be a valuation after examination of items was nothing of the kind." If the jewellery had in fact existed and had merely been over-valued, it seems unlikely that the decision would have been the same.

6.19   *(d) Circumstances of alteration to instrument.* By section 9(1)(*e*) to (*h*), an instrument which was originally made in precisely the circumstances in which it purports to have been made may nevertheless be false if it "tells a lie" about a subsequent alteration (real or fictitious). The requirements are precisely parallel to those relating to the making of the instrument. The instrument must purport to have been altered in some respect: this would not cover an instrument which had been altered in such a way as to give the impression that it had not been altered at all (though such an instrument would tell a lie about its making and be false under section 9(1)(*a*) or (*c*)). The alteration must purport to have been made:

54   [1984] 1 W.L.R. 1017 at p. 1018f.
55   See *supra*, para. 6.08.

(i) by a person who did not in fact make it[56] (*e.g.* because he did not exist),[57] or

(ii) on the authority of a person who did not in fact authorise it[58] (*quaere* whether this would apply where the person in question did not exist),[59] or

(iii) on a certain date, at a certain place or in certain circumstances, where that is not in fact the case.[60]

A doubtful case would be that of an instrument which gave no express indication of who made or authorised the alteration, or the circumstances in which it was made, but was nevertheless intended to convey a misleading impression as to one of these matters. Again the crucial question would be whether the instrument "purported" to have been altered in any particular circumstances.[61]

Making a false instrument

6.20   The *actus reus* of forgery is the making of a false instrument. This obviously includes the original production of an instrument which is false as soon as it is produced. But section 9(2) provides:

"A person is to be treated for the purposes of this Part of this Act as making a false instrument if he alters an instrument so as to make it false in any respect (whether or not it is false in some other respect apart from that alteration)."

In other words, "making a false instrument" includes

(i) making an instrument which is false,

(ii) making a genuine instrument false, and

(iii) making a false instrument even falser.

6.21   Where the defendant does not physically produce or alter the instrument himself, but provides false information or otherwise deceives an innocent victim into producing or altering it, it might be argued that it is the defendant who has "made" the instrument for the purposes of a forgery charge. Clearly the innocent maker would not be guilty of forgery: although section 1 does not expressly require that the maker of the instrument must realise that it is false, this must surely be implicit.[62]

---

56   s. 9(1)(*e*).
57   s. 9(1)(*h*).
58   s. 9(1)(*f*).
59   *Cf. supra*, para. 6.15.
60   s. 9(1)(*g*).
61   *supra*, para. 6.09ff.
62   The only obstacle to this reasoning is that section 2, which creates the offence of copying a false instrument, expressly requires not only an intention that the copy be accepted as genuine (*i.e.* as a copy of a genuine instrument) but also knowledge or belief that the original is false—thus suggesting that the latter requirement is not implicit in the former. But it is submitted that section 2 merely makes express what would otherwise be implied.

The defendant could therefore be regarded as having made the instrument himself, through an innocent agent. But such a charge might appear somewhat artificial. It might well be possible to frame an alternative charge of procuring the execution of a valuable security by deception,[63] which is a less serious offence than forgery but represents more accurately the nature of the defendant's conduct.

Acceptance of the instrument as genuine

6.22   The first element of the *mens rea* of forgery is that the maker of the false instrument must intend that he or another shall use it to induce somebody to accept it as genuine. Section 10(3) provides:

> "In this Part of this Act references to inducing somebody to accept a false instrument as genuine . . . include references to inducing a machine to respond to the instrument . . . as if it were a genuine instrument . . ."

The Act thus avoids the difficulties raised by the notion of deceiving a machine.[64] The offence might be committed by producing illicit copies of the cards used to operate bank cash dispensers, or by falsifying data held in a computer file, even if the false instrument were not intended to come to the attention of any human being but only of a machine. It must of course be established that what the defendant made was an "instrument" for the purposes of the Act; but "instrument" is defined so as to include discs, tapes and other devices for the storage of information,[65] so that the input of data into a computer would necessarily constitute "making an instrument". Even the computer's short-term memory is a device for the storage of information.

6.23   In the case of an instrument designed to deceive a human being, the phrase "to accept it as genuine" may perhaps be construed in the light of section 10(3): one accepts an instrument as genuine if one responds to it as if it were genuine. The verb "to accept" is clearly not to be confined to the sense of a physical taking, *i.e.* it is sufficient if the victim is intended to look at the instrument without touching it or keeping it. Presumably it is also sufficient if the maker of the instrument knows that the intended victim will be indifferent whether it is genuine or not—as will often be the case where stolen cheque cards and credit cards are concerned.[66] This situation raises less difficulty here than in the context of deception, because it is more natural to say that the apathetic victim "accepts" the card as genuine than that he is deceived as to the holder's right to use it.

---

63   Theft Act 1968 s. 20(2); *supra,* para. 3.40ff.
64   *Cf. supra,* para. 2.30.
65   s. 8(1)(*d*).
66   *Cf. supra,* para. 2.25ff

Prejudice

6.24 It must also be proved that the defendant intended the false instrument to be used so as to induce the person accepting it to (or not to do) some act to his own or someone else's prejudice. "Prejudice" is defined by section 10(1):

> "Subject to subsections (2) and (4) below, for the purposes of this Part of this Act, an act or omission intended to be induced is to a person's prejudice if, and only if, it is one which, if it occurs—
>
> (*a*) will result—
>
> > (i) in his temporary or permanent loss[67] of property; or
> > (ii) in his being deprived of an opportunity to earn remuneration or greater remuneration; or
> > (iii) in his being deprived of an opportunity to gain a financial advantage otherwise than by way of remuneration; or
>
> (*b*) will result in somebody being given an opportunity—
>
> > (i) to earn remuneration or greater remuneration from him; or
> > (ii) to gain a financial advantage from him otherwise than by way of remuneration; or
>
> (*c*) will be the result of his having accepted a false instrument as genuine . . . in connection with his performance of any duty."

6.25 Thus the concept of an intent to cause prejudice is very similar to that of intent to defraud under the old law:[68] it is sufficient if the maker of the instrument intends some other person to suffer financial loss[69] (or somebody else to gain a financial advantage at that person's expense, which seems to amount to the same thing) or to act in a manner contrary to his duty. In one respect prejudice may be a broader concept than fraud: section 10(1)(*c*) clearly extends to all duties, not merely "public" ones.[70] Strictly speaking it is not even necessary that the act or omission induced should be inconsistent with the duty in question, but only that it should be the result of the false instrument being accepted as genuine in connection with the performance of the duty. The effect is that it is sufficient if the person subject to the duty is induced to act in a manner which is in fact consistent with his duty, provided that his conduct is inconsistent with what his duty *would* have been had he known the instrument to be false. Section 10(4) adds that, where section 10(3) applies (*i.e.* where it is a machine which is intended to "accept" the instrument as genuine),

> "the act or omission intended to be induced by the machine responding to the instrument. . .shall be treated as an act or omission to a person's prejudice."

---

67 "Loss" includes not getting what one might get as well as parting with what one has: s. 10(5).

68 *Cf. supra,* para. 1.31ff.

69 *e.g.* where a bank is induced to honour a cheque with a forged indorsement: *Campbell (Mary)* [1984] Crim.L.R. 683.

70 *Cf. supra,* para. 1.42.

In effect, the machine is deemed to be a person acting in connection with the performance of a duty.

6.26 Under the old law there might be an intent to defraud if the defendant's intention was to obtain by deception something to which he was legally entitled, such as the payment of a debt.[71] Section 10(2) now provides:

> "An act which a person has an enforceable duty to do and an omission to do an act which a person is not entitled to do shall be disregarded for the purposes of this Part of this Act."

So it is not forgery if the maker of the instrument intends merely to induce another person to do what he is in any event legally obliged to do. But the effect of section 10(2) is limited: it does not provide a general defence that the maker of the instrument intended only to get what was his due, if the attainment of this objective involved inducing somebody to do something which he was *not* obliged to do. Thus it would be forgery to make out a false document for the purpose of backing up a tax claim,[72] even if the claim itself were a legitimate one, because the intention would be to induce the tax inspector to handle the claim in a particular way; and that is something which, irrespective of the soundness of the claim, he would be under no legal duty to do. It should be noted that forgery does not require any element of dishonesty.[73] This omission might allow scope for an argument that section 10(2) applies only if the act or omission induced was in fact legally required, and not if the defendant wrongly believed that it was. It is submitted that on general principles he should be treated as if his mistaken belief were in fact correct.[74]

Causation
6.27 The *mens rea* of forgery is in fact threefold: the maker of the false instrument must intend somebody else to be induced (i) to accept the instrument as genuine, (ii) to do (or not to do) some act to somebody's prejudice, and (iii) to do the latter "by reason of" doing the former. He must intend the accepting of the instrument to be, not presumably the *only* reason, but at least *a* reason for the act or omission. There must be at least a possibility that the person in question would act differently if he knew the instrument to be false.[75] The effect is similar to that of the old requirement that the document be false in a material particular, but it is now framed as a matter of causation (or rather *expected* causation). Thus

---

71 *Parker* (1910) 74 J.P. 208, *Smith* (1919) 14 Cr.App.R. 101.
72 *Cf. Patel* (1973) 48 T.C. 647.
73 *Horsey v. Hutchings* (1984) *The Times,* 8 November.
74 *Cf. Williams (Gladstone)* (1984) 78 Cr.App.R. 276.
75 *Cf. supra,* para. 2.56ff.

an instrument made in an assumed name is a false instrument,[76] but the maker would not be guilty of forgery if he thought that his identity would, in the circumstances of the intended transaction, be regarded as completely immaterial.[77]

Copying a false instrument

6.28 The act of making a copy of a false instrument is unlikely to constitute forgery, because the copy will not normally "tell a lie" about its own making but only about that of the original—though it might amount to forgery if the person making the copy intended to pass it off as the original. This is a somewhat technical distinction, since (as the Law Commission pointed out)[78] photocopies are commonly regarded more as duplicate originals than as mere copies. Hence section 2 of the Forgery and Counterfeiting Act 1981 provides:

> "It is an offence for a person to make a copy of an instrument which is, and which he knows or believes to be, a false instrument, with the intention that he or another shall use it to induce somebody to accept it as a copy of a genuine instrument, and by reason of so accepting it to do or not to do some act to his own or any other person's prejudice."

The offence carries the same penalties as forgery.[79]

6.29 Most of the elements of the offence are the same (*mutatis mutandis*) as those of forgery. The main difference is the express requirement that the maker of the copy must "know or believe" the original to be false.[80] The same distinction is drawn in the offence of handling stolen goods: in that context it must be proved that the defendant knew or believed the goods in question to be stolen.[81] He *knows* that they are stolen if he is told as much by someone with first-hand knowledge, such as the thief; he *believes* it if he says to himself "I cannot say I know for certain that those goods are stolen, but there can be no other reasonable conclusion in the light of all the circumstances." This latter state of mind is sufficient even if, in spite of all that he has seen and heard, the defendant refuses to accept what his brain tells him is obvious.[82] But it is not sufficient merely that he *suspects* the goods may be stolen,[83] nor that he has deliberately "closed his eyes" to that

---

76 *Supra,* para. 6.14.
77 *Cf. Gambling* [1975] Q.B. 207.
78 Law Com. No. 55, at para. 39.
79 s. 6(1), (2).
80 But it is suggested at para. 6.21, *supra,* that a similar requirement is implicit in s.1.
81 Theft Act 1968 s. 22(1).
82 *Hall (Edward)* [1985] Crim.L.R. 377.
83 *Grainge* [1974] 1 W.L.R. 619.

possibility,[84] nor even that he thinks they are *probably* stolen.[85] The same principles will presumably apply to the offence under section 2. The jury must be directed that the maker of the copy does not "believe" the original to be false merely because he suspects it may be; it is essential that in the light of the circumstances known to him there could be no other reasonable conclusion, and that he must have realised that that was so.

Using a false instrument

6.30 The old offence of uttering a forged document is replaced by section 3 of the 1981 Act, which provides:

> "It is an offence for a person to use an instrument which is, and which he knows or believes to be, false, with the intention of inducing somebody to accept it as genuine, and by reason of so accepting it to do or not to do some act to his own or any other person's prejudice."

The offence carries the same penalties as forgery.[86] Where the instrument is made by one person and used by another, the maker will normally be guilty of forgery and the user will commit the offence under section 3 (presumably with the maker as accessory). But there is no need for the instrument to be forged, in the sense that its maker must be guilty of forgery: it is sufficient if it is in fact false, provided that the user knows or believes that it is. Thus a person who deceives another into making a false instrument, and then uses it himself, would be guilty under section 3 even if the maker were completely innocent.[87]

Using a copy of a false instrument

6.31 The symmetry is completed by section 4, which provides:

> "It is an offence for a person to use a copy of an instrument which is, and which he knows or believes to be, a false instrument, with the intention of inducing somebody to accept it as a copy of a genuine instrument, and by reason of so accepting it to do or not to do some act to his own or any other person's prejudice."

The offence carries the same penalties as forgery.[88] It may in fact be redundant, since the use of a copy might be regarded as a use of the original within the meaning of section 3.[89] But the existence of section 4

---

84 *Griffiths* (1975) 60 Cr.App.R. 14, *Moys* (1984) 79 Cr.App.R. 72.
85 *Reader* (1978) 66 Cr.App.R. 33.
86 s. 6(1), (2).
87 He might also be guilty under s.1 (*supra*, para. 6.21) or s. 20(2) of the Theft Act 1968 (*supra*, para. 3.40ff).
88 s. 6(1), (2).
89 *Cf. Harris* [1966] 1 Q.B. 184.

suggests that section 3 is confined to cases where direct use is made of the original. Read literally, section 4 would appear not to apply if, by the time the copy is used, the original is no longer in existence or has been corrected so that it is no longer false, nor even if the user of the copy believes that that is so. It is submitted that such an interpretation would defeat the object of the section and should be rejected. It must be sufficient that the instrument was false when the copy was made and that the defendant knows or believes that it was.

Possession of specified false instruments

6.32 The Law Commission was of the opinion that the mere possession of certain types of false instrument should constitute an offence, on the grounds of the ease with which they may pass from hand to hand and be accepted as genuine.[90] The instruments in question are listed in section 5(5):

"The instruments to which this section applies are—
(*a*) money orders;
(*b*) postal orders;
(*c*) United Kingdom postage stamps;
(*d*) Inland Revenue stamps;
(*e*) share certificates;[91]
(*f*) passports and documents which can be used instead of passports;
(*g*) cheques;
(*h*) travellers' cheques;
(*j*) cheque cards;
(*k*) credit cards;
(*l*) certified copies relating to an entry in a register of births, adoptions, marriages or deaths and issued by the Registrar General, the Registrar General for Northern Ireland, a registration officer or a person lawfully authorised to register marriages; and
(*m*) certificates relating to entries in such registers."

6.33 There are two offences of possessing a false instrument within this list, one requiring the usual *mens rea* (*viz.* intent to pass the instrument off as genuine and thereby to cause prejudice) and one of mere possession without lawful excuse. Section 5(1) provides:

"It is an offence for a person to have in his custody or under his control an instrument to which this section applies which is, and which he knows or believes to be, false, with the intention that he or another shall use it to

---

90   Law Com. No. 55, at para. 63.
91   Defined as instruments entitling or evidencing the title of a person to a share or interest—
    (a) in any public stock, annuity, fund or debt of any government or state, including a state which forms part of another state; or
    (b) in any stock, fund or debt of a body (whether corporate or unincorporated) established in the United Kingdom or elsewhere: s. 5(6).

induce somebody to accept it as genuine, and by reason of so accepting it to do or not to do some act to his own or any other person's prejudice."

The offence carries the same penalties as forgery.[92]

6.34   Section 5(2) provides:

> "It is an offence for a person to have in his custody or under his control, without lawful authority or excuse, an instrument to which this section applies which is, and which he knows or believes to be, false."

This offence is punishable on conviction on indictment with two years' imprisonment.[93] There is no express requirement that the defendant should be aware that he has custody or control of the instrument, but this is presumably implied.[94] He will not have a "lawful excuse" for the possession merely because he has no intention to defraud or to cause "prejudice";[95] indeed it is hard to imagine what would constitute such an excuse, short of an intention to hand the instrument over to the police.[96]

Making and possession of materials for the making of specified instruments

6.35   The Law Commission pointed out that forgery itself is essentially a preparatory offence, and thought it unnecessary to go a step further by punishing acts which are preparatory to the commission of forgery.[97] The Act, however, includes two such offences relating to the making of the instruments listed in section 5(5).[98] Section 5(3) provides:

> "It is an offence for a person to make or to have in his custody or under his control a machine or implement, or paper or any other material, which to his knowledge is or has been specially designed or adapted for the making of an instrument to which this section applies, with the intention that he or another shall make an instrument to which this section applies which is false and that he or another shall use the instrument to induce somebody to accept it as genuine, and by reason of so accepting it to do or not to do some act to his own or any other person's prejudice."

The offence carries the same penalties as forgery.[99] The defendant must be proved to have *known* that the materials in question were designed or adapted for the making of specified instruments: mere belief is not enough. By analogy with the law of handling stolen goods it would seem to follow that the defendant must have been told of their function by

92   s. 6(1), (2).
93   s. 6(4).
94   *Cf. Harran* [1969] Crim.L.R. 662.
95   *Cf. Dickins v. Gill* [1896] 2 Q.B. 310.
96   *Wuyts* [1969] 2 Q.B. 476.
97   Law Com. No. 55, at para. 64.
98   *Supra,* para. 6.32.
99   s. 6(1), (2).

someone with first-hand knowledge.[1] There is no requirement that the materials be designed or adapted for the production of *false* instruments, but the defendant himself must have intended them to be used for that purpose.

6.36 Section 5(4) provides:

> "It is an offence for a person to make or to have in his custody or under his control any such machine, implement, paper or material, without lawful authority or excuse."

This offence carries the same penalties as that created by section 5(2).[2] The reference to "any such . . . material" clearly means not merely material designed or adapted for the making of the specified instruments, but material which the defendant knows to have been so designed or adapted. Since the materials in question include such comparatively harmless items as share certificate forms and cheque books, the notion of "lawful excuse" for their possession will need to be given a more generous interpretation than for the purposes of section 5(2).

Suppression of documents

6.37 The law of forgery is supplemented by two offences under section 20 of the Theft Act 1968. The offence of procuring the execution of a valuable security by deception, contrary to section 20(2), is considered above together with the other offences of deception:[3] it may be a useful alternative to forgery where the instrument is not made by the defendant himself but by a person whom he has deceived into making it. Section 20(1) provides:

> "A person who dishonestly, with a view to gain for himself or another or with intent to cause loss to another, destroys, defaces or conceals any valuable security, any will or other testamentary document or any original document of or belonging to, or filed or deposited in, any court of justice or any government department shall on conviction on indictment be liable to imprisonment for a term not exceeding seven years."

The offence is triable either way. The expressions "dishonestly", "view to gain. . .or. . .intent to cause loss" and "valuable security" have already been discussed;[4] it will be recalled that an intention to avoid the exposure of previous misconduct is sufficient to constitute a view to gain, and that "valuable security" is defined in such a way as to correspond roughly to the narrow interpretation of the word "instrument" in the Forgery and

---

1   See para. 6.29, *supra.*
2   *Supra,* para. 6.34.
3   *Supra,* para. 3.40ff.
4   *Supra,* para. 1.04ff. (dishonesty), 3.45 (gain and loss), 3.41 (valuable security).

Counterfeiting Act 1981. It does not extend to documents which do not themselves have any legal effect of any kind, such as internal accounting records.

6.38   Whereas the law of forgery is concerned with the making of false instruments, the offence under section 20(1) is primarily one of *suppressing* documents: the valuable security or other document must be destroyed, defaced or concealed. This might be done either because the fraud requires the absence of the document in question (*e.g.* where a testator's relative destroys a will which disinherits him) or because the document is to be replaced with a forged substitute. The making of the substitute itself would clearly not fall within section 20(1) and would have to be charged as forgery. Forgery committed by *altering* a document, however, might perhaps constitute "defacement" of the document within the meaning of section 20(1); indeed this might be a useful alternative if there were any doubt whether the alteration rendered the document "false" within section 9(1) of the Forgery and Counterfeiting Act 1981.[5] "Deface" is defined by the *Shorter Oxford English Dictionary* as "to mar the face or appearance of; . . .to disfigure". It is arguable that a document is defaced if it is altered in any way. It is submitted, however, that the word is to be construed *ejusdem generis* with "destroys" and "conceals"; *i.e.* that an alteration does not amount to defacement for this purpose unless it renders some of the document illegible. It might not be necessary to do this even if the intention were to pass off the altered document as having been originally executed in that form, as where letters and numbers are added to a cheque in order to increase the amount; and *a fortiori* if there were no attempt to disguise the fact that the document had been altered, but only some form of deceit as to the circumstances of the alteration.

FALSIFICATION AND SUPPRESSION OF ACCOUNTS AND OTHER RECORDS

6.39   There may be two distinct motives for the falsification of business records. On the one hand it may be done simply to cover up straightforward theft or improper expenditure such as corrupt payments.[6] Alternatively, the falsification may itself be an integral part of the fraud. Thus a company's accounts may be doctored so as to over-state the profits (with a view to obtaining credit, or facilitating a take-over) or

---

5   *Supra*, para. 6.08ff.
6   But if theft is the essence of the alleged misconduct, it should be charged as such and not as false accounting: *Eden* (1971) 55 Cr.App.R. 193 at p. 198 f., *per* Sachs L.J.

to under-state them (for tax purposes). The organisation itself may be defrauded by the manipulation of records, whether in documentary or electronic form. Fictitious employees may be put on the payroll so that their wages can be pocketed. Debts owed by employees or their friends and relatives may be recorded as paid. In a bank or similar organisation, computer staff may siphon off small sums from a large number of accounts into their own—the so-called "salami" method.

6.40   In appropriate circumstances the falsification of records might be charged as forgery. Such a charge would, however, entail two difficulties for the prosecution. First it would have to be established that the record in question was an "instrument" within the meaning of the Forgery and Counterfeiting Act 1981. It will be recalled that the word "instrument" was selected to denote documents which are *used* in commercial dealings as against merely recording them; but the definition of an "instrument" in section 8(1), if read literally, includes documents of any description.[7] In any event, records kept in mechanical or electronic form are expressly included by section 8(1)(*d*), so that in the case of the fraudulent use of a computer system this difficulty would not arise. The second problem is that traditionally it is not forgery merely to make a record which is incorrect: it must "tell a lie about itself", *e.g.* by purporting to have been made by someone who did not in fact make it.[8] Dicta in *Hopkins and Collins*[9] suggesting that any case of false accounting could be charged as forgery were disapproved in *Dodge and Harris*,[10] and the 1981 Act was certainly not intended to alter the position in this respect. It may be that an inaccurate record must now be regarded as a "false" instrument by virtue of section 9(1)(*g*), as interpreted in *Donnelly (Ian)*,[11] because it purports to have been made in circumstances in which it was not in fact made (*viz.* after the occurrence of the facts recorded); but it is submitted that *Donnelly* should not be extended beyond its own facts. A record is not necessarily false merely because it is untrue, and the falsification of records should normally be charged under the provisions discussed in this section rather than as forgery.

False accounting

6.41   The offences of the most general application are those created by section 17 of the Theft Act 1968. Section 17(1) provides:

7   *Supra,* para. 6.04ff.
8   *Supra,* para. 6.08.
9   (1957) 41 Cr.App.R. 231.
10   [1972] 1 Q.B. 416.
11   [1984] 1 W.L.R. 1017; *supra,* para. 6.17.

"Where a person dishonestly, with a view to gain for himself or another or with intent to cause loss to another—

(*a*) destroys, defaces, conceals or falsifies any account or any record or document made or required for any accounting purpose; or

(*b*) in furnishing information for any purpose produces or makes use of any account, or any such record or document as aforesaid, which to his knowledge is or may be misleading, false or deceptive in a material particular;

he shall, on conviction on indictment, be liable to imprisonment for a term not exceeding seven years."

Both offences are triable either way.

Accounts and accounting purposes

6.42 The article which is suppressed, falsified, produced or made use of (as the case may be) must be *either* an account *or* a record or document which, though not itself an account, is made or required for an accounting purpose. "Account" is not defined, but there seems no reason to confine it to accounts in documentary form.[12] The same applies to records made or required for an accounting purpose. Thus in *Edwards v. Toombs*[13] the Divisional Court refused to interfere with the justices' finding that a turnstile which recorded the number of people passing through it was a record made for an accounting purpose.

6.43 The words "made or required for any accounting purpose" were considered in *Attorney-General's Reference (No. 1 of 1980)*.[14] It was held by the Court of Appeal that personal loan proposal forms addressed to a finance company, though not *made* for an accounting purpose, were nevertheless *required* for one in that they would be used in the compiling of the company's accounts in the event of the proposals being accepted. Lord Lane C.J. said:

". . . it is to be observed that section 17(1)(*a*) in using the words 'made or required' indicates that there is a distinction to be drawn between a document made specifically for the purpose of accounting and one made for some other purpose but which is required for an accounting purpose. Thus it is apparent that a document may fall within the ambit of the section if it is made for some purpose other than an accounting purpose but is required for an accounting purpose as a subsidiary consideration."[15]

Nor is it necessary that the part of the document which is falsified should be required for an accounting purpose: it is sufficient if the document as a whole is so required, and part of the document is falsified.[16] It is

12 *Cf. Solomons* [1909] 2 K.B. 980 (a taxi-meter).
13 [1983] Crim.L.R. 43.
14 [1981] 1 W.L.R. 34.
15 *Ibid.* at p. 38.
16 *Ibid.; cf. Mallett* [1978] 3 All E.R. 10, *infra,* para. 6.46.

submitted with respect that the decision goes too far in extending the offence to cover documents which are not primarily required for accounting purposes but only as a secondary consideration. If a given purpose is not the document's main purpose, why is the document *required* for that purpose but not *made* for it? A more natural interpretation would be simply that "made" refers to the intentions of the person making the document, whereas "required" refers to those of the person for whom it is made. On this view the distinction does not necessarily imply, as the Court of Appeal take it to imply, that a purely subsidiary purpose will do.

Falsification

6.44   Section 17(1)(*a*) requires that the account, record or document be destroyed, defaced, concealed or falsified. The first three verbs are the same as those used in section 20(1) with reference to the suppression of valuable securities and other documents. However, the question whether a document is defaced by being altered is academic in this case, since the offence is committed if the account, record or document is *falsified*. Section 17(2) provides:

> "For purposes of this section a person who makes or concurs in making in an account or other document an entry which is or may be misleading, false or deceptive in a material particular, or who omits or concurs in omitting a material particular from an account or other document, is to be treated as falsifying the account or document."

It was held in *Edwards v. Toombs*[17] that this is not an exhaustive definition: if the defendant's conduct amounts to falsification in the ordinary sense of that word, it is immaterial that it does not fall within the precise terms of section 17(2). Presumably the word's ordinary meaning would include any case where the account, record or document is deliberately rendered inaccurate, even if (as in *Edwards v Toombs)* it is not rendered "false" for the purposes of the law of forgery.

6.45   In so far as section 17(2) extends the meaning of "falsify" beyond its ordinary meaning, it only applies to accounts and other documents— not (unlike section 17(1)) to records which are neither accounts nor documents. It is doubtful how large a gap this leaves. The turnstile in *Edwards v. Toombs* was regarded as a record of the number of people passing through it, but it might have qualified as an account.[18] Computer files are not necessarily accounts, but they could arguably be treated as documents.[19] It is submitted, however, that some significance must be

---

17   [1983] Crim.L.R. 43.
18   *Cf. Solomons* [1909] 2 K.B. 980.
19   *Cf. supra,* para. 3.41.

attached to the inclusion of the word "record" in section 17(1) and its omission from section 17(2). There must be some records which are not documents; if those records are not accounts either, section 17(2) does not apply to them, and they are "falsified" only by conduct falling within the word's ordinary meaning.

6.46 Section 17(2) refers to the making of an entry "which is or may be misleading, false or deceptive in a material particular". In *Mallett*[20] a finance company was induced to enter into a hire-purchase agreement by an application form which falsely stated that the hirer had for eight years been a director of a certain company. It was not disputed that the form was required for an accounting purpose (and in the light of *Attorney-General's Reference (No. 1 of 1980)*[21] it presumably was so required) but it was argued that the false statement was not "material" because it was not connected with the accounting purpose for which the form was required. The argument was rejected by the Court of Appeal.

> "The material particular in question does not have to be one which is directly connected with the accounting purpose of the document. The document itself has to be made or required for an accounting purpose. But once the document qualifies in that relevant respect ... then if that document contains a false statement in a material particular the person who is guilty of dishonestly furnishing that information for any purpose is, in our view, guilty of an offence against the section."[22]

A statement cannot be material in the abstract: it can only be material for a particular purpose. Yet a statement in a document required for an accounting purpose may, it seems, be "material" even if it is not material to the accounting purpose. Presumably the explanation is to be found in *Attorney-General's Reference (No. 1 of 1980)*:[23] a document may be required for an accounting purpose even if it is primarily required for some other purpose. A statement in such a document will be "material" not only if it is material to the accounting purpose but also if it is material to the primary purpose. In certain circumstances it might be necessary to adduce evidence that the statement was material for at least one of the purposes of the document, but often (as in *Mallett*) this will be an irresistible inference.

6.47 Whether a particular set of accounts is in fact "misleading, false or deceptive" may be a difficult question. In the case of company accounts, the overriding principle is that they should present a "true and fair view"

20 [1978] 3 All E.R. 10.
21 [1981] 1 W.L.R. 34; *supra*, para. 6.43.
22 [1978] 3 All E.R. 10 at p. 12, *per* Roskill L.J.
23 [1981] 1 W.L.R. 34; *supra*, para. 6.43.

of the company's financial position,[24] but this requirement is notoriously imprecise. The process of valuing a company's assets is bound to involve an element of subjectivity. There is, moreover, a twilight zone between those accounting practices which are clearly acceptable and those which clearly are not. One such dubious practice is that of "window-dressing", *i.e.* borrowing for a short period over the end of the financial year so as to create a false impression of liquidity. The accountancy profession is not united in the condemnation of this device,[25] presumably because the picture of the company's assets and liabilities which is drawn by the balance-sheet is in fact perfectly accurate as at the date in question—though not representative of the company's normal position. If a substantial body of expert opinion believes a given practice to be legitimate it may well be difficult to establish that a particular instance of that practice was dishonest: the defence will be able to argue plausibly either that what was done was not dishonest according to ordinary standards or that, even if it was, the defendant did not realise that it was.[26] But the issue of dishonesty is quite distinct from that of whether the accounts are misleading, false or deceptive. For this purpose it is clearly sufficient if they make an implied statement which is untrue. But that is not essential, if the concept of deception presented above[27] is accepted: all that is required is that the accounts should be likely to induce their readers (or some of them) to believe in the truth of certain propositions which are in fact false. Thus a valuation of an asset suggests that the valuation is genuinely believed to be a fair one; in the absence of such belief, the valuation is deceptive. Window-dressing is calculated to give the impression that the company normally has a certain level of liquidity which it does not in fact have. Accounts which incorporate the effects of window-dressing are therefore deceptive accounts.

6.48   It is therefore essential to distinguish between expert evidence as to the legitimacy of a particular accounting practice and evidence as to the impression which it is likely to create. If it appeared that a balance-sheet is not in fact commonly expected to reflect the company's normal position but only the position at the year end, window-dressing would involve no deception—however abnormal and artificial the year-end position might be. In *Williams*[28] the defendant entered in his accounts a certain sum as "balance in hand". That sum was in fact correct in the sense that it represented the difference between receipts and expenditure, but the defendant was unable to produce it. He was held not to have

---

24 *Infra,* para. 6.63.
25 L.H. Leigh, *The Control of Commercial Fraud* at p. 212.
26 *Cf. supra,* para. 1.16ff.
27 *Supra,* ch. 2.
28 (1899) 19 Cox 239.

falsified the accounts. Presumably the accounts would have been false if "balance in hand" meant that the sum in question could be immediately produced. In any event the appropriate charge would be one of theft rather than false accounting.[29]

6.49   The reference in section 17(2) to an entry which "is *or may be*[30] misleading, false or deceptive" is curious. An entry is false if it makes a statement which is not true. It is misleading or (which comes to the same thing) deceptive if it has a tendency to induce somebody to believe that a proposition is true which is not. Under what circumstances could it properly be said that an entry *may* be misleading, false or deceptive but not that it *is*? It can hardly be intended that section 17(2) is to apply where it is uncertain whether the proposition stated or suggested is true or not. It is submitted that the alternative "or may be" applies only to the words "misleading" and "deceptive" and not to the word "false", the object being to rule out any argument that the entry must be *certain* to mislead or deceive and not merely *capable* of doing so.

6.50   Where section 17(2) applies, it is sufficient not only if a false entry is made but also if a material particular is omitted. Clearly this does not mean that the account or document is deemed to have been falsified unless it includes all the information which might conceivably be relevant to any of the purposes for which it is made or required. The phrase "material particular" must, it is submitted, be read in a narrower sense in this context than in that of a false entry: an omission is not "material" merely because it would have been regarded as relevant had it been included, but only if in the circumstances it results in the account or document giving a false impression. It has already been noted in the context of deception that a half-truth may be as deceptive as a downright lie.[31] Whether an omission has this effect will obviously depend on the nature of the account or document and the nature of the omission. In *Keatley*[32] a submission of no case was accepted where an employee had made unauthorised purchases and sales without disclosing them in his accounts. The judge ruled that there was in the circumstances no duty to include the transactions in the accounts. Presumably the accounts were not regarded as a *complete* statement of the employee's sales or purchases: had they been so regarded, the omission would clearly have constituted falsification.

---

29   *Eden* (1971) 55 Cr.App.R. 193 at p. 198f.
30   Italics supplied.
31   *Supra*, para. 2.36.
32   [1980] Crim.L.R. 505.

6.51   Finally it is sufficient under section 17(2) if the defendant does not himself make a false entry or omit a material particular, but "concurs in" the making of such an entry or the omission of such a particular by someone else. In *Attorney-General's Reference (No. 1 of 1980)*,[33] for example, the offending forms were filled in by the defendant's customers at his instigation. On those facts the defendant would in any event have been guilty as a secondary party, but the expression "or concurs in" might perhaps extend to acquiescence falling short of encouragement and not therefore amounting to secondary participation. The phrase does not seem apt for the situation where the actual maker of the account is unaware of the inaccuracy and is in effect the innocent agent of the person supplying the information; but in that case the party who knowingly provided false information would be regarded as having "made" the entry himself.[34] It seems the offence is committed when and where the accounts are made up, so that there may be jurisdiction even if the information is sent from abroad.[35]

Mens rea

6.52   The *mens rea* of false accounting involves two elements: dishonesty, and a view to gain or intent to cause loss. The latter requirement is discussed in connection with the offence under section 20(2) of the Theft Act 1980.[36] It will be recalled that the gain or loss must be financial, but that an intention to make a temporary gain by concealing previous misconduct is sufficient. The element of dishonesty may involve particular difficulty in the context of accounting, where the views of businessmen on commercial morality may not coincide with those of the man in the street. It is submitted that the crucial question is not whether accountants would condone the deception, but whether ordinary people would think it dishonest and whether the defendant realised that they would. This problem is discussed further in chapter 1.[37]

Using a false account

6.53   Section 17(1)(*b*) creates an offence of *using* a false account (or record or document made or required for an accounting purpose). The *mens rea* involves not only dishonesty and a view to gain or intent to cause loss, but also knowledge that the account, record or document is (or may be) misleading, false or deceptive. It is arguable that the phrase "which to his knowledge. . .may be misleading. . ." would include a

---

33   [1981] 1 W.L.R. 34; *supra,* para. 6.43.
34   *Butt* (1884) 15 Cox 564, *Oliphant* [1905] 2 K.B. 67.
35   *Oliphant* [1905] 2 K.B. 67, following *Munton* (1793) 1 Esp. 62; *cf. infra,* para. 11.10ff.
36   *Supra,* para. 3.45.
37   At para. 1.30.

person who was not sure whether the account was misleading but realised that it might be—*i.e.* a case of recklessness in the subjective sense. It is submitted, however, that the words "or may be" should be read simply as referring to an account which is capable of misleading but not certain to do so. The requirement of knowledge should be read as excluding recklessness: in other words, the prosecution must prove that the account was in fact capable of misleading and that the defendant knew it was. The account must be used "in furnishing information for any purpose". There is no requirement of an intent to mislead, and it is clearly sufficient if the defendant realises that there is a risk of somebody being misled without positively intending him to be. The offence might therefore be committed where a charge of attempted deception would fail due to the absence of an intention to deceive.

Liability of directors and other officers

6.54 Section 18 of the Theft Act 1968, which imposes liability on company directors and other officers who consent to or connive at the commission by the company of offences of deception, applies equally where the company is guilty of false accounting. It is unlikely to be significant in this context, since an officer who consented to the falsification or connived at it would presumably be "concurring" in it, and would therefore fall squarely within the terms of section 17.

False statements by company directors etc.

6.55 An offence which will often be committed where a company's annual accounts are misleading, and which may therefore be regarded as an alternative to false accounting, is created by section 19 of the Theft Act 1968. Section 19(1) provides:

> "Where an officer of a body corporate or unincorporated association (or person purporting to act as such), with intent to deceive members or creditors of the body corporate or association about its affairs, publishes or concurs in publishing a written statement or account which to his knowledge is or may be misleading, false or deceptive in a material particular, he shall on conviction on indictment be liable to imprisonment for a term not exceeding seven years."

The offence is triable either way.

6.56 The defendant must[38] be (or purport to be) an "officer" of the corporation or association. "Officer" is not defined, but section 744 of the Companies Act 1985 provides that in relation to a company that expression includes a director, manager or secretary. An auditor is an

---

38   Subject to s. 19(3), *infra.*

officer if he is appointed to fill the office of auditor and not merely "*ad hoc* for a limited purpose".[39] Thus the offence would be committed by an auditor who was corruptly induced to refrain from qualifying his report. Section 19(3) of the Theft Act adds:

> "Where the affairs of a body corporate or association are managed by its members, this section shall apply to any statement which a member publishes or concurs in publishing in connection with his functions of management as if he were an officer of the body corporate or association."

6.57 The *actus reus* of the offence is the publication of a *written* statement or account which is or may be misleading, false or deceptive in a material particular. As in the case of section 17, it is submitted that this means the statement or account must either be false or be at least *capable* of giving a false impression.[40] The requirement of falsehood (*etc.*) "in a material particular", in the light of the required mental element, presumably means merely that the falsehood must relate to the affairs of the corporation or association. It is also sufficient if the defendant does not publish the statement or account himself but concurs in its publication by someone else. Professor L.H. Leigh has suggested that section 19

> ". . . does not apply to exuberant oral statements by directors to the press, even though those may substantially affect public views of the company . . ."[41]

But it is arguable that if a director makes a statement to the press he is "concurring" in the statement's subsequent publication.

6.58 The *mens rea* of the offence does not include the element of dishonesty. Two elements are required: first (and somewhat superfluously in the light of the second element), knowledge that the statement or account is or may be misleading, false or deceptive; and second, an intent to deceive members or creditors[42] of the corporation or association about its affairs. The intent to deceive should, it is submitted, be interpreted as an intent to induce a belief in a proposition of fact which is false.[43] An intent to deceive *prospective* members or creditors does not appear to be sufficient, but a deception of this type might well constitute one of the offences discussed in connection with investment fraud.[44]

---

39 *Shacter* [1960] 2 Q.B. 252.
40 *Cf. supra*, para. 6.49.
41 *The Control of Commercial Fraud*, p. 83.
42 Including persons who have entered into a security for the benefit of the corporation or association: s. 19(2).
43 *Cf.* ch. 2, *supra*.
44 Ch. 8, *infra*.

False statements in documents required by statute

6.59 A further offence which might be committed by the submission of false accounts, tax returns[45] *etc.* is that created by section 5 of the Perjury Act 1911, which provides:

"If any person knowingly and wilfully makes (otherwise than on oath) a statement false in a material particular, and the statement is made—

(*a*) in a statutory declaration;[46] or

(*b*) in an abstract, account, balance sheet, book, certificate, declaration, entry, estimate, inventory, notice, report, return, or other document which he is authorised or required to make, attest, or verify, by any public general Act of Parliament for the time being in force; or

(*c*) in any oral declaration or oral answer which he is required to make by, under, or in pursuance of any public general Act of Parliament for the time being in force;

he shall be . . . liable on conviction thereof on indictment to imprisonment . . . for any term not exceeding two years . . ."

Section 5(*b*) would seem to cover the accounting records, annual accounts, annual returns and multifarious other documents required by the companies legislation. But for the purposes of section 5(*b*), unlike section 5(*c*), the document must be authorised or required by the public general Act itself, not merely by secondary legislation or executive action under it. The statement must be known to be false: recklessness is not enough. The requirement of wilfulness appears to add little apart from leaving open the defence of lawful excuse.

False statements to or by agents

6.60 A somewhat surprising source of what is essentially an offence of false documentation is the Prevention of Corruption Act 1906. Section 1(1) makes it an offence for a person to give to an agent, or for an agent to use, a document containing a false statement and intended to mislead the agent's principal. In spite of the context in which the offence appears, it is not confined to cases of corruption and may be committed even if the agent receiving the document is unaware of its falsity;[47] but it does not apply to the falsification of a purely internal document.[48] The offence is considered in detail below.[49]

---

45 *e.g. Bradbury and Edlin* [1921] 1 K.B. 562.
46 See the Statutory Declarations Act 1835.
47 *Sage v. Eicholz* [1919] 2 K.B. 171.
48 *Tweedie* [1984] Q.B. 729.
49 *Infra,* para. 7.15ff.

Company records and accounts

Accounting records

6.61 The falsification of accounts and accounting records may often be charged under the specific provisions of the Companies Act 1985. Section 221[50] requires every company to cause accounting records to be kept. These records must be sufficient to show and explain the company's transactions, and must be such as to disclose with reasonable accuracy, at any time, the company's financial position at that time, and to enable the directors to ensure that any balance sheet or profit and loss account prepared by them complies with the requirements of the Act.[51] In particular they must contain the following information:

(a) entries from day to day of all sums of money received and expended by the company, and the matters in respect of which the receipt and expenditure take place;

(b) a record of the company's assets and liabilities;[52] and

(c) where the company's business involves dealing in goods,

(i) statements of stock held by the company at the end of each financial year of the company;

(ii) all statements of stocktakings from which statements in (i) have been or are to be prepared; and

(iii) (except in the case of goods sold by way of ordinary retail trade) statements of all goods sold and purchased showing the goods, the buyers and the sellers in sufficient detail to enable them all to be identified.[53]

If a company fails to comply with these requirements, every officer of the company who is in default is guilty of an offence (punishable on conviction on indictment with two years' imprisonment)[54] unless he shows that he acted honestly[55] *and* that in the circumstances in which the company's business was carried on the default was excusable.[56] A private company must preserve its accounting records for three years and a public company for six;[57] any officer failing to take reasonable steps for securing the company's compliance with this requirement, or intentionally causing any default by the company in so complying, is also guilty of an offence (punishable as above).[58]

---

50 Replacing Companies Act 1976 s. 12 with effect from 1 July 1985.
51 s. 221(2).
52 s. 221(3).
53 s. 221(4).
54 s. 223(3), Sch. 24. On summary conviction the offence carries six months' imprisonment or a fine of the statutory maximum or both.
55 *Cf. supra,* para. 1.04ff.
56 s. 223(1).
57 s. 222(4).
58 s. 223(2).

Falsification and suppression of records

6.62   There are several offences of falsifying or suppressing company records. Under section 450(1) of the Companies Act 1985[59] an officer of a company is guilty of an offence, punishable on conviction on indictment with seven years' imprisonment,[60] if he

(a) destroys, mutilates or falsifies a document affecting or relating to the company's property or affairs,
(b) makes a false entry in such a document, or
(c) is privy to one of the acts in (a) or (b),

unless he proves that he had no intention to conceal the state of the company's affairs or to defeat the law.[61] Under section 450(2) such an officer is also guilty of an offence (punishable as above) if he

(a) fraudulently parts with, alters or makes an omission in such a document, or
(b) is privy to any such fraudulent conduct.

Although these offences appear in Part XIV of the Act, which is primarily concerned with the inspection of companies' books by the Department of Trade and Industry, on a literal reading they do not appear to be confined to companies which are the subject of such inspection. But it is arguable that in the light of the context a qualification to that effect must be implied.[62] There are similar provisions dealing with the falsification of records where the company in question is being wound up, and these are discussed in the context of insolvency fraud.[63]

Annual accounts

6.63   The directors of a company must prepare, in respect of each accounting reference period of the company,[64] a balance sheet, a profit and loss account[65] and a directors' report.[66] These documents, together with the auditors' report on them,[67] constitute the company's annual accounts. They must give a "true and fair view" of the state of the company's affairs, and (subject to that overriding principle) must comply with the requirements of Schedule 4 of the Companies Act 1985.[68] Of particular importance in the context of fraud is the requirement that the accounts must disclose all transactions, arrangements and agreements of

---

59   Replacing Companies Act 1967 s. 113(1) with effect from 1 July 1985.
60   s. 450(3), Sch. 24. On summary conviction the offence carries six months' imprisonment or a fine of the statutory maximum or both.
61   *Cf. infra*, para. 9.12.
62   *Cf. D.P.P. v. Schildkamp* [1971] A.C. 1.
63   *Infra*, para. 9.11f.
64   Companies Act 1985 s. 224.
65   s. 227.
66   s. 235.
67   s. 236.
68   s. 228.

the kinds regulated by section 330 (*i.e.* loans, quasi-loans *etc.* to directors and persons connected with them).[69] Failure to comply with the requirements of the legislation as to the contents of the accounts is an offence (punishable on conviction on indictment with a fine) on the part of each director, unless he proves that he took all reasonable steps to secure such compliance.[70]

False statements to auditors

6.64 Under section 393 of the Companies Act 1985[71] an offence is committed by an officer of a company who knowingly or recklessly makes an oral or written statement to the company's auditors which

(a) conveys (or purports to convey) any information or explanation which they require (or are entitled to require) as auditors of the company, and

(b) is misleading, false or deceptive in a material particular.

The offence is punishable on conviction on indictment with two years' imprisonment.[72] The phrase "misleading, false or deceptive in a material particular" has been discussed in connection with the offence of false accounting.[73] It is arguable that a statement is not made recklessly unless the maker has no genuine belief in its truth, but it is probably sufficient that he has no grounds for such a belief.[74]

---

69 s. 232; *cf. supra*, para. 5.02ff.
70 s. 245.
71 Replacing Companies Act 1976 s. 19 with effect from 1 July 1985.
72 Sch. 24. On summary conviction it carries six months' imprisonment or a fine of the statutory maximum or both.
73 *Supra*, para. 6.46ff.
74 *Cf. infra*, para. 8.07.

CHAPTER 7

Corruption

7.01 Many frauds require some degree of co-operation from those in the employment of the victim, and such co-operation will normally be procured by dint of bribery or other forms of corruption. Often there will be an offence such as theft or deception[1] which is facilitated by the corruption and to which the corrupt employee or agent will be at least an accessory. In addition, however, there will probably be one or more offences under the interlocking provisions of the Public Bodies Corrupt Practices Act 1889, the Prevention of Corruption Act 1906 and the Prevention of Corruption Act 1916 (known collectively as the Prevention of Corruption Acts). Corruption in public bodies is dealt with by the 1889 Act and corruption of agents in general by the 1906 Act; the provisions of the 1916 Act are purely ancillary. We shall also consider briefly the position of public officers.

CORRUPTION IN PUBLIC BODIES

7.02 Section 1 of the Public Bodies Corrupt Practices Act 1889 provides:

"(1) Every person who shall by himself or by or in conjunction with any other person, corruptly solicit or receive, or agree to receive, for himself, or for any other person, any gift, loan, fee, reward, or advantage whatever as an inducement to, or reward for, or otherwise on account of any member, officer, or servant of a public body as in this Act defined, doing or forbearing to do anything in respect of any matter or transaction whatsoever, actual or proposed, in which the said public body is concerned, shall be guilty of an offence.

(2) Every person who shall by himself or by or in conjunction with any other person corruptly give, promise, or offer any gift, loan, fee, reward, or advantage whatsoever to any person, whether for the benefit of that person or of another person, as an inducement to or reward for or otherwise on account of any member, officer, or servant of any public body as in this Act defined, doing or forbearing to do anything in respect of any matter or transaction whatsoever, actual or proposed, in which such public body as aforesaid is concerned, shall be guilty of an offence."

---

1 *Supra*, ch. 3.

These offences are punishable on conviction on indictment with two years' imprisonment or a fine or both;[2] but the maximum term of imprisonment is extended to seven years if the matter or transaction in relation to which the offence is committed is a contract or a proposal for a contract with Her Majesty or any Government department or public body,[3] or a sub-contract to execute any work comprised in such a contract.[4] A prosecution may not be brought without the consent of the Attorney-General.[5]

Public bodies

7.03 The main limitation on the scope of these offences is the requirement that the person for whose favour the bribe is given (or solicited, offered *etc.*) must be a member, officer or servant of a "public body". This phrase is defined by section 7 of the 1889 Act:

> "The expression 'public body' means any council of a county or council of a city or town, any council of a municipal borough, also any board, commissioners, select vestry, or other body which has power to act under and for the purposes of any Act relating to local government, or the public health, or to poor law or otherwise to administer money raised by rates in pursuance of any public general Act, but does not include any public body as above defined existing elsewhere than in the United Kingdom . . ."

This definition has been said to be "clearly . . . confined to local authorities".[6] But it is extended by section 4(2) of the Prevention of Corruption Act 1916, which provides:

> "In this Act and in the Public Bodies Corrupt Practices Act 1889, the expression 'public body' includes in addition to the bodies mentioned in the last-mentioned Act, local and public authorities of all descriptions."

It is apparently sufficient if the authority is local *or* public,[7] though a private local authority is hard to imagine. At any rate all public authorities of any description, local or otherwise, are public bodies for the purposes of the 1889 Act. A public authority is a body which has public or statutory duties to perform and which performs those duties and carries out its transactions for the benefit of the public and not for private profit,[8] whether or not it is expressly described as a public authority in the legislation creating it (if any).[9] This definition includes a

2 s. 2(a).
3 For the definition of a public body see *infra*, para. 7.03.
4 Prevention of Corruption Act 1916 s. 1.
5 Public Bodies Corrupt Practices Act 1889 s. 4.
6 *Joy and Emmony* (1976) 60 Cr. App. R. 132 at p. 133, *per* Judge Rigg.
7 *Hirst and McNamee* (1975) 64 Cr. App. R. 151 at p. 152, *per* Judge Buzzard.
8 *The Johannesburg* [1907] P. 65, decided under the Public Authorities Protection Act 1893 but equally applicable to the Prevention of Corruption Acts: *D.P.P. v. Holly and Manners* [1978] A.C. 43.
9 *D.P.P. v. Holly and Manners* [1978] A.C. 43.

corporation administering a nationalised industry,[10] but presumably not a company which is only partly in public ownership.

Inducements and rewards

7.04 The offences require the giving (or offering, solicitation etc.) of a "gift, loan, fee, reward, or advantage". The last and apparently widest of these terms is also defined by section 7, 1889 Act:

> "The expression 'advantage' includes any office or dignity, and any forbearance to demand money or money's worth or valuable thing, and includes any aid, vote, consent, or influence, or pretended aid, vote, consent, or influence, and also includes any promise or procurement of or agreement or endeavour to procure, or the holding out of any expectation of any gift, loan, fee, reward, or advantage, as before defined."

The advantage (*etc.*) must be given (*etc.*):

(a) as an *inducement* to a member (*etc.*) of a public body to do or forbear to do something in respect of a matter or transaction, actual or proposed, in which the public body is concerned; or

(b) as a *reward* for such a person's doing or forbearing to do such a thing; or

(c) otherwise *on account of* such a person's doing or forbearing to do such a thing.

It is not clear what, if anything, the third alternative adds to the first two. Of course a bribe may be both a reward for past favours and an inducement to repeat them in future.[11] But a reward for past favours is sufficient even if there is no element of inducement for the future and even if there was no agreement in advance that a reward would be forthcoming.[12]

7.05 The conduct in respect of which the inducement or reward is given (*etc.*) may consist of any action in respect of any of the public body's affairs, or even a forbearance from such action. The reference to "any matter or transaction" suggests that the bribe must relate to some specific matter, and that it is not sufficient if the intention is merely to render the recipient generally well-disposed towards the giver. It is noteworthy that the Prevention of Corruption Act 1906, by contrast, expressly provides an alternative of "showing or forbearing to show favour or disfavour to any person".[13] But in *Grierson and Powdrill*[14] the Court of Criminal

---

10 *Ibid.*
11 *Cf. Morgan v. D.P.P.* [1970] 3 All E.R. 1053.
12 *Andrews Weatherfoil Ltd* [1972] 1 W.L.R. 118.
13 *Infra*, para. 7.11.
14 [1960] Crim. L.R. 773.

Appeal held that it is an offence under the 1889 Act to bribe an officer of a public body to "show favour": one cannot show favour without either doing something or forbearing from doing something. The 1906 Act had merely made express what in the 1889 Act was implicit.

"Corruptly"

7.06   The offences under the 1889 Act (and the corresponding offences under the 1906 Act) are not committed unless the bribe is given (or solicited, offered *etc.*) "corruptly". This term is not defined. It has been stated that it implies an element of dishonesty[15] and that mere sharp practice is not enough;[16] but it seems that this is not so.[17] In *Smith*[18] it was held not to be necessary that the defendant should act with a corrupt motive, only that he must purposely do an act which the law forbids as tending to corrupt: therefore the offence was committed when a bribe was offered with the intention of exposing the recipient. On this interpretation it is not immediately obvious what the word "corruptly" adds to the other ingredients of these offences. Lord Parker C.J. suggested in *Smith* that it may add something in the case of a reward for past favours even if it is redundant in the case of an inducement for the future;[19] in other words, that the offer or acceptance of an inducement to show favour in the future may well be "corrupt" by definition, but that it is not necessarily corrupt to offer or accept a reward for favour already shown. The circumstances in which such a reward would *not* be corrupt were not explained.

7.07   It is submitted that Lord Parker's distinction between inducements and rewards is at best a partial explanation of the mental element required. We may distinguish five different situations where it might be argued that a suspect transaction is not corrupt.

(a) Neither party to the transaction intends it to be corrupt: *e.g.* a payment is made which is understood by both parties to be gratuitous or to be in respect of some innocent consideration. Obviously the payment is not made corruptly, but that requirement adds nothing because the payment is not made as an inducement to show favour or as a reward for doing so.

(b) One party intends the transaction to be corrupt but the other does not: *e.g.* a payment is made which is intended by the donor to be an inducement to show favour but is understood by the recipient to be

---

15   *Lindley* [1957] Crim. L.R. 321. For dishonesty see *supra*, para. 1.04ff.
16   *Calland* [1967] Crim. L.R. 236.
17   *Wellburn* (1979) 69 Cr. App. R. 254.
18   [1960] 2 Q.B. 423.
19   At p. 428 f.

gratuitous or to be in respect of an innocent consideration. The donor is acting corruptly; the recipient (even if he can be said to receive the payment *as* an inducement) is not.[20]

(c) One party intends the transaction to be corrupt; the other knows that that is the intention, but in his own mind justifies his participation on the basis of some non-corrupt consideration which he has provided or intends to provide. For example, a payment is made which is intended by the donor to be a reward for past favours, and which is understood by the recipient tc be so intended, but to which the recipient believes he is entitled (either legally or morally) by virtue of services innocently rendered by him. His conduct may not be dishonest, but it is nevertheless corrupt.[21]

(d) One party intends the transaction to be corrupt; the other knows that that is the intention, but has no intention of performing his side of the bargain. This situation by its nature can only arise in the case of inducements rather than rewards. There may in addition be the element of supposed justification ((c) above) for accepting the bribe without showing favour in return (or *vice versa*). With or without that element, the transaction is still corrupt on both sides.[22]

(e) One party intends the transaction to be corrupt; the other knows that that is the intention, and co-operates only for the purpose of subsequently exposing the first party. The Court of Appeal has said that such conduct "would plainly not be corrupt";[23] but in the case of a person *offering* a bribe, the intention to expose the recipient is not a defence,[24] and it is not clear why the two situations are distinguishable. Possibly it is corrupt to instigate the transaction, irrespective of one's motives for so doing, but not merely to accept another's proposal with a view to securing evidence against him.

Presumption of corrupt inducement or reward

7.08   The task of proving that a transaction was made by way of an inducement to show favour or a reward for past favours, and (in so far as it is a separate requirement) that it was made corruptly, may be eased for the prosecution by the provisions of section 2 of the Prevention of Corruption Act 1916:

"Where in any proceedings against a person for an offence under the Prevention of Corruption Act 1906, or the Public Bodies Corrupt Practices Act 1889, it is proved that any money, gift, or other consideration has been

20   *Millray Window Cleaning Co. Ltd* [1962] Crim. L.R. 99.
21   *Mills* (1978) 68 Cr. App. R. 154.
22   *Carr* [1957] 1 W.L.R. 165; *Mills, supra.*
23   *Mills, supra,* at p. 159, *per* Geoffrey Lane L.J.; *cf. Carr* [1957] 1 W.L.R. 165.
24   *Smith* [1960] 2 Q.B. 423.

paid or given to or received by a person in the employment of [Her] Majesty or any Government Department or a public body by or from a person, or agent of a person, holding or seeking to obtain a contract from [Her] Majesty or any Government Department or public body, the money, gift, or consideration shall be deemed to have been paid or given and received corruptly as such inducement or reward as is mentioned in such Act unless the contrary is proved."

In *Braithwaite and Girdham*[25] Lord Lane C.J. explained how this presumption operates:

"The effect of [section 2] is that when the matters in that section have been fulfilled, the burden of proof is lifted from the shoulders of the prosecution and descends on the shoulders of the defence. It then becomes necessary for the defendant to show, on a balance of probabilities, that what was going on was not reception corruptly as inducement or reward. In an appropriate case it is the judge's duty to direct the jury first of all that they must decide whether they are satisfied so as to feel sure that the defendant received money or gift or consideration, and then to go on to direct them that if they are so satisfied, then under section 2 of the 1916 Act the burden of proof shifts."[26]

Thus in *Evans-Jones and Jenkins*[27] it was held that where the presumption is raised, the jury may properly be directed to convict if they are left in any doubt whether the payment was corrupt. It is for the defence to satisfy them, on the balance of probabilities, that it was not. The presumption can be rebutted only by evidence of an innocent explanation, not merely by the defendant's unsupported assertion that such an explanation existed.[28]

7.09 Section 2 applies to all payments made to employees of public bodies as defined by section 7 of the 1889 Act and section 4(2) of the 1916 Act, even if the charge is brought under the 1906 Act and does not therefore require proof that the payment was made to such an employee. But it applies only to employees, not to members such as local councillors, and only where a *contract* is involved rather than an exercise of discretion such as a grant of planning permission.[29]

7.10 If the prosecution can establish that some "money, gift, or other consideration" was received by such an employee, it remains only to show that the person providing the consideration (or the person for whom he was acting) was holding or seeking to obtain a contract from Her Majesty or a Government department or public body. In *Braithwaite*

25 [1983] 1 W.L.R. 385.
26 At p. 389.
27 (1923) 17 Cr. App. R. 121.
28 *Mills* (1978) 68 Cr. App. R. 154.
29 *Cf. Dickinson and De Rable* (1948) 33 Cr. App. R. 5.

and Girdham[30] the question arose of what the prosecution must do in order to establish such a receipt so as to bring the presumption into play. The appellants admitted receiving goods and services respectively, but claimed that they had paid for them in full and that it was for the prosecution to prove that they had not. The Court of Appeal held that on the contrary it was for the appellants to prove that they had, because the receipt of the goods or services was either a gift or a consideration and therefore brought section 2 into play. Delivering the judgement of the court, Lord Lane C.J. said:

> "In our judgment the word 'consideration' connotes the existence of something in the shape of a contract or a bargain between the parties. In the context of the present case, take E as the employee of the public body and A as the agent of the contractor. E, the employee, promises to pay A, the agent of the contractor, £x. The consideration for that promise is that the contractor will supply tyres for E's car, or will do work on E's car, as the case may be. That is the consideration, namely the work done on the car or the supplying of the tyres for the car. If that is correct, then on proof of the receipt of the tyres or the doing of the work, the defendant is called upon for an explanation. In our view the word 'gift', according to the Crown's argument, is not otiose. The word 'gift' is the other side of the coin, that is to say it comes into play where there is no consideration and no bargain. Consideration deals with the situation where there is a contract or a bargain and something moving the other way."[31]

It follows that any benefit received in the circumstances set out in section 2 will be sufficient to put the burden of proof on the defence: either there is consideration for the benefit (in which case the benefit is itself a "consideration" within the meaning of section 2) or there is not (in which case the benefit is a "gift"). In either case the receipt of the benefit may or may not be corrupt: the existence of a bargain between the parties is neither necessary nor sufficient to establish liability. But it will be for the defence to prove that the benefit was conferred either in exchange for an innocent consideration or out of pure philanthropy.

CORRUPTION OF AGENTS

7.11 Section 1(1) of the Prevention of Corruption Act 1906 provides:

> "If any agent corruptly accepts or obtains, or agrees to accept or attempts to obtain, from any person, for himself or for any other person, any gift or consideration as an inducement or reward for doing or forbearing to do, or for having after the passing of this Act done or forborne to do, any act in relation to his principal's affairs or business, or for showing or forbearing

---

30 [1983] 1 W.L.R. 385. The Appeal Committee of the House of Lords dismissed a petition for leave to appeal: [1983] 1 W.L.R. 973.
31 At p. 391.

to show favour or disfavour to any person in relation to his principal's affairs or business; or if any person corruptly gives or agrees to give or offers any gift or consideration to any agent as an inducement or reward for doing or forbearing to do, or for having after the passing of this Act done or forborne to do, any act in relation to his principal's affairs or business, or for showing or forbearing to show favour or disfavour to any person in relation to his principal's affairs or business; or if any person knowingly gives to any agent, or if any agent knowingly uses with intent to deceive his principal, any receipt, account, or other document in respect of which the principal is interested, and which contains any statement which is false or erroneous or defective in any material particular, and which to his knowledge is intended to mislead the principal; he shall be guilty of an offence and shall be liable on conviction on indictment to imprisonment . . . for a term not exceeding two years, or to a fine . . . or to both such imprisonment and such fine . . ."[32]

Again the maximum term of imprisonment is extended to seven years where a contract with a public body is involved.[33] A prosecution may not be brought without the consent of the Attorney-General or the Solicitor-General.[34]

Agents

7.12   The offences created by the 1906 Act (unlike those under the 1889 Act) are not confined to corruption in public bodies but extend to all "agents". Moreover it is expressly provided that the expression "agent" includes any person employed[35] by or acting for another,[36] and any person serving under the Crown or under any corporation or any borough, county, or district council, any board of guardians,[37] or any public body.[38] A person may be "serving under" the Crown or a public body even if he is not strictly an employee.[39] The expression "acting for another" is somewhat vague. It might be argued that it includes any person who provides another with his services, even if he is neither an employee nor an agent in the normal sense but merely an independent contractor acting as a principal in his own right. It is submitted, however, that in a penal provision the narrower construction is to be preferred; in other words, that a person does not act *for* another unless he acts on his behalf, *i.e.* as his agent in the strict sense. In that case the Act

---

32   Offences under the 1906 Act (unlike those under the 1889 Act) are triable either way, and on summary conviction carry four months' imprisonment or a fine of the prescribed sum or both.
33   Prevention of Corruption Act 1916 s. 1: *supra*, para. 7.02.
34   Prevention of Corruption Act 1906 s. 2(1).
35   The expression "principal" includes an employer: s. 1(2).
36   s. 1(2).
37   s. 1(3).
38   Prevention of Corruption Act 1916 s. 4(3). For the definition of a public body, see *supra*, para. 7.03.
39   *Barrett* [1976] 1 W.L.R. 946.

would apply to employees (whether or not they are strictly agents), agents in the strict sense (whether employees or independent contractors) and persons serving under the Crown, public bodies *etc.* (whether or not they are employees or agents in the strict sense). This interpretation might involve the application of the fine distinctions drawn by the civil law between an employee and an independent contractor on the one hand and between an agent and a principal on the other.[40]

Inducements and rewards

7.13   With the exception of the offence of deceiving the agent's principal, which is considered below,[41] the offences created by the 1906 Act broadly correspond to those under the 1889 Act: again the corrupt[42] payment of an inducement or reward is an offence on the part of both the donor and the recipient. There are certain differences which are probably more apparent than real. Whereas the 1889 Act expressly prohibits the *soliciting* of an inducement or reward, the 1906 Act refers instead to an attempt to obtain it. It is doubtful whether the mere solicitation of a bribe is sufficiently proximate to the obtaining to be properly described as an attempt, or (in the terminology of the Criminal Attempts Act 1981) whether it is "more than merely preparatory";[43] but it is hard to imagine what else might amount to an attempt to obtain but not an agreement to receive. The 1889 Act also appears to be somewhat wider in terms of the parties involved. The 1906 Act does not expressly prohibit a person other than the agent himself from accepting a bribe on his behalf, nor a third party from offering a bribe to such a person. But the intermediary will commit an offence when he passes the bribe on to the agent, or offers to do so, and both he and the original briber are presumably guilty of a conspiracy to commit that offence. The inducement or reward itself must be a "gift, loan, fee, reward, or advantage" for the purposes of the 1889 Act, but a "gift or consideration"[44] under the 1906 Act. If the agent innocently provides some service (or property) for which he receives fair but not excessive payment, he does no doubt accept a consideration,[45] whether or not it is a "reward" or "advantage"; but obviously the

---

40   *Cf. supra,* para. 4.15ff.
41   Para. 7.15ff.
42   For the element of corruption, see *supra,* para. 7.06. The presumption created by s. 2 of the 1916 Act (*supra,* para. 7.08) is applicable.
43   Strictly speaking the statutory formula is probably not applicable by virtue of s. 3(3) of the 1981 Act, since that provision applies only to an offence which "is expressed as an offence of attempting to commit *another* offence" (s. 3(2)(*b*), italics supplied). In this case there would seem to be one offence which can be committed either by obtaining the bribe or by attempting to do so.
44   "Consideration" includes valuable consideration of any kind: s. 1(2).
45   *Cf. Braithwaite and Girdham* [1983] 1 W.L.R. 385; *supra,* para. 7.10.

consideration cannot be regarded either as corrupt or as an inducement to show favour or a reward for doing so.[46]

7.14 Under the 1906 Act the gift or consideration must be an inducement or reward either for doing (or forbearing to do) any act in relation to the agent's principal's affairs or business, or for showing (or forbearing to show) favour or disfavour to any person in relation to those affairs or business. Clearly the bribe need not relate to any particular transaction and general "sweeteners" are sufficient. Moreover the expression "in relation to his principal's affairs or business" is "designedly very wide".[47] The corrupt payment need not relate to work with which the agent's duties bring him into direct contact,[48] nor even to matters in respect of which he owes his principal any duty at all: thus a trade union official commits the offence if he accepts a bribe in respect of the union's affairs.[49] *A fortiori* it would seem that an employee who accepts a bribe to move to another job is being induced to do an act in relation to his employer's affairs, *viz.* to hand in his notice; yet the Court of Criminal Appeal once approved a direction that such a bribe is not illegal.[50] Perhaps the explanation is simply that it is not corrupt. The employer has no legally protected interest in retaining the employee's services beyond the required period of notice. Indeed the situation is scarcely distinguishable from the mere offer of a higher salary as an inducement to change jobs.

Deception of principal

7.15 As well as the offences of bribery corresponding to those in the 1889 Act, section 1(1) of the 1906 Act also provides that it is an offence

". . . if any person knowingly gives to any agent, or if any agent knowingly uses with intent to deceive his principal, any receipt, account, or other document in respect of which the principal is interested, and which contains any statement which is false or erroneous or defective in any material particular, and which to his knowledge is intended to mislead the principal . . ."

The Royal Commission on Standards of Conduct in Public Life was advised by the then Attorney-General that this provision was useful,

" . . . since it may sometimes be easier to prove the intention to mislead than to demonstrate any associated bribery."[51]

---

46 *Bateman and Linnecor* [1955] Crim. L.R. 108.
47 *Dickinson and De Rable* (1948) 33 Cr. App. R. 5 at p. 9, *per* Pritchard J.
48 *Ibid.*
49 *Morgan v. D.P.P.* [1970] 3 All E.R. 1053.
50 *Huessener and Schroeder* (1911) 6 Cr. App. R. 173.
51 Cmnd. 6524 (1976) at para. 78.

Not only is there no requirement that the agent be bribed to co-operate in the deception: it is not even necessary that he should knowingly be a party to it. In *Sage v. Eicholz*[52] it was held by the Divisional Court that the offence was committed where the defendant gave a document containing a false statement to an agent of the Metropolitan Water Board, with the intention of deceiving the agent's superiors, even though the agent was unaware that the statement was false. In the expression "which to his knowledge is intended to mislead the principal" the word "his" was held to refer to the defendant, not necessarily the agent. The court pointed out that the element of corruption, which is expressly required in the preceding provisions of section 1(1), is not here referred to. But the explanation for the omission may be simply that corruption was thought to involve not merely disloyal conduct but disloyal conduct *procured by bribery*. In essence the defendant simply made a false statement in writing. The appropriate charge would now be one of deception.

7.16 However, in spite of the somewhat literal-minded approach taken in *Sage v. Eicholz,* the courts have stopped short of applying this provision where no third party is involved at all. In *Tweedie*[53] the defendant submitted to his employer's accounting staff details of transactions which he had not in fact made. The prosecution argued, without success, that this conduct fell within the plain wording of section 1(1) since the defendant had knowingly used a document containing a false statement with intent to deceive his principal. Speaking for the Court of Appeal, Lawton L.J. said:

> "If this paragraph had stood by itself as a separate section creating an offence, the argument might have had more force; but it does not. It is part of one subsection which deals in the first two paragraphs with dishonest conduct, either as a fact or in contemplation, between an employee and a third party. It would be odd drafting for the last part of this subsection to create an offence which made an employee criminally liable for using a document which did not have any connection with a third party or was not intended to go to a third party. As Hobhouse J. pointed out in the course of argument, the words 'receipt' and 'account' in the third paragraph, as a matter of the ordinary use of English, refer to documents *inter partes* either in creation or in use. A receipt is made out to someone who has paid a debt. An account is rendered by one person to another. The words 'or other document' should, in our judgment, be construed as meaning a document which would pass *inter partes*. Such documents are capable of being *given* by a third party and then *used* by an employee. Both or one or other can be guilty of the offence created by the third paragraph if there is proof of the knowledge and intent specified. All the words following 'intent to deceive

52 [1919] 2 K.B. 171.
53 [1984] Q.B. 729.

his principal' are words common to the definition of an offence by a third party or an employee . . . If the prosecution's contention were right, the third paragraph would apply to any false document knowingly used by an employee with intent to deceive or mislead his employers. An employee who put a false entry on his time sheet would be guilty of an offence under the Act of 1906. Parliament could not have intended that this should be so."[54]

7.17 The reasoning in *Tweedie* does not sit happily with *Sage v. Eicholz*.[55] The decision might have been based on the narrower ground that an agent cannot commit the offence by *using* a document which has no connection with anyone outside the employer's organisation; this would have left open the possibility that the offence might be committed if one agent *gave* such a document to another agent of the same employer. According to *Sage v. Eicholz* the innocence of the second agent would not in itself be a defence. But the case might have been presented on this basis in *Tweedie* itself, and the court did not suggest that the conviction would then have been legitimate. On the contrary, Lawton L.J. concluded that "the third paragraph did not apply to the facts of this case".[56] It would seem, therefore, that a person outside the organisation commits the offence if he gives a false document to an agent within it, even if the agent is totally innocent; but a person within the organisation who gives an internal document to a fellow employee does not commit the offence even if the recipient is a party to the fraud. Yet the latter case appears to have more to do with corruption (with which the Act purports to deal) than does the former. It is submitted that *Sage v. Eicholz* fails to take adequate account of the legislative context which in *Tweedie* was regarded as decisive, and that it should now be reconsidered.

CORRUPTION OF PUBLIC OFFICERS

7.18 Many public officers are "serving under" the Crown[57] or are members, officers or servants of public bodies, in which case corruption and attempted corruption will be covered by the Prevention of Corruption Acts. Members and officers of local authorities are also under a statutory obligation to disclose a pecuniary interest in proposed contracts or (in the case of members) other matters,[58] but failure to do so is only a summary offence punishable with a fine.[59] Members of

---

54   At p. 734.
55   [1919] 2 K.B. 171; *supra,* para. 7.15.
56   At p. 612.
57   *e.g. Barrett* [1976] 1 W.L.R. 946.
58   Local Government Act 1972 ss. 94-98, 117; see Diane M. Hare, "The Need for New Anti-Corruption Laws in Local Government" [1974] P.L. 146.
59   s. 94(2).

Parliament are subject to no such statutory requirements, but it has been plausibly argued that the House of Commons is a "public authority" and therefore a public body within the meaning of the Public Bodies Corrupt Practices Act 1889.[60] There are in addition offences at common law of misbehaviour in a public office[61] and of bribery of a public officer.[62] The definition of a public officer for the purposes of the latter offence (and presumably the former too) is as follows:

> "A public officer is an officer who discharges any duty in the discharge of which the public are interested, more clearly so if he is paid out of a fund provided by the public. If taxes go to supply his payment and the public have an interest in the duties he discharges, he is a public officer."[63]

This definition appears to be wide enough to embrace not only Ministers of the Crown but any Member of Parliament.[64] It seems likely, however, that both of these common law offences involve an element of dishonesty or corruption;[65] and in view of the accepted practice of M.P.s acting as paid consultants to particular organisations this element might prove impossible to establish.

---

60 G. Zellick, "Bribery of Members of Parliament and the Criminal Law" [1979] P.L. 31.
61 *Llewellyn-Jones* [1968] 1 Q.B. 429; *cf. Bembridge* (1783) 22 St. Tr. 1.
62 *Pollman* (1809) 2 Camp. 229, *Whitaker* [1914] 3 K.B. 1283. A *conspiracy* to bribe a public officer would no doubt be a conspiracy to defraud at common law (*cf. supra,* para. 1.44), but should now be charged as a conspiracy to commit the substantive offence (*infra*, para. 12.34ff).
63 *Whitaker* [1914] 3 K.B. 1283 at p. 1296, *per* Lawrence J.
64 G.Zellick, *op. cit.*
65 *Llewellyn-Jones* [1968] 1 Q.B. 429.

CHAPTER 8

Frauds on Investors

8.01 The process of investment, by its very nature, involves a certain risk of fraud. The investor is generally required to hand over his money before he sees any tangible return on it, and he may end up with neither money nor return. But a bad investment is not the same as a fraudulent one. Before fraud can be established it will normally have to be proved either that the investor was deceived in some way or that his money was misapplied for some unauthorised purpose. In either case at least one of the offences already considered will probably have been committed. If the investor is deceived into investing in the first place, there will be an offence of obtaining property by deception;[1] if he is deceived into accepting less than he is owed, there will be an evasion of liability by deception.[2] The deception may involve offences of false accounting[3] or of publishing misleading statements about a company's affairs.[4] Misapplication of the money invested will probably amount to theft,[5] provided the investor has a legal right that it be applied as he intended.[6] And where no substantive offence is involved (but not otherwise)[7] it may be possible to fall back on a charge of conspiracy to defraud. For example, a scheme to create a false market in securities by buying them at a fictitious premium was an indictable conspiracy at common law;[8] today it would still be an indictable conspiracy, but it might be necessary (depending whether the sham purchases could be said to involve a deception)[9] to charge it as a statutory conspiracy to obtain money by deception.

8.02 These offences are however supplemented by several offences specifically relating to investment fraud. These offences fall into two

1 *Supra*, para. 3.02ff.
2 *Supra*, para. 3.29ff.
3 *Supra*, para. 6.41ff.
4 *Supra*, para. 6.55ff.
5 *Supra*, para. 3.02ff.
6 *Supra*, para. 4.07ff. The White Paper *Financial Services in the United Kingdom* (Cmnd. 9432, at para. 7.9) proposes to require all investment businesses (other than banks, licensed deposit takers and building societies) holding funds on behalf of a client to place them in a segregated trust account: misapplication of them will then clearly constitute theft.
7 *Infra*, para. 12.34ff.
8 *Scott v. Brown, Doering, McNab & Co.* [1892] 2 Q.B. 724.
9 *Cf. supra*, para. 2.07.

categories: those which consist essentially of deceiving the prospective investor into parting with his money, and those which prohibit certain transactions altogether on the grounds of an unfair imbalance of information. These offences will be superseded if the recommendations of Professor L. C. B. Gower's *Review of Investor Protection*[10] are implemented.

DECEPTION OF INVESTORS

False statements in company prospectuses

8.03   Section 70(1) of the Companies Act 1985[11] provides that a person who authorises[12] the issue of a prospectus is guilty of an offence (punishable on conviction on indictment with two years' imprisonment or a fine or both)[13] if the prospectus includes any untrue statement, unless he proves *either* that the statement was immaterial *or* that he had reasonable ground to believe, and did believe up to the time of the issue of the prospectus, that the statement was true. An intent to deceive or defraud is not required. Moreover the offence is not confined to statements which are literally untrue: it extends to any statement in a prospectus which is "misleading in the form and context in which it is included"[14]—*i.e.*, presumably, any statement likely to give a false impression. This would clearly include the "half-truth" which is misleading by virtue of what is left unsaid.[15]

8.04   It is however essential that the misleading statement be included in a *prospectus* (or in a report or memorandum appearing on the face of a prospectus or by reference incorporated therein or issued therewith).[16] It is expressly provided that where a company allots or agrees to allot its shares or debentures with a view to their being offered for sale to the public, any document by which the offer for sale to the public is made is deemed for all purposes to be a prospectus issued by the company.[17] More generally, the term "prospectus" is defined as "any prospectus, notice, circular, advertisement, or other invitation, offering to the public for subscription or purchase any shares in or debentures of a

---

10   Cmnd. 9125. See also *Financial Services in the United Kingdom* (Cmnd. 9432).
11   Replacing s. 44(1) of the Companies Act 1948 with effect from 1 July 1985.
12   A person does not authorise the issue of a prospectus merely by consenting to the inclusion therein of a statement purporting to be made by him as an expert: s. 70(2).
13   Sch. 24. On summary conviction the offence carries six months' imprisonment or a fine of the statutory maximum or both.
14   s. 71(*a*).
15   *Cf. Kylsant* [1932] 1 K.B. 442.
16   s. 71(*b*).
17   s. 58(1).

company".[18] "Subscription" refers to the acquisition of securities at the time of issue, "purchase" to a subsequent acquisition; in either case the acquisition must be for cash. Thus a document offering securities of one company in exchange for those of another is not a prospectus.[19] The securities must, moreover, be offered "to the public". This expression includes an offer to any *section* of the public, whether selected as members or debenture holders of the company concerned or as clients of the person issuing the prospectus or in any other manner;[20] but it does not include an offer which can properly be regarded, in all the circumstances,

(a) as not being calculated to result, directly or indirectly, in the shares or debentures becoming available for subscription or purchase by persons other than those receiving the offer or invitation, or

(b) otherwise as being a "domestic concern" of the persons making and receiving it.[21]

Other false statements to prospective investors

8.05 Section 13(1) of the Prevention of Fraud (Investments) Act 1958, as amended,[22] provides as follows:

> "Any person who, by any statement, promise or forecast which he knows to be misleading, false or deceptive, or by any dishonest concealment of material facts, or by the reckless making (dishonestly or otherwise) of any statement, promise or forecast which is misleading, false or deceptive, induces or attempts to induce another person—
>
> (*a*) to enter into or offer to enter into—
>
>   (i) any agreement for, or with a view to, acquiring, disposing of, subscribing for or underwriting securities . . ., or
>
>   (ii) any agreement the purpose or pretended purpose of which is to secure a profit to any of the parties from the yield of securities or by reference to fluctuations in the value of securities, or
>
> (*b*) to take part or offer to take part in any arrangements with respect to property other than securities, being arrangements the purpose or effect, or pretended purpose or effect, of which is to enable persons taking part in the arrangements (whether by becoming owners of the property or any part of the property or otherwise) to participate in or receive profits or income alleged to arise or to be likely to arise from the acquisition, holding, management or disposal of such property,

---

18 s. 744.
19 *Government Stock & Other Securities Investment Co. Ltd v. Christopher* [1956] 1 W.L.R. 237.
20 s. 59(1).
21 s. 60(1). In the case of private companies (which are prohibited from offering their securities to the public at all: s. 81(1)) there is a rebuttable presumption that an offer is a domestic concern if it is made to members or employees of the company, or their families, or existing debenture-holders, or if the securities are to be held under an employees' share scheme: s. 60(3)-(6).
22 Protection of Depositors Act 1963 ss. 1(3), 21; Banking Act 1979 Sch. 6.

or sums to be paid or alleged to be likely to be paid out of such profits or income, or

(c) to enter into or offer to enter into an agreement the purpose or pretended purpose of which is to secure a profit to any of the parties by reference to fluctuations in the value of any property other than securities,

shall be guilty of an offence, and liable to imprisonment for a term not exceeding seven years."[23]

The falsehood

8.06 The falsehood may take any of three forms:

(a) the making of a statement, promise or forecast which the defendant *knows* to be misleading, false or deceptive;

(b) the *dishonest concealment* of material facts; or

(c) the *reckless* making of a statement, promise or forecast which is in fact misleading, false or deceptive.

A statement may be misleading or deceptive if, though literally true, it is likely to give a false impression. Promises and forecasts are regarded for legal purposes as being incapable of truth or falsehood, since they relate to the future, but may be misleading or deceptive if they give a false impression of present facts (*e.g.* that the maker of a promise intends to keep it, or that there are reasonable grounds for believing that a forecast will prove correct).[24] A single count may allege several statements, promises and forecasts,[25] and it is sufficient if any of them is proved; but at least one of them must be proved to the satisfaction of the whole jury.[26] It is not sufficient that different members of the jury are satisfied as to different statements.[27]

8.07 The words "dishonestly or otherwise", referring to the *reckless* making of a misleading statement (*etc.*) were inserted by the Protection of Depositors Act 1963.[28] The intention was to resolve a difference of judicial opinion over the interpretation of the word "reckless", and to reject the view taken in *Mackinnon*[29] that a statement is not reckless unless it is made without any genuine belief in its truth.[30] Clearly the defendant need not be subjectively aware that the statement may be misleading. There is some room for argument as to what degree of fault *is*

---

23 The White Paper *Financial Services in the United Kingdom* (Cmnd. 9432, at para. 7.5) proposes extending s. 13(1) to cover any person who knowingly or recklessly engages in any act, device, scheme, practice or course of conduct in relation to investment business which is likely to defraud, deceive or mislead.
24 *Cf. supra*, para. 2.14ff.
25 *Linnell* [1969] 1 W.L.R. 1514.
26 Subject to the possibility of a majority verdict.
27 *Kevin Brown* (1983) 79 Cr.App.R. 115; *supra*, para. 2.34.
28 s. 21(1)(*a*).
29 [1959] 1 Q.B. 150.
30 *Cf. Derry v. Peek* (1889) 14 App. Cas. 337.

required. In *Bates*[31] Donovan J. ruled that it was sufficient if there was "a high degree of negligence without dishonesty",[32] and the Court of Criminal Appeal, *obiter,* expressed its agreement.[33] In *Grunwald*[34] Paull J. interpreted *Bates* as suggesting that mere carelessness is sufficient (which is not what Donovan J. said) and disagreed. In his view a statement was not reckless unless it was "a rash statement to make" and the defendant had no real basis of facts on which he could support it. The gap between these two interpretations is not wide. Probably the word should now be construed in the light of the House of Lords' decision in *Caldwell:*[35] *i.e.* it is sufficient if there was an obvious risk that the statement might not be true and the defendant failed to address his mind to that possibility.

8.08 As well as ruling out the subjective interpretation of the word "reckless", the insertion of the words "dishonestly or otherwise" has a side-effect: it precludes any suggestion that (in cases of positively false statements rather than mere concealment) the offence requires dishonesty as that term is now construed in the context of the Theft Acts. On a deception charge the defendant may argue that although he did not believe his statement to be true, it was not dishonest of him to make it.[36] But on a charge of making false statements contrary to the 1958 Act the argument would be irrelevant. Not only does section 13 not expressly require dishonesty as the deception offences do: it expressly provides that in the case of reckless statements dishonesty is not required. *A fortiori* it cannot be required in the case of statements *known* to be false.[37] It is true that the 1963 amendment was not intended to achieve this result, since the element of dishonesty as it is now understood was not then regarded as a distinct ingredient of criminal liability. But it could scarcely be argued that dishonesty is implicitly required under a provision which expressly states that it is not.

8.09 It is not entirely clear what constitutes a "dishonest concealment of material facts". It is arguable that this possibility was provided for *ex abundanti cautela* and adds nothing to the other two forms of the offence. In *Mackinnon*[38] Salmon J. said:

"If any fact that is omitted from a statement, promise or forecast is material, it can only be material in that its omission makes what has been

31   (1952) 36 Cr.App.R. 175.
32   At p. 183.
33   *Sub. nom. Russell* [1953] 1 W.L.R. 77.
34   [1963] 1 Q.B. 935.
35   [1982] A.C. 341.
36   *Supra*, para. 1.16ff.
37   But *cf. Clegg* [1977] C.L.Y. 619.
38   [1959] 1 Q.B. 150.

said misleading, false or deceptive. If the omission is dishonest, it can only be dishonest because the person who makes it knows that what he has said is misleading, false or deceptive by reason of that omission."[39]

The authority of this dictum is perhaps undermined by the fact that his Lordship's conclusions on the interpretation of the word "reckless" were subsequently overruled by Parliament.[40] In any case the reasoning is not convincing. A fact is material if a reasonable man would take it into account in deciding on his course of action. In the context of a prospective investment the number of material facts may be considerable. It can hardly be maintained that the omission of any one of those facts *per se* renders a statement of the others misleading. A statement of part of the truth *may* be misleading,[41] but it is not *necessarily* so. Therefore a deliberate omission may be a concealment of material facts even if what *is* stated is not positively misleading.

8.10 However, it is not sufficient for liability under section 13 that the defendant merely conceals material facts: he must conceal them *dishonestly*. The Act does not define what makes a concealment dishonest, and the authorities on the concept of dishonesty in other offences are presumably applicable. In that case there is no offence unless ordinary people would think it dishonest in the circumstances to conceal the facts in question, and the defendant realises that they would think so.[42] It is submitted, however, that this proposition alone does not give full weight to the requirement of dishonesty. In general the law does not require one party to a contract to disclose all material facts to the other: *caveat emptor*. If a person conceals facts which are material but which he is under no obligation to disclose, is he really guilty of an offence merely because ordinary people would think it dishonest of him to stand on his legal rights? The solution, it is submitted, lies in a conception of dishonesty which reflects not only moral considerations but also legal ones. It was argued above[43] that, irrespective of current moral opinion, conduct which is entirely lawful according to the civil law cannot be regarded as dishonest for the purposes of criminal liability. On this view, the concealment of facts would not be "dishonest" within the meaning of section 13 unless the civil law imposed a duty to disclose those facts (which would be exceptional). In effect the position would be the same as that tentatively suggested above in the context of deception:[44] *i.e.* there

---

39   At p. 154.
40   *Supra*, para. 8.07.
41   *e.g. Linnell* [1969] 1 W.L.R. 1514. In *Delmayne* [1970] 2 Q.B. 170 the failure to disclose a material fact was treated as a dishonest concealment, but it probably amounted to a positive misrepresentation.
42   *Ghosh* [1982] Q.B. 1053; *supra*, para. 1.23.
43   Para. 1.10ff.
44   Para. 2.10f.

must be *either* a positive misrepresentation *or* a breach of a duty of disclosure. The difference is that in the context of deception even a positive misrepresentation must be dishonest according to current opinion, whereas under section 13 that test is relevant only to concealment.

The agreement or arrangements

8.11 The agreement into which the victim is to be induced to enter, or the arrangements in which he is to be induced to take part, may relate either to "securities" as defined by the Act[45] or to property other than securities. But the arrangements referred to in paragraph (*b*) must relate to some property *in which* the victim is to invest, not the property which he himself is to put up *as* his investment:[46] thus the section would not cover a scheme under which property already owned by the victim was to be managed on his behalf. Moreover the purpose or effect (or pretended purpose or effect) of the arrangements must be to enable persons taking part to participate in or receive profits or income arising from the acquisition, holding, management or disposal of the property in question (or sums to be paid out of such profits or income). It has been held that this does not extend to an arrangement under which persons are to buy goods from the defendant at wholesale prices and sell them to the public at a profit[47]—an interpretation more in keeping with the spirit of the section than its wording. An offence is committed not only if the victim is induced actually to enter into an agreement (or to take part in any arrangements) of the types specified, but also if he is induced merely to *offer* to do so. These alternatives constitute distinct offences, but they are not mutually exclusive. Thus an offence is committed if the investor does in fact take part in an arrangement within the jurisdiction, even if his *offer* to do so was procured abroad, and even if the acts within the jurisdiction which constitute "taking part" are performed by his agents on his behalf.[48]

8.12 It is also sufficient for the full offence if the defendant merely *attempts* by means of the false statement (*etc.*) to induce the victim to

---

45 *i.e.* (a) shares or debentures, or rights or interests (described whether as units or otherwise) in any shares or debentures, or (b) securities of the Government of the U.K. or of Northern Ireland or the Government of any country or territory outside the U.K., or (c) rights (whether actual or contingent) in respect of money lent to, or deposited with, any industrial and provident society or building society, or (d) rights or interests (whether described as units or otherwise) which may be acquired under any unit trust scheme under which all property for the time being subject to any trust created in pursuance of the scheme consists of securities within (a) to (c) above.

46 *Hughes v. Trapnell* [1963] 1 Q.B. 737. This case was decided on the original wording of the section, but the amendment effected by s. 21(1)(*b*) of the Protection of Depositors Act 1963 does not appear to affect the reasoning.

47 *Newton and Wright* (1966) 110 S.J. 185.

48 *Secretary of State for Trade v. Markus* [1976] A.C. 35; *infra*, para. 11.04.

enter into an agreement (or to take part in any arrangements) of the types specified, or to offer to do so. This form of the offence clearly requires an *intention* to induce the victim to do one of these things. In *Tarling (No. 1) v. Government of the Republic of Singapore,*[49] in the context of an alleged *conspiracy* to commit the offence, the House of Lords gave a curiously restricted interpretation to the requirement of an intention to induce persons to invest. The alleged conspiracy involved the concealment of certain highly profitable transactions entered into by a company, by the device of transferring the proceeds to a unit trust and then retrieving them in instalments over several years. The objective was to stabilise the price of the company's shares by giving the impression of steady growth rather than isolated killings. A bare majority of the House of Lords held that there was no evidence of a conspiracy to induce members of the public to buy the company's shares by means of false and misleading statements in the company's accounts. The reason advanced by Lord Wilberforce was that there was no evidence of dishonesty;[50] but dishonesty is required only in the case of concealment, not where statements are made which are positively misleading. The other two members of the majority, Lord Salmon[51] and Lord Keith,[52] thought there was no evidence of an intention to induce the public to invest in the company, because the intention was merely to protect the company and its shareholders by supporting the price of the shares. The difficulty with this reasoning is that one cannot support the market price of a commodity without inducing people to buy it at that price. The scheme alleged would be futile unless investors were led to take a more optimistic view of the company's prospects than they otherwise would, and hence to buy the shares at a higher price than they otherwise would. It is submitted, with respect, that there was ample evidence of the intention required.

Liability of company officers
8.13   Section 19 of the 1958 Act provides:

> "Where any offence under this Act committed by a corporation is proved to have been committed with the consent or connivance of any director, manager, secretary or other officer of the corporation, he, as well as the corporation, shall be deemed to be guilty of that offence and shall be liable to be proceeded against and punished accordingly."

The corresponding provision in the Theft Act 1968 is discussed above.[53]

---

49   (1978) 70 Cr.App.R. 77.
50   At p. 112.
51   At p. 133.
52   At p. 139 f.
53   Para. 3.46.

Insurance and deposits

8.14   Section 13 of the 1958 Act does not extend to inducements to take out insurance policies[54] or (since 1963) to invest money on deposit.[55] However, in these cases corresponding offences are provided by specialised legislation. Section 73 of the Insurance Companies Act 1982 provides:

> "Any person who, by any statement, promise or forecast which he knows to be misleading, false or deceptive, or by any dishonest concealment of material facts, or by the reckless making (dishonestly or otherwise) of any statement, promise or forecast which is misleading, false or deceptive, induces or attempts to induce another person to enter into or offer to enter into any contract of insurance with an insurance company[56] shall be guilty of an offence."

On conviction on indictment the offence is punishable with two years' imprisonment or a fine or both.[57] Similarly section 39(1) of the Banking Act 1979 provides:

> "Any person who, . . . by any statement, promise or forecast which he knows to be misleading, false or deceptive, or by any dishonest concealment of material facts, or by the reckless making (dishonestly or otherwise) of any statement, promise or forecast which is misleading, false or deceptive, induces or attempts to induce another person—
> (*a*) to make a deposit[58] with him or with any other person, or
> (*b*) to enter into or offer to enter into any agreement for that purpose,
> shall be liable on conviction on indictment to imprisonment for a term not exceeding seven years or to a fine or both."

As from 1 July 1985 this provision replaced a similarly worded offence under section 1(1) of the Protection of Depositors Act 1963.

PROHIBITED TRANSACTIONS

Option dealings by directors

8.15   Certain transactions relating to securities are prohibited altogether

---

54   Insurance Companies Act 1982 s. 79. The *Review of Investor Protection* (Cmnd. 9125, at para. 8-34) recommends that s. 79 be repealed and that life policies be treated as investments under the provision proposed as a replacement for s. 13 of the 1958 Act.
55   Protection of Depositors Act 1963 s. 1(3).
56   *i.e.* a person or body of persons (whether incorporated or not) carrying on insurance business: s. 96(1).
57   s. 81(1). On summary conviction the offence carries a fine of £1,000 or (if greater) the prescribed sum under s. 32 of the Magistrates' Courts Act 1980. S.91 corresponds to s. 19 of the 1958 Act (*supra*, para1 8.13) but applies in cases of neglect by officers as well as of consent and connivance.
58   *i.e.* a sum of money paid on terms (a) under which it will be repaid, with or without interest or a premium, and either on demand or at a time or in circumstances agreed by or on behalf of the person making the payment and the person receiving it, and (b) which are not referable to the provision of property or services or to the giving of security: s. 1(4).

on the ground that they constitute (or are likely to constitute) "insider dealing", *i.e.* taking advantage of inside knowledge about a company's affairs for the purpose of making an unfair profit on dealings in its securities. Section 323(1) of the Companies Act 1985[59] prohibits one of the most blatant examples, *viz.* the purchase by company directors of options in the securities of their own companies. It provides:

> "It is an offence for a director[60] of a company to buy—
> (*a*) a right to call for delivery at a specified price and within a specified time of a specified number of relevant shares or a specified amount of relevant debentures;[61] or
> (*b*) a right to make delivery at a specified price and within a specified time of a specified number of relevant shares or a specified amount of relevant debentures; or
> (*c*) a right (as he may elect) to call for delivery at a specified price and within a specified time or to make delivery at a specified price and within a specified time of a specified number of relevant shares or a specified amount of relevant debentures."

The offence is punishable on conviction on indictment with two years' imprisonment or a fine or both.[62] "Relevant" shares and debentures are those of the director's own company, or of another company in the same group, which are listed on a stock exchange (whether in Great Britain or elsewhere).[63] Section 323 is extended by section 327 so as to apply to a director's spouse or infant child (including a step-child), but it is a defence for such a person to prove that he had no reason to believe that his or her spouse or parent (as the case may be) was a director of the company in question.

Insider dealing

8.16   A far more wide-ranging attack on the problem of insider dealing is to be found in the Company Securities (Insider Dealing) Act 1985.[64] Whereas section 323 of the Companies Act is confined to dealings in options, these provisions extend to other forms of dealing and even to the practice of giving unauthorised tip-offs; and whereas section 323 applies only to directors and their families, the insider dealing provisions cover a wide variety of persons who hold inside information by virtue of their

---

59   Replacing s. 25(1) of the Companies Act 1967 with effect from 1 July 1985.
60   Including a shadow director, *i.e.* a person in accordance with whose directions or instructions the directors are accustomed to act, unless they act merely on advice given by him in a professional capacity: s. 323(4), s. 741(2).
61   But the section does not prohibit a person from buying a right to *subscribe* for shares or debentures, or from buying convertible debentures: s. 323(5).
62   Sch. 24. On summary conviction the offence carries six months' imprisonment or a fine of the statutory maximum or both.
63   s. 323(3).
64   Replacing Part V of the Companies Act 1980 with effect from 1 July 1985.

position or have obtained it from such persons. Unfortunately the necessary evidence has proved hard to obtain and prosecutions have been few.[65] We shall examine first the key concept of "unpublished price sensitive information", and the persons affected by the legislation ("insiders" and "tippees"),[66] before turning to the offences themselves and the exceptions to them.

Unpublished price sensitive information
8.17 The crucial limitation on the scope of the offences created by the Act is that the defendant must be in possession of unpublished price sensitive information in relation to a company's securities.[67] In this context "company" means *any* company, whether or not a company within the meaning of the Companies Act 1985, and therefore includes a foreign company.[68] "Securities", in the case of a company within the meaning of the Companies Act, a company registered under Chapter II of Part XXII of that Act or an unregistered company,[69] includes any shares or debentures or any right to subscribe for, call for or make delivery of a share or debenture (*i.e.* an option);[70] but the prohibitions are confined to dealings on a recognised stock exchange[71] or an investment exchange[72] or on the "over the counter" markets.[73] In the case of other companies (*e.g.* foreign companies) the term "securities" is restricted to securities listed on a recognised stock exchange.[74] "Unpublished price sensitive information" in relation to any securities of a company is defined as information which

---

65 The White Paper *Financial Services in the United Kingdom* (Cmnd. 9432, at para. 14.3) proposes giving to those investigating alleged insider dealing powers similar to those of an inspector appointed under s. 432 of the Companies Act 1985, enabling them to require any person who has bought or sold securities to disclose details of a transaction.
66 We follow common usage in adopting these terms although the latter is not used in the legislation and the former is used only in a marginal note.
67 The White Paper *Financial Services in the United Kingdom* (Cmnd. 9432, at para. 14.1), following the *Review of Investor Protection* (Cmnd. 9125, at para. 9-34), proposes to extend the offences so as to cover *all* securities, including units in unit trusts, Government and local authority stocks, options and futures contracts based on them.
68 s. 11(*a*).
69 *i.e.* any body corporate to which the provisions of the Companies Act 1985 specified in Sch. 22 to that Act apply by virtue of s. 718 of that Act: s. 16(1).
70 s. 12(*a*).
71 *i.e.* any body of persons which is for the time being a recognised stock exchange for the purposes of the Prevention of Fraud (Investments) Act 1958: s. 16(1). But there is no need for the securities dealt in to be *listed* on that stock exchange: *e.g.* dealings under the Stock Exchange's rule 163(2) are probably dealings "on" a recognised stock exchange. See Barry A.K. Rider, *Insider Trading* at para. 1.2.3.
72 References in the legislation to dealing on a recognised stock exchange include dealing through an investment exchange: s. 13(1). An investment exchange is defined as an organisation maintaining a system whereby an offer to deal in securities made by a subscriber to the organisation is communicated, without his identity being revealed, to other subscribers to the organisation, and whereby any acceptance of that offer by any of those other subscribers is recorded and confirmed: s. 13(2).
73 *Infra*, para. 8.20.
74 s. 12(*a*), (*b*). S. 13(1) (*supra*, n. 72) does not affect the definition of securities itself.

"(*a*) relates to specific matters relating or of concern (directly or indirectly) to that company, that is to say, is not of a general nature relating or of concern to that company, and

(*b*) is not generally known to those persons who are accustomed or would be likely to deal in those securities but which would if it were generally known to them be likely materially to affect the price of those securities."[75]

It will be noted that the word "specific" in paragraph (*a*) governs the word "matters" rather than the phrase "relating . . . to that company"; in other words, the information need not relate to that company *in particular* (*i.e.* as against any other company or person), provided it is information as to specific *matters* (*i.e.* "not of a general nature"). There is no requirement that the defendant should be *influenced* by the information: it is sufficient that he has it and that he knows it is unpublished price sensitive information in relation to the securities in question.[76]

Insiders

8.18 A person is not subject to the prohibitions imposed by the Act merely because he is in possession of unpublished price sensitive information in relation to a company's securities: he must in addition be either an "insider" or a "tippee". An insider is an individual[77] who, by virtue of holding one of the following positions,[78] has unpublished price sensitive information in relation to any securities of a company and who knows[79] that the information is unpublished price sensitive information in relation to those securities:[80]

---

75   s. 10.
76   Rider (*op. cit.*, at para. 1.2.1) states that a person who deals in securities whilst in possession of inside information relating to them is rebuttably presumed to have used the information in arriving at his decision to deal. With respect, there is no presumption, rebuttable or otherwise. The weight attached to the information (if any) is simply not an element of the offence.
77   *i.e.* not a corporation; but a company might be liable as an accessory.
78   In the case of (3) below, *i.e.* the take-over bidder, there is no express requirement that he should have the information by virtue of his position; but in this case the information must be either that the offer is contemplated or that it is no longer contemplated, and the bidder could hardly have that information *otherwise* than by virtue of his position.
79   Recklessness is clearly *not* sufficient, as Rider suggests (*op. cit.* at para. 1.2.6.).
80   As a matter of ordinary usage it might be more accurate to say that a person is an insider if he *has* unpublished price sensitive information by virtue of his position, whether or not he *knows* it is unpublished price sensitive information, although he does not commit an *offence* by dealing in the securities in question unless he knows that the information is unpublished price sensitive information in relation to those securities; but the term "insider" is introduced only for the purpose of exposition, and for that purpose it seems simpler to regard the mental element as part of its definition. It should however be remembered that a person may be a *tippee* although the "insider" from whom he obtained the information did not know that it was unpublished price sensitive information: *infra*, para. 8.19.

(1) A person who is (or at any time in the preceding six months has been) knowingly[81] connected with the company in question, provided that it would be reasonable to expect a person so connected and in the position by virtue of which he is so connected not to disclose the information except for the proper performance of the functions attaching to that position.[82] A person is connected with a company if, but only if,

"(a) he is a director of that company or a related company;[83] or
(b) he occupies a position as an officer (other than a director) or employee of that company or a related company or a position involving a professional or business relationship between himself (or his employer or a company of which he is a director) and the first company or a related company which in either case may reasonably be expected to give him access to information which, in relation to securities of either company, is unpublished price sensitive information, and which it would be reasonable to expect a person in his position not to disclose except for the proper performance of his functions."[84]

(2) A person who is (or at any time in the preceding six months has been) knowingly connected with *another* company, provided that
(a) the information relates to a transaction (actual or contemplated) involving both companies, or involving one of them and securities of the other, or to the fact that such transaction is no longer contemplated, and
(b) it would be reasonable to expect a person so connected and in the position by virtue of which he is so connected not to disclose the information except for the proper performance of the functions attaching to that position.[85]

(3) A person who is contemplating (or has contemplated) making a take-over offer[86] for the company in question, whether with or without another person; but only in respect of the information that the offer is (or is no longer) contemplated.[87]

(4) A Crown servant[88] or former Crown servant, provided that it

---

81 Again the requirement of knowledge might alternatively be regarded as essential to the *offence* rather than to the definition of an insider: see *supra*, n.80.
82 s. 1(1).
83 *i.e.* any body corporate in the same group: s. 11(b).
84 s. 9.
85 s. 1(2).
86 *i.e.* an offer made to all the holders (or all the holders other than the person making the offer and his nominees) of the shares in the company to acquire those shares or a specified proportion of them, or to all the holders (or all the holders other than the person making the offer and his nominees) of a particular class of those shares to acquire the shares of that class or a specified proportion of them: s. 14.
87 s. 1(5).
88 *i.e.* an individual who holds office under, or is employed by, the Crown: s. 16(1). The White Paper *Financial Services in the United Kingdom* (Cmnd. 9432, at para. 14.2), following the *Review of Investor Protection* (Cmnd. 9125, at para. 9-34) proposes extending this provision so as to include not only Crown servants but all public servants, *e.g.* local government officers.

would be reasonable to expect a person in that position[89] not to disclose the information except for the proper performance of the functions attaching to that position.[90]

Tippees

8.19 A tippee is an individual[91] who

(a) has unpublished price sensitive information in relation to any securities of a company;

(b) knows that the information is unpublished price sensitive information in relation to those securities;

(c) knowingly obtained the information (directly or indirectly)[92] from a person who was at that time an insider;[93]

(d) knows or has reasonable cause to believe that the insider held the information by virtue of his connection or position (as the case may be);[94] and

(e) (where the insider was an insider by virtue of being connected with a company) knows or has reasonable cause to believe that, because of the insider's connection and position, it would be reasonable to expect him not to disclose the information except for the proper performance of the functions attaching to that position.[95]

Offences

8.20 Subject to the exceptions referred to below, it is an offence punishable with two years' imprisonment[96] for an insider or a tippee to:

(a) deal[97] on a recognised stock exchange or an investment exchange in the securities to which the information relates;[98] or

(b) counsel or procure any person to deal in those securities, knowing (or having reasonable cause to believe) that that person would[99] deal in them on a recognised stock exchange or an investment

---

89   *i.e.*, in the case of a former Crown servant, his *former* position.
90   s. 2(1), (2).
91   *i.e.* not a corporation.
92   Subject to the requirement of knowledge, this would seem to include a person who obtains the information at second or third hand (a "sub-tippee").
93   Except that the person from whom the information was obtained need not have known that it was unpublished price sensitive information, nor, where he was or had been connected with a company, that he was or had been so connected.
94   Except where the insider was a take-over bidder: see *supra*, n. 78.
95   s. 1(3), (6); s.2(1), (2).
96   s. 8(1). On summary conviction the offences carry six months' imprisonment or a fine of the statutory maximum or both.
97   A person deals in securities if (whether as principal or agent) he buys or sells them or agrees to do so: s. 13(1).
98   s. 1(1)-(6), s. 2(3)(*a*).
99   *i.e.* presumably, if he *did* deal in them.

exchange or on any stock exchange outside Great Britain;[1] or

(c) communicate the information to any other person, knowing (or having reasonable cause to believe) that that or some other person will make use of it for the purpose of dealing in those securities on a recognised stock exchange or an investment exchange or on any stock exchange outside Great Britain, or of counselling or procuring any other person to do so.[2]

Provided that the securities in question are "advertised securities",[3] it is also an offence for an insider or a tippee to:

(d) deal in those securities otherwise than on a recognised stock exchange or an investment exchange, either

(i) *through* an off-market dealer[4] who is making a market in those securities,[5] in the knowledge that he is an off-market dealer, that he is making a market in those securities and that the securities are advertised securities, or

(ii) *as* an off-market dealer[6] who is making a market in those securities or as an officer, employee or agent of such a dealer acting in the course of the dealer's business;[7] or

---

1 s. 1(7), s. 2(3)(*b*), s. 5(1)(*a*). The reference to stock exchanges outside Great Britain makes it impossible to evade the legislation simply by dealing on a foreign stock exchange: the offence would still be committed within the jurisdiction unless the defendant went abroad before giving instructions to his broker or other intermediary (who would also need to be abroad: *cf. Secretary of State for Trade v. Markus* [1976] A.C. 35, *infra* at para. 11.04). Rider (*op. cit.*, at para. 1.10) thinks it "most unlikely" that instructing a broker to deal amounts to counselling or procuring him to do so, but gives no reasons for this view. An insider who instructed a broker to deal on the Stock Exchange would no doubt be charged with dealing rather than counselling and procuring: but the broker would also be dealing ("dealing" includes dealing as principal or agent: s.13(1)) and the insider would therefore be counselling and procuring him to deal. If the deal was to be effected on a foreign stock exchange, the insider would not be guilty of dealing but (provided he was in England or Wales when he gave the instructions) he would still be guilty of counselling and procuring.
2 s. 1(8), s. 2(3)(*c*), s. 5(1)(*b*).
3 *i.e.* securities listed on a recognised stock exchange, or securities in respect of which information indicating the prices at which persons have dealt or were willing to deal in those securities has been published within the previous six months for the purpose of facilitating deals in those securities: s. 12(*c*).
4 *i.e.* a person who (a) holds a licence under s. 3 of the Prevention of Fraud (Investments) Act 1958 (principals' and representatives' licences for dealers in securities), or (b) is a member of a recognised stock exchange or recognised association of dealers in securities within the meaning of that Act, or (c) is an exempted dealer within the meaning of that Act: s. 13(3). An individual deals through an off-market dealer if the latter is a party to the transaction, is an agent for either party to the transaction or is acting as an intermediary in connection with the transaction: s. 13(5).
5 An off-market dealer makes a market in securities if in the course of his business as an off-market dealer he holds himself out both to prospective buyers and to prospective sellers of those securities (other than particular buyers or sellers) as willing to deal in them otherwise than on a recognised stock exchange: s. 13(4)(*b*).
6 An off-market dealer deals in advertised securities not only if he deals in them as defined *supra* at n. 97, but also if he acts as an intermediary in connection with deals in them made by other persons: s. 13(4)(*a*).
7 s. 4(*a*).

(e) counsel or procure any person to deal in those securities in the knowledge (or with reasonable cause to believe) that he would deal in them as in (d) above;[8] or

(f) communicate the information in the knowledge (or with reasonable cause to believe) that it will be used for such dealing or such counselling or procuring.[9]

Prosecutions for these offences may not be brought except by the Secretary of State or by (or with the consent of) the Director of Public Prosecutions.[10]

Exceptions

8.21 The prohibitions set out above are subject to the following exceptions:

(1) A person who is an insider because he is contemplating (or has contemplated) making a take-over offer for the company may deal in the company's securities provided that he does so in the *same capacity* as that in which he is contemplating (or has contemplated) making the offer, *e.g.* for the purpose of building up his holding before making the offer.[11]

(2) A person is not prohibited from doing any particular thing otherwise than with a view to the making of a profit or the avoidance of a loss (whether for himself or another person) by the use of the information in question.[12] A trustee or personal representative (or, where a trustee or personal representative is a body corporate, an individual acting on its behalf) is presumed to be within this exception if he acted on the advice of a person who

(a) appeared to him to be an appropriate person from whom to seek such advice, and

(b) did not appear to him to be prohibited from dealing in the securities in question.[13]

(3) A person is not prohibited from entering a transaction in the course

---

8 s. 4(*b*).

9 s. 4(*c*).

10 s. 8(2).

11 s. 1(5). It is arguable that a side-effect of this exception is to exclude the prohibitions of counselling and procuring and on communicating the information, since the provisions in question (s. 1(7),(8)) apply only to "an individual who is for the time being prohibited . . . from dealing" in the securities: the take-over bidder is not prohibited from dealing, only from dealing in another capacity. It is submitted, however, that for this purpose a person should be regarded as being "prohibited" from dealing not only if he is prohibited altogether from doing so but also if his freedom to do so is in any way curtailed—*i.e.* if he is an insider or a tippee.

12 s. 3(1)(*a*), s. 5(2).

13 s. 7. *Quaere* whether the test here is necessarily subjective, as Rider assumes (*op. cit.* at para. 1.7). Does a person "appear" to be an appropriate person (or a person who is not prohibited from dealing) merely because the trustee or personal representative believes that he is, whether or not there are reasonable grounds for the belief?

of the exercise in good faith of his functions as a liquidator, receiver or trustee in bankruptcy.[14]

(4) A person is not prohibited from doing any particular thing if the information in question

(a) was obtained by him in the course of a business of a jobber[15] in which he was engaged or employed, and

(b) was of a description which it would be reasonable to expect him to obtain in the ordinary course of that business,

and he does that thing in good faith in the course of that business.[16]

(5) With the exception of deals in a company's securities by an individual who is (or at any time in the preceding six months has been) connected with that company, or by his tippee, an individual who has information relating to a particular transaction is not thereby prohibited from doing any thing if he does it in order to facilitate the completion or carrying out of the transaction.[17]

(6) There is a special exception for dealers in the Eurobond market. Where an issue manager[18] for an international bond issue,[19] by virtue of his position, holds information which it would be reasonable to expect him to have obtained in that capacity, he is not prohibited from doing anything in relation to a debenture (or a right to subscribe for, call for or make delivery of a debenture) if

(a) he does it in good faith in connection with that issue not later than three months after the issue date,[20] or (if the issue is not proceeded with) before the decision is taken not to proceed, or

(b) he is making a market in that debenture or right, and he does the thing in question in good faith as a person making a market in that debenture or right.[21]

---

14 s. 3(1)(*b*), s. 5(2).
15 *i.e.* an individual, partnership or company dealing in securities on a recognised stock exchange and recognised by the Council of the Stock Exchange as carrying on the business of a jobber: s. 3(1)(*c*).
16 s. 3(1)(*c*), s. 5(2).
17 s. 3(2).
18 *i.e.* (a) an off-market dealer acting as an agent of the issuing company for the purposes of an international bond issue, or (b) where the issuing company issues or proposes to issue the debentures to an off-market dealer under an arrangement in pursuance of which he is to sell the debentures to other persons, that off-market dealer: s. 15(1)(*c*).
19 *i.e.* an issue of debentures of a company, (a) all of which are offered (or to be offered) by an off-market dealer to persons (whether principals or agents) whose ordinary business includes the buying or selling of debentures, and (b) where the debentures are denominated in sterling, not less than 50% in nominal value of the debentures are or are to be so offered to persons who are neither British citizens, British Dependent Territories citizens nor British Overseas citizens, nor companies incorporated or otherwise formed under the law of any part of the U.K.: s. 15(1)(*a*), (3).
20 *i.e.* the date on which the first of the debentures is issued by the issuing company: s. 15(1)(*b*).
21 s. 6(1).

The exception extends to the officers, employees and agents of such an issue manager.[22] A person within this exception is also exempted (as regards the information in question) from the prohibitions on counselling or procuring persons to deal on a non-recognised stock exchange outside Great Britain, and on communicating the information so as to enable other persons so to deal or to counsel or procure other persons so to deal[23]—even, it would seem, if he does so otherwise than in good faith.[24]

---

22 *Ibid.*
23 s. 6(2).
24 s. 6(2) provides that if, by virtue of s. 6(1), he is not prohibited by s. 1 from doing anything, then he is not prohibited by s. 5 from doing any other thing. In other words, if he is a person to whom s. 6(1) applies, s. 5 does not apply to him at all.

CHAPTER 9
Frauds on Creditors

9.01 Frauds on creditors may be divided into three basic types. Firstly, they may consist simply of incurring debts which the debtor has no intention of paying (*e.g.* the "long firm" fraud) or which he does not expect to be *able* to pay. In both cases a large-scale fraud is likely to involve the use of a company to obtain credit, perhaps an existing company whose suppliers are unaware of a change of ownership; or a subsidiary may be deliberately created with insufficient capital, the parent company not only escaping liability on the subsidiary's insolvency but perhaps even claiming preferential treatment as a secured creditor.[1] Secondly, the fraud may consist in the evasion of debts already incurred (innocently or otherwise), *e.g.* by deception of creditors, by absconding, or by abstracting property out of which the debts might be paid: the practice of directors siphoning off a company's assets, discussed in chapters 4 and 5 above, may well constitute a fraud on the company's creditors rather than, or as well as, its shareholders. Thirdly, there may be sharp practice in the course of insolvency proceedings. The debtor may try to conceal the true state of his finances (*e.g.* by destroying accounts) or act in collusion with some creditors to the detriment of others. Aspersions have often been cast on the integrity of liquidators, particularly where the controllers of the insolvent company immediately set up a new company which buys up the stock and plant of the old one at an undervalue (the "phoenix syndrome").

9.02 Sometimes these frauds will give rise to liability for the offences of general application discussed in previous chapters. Frauds of the first type may involve an offence of obtaining property or services by deception,[2] if it can be argued that the incurring of the debt amounted to a deception as to either the debtor's solvency or his intention to pay. The creditor will presumably have made assumptions as to both, but it may be easier to establish that the latter assumption was induced by the debtor: the mere fact of trading does not in itself imply that the trader is solvent.[3] On the other hand if there *is* a representation of solvency, it will be

---

1 See *Re Southard & Co. Ltd* [1979] 1 W.L.R. 1198 at p. 1208, *per* Templeman L.J.
2 *Supra,* para. 3.02ff., 3.25ff.
3 *Parker and Bulteel* (1916) 25 Cox 145 at p. 149, *per* Avory J.

comparatively easy to disprove, whereas it may be hard to establish that the defendant never intended to pay. Dishonesty can often be disguised as misplaced optimism. Where there is deception in respect of an existing debt, the appropriate charge will probably be one of evading liability by deception.[4] The misapplication of company assets, or of funds to which a creditor is specifically entitled, may constitute theft.[5] A scheme to defraud creditors may amount to a conspiracy to defraud at common law,[6] even if the debtor is not yet insolvent[7] and even if no creditor yet has more than an unliquidated claim;[8] but normally such a scheme would involve a substantive offence and could not therefore be charged at common law.[9] There are a number of statutory offences specifically directed at frauds on creditors, and it is to these that we now turn. We consider first the offence of fraudulent trading by a company, next various offences relating to insolvency (both corporate and individual), and finally the offence of making off without payment where payment on the spot is expected.

FRAUDULENT TRADING

9.03   Section 458 of the Companies Act 1985[10] provides:

> "If any business of a company is carried on with intent to defraud creditors of the company or creditors of any other person, or for any fraudulent purpose, every person who was knowingly a party to the carrying on of the business in that manner is liable to imprisonment or a fine, or both. . ."

The maximum term of imprisonment on conviction on indictment is seven years.[11] It will be noted that the offence can be committed only where the fraudulent enterprise is a company: the Committee on Insolvency Law and Practice (the Cork Committee) recommended the creation of a parallel offence of fraudulent trading by individuals,[12] but this proposal has not yet been adopted. Section 458's predecessor, section 332(3) of the Companies Act 1948, appeared in the part of the Act concerned with winding up, and in a section primarily concerned with the personal liability of directors and others where fraudulent trading came to light in the course of winding up. In the light of this context it was held that the offence under section 332(3), though not expressly so restricted,

---

4   *Supra,* para. 3.29ff.
5   *Supra,* ch. 4.
6   *Potter* [1953] 1 All E.R. 296; but *cf. Zemmel and Melik* [1985] Crim.L.R. 213.
7   *Hall* (1858) 1 F. & F. 33; *Heymann* (1873) L.R. 8 Q.B. 102 at p. 105. *per* Blackburn J.
8   *Seillon* [1982] Crim.L.R. 676.
9   *Infra,* para. 12.34ff.
10   Replacing Companies Act 1948 s. 332(3) with effect from 1 July 1985.
11   Sch. 24. On summary conviction the offence carries six months' imprisonment or a fine of the statutory maximum or both.
12   Cmnd. 8558 at para. 1890.

could not be charged unless the company was in liquidation.[13] This restriction was removed by section 96 of the Companies Act 1981, and section 458 of the consolidating 1985 Act now provides:

> "This applies whether or not the company has been, or is in the course of being, wound up."

Section 96 of the 1981 Act came into force on 22 December 1981,[14] and the question has arisen of whether it is retrospective in its effect: *i.e.* whether fraudulent trading before that date may now be the subject of a prosecution although the company in question has not gone into liquidation. In *Redmond and Redmond*[15] the Court of Appeal, overruling the view of a trial judge in *Sutcliffe-Williams and Gaskell*,[16] held that section 96 is indeed retrospective. It does not render unlawful acts which were formerly lawful, but merely removes a condition precedent to a prosecution which formerly existed. Hence it does apply to acts committed before it came into force.

Carrying on business

9.04 In a prosecution under section 458 it must first be shown that the company was carrying on business. In *Re Murray-Watson Ltd*[17] Oliver J. said:

> "[Section 458] is aimed at the carrying on of a business. . . and not at the execution of individual transactions in the course of carrying on that business. I do not think that the words 'carried on' can be treated as synonymous with 'carried out', nor can I read the words 'any business' as synonymous with 'any transaction or dealing'. The director of a company dealing in second-hand motor cars who wilfully misrepresents the age and capabilities of a vehicle is, no doubt, a fraudulent rascal, but I do not think that he can be said to be carrying on the company's business for a fraudulent purpose, although no doubt he carries out a particular business transaction in a fraudulent manner."

In *Re Gerald Cooper Chemicals Ltd*[18] Templeman J. suggested that the reason why Oliver J.'s hypothetical car dealer was not guilty of fraudulent trading was not that there was only one transaction but that he intended to defraud a customer, not a creditor. His Lordship held that the section could apply even if there was only one transaction:

> "In the present case, the Cooper companies were carrying on the business of selling indigo. In my judgement, they carried on that business with intent

13 *D.P.P. v. Schildkamp* [1971] A.C. 1.
14 (1981) S.I. no. 1684.
15 [1984] Crim.L.R. 292.
16 [1983] Crim.L.R. 255.
17 6 April 1977, unreported.
18 [1978] Ch. 262.

to defraud creditors if they accepted deposits knowing that they could not supply the indigo and were insolvent. They were carrying on business with intent to defraud creditors as soon as they accepted one deposit knowing that they could not supply the indigo and would not repay the deposit. It does not matter for the purposes of section [458] that only one creditor was defrauded, and by one transaction, provided that the transaction can properly be described as a fraud on a creditor perpetrated in the course of carrying on business."[19]

And in *Re Sarflax Ltd*[20] Oliver J. conceded that his observations in *Re Murray-Watson Ltd* might require some qualification in the light of Templeman J.'s decision.[21] He went on to hold that, whether or not the "carrying on of. . . business" implied a course of conduct rather than just one transaction, it was not restricted to the carrying on of trading activities and could include the collection and distribution of a company's assets after it had ceased trading.

Fraudulent purpose

9.05   The company's business must be carried on either with intent to defraud creditors (whether the company's or someone else's) or for some other fraudulent purpose. It has been said that the section creates two offences.[22] However, it is not clear how much the latter alternative adds to the former. It may be that they should be construed *ejusdem generis,* and that an intent to defraud someone other than a creditor is not necessarily sufficient. Thus Oliver J., in the passage from his judgment in *Re Murray-Watson Ltd* quoted above, said that the car dealer who fraudulently misdescribed a vehicle was not carrying on business for a fraudulent purpose. Possibly he meant that the section could not apply to a single transaction; but Templeman J., who in *Re Gerald Cooper Chemicals Ltd* rejected this limitation, appeared to agree with Oliver J.'s conclusion.

"In the example given by Oliver J. the dealer was carrying on the business of selling motor cars. He did not carry on that business with intent to defraud creditors if he told lies every time he sold a motor car to a customer or only told one lie when he sold one motor car to one single customer. When the dealer told a lie, he perpetrated a fraud on a customer, but he did not intend to defraud a creditor. It is true that the defrauded customer had a right to sue the dealer for damages, and to the extent of the damages was a contingent creditor, but the dealer did nothing to make it impossible for the customer, once he had become a creditor, to recover the sum due to him as a creditor."[23]

19   At p. 267f.
20   [1979] Ch. 592.
21   At p. 598.
22   *Inman* [1967] 1 Q.B. 140.
23   [1978] Ch. 262 at p. 267.

Certainly the dealer intends to defraud, and if the sale amounts to the carrying on of business, then he is surely carrying on business for a fraudulent purpose in the ordinary sense of those words. Nevertheless it is submitted with respect that these dicta are correct in effectively confining the section to insolvency frauds, and that its use as a general purpose offence, embracing any form of fraudulent conduct on the part of a corporate enterprise, is misconceived. It can hardly be supposed that if Parliament intended to create such an offence, wider in scope than any substantive offence of fraud which may be committed by an individual, it would bury it in the provisions on winding up. The fact that the section no longer appears among those provisions is beside the point, since the 1985 Act is purely a consolidation. Section 96 of the 1981 Act[24] removed a procedural bar to a prosecution but there are no grounds for supposing that it altered the meaning of the words "or for any fraudulent purpose". This narrow interpretation does not necessarily render those words redundant. For example, a person who has a claim for an unliquidated sum is not strictly speaking a creditor, and it has been held that an intent to avoid satisfying such a claim is not therefore an intent to defraud a creditor;[25] but it can certainly constitute a "fraudulent purpose" on even the narrowest interpretation of those words.[26]

9.06 In a typical case of fraudulent trading the company will have incurred liabilities which either its controllers had no intention of meeting or which it would obviously be unable to meet. In the latter case it may be a question of degree whether the company's prospects were so bad as to make it fraudulent to go on incurring credit. Clearly it is not fraudulent to incur a debt during a temporary cash-flow crisis which will merely entail a slight delay in payment. In *Re White and Osmond (Parkstone) Ltd*[27] Buckley J. appeared to go further and to suggest that the directors must realise the company will *never* be able to pay. This suggestion was however rejected by the Court of Appeal in *Grantham*,[28] where it was held to be sufficient if the directors knew that the company would be unable to pay the debt when it fell due or shortly thereafter. If it is no defence that the debt would be paid eventually, it may be asked why even a *short* delay is not sufficient: *any* delay represents a loss to the creditor in that he is deprived of the use of his money.[29] There are two possible answers. One is

---

24   *Supra*, para. 9.03.
25   *Hopkins and Ferguson* [1896] 1 Q.B. 652; but *cf. Seillon* [1982] Crim.L.R. 676, *infra* para. 9.10.
26   This appears to have been assumed in *Re Sarflax Ltd* [1979] Ch. 592, *infra* para. 9.07.
27   30 June 1960, unreported.
28   [1984] Q.B. 675.
29   The principle that it is fraudulent to deceive another into taking a financial risk (*supra* para. 1.35), though relied upon by the court, is not strictly relevant. The directors *intend* to cause this loss.

that if the delay is expected to be short there is no deception, because debts are not normally paid at the very instant when they become due; it might therefore be unreasonable for the creditor to assume that the debtor *intended* to pay the debt at once, or for that matter that he would be *able* to. The alternative explanation is that, for much the same reasons, if there *is* a deception, it is not dishonest. Dishonesty is an essential element of fraud in general[30] and of fraudulent trading in particular,[31] and a jury will hardly regard the incurring of a debt as dishonest unless the delay in paying it was likely to be substantial. On the other hand the requirement of dishonesty is unlikely to present difficulty if there was no prospect of the company being able to pay in the foreseeable future or (*a fortiori*) at all. Maugham J., who recognised that dishonesty was essential,[32] nevertheless expressed the distinctly moderate view that

> " . . . if a company continues to carry on business and to incur debts at a time when there is to the knowledge of the directors no reasonable prospect of the creditors ever receiving payment of their debts, it is, in general, a proper inference that the company is carrying on business with intent to defraud."[33]

But of course the jury must not be told that this is so as a matter of law. Ultimately the issue of dishonesty is for them.[34]

9.07 Fraudulent trading may consist not only in the incurring of fresh liabilities but also in the evasion of existing ones. For an insolvent company to dispose of its assets for inadequate consideration would clearly be a fraud on its creditors. However, the payment of a genuine debt to one creditor is not a fraud on the others. If made within six months before the commencement of the company's winding up, such a payment might be deemed to be a fraudulent preference (and therefore invalid) by virtue of section 615(1) of the Companies Act 1985;[35] but it is not in itself "fraudulent" for the purposes of section 458. Subject to section 615(1) and its equivalent in the bankruptcy legislation,[36] a debtor may pay his creditors in any order he likes.[37] It seems that this is so even if he has a direct financial interest in preferring one creditor to another. In *Re Sarflax Ltd*[38] a company was faced with a claim for damages by an Italian company. It passed a resolution to cease trading and applied its assets to the payment of its other creditors, chief among them being its

---

30 *Supra,* para. 1.04ff.
31 *Cox and Hodges* (1982) 75 Cr.App. R. 291.
32 *Re Patrick & Lyon Ltd* [1933] 1 Ch. 786 at p. 790; *supra* para. 1.16.
33 *Re William C. Leitch Bros Ltd* [1932] 2 Ch. 71 at p. 77.
34 *Supra,* para. 1.19.
35 Replacing Companies Act 1948 s. 320 with effect from 1 July 1985.
36 Bankruptcy Act 1914 s. 44.
37 *Glegg v. Bromley* [1912] 3 K.B. 474 at p. 485, *per* Fletcher Moulton L.J.
38 [1979] Ch. 592.

parent company. This left virtually nothing with which to meet the Italian company's claim. The liquidator sought a declaration under section 332 of the Companies Act 1948 that the company's business had been carried on with intent to defraud the Italian company and that the directors were therefore personally liable for the Italian company's loss. Oliver J. struck out the summons as disclosing no reasonable cause of action. It made no difference that one of the creditors who were paid in full was the parent company, in which the directors of the insolvent company held the majority shareholding. They were under no duty to put the other creditors first, or even to refrain from putting them second. Oliver J. concluded:

> "It is unnecessary for me to decide, and I do not decide, that there may not be circumstances of a very peculiar nature involving preferential payments from which the intention required by section 332 could be inferred. What is alleged here—and it is all that the liquidator relies on—is the bare fact of preference and . . . the proposition that that, *per se*, constitutes fraud within the meaning of the section is not one which is, in my judgment, arguable with any prospect of success."[39]

But if the circumstances of *Sarflax* itself did not render the preference fraudulent, it is hard to imagine what circumstances would.

Implication in fraudulent purpose

9.08 Where a company has been carrying on business fraudulently, the offence is committed by any person who is knowingly a party to the fraud. Clearly the defendant must either himself be in control of the company or must be aware that those who are in control are carrying on business with intent to defraud. Where he is not himself controlling the company's activities, he is not a party to them unless he participates or at least concurs in them;[40] and it has been said that this involves the taking by him of some positive steps.[41] Thus mere acquiescence on the part of the company's secretary and financial adviser is not sufficient.[42] Acquiescence on the part of a director, however, might be a different matter: the directors, unlike the secretary, are responsible for the management of the company. For the purposes of the law of secondary criminal liability a person may be a party to an offence merely by failing to intervene so as to prevent the offence where he has the authority to do so.[43] A director who turned a blind eye to the fraudulent activities of his colleagues might, by analogy, be said to be a party to the fraud; in any

---

39 At p. 612.
40 *Re Maidstone Buildings Provisions Ltd* [1971] 1 W.L.R. 1085.
41 *Ibid.* at p. 1092, *per* Pennycuick V.-C.
42 *Ibid.*
43 *Tuck v. Robson* [1970] 1 W.L.R. 741.

event, if he were not guilty as a principal offender he would presumably be an accessory. Even a creditor may be a party to a fraud on another creditor, *e.g.* where he accepts in payment money which he knows to have been obtained by carrying on business fraudulently for the purpose of making the payment:[44] "... a man who warms himself with the fire of fraud cannot complain if he is singed."[45]

INSOLVENCY OFFENCES

Offences in winding up

False declaration of solvency

9.09   Section 577(1) of the Companies Act 1985[46] provides that where it is proposed to wind up a company voluntarily a majority of the directors may make a statutory declaration of solvency, stating that they have made a full inquiry into the company's affairs and have formed the opinion that the company will be able to pay its debts in full within such period (not exceeding twelve months from the commencement of the winding up) as may be specified in the declaration. The significance of the declaration is that, if it is made, the winding up will be a *members'* voluntary winding up; otherwise it will be a *creditors'* voluntary winding up.[47] Under section 577(4) it is an offence, punishable on conviction on indictment with two years' imprisonment or a fine or both,[48] for a director to make the declaration without having reasonable grounds for the opinion that the company will be able to pay its debts in full within the period specified. There is no requirement that he should know the true position: negligence is sufficient. Moreover, it is provided that if the company is wound up in pursuance of a resolution passed within five weeks after the making of the declaration, but its debts are not paid or provided for in full within the period specified in the declaration, it is to be presumed unless the contrary is shown that the director did not have reasonable grounds for his opinion.[49]

Concealment or disposal of property

9.10   When a company is ordered to be wound up by the court, or passes a resolution for voluntary winding up, an offence is deemed to have been committed if:

---

44   *Re Gerald Cooper Chemicals Ltd* [1978] Ch. 262.
45   At p. 268, *per* Templeman J.
46   Replacing Companies Act 1948 s. 283(1) with effect from 1 July 1985.
47   s. 578.
48   Sch. 24. On summary conviction the offence carries six months' imprisonment or a fine of the statutory maximum or both.
49   s. 577(5).

(1) a person who was at that time an officer[50] of the company, with intent to defraud its creditors, has

(a) made (or caused to be made) any gift or transfer of, or charge on, the company's property,[51] or

(b) caused or connived at the levying of any execution against such property, or

(c) concealed or removed any part of such property since (or within two months before) the date of any unsatisfied judgment or order for the payment of money obtained against the company;[52] or

(2) a past or present officer of the company (including a shadow director, past or present),[53] within the twelve months immediately preceding the commencement of the winding up or at any time thereafter, has

(a) concealed any part of the company's property to the value of £120[54] or more, or

(b) concealed any debt due to or from the company, or

(c) fraudulently removed any part of the company's property to the value of £120[54] or more, or

(d) pawned, pledged or disposed of any property of the company which was obtained on credit and has not been paid for (unless the pawning, pledging or disposal was in the ordinary way of the company's business).[55]

In the case of the offences under (1) and (2)(c), fraud is an essential ingredient and must be proved by the prosecution.[56] Under (2)(a), (b) and (d) it is for the defence to prove that there was *no* intent to defraud,[57] though all the other elements of the offence must still be proved by the prosecution.[58] In view of this reversal of the burden of proof it is curious that the offences under (2) are punishable on conviction on indictment with seven years' imprisonment, but those under (1) with only two years.[59] What constitutes an intent to defraud has already been

---

50 Including a director, manager or secretary: s. 744.

51 The cancellation of a debt owed to the company is not a transfer of its property: *Davies* [1955] 1 Q.B. 71.

52 Companies Act 1985 s. 625, replacing Companies Act 1948 s. 330 with effect from 1 July 1985.

53 s. 624(3). A shadow director is a person in accordance with whose directions or instructions the directors of the company are accustomed to act, unless they act merely on advice given by him in a professional capacity: s. 741(2).

54 This sum may be altered by regulations under s. 664: s. 624(7).

55 Companies Act 1985 s. 624(1)(*a*), (*b*), (*f*), replacing Companies Act 1948 s. 328(1)(*d*), (*e*), (*o*). Where a person is guilty of an offence under (2)(d), an offence (similarly punishable) is committed by any person who takes the property in pawn or pledge, or otherwise receives it, knowing it to be pawned, pledged or disposed of in circumstances constituting the offence: s. 624(5).

56 *Cf. Lusty* [1964] 1 W.L.R. 606.

57 s. 624(4)(*a*).

58 *Cf. R. v. Governor of Brixton Prison, ex p. Shure* [1926] 1 K.B. 127.

59 s. 625(2), s. 624(6), Sch. 24. On summary conviction all the offences carry six months' imprisonment or a fine of the statutory maximum or both.

considered.[60] It might consist in an intent either to cause loss to another (*e.g.* a creditor[61] or shareholder) or to cause the liquidator (or any person concerned in the resolution of the company's affairs) to act in a way in which he would not act if he knew the true position.[62] But what is required under (1) above is not merely an intent to defraud but an intent to defraud *creditors*. A person with an unliquidated claim against the company is not strictly a creditor, and it has therefore been held that an intent to defeat such a claim is not an intent to defraud a creditor.[63] This reasoning appears to overlook the fact that intent relates to the future. In principle it is immaterial whether any creditors are yet in existence: it should be sufficient if there is an intention at some future date to defraud persons who will by that time be creditors.[64]

Falsification of documents

9.11 The general offences relating to the falsification of documents, discussed in chapter 6 above, are supplemented by specific offences which apply only in the context of winding up. Section 627(1) of the Companies Act 1985[65] provides:

> "When a company is being wound up, an officer or contributory of the company commits an offence if he destroys, mutilates, alters or falsifies any books, papers or securities, or makes or is privy to the making of any false or fraudulent entry in any register, book of account or document belonging to the company with intent to defraud or deceive any person."

The offence is punishable on conviction on indictment with seven years' imprisonment or a fine or both.[66] The interpretation section provides that, unless the contrary intention appears, "books and papers" includes accounts, deeds, writings and documents;[67] the first of these terms, at least, seems wide enough to cover a computer-based accounting system. Whether the same can be said of the phrase "register, book of account or document" is dubious, though it may be that a computer file is a "document".[68] The drafting of the section does not make it clear whether the phrase "belonging to the company" governs "books, papers or securities" as well as "register, book of account or document", but it is submitted that it must do so: otherwise the offence might be committed by the falsification of papers which have nothing to do with the company

---

60 *Supra,* ch. 1.
61 But not, it seems, simply by paying another creditor: *supra,* para. 9.07.
62 *Welham v. D.P.P.* [1961] A.C. 103, *supra* para. 1.40.
63 *Hopkins and Ferguson* [1896] 1 Q.B. 652.
64 *Cf. Seillon* [1982] Crim.L.R. 676.
65 Replacing Companies Act 1948 s. 329 with effect from 1 July 1985.
66 s. 627(2), Sch. 24. On summary conviction the offence carries six months' imprisonment or a fine of the statutory maximum or both.
67 s. 744.
68 *Cf. supra,* para. 3.41.

at all. If this is the correct reading, it follows that the "intent to defraud or deceive" is required on a charge of the destruction (*etc.*) of books, papers or securities, and not merely on one of making false or fraudulent entries. If "belonging to the company" applies to both limbs of the subsection it could scarcely be argued that the succeeding phrase "with intent to defraud or deceive" applies only to the second. An intent to deceive is sufficient but not essential. Thus if the defendant destroys records in order to suppress evidence of dubious transactions, it might be difficult to argue that he intends to deceive others into believing that those transactions did not take place; but fraud does not require deception, and a dishonest intention to avoid the consequences of his misconduct would probably suffice.[69]

9.12   An offence is also deemed to have been committed if a company is ordered to be wound up by the court or passes a resolution for voluntary winding up, and, within the twelve months immediately preceding the commencement of the winding up or at any time thereafter, a past or present officer of the company (including a shadow director, past or present)[70] has

    (a) concealed, destroyed, mutilated or falsified any book or paper affecting or relating to the company's property or affairs, or

    (b) made any false entry in any such book or paper, or

    (c) fraudulently parted with, altered or made any omission in any document affecting or relating to the company's property or affairs, or

    (d) been privy to the doing by others of any of the things mentioned in (a) to (c) above.[71]

These offences are punishable on conviction on indictment with seven years' imprisonment or a fine or both.[72] Under (a) and (b), and on a charge under (d) of being privy to the actions in (a) or (b), there is no need to prove fraud, but it is a defence for the defendant to prove that he had no intent to conceal the state of affairs of the company or to defeat the law.[73] This last phrase is somewhat obscure and it may be doubted whether it is a true alternative: if a defendant has done one of the things set out in (a) or (b), but has proved that he did not intend to conceal the state of the company's affairs, it is hard to see how he could be convicted on the grounds that he has not disproved an intent to defeat the law.

69   *Cf. Welham v. D.P.P.* [1961] A.C. 103, *supra* para. 1.40.
70   s. 624(3).
71   Companies Act 1985 s. 624(1)(*c*)—(*e*), (2), replacing Companies Act 1948 s. 328(1)(*i*)—(*k*) with effect from 1 July 1985.
72   s. 624(6), Sch. 24. On summary conviction they carry six months' imprisonment or a fine of the statutory maximum or both.
73   s. 624(4)(*b*).

Deception of creditors

9.13 Section 629(1) of the Companies Act 1985[74] provides that, where a company is being wound up (whether by or under the supervision of the court or voluntarily), a past or present officer of the company (including a shadow director, past or present)[75] commits an offence if he makes any false representation or commits any other fraud for the purpose of obtaining the consent of the company's creditors (or any of them) to an agreement with reference to the company's affairs or to the winding up. If the company is not yet being wound up at the time of the false representation or fraud, the officer is deemed to have committed an offence as soon as the winding up begins.[76] The offence is punishable on conviction on indictment with seven years' imprisonment or a fine or both.[77] It may be that in this context the term "fraud" should be construed not in its ordinary sense but as *ejusdem generis* with "false representation" and therefore confined to deception. This would not make it redundant if, as has been argued above,[78] it is possible to deceive without making a false representation. Even on this interpretation the word "fraud" would presumably retain its normal implication of dishonesty. In the case of a false representation, however, there is no express requirement of fraud or dishonesty. It has been held in the context of the corresponding provision of the bankruptcy legislation[79] that "false" means "fraudulent",[80] but this probably means only that the defendant must have no genuine belief in the truth of the representation: it does not follow that he must have acted dishonestly. Even proof that the representation was *not* dishonest does not appear to be a defence.

Material omissions in statements

9.14 Under section 628 of the Companies Act 1985[81] an offence is committed by a past or present officer of a company (including a shadow director, past or present)[82] if

(a) when the company is being wound up (whether by or under the supervision of the court or voluntarily), he makes any material omission in any statement relating to the company's affairs,[83] or

(b) he makes any such omission and the company is subsequently

---

74 Replacing Companies Act 1948 s. 328(1)(*p*) with effect from 1 July 1985.
75 s. 629(2).
76 s. 629(1)(*b*).
77 s. 629(3), Sch. 24. On summary conviction it carries six months' imprisonment or a fine of the statutory maximum or both.
78 Para. 2.06ff.
79 Now Bankruptcy Act 1914 s. 154(1)(*16*), *infra* para. 9.21.
80 *Cherry* (1871) 12 Cox 32.
81 Replacing Companies Act 1948 s. 328(1)(*f*) with effect from 1 July 1985.
82 s. 628(3).
83 s. 628(1).

ordered to be wound up by the court or passes a resolution for voluntary winding up.[84]

The offence is punishable on conviction on indictment with seven years' imprisonment or a fine or both.[85] It is not necessary to prove that the omission was fraudulent, or even deliberate, but it is a defence for the defendant to prove that he had no intent to defraud.[86] On a literal reading the offence would be remarkably wide: it is not confined to written statements, and it applies to mere omissions rather than positive misstatements. An omission is material if the fact omitted is material. Yet it can hardly be the law that an officer of a company being wound up must not make any statement about the company's affairs unless he includes everything which his hearer would regard as material. It is submitted that the offence can be kept within reasonable bounds only by construing "material omission" to mean an omission which has the effect of rendering what *is* said misleading.

Other misconduct

9.15 Under section 626 of the Companies Act 1985[87] an offence is committed if a company is being wound up (whether by or under the supervision of the court or voluntarily), and a past or present officer of the company (including a shadow director, past or present):[88]

(a) does not to the best of his knowledge and belief fully and truly discover to the liquidator all the company's property, and how and to whom and for what consideration and when the company disposed of any part of that property (except such part as has been disposed of in the ordinary way of the company's business), or

(b) does not deliver up to the liquidator (or as he directs) all such part of the company's property as is in his custody or under his control, and which he is required by law to deliver up, or

(c) does not deliver up to the liquidator (or as he directs) all books and papers in his custody or under his control belonging to the company and which he is required by law to deliver up, or

(d) knowing or believing that a false debt has been proved by any person in the winding up, fails for the period of a month to inform the liquidator of it, or

(e) after the commencement of the winding up, prevents the production

---

84 s.628(2).
85 s. 628(5), Sch. 24. On summary conviction it carries six months' imprisonment or a fine of the statutory maximum or both.
86 s. 628(4).
87 Replacing Companies Act 1948 s. 328(1)(*a*)—(*c*), (*g*), (*h*), (*l*) with effect from 1 July 1985.
88 s. 626(3).

of any book or paper affecting or relating to the company's property or affairs, or

(f) attempts to account for any part of the company's property by fictitious losses or expenses, or has so attempted at any meeting of the company's creditors within the twelve months immediately preceding the commencement of the winding up.

These offences are punishable on conviction on indictment with seven years' imprisonment or a fine or both.[89] None of them require proof of fraud; but it is a defence for the defendant to prove, in the case of (a) to (c) that he had no intent to defraud, and in the case of (e) that he had no intent to conceal the state of affairs of the company or to defeat the law.[90]

Offences in bankruptcy

9.16 Fraudulent conduct on the part of an individual insolvent may constitute one or more of a variety of offences under the Bankruptcy Act 1914 (as amended) or other legislation.[91] Most of these offences correspond closely to the offences of corporate insolvency already considered, and for further discussion the reader is referred to the appropriate passage in the preceding section. There are however some additional offences which have no counterpart in the provisions relating to corporate insolvency.

Concealment or disposal of property

9.17 An offence, punishable on conviction on indictment with one year's imprisonment,[92] is committed by any person who, with intent to defraud his creditors (or any of them),

(a) makes (or causes to be made) any gift, delivery or transfer of, or charge on, his property, or
(b) conceals or removes any part of his property after, or within two months before, the date of any unsatisfied judgment or order for payment of money obtained against him.

These offences are created in virtually identical terms by both the Debtors Act 1869[93] and the Bankruptcy Act 1914,[94] the main difference being that

---

89 s. 626(5), Sch. 24. On summary conviction they carry six months' imprisonment or a fine of the statutory maximum or both.
90 s.626(4). On intent to defeat the law, *cf. supra* para. 9.12.
91 Chapter VII of Part III of the Insolvency Bill 1985 would restate most of these offences with minor amendments and revised penalties.
92 On summary conviction the offence carries six months' imprisonment if charged under the Debtors Act 1869 but twelve months if charged under the Bankruptcy Act 1914 (s. 164(1)).
93 s. 13.
94 s. 156.

the offences under the Bankruptcy Act are committed only if the defendant has been adjudged bankrupt or a receiving order has been made in respect of his estate. It is not entirely clear whether the offence is deemed to have been committed if a receiving order is made *after* the defendant has done one of the things specified; the Cork Committee recommended making it clear that it is immaterial when the receiving order is made.[95] For the purposes of the Bankruptcy Act offence under (a) above, it is expressly declared ("for the removal of doubts") that a person is deemed to make a transfer of or charge on his property if he causes or connives at the levying of any execution against his property.[96] Probably the same applies in the case of the Debtors Act.

9.18 A person who has been adjudged bankrupt, or in respect of whose estate a receiving order has been made, is also deemed to have committed an offence under the Bankruptcy Act 1914 if:

(a) within a period of twelve months ending with the presentation of a bankruptcy petition by or against him, or at any time thereafter, he has

  (i) concealed any part of his property to the value of £120 or more, or

  (ii) concealed any debt due to or from him, or

  (iii) fraudulently removed any part of his property to the value of £120 or more;[97] or if

(b) within a period of twelve months ending with the presentation of a bankruptcy petition by or against him (or the making of a receiving order under section 107 of the Act), or after the presentation of a bankruptcy petition but before the making of a receiving order, he has pawned, pledged or disposed of any property (otherwise than in the ordinary way of his trade, if any) which he obtained on credit and has not paid for.[98]

The offences under (a) are punishable on conviction on indictment with two years' imprisonment,[99] that under (b) with five years.[1] The offence under (a)(iii) requires proof of fraud;[2] the rest do not, but it is a defence for the defendant to prove that he had no intent to defraud.

---

95   Cmnd. 8558 at para. 1886. The Insolvency Bill 1985 would make this point clear.
96   Bankruptcy (Amendment) Act 1926 s. 6.
97   s. 154(1)(*4*), (*5*), as amended by Insolvency Act 1976 Sch. 1.
98   s. 154(1)(*15*). Where a person is guilty of this offence, an offence punishable with seven years' imprisonment is committed by any person who takes the property in pawn or pledge, or otherwise receives it, knowing it to be pawned, pledged or disposed of in circumstances constituting the offence: s. 154(3).
99   s. 164(1). On summary conviction they carry twelve months' imprisonment.
1   s. 154(2). On summary conviction it carries twelve months' imprisonment.
2   *Lusty* [1964] 1 W.L.R. 606. Under the Insolvency Bill 1985 the burden of proof would be reversed as in the case of the other offences.

Absconding with property

9.19   Under section 159 of the Bankruptcy Act 1914, as amended,[3] an offence (punishable on conviction on indictment with two years' imprisonment)[4] is committed by a person who has been adjudged bankrupt, or in respect of whose estate a receiving order has been made, and who, within a period of six months ending with the presentation of a bankruptcy petition by or against him or at any time thereafter, has left England and taken with him any part of his property (to the amount of £250 or more) which ought by law to be divided amongst his creditors, or has attempted or made preparations to do so. It is a defence for him to prove that he had no intent to defraud.

Falsification of documents

9.20   A person who has been adjudged bankrupt, or in respect of whose estate a receiving order has been made, is guilty of an offence if, within a period of twelve months[5] ending with the presentation of a bankruptcy petition by or against him, or at any time thereafter, he has

(a) concealed, destroyed, mutilated or falsified any book or document affecting or relating to his property or affairs, or

(b) made any false entry in any such book or document, or

(c) fraudulently parted with, altered or made any omission in any such document, or

(d) been privy to any of the actions in (a) to (c).[6]

The offences are punishable on conviction on indictment with two years' imprisonment.[7] In the case of the actions under (c) (or being privy to such actions) fraud must be proved;[8] in the other cases it is a defence if the defendant proves that he had no intent to conceal the state of his affairs or to defeat the law.[9]

Deception of creditors

9.21   A person who has been adjudged bankrupt, or in respect of whose estate a receiving order has been made, commits an offence (punishable on conviction on indictment with two years' imprisonment)[10] if he is guilty of any false representation or other fraud for the purpose of obtaining the consent of his creditors (or any of them) to an agreement

---

3   Insolvency Act 1976 Sch. 1.
4   s. 164(1). On summary conviction it carries twelve months' imprisonment.
5   In the case of the books of account required by s. 158 (*infra* para. 9.24), the period is extended to two years: s. 158(4).
6   s. 154(1)(*9*)—(*11*).
7   s. 164(1). On summary conviction they carry twelve months' imprisonment.
8   The Insolvency Bill 1985 would reverse the burden of proof as in the other cases.
9   *Cf. supra*, para. 9.12.
10   s. 164(1). On summary conviction it carries twelve months' imprisonment.

with reference to his affairs or to his bankruptcy.[11] The offence corresponds to that under section 629 of the Companies Act 1985.[12] The Cork Committee expressed the view that it was not clear whether the offence was limited to conduct prior to the bankruptcy or extended to conduct after it.[13] With respect, it seems entirely clear that conduct after the bankruptcy is covered: what is debatable is the case of conduct before it. In any event the Committee recommended that the offence should extend to both.[14]

Material omissions in statements

9.22 A person who has been adjudged bankrupt, or in respect of whose estate a receiving order has been made, is guilty of an offence (punishable on conviction on indictment with two years' imprisonment)[15] if he makes any material omission in any statement relating to his affairs, unless he proves that he had no intent to defraud.[16] The question of what constitutes a material omission is considered above in relation to the corresponding offence under section 628 of the Companies Act 1985.[17]

Other misconduct in relation to bankruptcy proceedings

9.23 A person who has been adjudged bankrupt, or in respect of whose estate a receiving order has been made, is guilty of an offence (punishable on conviction on indictment with two years' imprisonment)[18] if he

(a) does not to the best of his knowledge and belief fully and truly discover to the trustee[19] all his property, real and personal, and how and to whom and for what consideration and when he disposed of any part thereof (except such part as has been disposed of in the ordinary way of his trade, if any, or laid out in the ordinary expense of his family), or

(b) does not deliver up to the trustee (or as he directs) all such part of his real and personal property as is in his custody or under his control, and which he is required by law to deliver up, or

(c) does not deliver up to the trustee (or as he directs) all books, documents, papers and writings in his custody or under his control relating to his property or affairs, or

---

11 s. 154(1)(*16*).
12 *Supra,* para. 9.13.
13 Cmnd. 8558 at para. 1884.
14 The Insolvency Bill 1985 would implement this proposal.
15 s. 164(1). On summary conviction it carries twelve months' imprisonment.
16 s. 154(1)(*6*).
17 *Supra,* para. 9.14.
18 s. 164(1). On summary conviction these offences carry twelve months' imprisonment.
19 *i.e.* the official receiver of his estate or the trustee administering it for the benefit of his creditors: s. 154(1).

(d) knowing or believing that a false debt has been proved by any person under the bankruptcy, fails for the period of a month to inform the trustee thereof, or

(e) after the presentation of a bankruptcy petition by or against him, prevents the production of any book, document, paper or writing affecting or relating to his property or affairs, or

(f) after the presentation of a bankruptcy petition by or against him, or at any meeting of his creditors within the twelve months before such presentation, attempts to account for any part of his property by fictitious losses or expenses.[20]

It is a defence for the defendant to prove, in the case of (a) to (c) that he had no intent to defraud, and in the case of (e) that he had no intent to conceal the state of his affairs or to defeat the law.[21]

Failure to keep proper accounts

9.24   For an individual trader, unlike a company,[22] it is not an offence in itself to fail to keep proper books of account; but it becomes an offence if he subsequently becomes insolvent. The justification for this offence is not only that the absence of proper accounts may conceal improper transactions which might otherwise be revealed, but also that it may itself be a factor contributing to the insolvency. The Cork Committee pointed out:

> "In all insolvencies of substance, a crucial element contributing to the collapse is the wilful—or at least grossly negligent—failure of the insolvent to have kept proper books of account, or a refusal on his part to inspect them or to believe what they reveal or what he is told about them."[23]

Brett M.R. once went as far as to say:

> "In my opinion, the not keeping of books is one of the greatest offences which can be committed by a trader. . . You may be almost certain that a trader who does not keep books will sooner or later become a bankrupt."[24]

9.25   Under section 158(1) of the Bankruptcy Act 1914 (as amended)[25] an offence is committed by a person who has been adjudged bankrupt, or in respect of whose estate a receiving order has been made, if

(a) he was engaged in any trade or business during any period in the two years immediately preceding the date of the presentation of the

---

20   s. 154(1)(*1*)—(*3*), (*7*), (*8*), (*12*).
21   *Cf. supra,* para. 9.12.
22   *Cf. supra,* para. 6.61.
23   Cmnd. 8558 at para. 217.
24   *Re Wallace, ex p. Campbell* (1885) 15 Q.B.D. 213 at p. 217.
25   Bankruptcy (Amendment) Act 1926 s. 7, Insolvency Act 1976 Sch. 1.

bankruptcy petition (or the making of a receiving order under section 107 of the Act),[26] *and*

(b) he has
  (i) not kept proper books of account throughout that period, and throughout any further period in which he was so engaged between the date of the presentation of the petition and the date of the receiving order, *or*
  (ii) not preserved all books of account so kept.

The offence is punishable on conviction on indictment with two years' imprisonment.[27] A prosecution may not be instituted without an order of the court.[28] It is a defence if

(a) the bankrupt's unsecured liabilities at the date of the receiving order did not exceed £6,000 (or £1,200 if he has previously been adjudged bankrupt or made a composition or arrangement with his creditors), or
(b) he proves that, in the circumstances in which he traded or carried on business, the omission was honest and excusable. It is not sufficient that the omission was honest if it was not excusable.[29]

9.26 The books of account required must be such as are necessary to exhibit or explain the trader's transactions and financial position in his trade or business, including:

(a) a book or books containing entries from day to day in sufficient detail of all cash received and cash paid, and
(b) where the trade or business has involved dealings in goods,
  (i) statements of annual stocktakings and
  (ii) (except in the case of goods sold by way of retail trade to the actual consumer) accounts of all goods sold and purchased, showing the buyers and sellers thereof in sufficient detail to enable the goods and the buyers and sellers to be identified.[30]

Moreover the following dictum of Lord Esher is undoubtedly still applicable:

"It is not enough that there should be books with entries in them which would require a prolonged examination by a skilled accountant in order to ascertain the result of them. That is not keeping proper books. The books should be properly kept and balanced from time to time, so that at any moment the real state of the trader's affairs may at once appear."[31]

---

26 s. 158(5).
27 s. 164(1). On summary conviction it carries twelve months' imprisonment.
28 s. 158(2).
29 *Dandridge* (1931) 22 Cr.App.R. 156.
30 s. 158(3).
31 *Re Reed and Bowen* (1886) 17 Q.B.D. 244 at p. 254.

Gambling, speculation and other losses

9.27 With or without the assistance of books of account, a bankrupt trader may be required to give an account of the losses he has sustained, and may be guilty of an offence if he cannot offer a satisfactory explanation. Under section 157(1) of the Bankruptcy Act 1914 an offence is committed by a person who

(a) has been adjudged bankrupt, or has had a receiving order made in respect of his estate,

(b) has been engaged in any trade or business,

(c) at the date of the receiving order has outstanding any debts contracted in the course and for the purposes of such trade or business,[32] and

(d) *either*

    (i) on being required by the Official Receiver at any time (or in the course of his public examination by the court) to account for the loss of any substantial part of his estate incurred up to a year before the date of the presentation of the bankruptcy petition,[33] or between that date and the date of the receiving order, fails to give a satisfactory explanation of the manner in which such loss was incurred, *or*

    (ii) has materially contributed to or increased the extent of his insolvency within the two years before the presentation of the bankruptcy petition, or has lost any part of his estate between that date and the date of the receiving order, by gambling or rash and hazardous speculations which (in either case) were unconnected with his trade or business.

The offences are punishable on conviction on indictment with two years' imprisonment.[34] A prosecution may not be instituted without an order of the court.[35]

9.28 A bankrupt who falls within the scope of section 157(1) escapes liability only if he can give a satisfactory explanation *and* that explanation does not reveal gambling or rash and hazardous speculations unconnected with his trade or business. This suggests that an explanation is not unsatisfactory merely because it does reveal such gambling or speculations: otherwise the offence under (d)(ii) above would be redundant. And if the elements of gambling and rash speculation do not render the explanation unsatisfactory, presumably nor do other repre-

---

32 This does not include tax liabilities: *Vaccari* [1958] 1 W.L.R. 297.
33 References to the presentation of a bankruptcy petition include the making of a receiving order under s. 107: s. 157(3).
34 s. 164(1). On summary conviction they carry twelve months' imprisonment.
35 s. 157(2).

hensible factors such as wanton extravagance. But an explanation is obviously not satisfactory if it is false, nor if it is incomplete; and a bankrupt who cannot give the required explanation is guilty of the offence even if he is doing his best. Fraud is not required.[36]

9.29 What constitutes a rash and hazardous speculation is not entirely clear. It is expressly provided that the defendant's financial position at the time of the speculations is a relevant factor:[37] what is an acceptable risk for a millionaire may be rash for a pauper. Lord Westbury L.C. suggested that a speculation is rash if it is one which no reasonable man would enter into;[38] but the suggestion was subsequently criticised by Brett M.R.,[39] and it is clear that mere imprudence is not enough.[40] On the other hand there is no requirement of an intent to defraud, and it is unnecessary to prove that the defendant actually realised the risk was unacceptable. It is sufficient that that fact should have been obvious. If understood in that sense, the term "recklessness" may perhaps approximate to the required degree of culpability.[41] It should be noted that even rash and hazardous speculations will not give rise to liability if they are connected with the defendant's trade or business. The offence is aimed not at bad businessmen but at businessmen whose private affairs are financed at their creditors' expense.

Engaging in trade or business
9.30 Undischarged bankrupts, unlike directors of insolvent companies, are automatically subject to certain disabilities in respect of their business activities. Under section 302(1) of the Companies Act 1985[42] an undischarged bankrupt commits an offence if (without the leave of the court by which he was adjudged bankrupt) he acts as director or liquidator of a company, or (directly or indirectly) takes part in or is concerned in its promotion, formation or management. The offence is punishable on conviction on indictment with two years' imprisonment.[43] It would seem to cover a bankrupt who plays any part whatsoever in a company's management, even if he is neither a director nor an employee but (*e.g.*) a management consultant.[44]

---

36 *Salter* [1968] 2 Q.B. 793, disapproving *Phillips* (1921) 85 J.P. 120.
37 s. 157(1).
38 *Re Downman* (1863) 32 L.J.Bcy 49 at p. 50.
39 *Re Young* (1885) 2 Morr. 37 at p. 40.
40 *Re Barnard* (1862) 31 L.J.Bcy 63.
41 *Cf. Caldwell* [1982] A.C. 341.
42 Replacing Companies Act 1948 s. 187 with effect from 1 July 1985.
43 Sch. 24. On summary conviction it carries six months' imprisonment or a fine of the statutory maximum or both.
44 *Cf. Campbell (A.J.)* (1984) 78 Cr.App.R. 95.

9.31 It is also an offence, under section 155(*b*) of the Bankruptcy Act 1914, for an undischarged bankrupt to engage in *any* trade or business (including an unincorporated one) under a name other than that under which he was adjudicated bankrupt, without disclosing the latter name (but not necessarily the fact of his bankruptcy) to all persons with whom he enters into any business transaction. The offence is punishable on conviction on indictment with two years' imprisonment.[45] The reference to business transactions entered into by the bankrupt himself makes it clear that he must be running the business in person rather than merely advising behind the scenes. On the other hand it is no defence that some other person is acting as a "front" for a business which is in fact the bankrupt's:[46] the firm's transactions will still be entered into by him, albeit through an agent.

Obtaining credit

9.32 Under section 155(*a*) of the Bankruptcy Act 1914[47] an offence is committed by an undischarged bankrupt who, either alone or jointly with any other person, obtains credit to the extent of £50 or upwards from any person without informing that person that he is an undischarged bankrupt. The offence is punishable on conviction on indictment with two years' imprisonment.[48] Unlike most of the other bankruptcy offences, section 155(*a*) is concerned not with the evasion of existing debts but with the incurring of fresh ones. The Cork Committee regarded it as essentially an offence of deception:

> "Logically, in our view, the wrong consists, not in the failure to pay the debt (which is a civil wrong), but in the deception practised on the creditor by obtaining credit from him knowing that he would not extend it if he knew the circumstances. Even where the bill is paid at once, the creditor was still put unjustifiably at risk."[49]

We have seen that deceiving another into taking a financial risk is one of the established forms of criminal fraud.[50]

9.33 The offence created by section 155(*a*) has given rise to a surprising amount of difficulty, chiefly with regard to the concept of "credit". Some of the cases were decided on section 13(1) of the Debtors Act 1869 (now repealed)[51] but they are equally relevant to section 155(*a*).[52] It is now

---

45   s. 164(1). On summary conviction it carries twelve months' imprisonment.
46   *Doubleday* (1964) 49 Cr.App.R. 62.
47   As amended by Insolvency Act 1976 Sch. 1.
48   s. 164(1). On summary conviction it carries twelve months' imprisonment.
49   Cmnd. 8558 at para. 1844.
50   *Allsop* (1976) 64 Cr.App.R. 29; *supra,* para. 1.35.
51   Theft Act 1968 s. 33(3) and Sch. 3.
52   *Fisher v. Raven* [1964] A.C. 210.

established, earlier authority to the contrary notwithstanding,[53] that credit consists of an obligation to pay *money*: an obligation to provide goods or services, even if they are paid for in advance, is not sufficient.[54] The Court of Appeal has stated:

> "The obtaining of credit, in our view, means obtaining some benefit from another, without immediately giving the consideration in return for which that benefit is confirmed."[55]

A loan is clearly a form of credit.[56] The fact that the bankrupt provides security for the loan does not necessarily make any difference, though it may do so if the security is obviously worth more than the amount lent.[57] Another clear case is the purchase of goods, or the obtaining of services, on the basis that payment is deferred until later—even if the delay is to be very short, as where a meal is provided in a restaurant and the customer is expected to pay after the meal but before he leaves the premises.[58]

9.34 Other types of transaction present more difficulty. In *Smith*[59] it was treated as self-evident that an agreement for the letting of a house at a monthly rent involved the obtaining of credit by the lessee. But this is not necessarily so. It is not sufficient that the bankrupt incurs an obligation to pay money at some future date: the essence of credit is that payment is not to be made until after receipt of the benefit in question. In principle, therefore, it should be crucial whether the rent is payable in advance or in arrears.[60] It is only in the latter case that credit is obtained. In the case of hire-purchase agreements, on the other hand, it has sometimes been assumed that credit is *not* obtained, because title to the goods does not pass until all the instalments have been paid.[61] But in theory the instalments are by way of payment for the hire of the goods: logically, therefore, the same considerations should apply as in the case of rental and hire agreements. The question should be whether each

---

53 *Ingram* [1956] 2 Q.B. 424.
54 *Laker* (1949) 34 Cr.App.R. 37, *Fisher v. Raven* [1964] A.C. 210.
55 *Miller* [1977] 1 W.L.R. 1129 at p. 1134. "Confirmed" is presumably a misprint for "conferred".
56 *Pryce* (1949) 34 Cr.App.R. 21.
57 *Fryer* (1912) 7 Cr.App.R. 183.
58 *Jones* [1898] 1 Q.B. 119. In other words, credit may be obtained even if payment "on the spot" is required for the purposes of the offence of making off without payment (Theft Act 1978 s. 3, *infra*, para. 9.42).
59 (1915) 11 Cr.App.R. 81.
60 *Cf. Miller* [1977] 1 W.L.R. 1129 at p. 1132, where Roskill L.J. explained the decision in *Hartley* [1972] 2 Q.B. 1 (that the defendant obtained credit by falling behind with the rent) on the basis that "the rent in question was rent in arrears and not in advance". With respect, this was clearly not the ground of the decision in *Hartley* (see *infra*), but logically the distinction ought to be crucial.
61 *Garlick* (1958) 42 Cr.App.R. 141 (where the point was conceded by the Crown), *Inman* [1967] 1 Q.B. 140. In *Miller, supra,* the Court of Appeal declined to express an opinion on the point.

instalment is payable in advance of the period to which it relates, or in arrears.

9.35 The question has arisen whether it is sufficient to constitute an obtaining of credit merely that the defendant does in fact obtain the benefit in question before paying for it, or whether there must be some agreement to this effect on the part of the creditor. This issue may be subdivided into two: firstly, is it necessary that the defendant be legally *entitled* to defer payment? And if not, is it at least necessary that the creditor should *consent* to the delay?

9.36 A leading authority on the former question is *Peters*,[62] where the defendant, an undischarged bankrupt living in Newcastle, bought a horse on f.o.b. terms from a man living in County Antrim, and having taken delivery of the horse failed to pay the price. His conviction of an offence under the predecessor of section 155(*a*) was upheld. Lord Coleridge C.J., speaking for the majority of the Court for Crown Cases Reserved, said:

> "The words of the section are 'obtains credit'. Did the prisoner obtain credit? It is said that he did not, because he did not stipulate for it; but the Act does not say that there must be a stipulation for credit, or that it must be obtained on a specific contract to give credit. In such a case as the present, where a man obtains goods and does not pay for them for a substantial period of time, I am not prepared to say that we ought to limit the plain meaning of the words in the Act of Parliament. The prisoner has obtained credit and has had it, whether or no he stipulated for it at the time of purchase."[63]

This would seem to imply that under the terms of the contract the defendant had no *right* to defer payment until after taking delivery of the horse (and indeed that was the ground of Manisty J.'s dissenting judgment), but that the absence of such a right was immaterial. In *Miller*,[64] however, the Court of Appeal explained the decision as resting on the fact that there *was* such a right, because in the absence of an express term as to payment it was implied that Peters was not obliged to pay the price as soon as the horse was put on board ship (and title therefore passed to him) but only within a reasonable time.[65] The court expressed its agreement with this reasoning, and went on to say that credit is obtained only if the creditor does not acquire an immediate cause of action for the money due. The acquisition of such a cause of action

---

62 (1885) 16 Q.B.D. 636.
63 At p. 640f.
64 [1977] 1 W.L.R. 1129.
65 With respect, this interpretation is open to question. In a contract of sale, payment and delivery are concurrent conditions unless otherwise agreed (Sale of Goods Act 1979 s. 28). In the absence of any stipulation to the contrary, the vendor would therefore be entitled to payment against the shipping documents.

was described as "the antithesis of giving credit".[66] It follows that the defendant does not obtain credit unless he is entitled to defer payment; and accordingly it was held that the mere failure to pay a debt when it falls due does not constitute an obtaining of credit. However, the court also suggested that the position might be otherwise if, instead of simply defaulting, the defendant asked the creditor for more time to pay—assuming, presumably, that the creditor agreed, since the request in itself could hardly convert the default into an obtaining of credit. But this is hard to reconcile with the court's earlier reasoning, since even if the creditor agreed not to press for payment he would still have a cause of action when the debt became due. In *Hartley*[67] it was held that the defendant obtained credit by writing cheques which were honoured by the bank although his account was overdrawn. Yet he was not *entitled* to an overdraft facility under the terms of his contract with the bank, and it seems clear that on honouring each cheque the bank acquired an immediate cause of action against him for reimbursement of the amount paid out.

9.37 Whether or not *Miller* is correct in suggesting that credit necessarily involves a *right* to defer payment, it does at least appear to require some degree of consent on the part of the creditor. The decision is that one does not obtain credit merely by failing to pay a debt when it falls due, though it may be otherwise if the creditor agrees to wait. This less radical interpretation is easily reconciled with *Peters,* since the vendor in that case, by not insisting on payment against documents, did by implication allow the defendant to have credit. *Hartley*, however, is still an obstacle: the Court of Appeal there held that the defendant had obtained credit not only by overdrawing on his bank account (with the bank's consent) but also by falling into arrears with his rent (without the consent of his landlord). On the latter point the decision seems flatly inconsistent with *Miller*. The only ground of distinction suggested in *Miller* is that in *Hartley* the rent was payable in arrears, not in advance. This fact might indeed have been crucial if the defendant had been charged with obtaining credit by entering into the rental agreement in the first place;[68] but that was not the way in which the case was presented. It is submitted that on this point *Hartley* must be taken to be implicitly overruled by *Miller*.

9.38 The credit obtained by the defendant must amount to at least £50, but there is no requirement that this sum be attributable to any one

66 At p. 1134.
67 [1972] 2 Q.B. 1.
68 *Cf. supra,* para. 9.34.

transaction: it is the *aggregate* amount which is crucial.[69] However, it is clear from the wording of section 155(*a*) ("obtains credit . . . to the extent of £50 or upwards from any person . . .") that the £50 must all be owed to the same creditor.

9.39 The requirement that the credit be "obtained" would not at first sight appear to involve any difficulty beyond that inherent in the concept of credit itself. In *Hartley*[70] Sachs L.J. said:

". . . if a person charged has by words or conduct secured that credit be given to him to the extent of [£50] or more, he has obtained that credit."[71]

This dictum was approved in *Miller*,[72] though it must now be read in the light of that decision. In *Hayat*,[73] however, the Court of Appeal appears to have envisaged that one may act in such a way as to be given credit without thereby obtaining credit. The defendant's bank account became overdrawn when one of his customers stopped two cheques. Clearly the bank *gave* him credit by honouring his cheques; but the court held that it should have been left to the jury to decide whether he had *obtained* credit. It is not clear on what grounds a reasonable jury might have decided that he had not. Presumably it was thought that the word "obtain" has connotations of *intentional* conduct, or at least that a jury might think it had. It may be that although the prosecution need not prove an intent to defraud[74] they must at least prove an intent to obtain credit.

9.40 Another question which must be left to the jury is that of whether the credit is given to the defendant himself or to some other person such as a relative or a company with which the defendant is associated.[75] In *Godwin*[76] Kilner Brown J. said, giving the judgment of the court:

"The critical question always is whether on the evidence the bankrupt holds himself out as the person for whom credit is sought, or whether it is for a genuine and separate business and not a charade to disguise the fact that he is the person seeking credit."[77]

The reference to a "charade" is, with respect, misleading. In principle the crucial question is simply whether it is the defendant who incurs the obligation to pay or somebody else, a question which falls to be answered according to the civil law of contract and agency. If it is someone other

---

69 *Juby* (1886) 16 Cox 160, *Hartley* [1972] 2 Q.B. 1.
70 [1972] 2 Q.B. 1.
71 At p. 7.
72 [1977] 1 W.L.R. 1129, *supra* para. 9.36.
73 (1976) 63 Cr.App.R. 181.
74 *Dyson* [1894] 2 Q.B. 176.
75 *Goodall* (1959) 43 Cr.App.R. 24.
76 (1980) 71 Cr.App.R. 97.
77 At p. 99.

than the bankrupt who undertakes the liability, then the case falls outside the mischief attacked by the offence, because the credit is not given to someone who is, unknown to the creditor, already insolvent; and this is so even if that person's sole objective is to assist the bankrupt. But if he is in fact the bankrupt's agent, it will of course be the bankrupt himself who is obtaining credit. If the bankrupt is running a business there may in addition be an offence under section 155(*b*).[78]

9.41 The offence under section 155(*a*) is not committed if the defendant informs the creditor that he is an undischarged bankrupt. He need not disclose the fact at the very moment of obtaining the credit: it is sufficient if he does so at about that time.[79] But of course the creditor must be told *before* the transaction is effected. The section does not require an intent to defraud,[80] and it is no defence that the defendant reasonably believed the creditor had been told.[81]

MAKING OFF WITHOUT PAYMENT

9.42 The mere failure to pay a debt, unaccompanied by deception,[82] is not in itself an offence. If a defaulting debtor cannot be proved to have acted dishonestly in incurring the debt in the first place,[83] he may therefore escape criminal liability altogether. This was found to be unsatisfactory in the situation where there is no intention of granting credit in the ordinary sense[84] but, as a matter of convenience, payment is not required until after the provision of the benefit in question. For example, a person who left a restaurant without paying the bill could not be charged with theft of the meal,[85] and deception might be hard to establish.[86] This situation is now the subject of section 3 of the Theft Act 1978, which provides:

"Subject to subsection (3) below,[87] a person who, knowing that payment on the spot for any goods supplied or service done is required or expected

---

78 *Supra*, para. 9.31.
79 *Zeitlin* (1932) 23 Cr.App.R. 163.
80 *Dyson* [1894] 2 Q.B. 176.
81 *Duke of Leinster* [1924] 1 K.B. 311.
82 For the evasion of liability by deception see para. 3.29ff.
83 If he never intended to pay, he will be guilty of an offence under ss. 15 or 16 of the Theft Act 1968 or under s. 1 or s. 2(1)(*c*) of the Theft Act 1978: see ch. 3.
84 But technically credit is obtained: *Jones* [1898] 1 Q.B. 119.
85 *Corcoran v. Whent* [1977] Crim.L.R. 52.
86 But the House of Lords managed to overcome the difficulty in *D.P.P. v. Ray* [1974] A.C. 370.
87 Subsection (3) provides that subsection (1) shall not apply where the supply of the goods or the doing of the service is contrary to law, or where the service done is such that payment is not legally enforceable. Presumably the offence may be committed where *goods* are supplied in such circumstances that payment is not legally enforceable, *e.g.* where non-necessaries are supplied to a minor: J.C. Smith, *The Law of Theft* (5th ed.) para. 246.

from him, dishonestly makes off without having paid as required or expected and with intent to avoid payment of the amount due shall be guilty of an offence."

The offence is punishable on conviction on indictment with two years' imprisonment,[88] and there is an express power of arrest.[89]

9.43   For the offence under section 3 to be committed, some goods must have been supplied or some service done. Neither expression is defined,[90] but there will seldom be any difficulty in bringing a case within one or the other. The defendant must be "required or expected"[91] to pay for the goods or the service "on the spot"—*i.e.* presumably, not just *at* the place where the goods are supplied or the service done,[92] but *before leaving* that place. Section 3(2) provides, perhaps somewhat unnecessarily, that "payment on the spot" includes payment at the time of collecting goods on which work has been done or in respect of which service has been provided. It is submitted that payment on the spot may still be required or expected even if the provider of the goods or service is known to accept cheques or credit cards, because the use of a credit card (or of a cheque backed by a cheque card) replaces the trader's claim against the customer with a claim against the credit card company (or the customer's bank) and can therefore be regarded as a form of payment.[93] The position might be more doubtful if the trader were known to accept cheques unsupported by cheque cards. Admittedly it is said that the tender of a cheque operates as conditional payment,[94] but it is arguable that the acceptance of an unsupported cheque is in practice closer to giving credit than to exacting payment in any real sense. In any case the question would only arise in the unlikely event of customers being neither required nor even expected to use a cheque card.

9.44   Similar difficulties are raised by the expression "makes off without having paid as required or expected". It is submitted that a customer who presents an apparently valid credit card (or a cheque backed by an

---

88   s. 4(2)(*b*). On summary conviction it carries six months' imprisonment or a fine of the prescribed sum or both.

89   s. 3(4).

90   Therefore "service" is not necessarily synonymous with "services" in s. 1, which is so defined as to extend beyond its ordinary meaning: *supra*, para. 3.25ff.

91   Presumably one may be *expected* to pay on the spot although one is under no legal obligation (*i.e.* not *required*) to do so. But there must normally be a legal obligation to pay eventually, because s. 3(3) provides that payment for the service done (though not for goods supplied) must be legally enforceable: *cf.* n. 87 *supra*.

92   If the service involves transporting the defendant from one place to another (*e.g.* a ride in a taxi), the "spot" on which payment must be due is presumably the destination—or perhaps the vehicle?

93   *Cf. supra,* para. 3.34.

94   *e.g. D. & C. Builders Ltd v. Rees* [1966] 2 Q.B. 617 at p. 628, *per* Winn L.J. *Cf. Hammond* [1983] Crim.L.R. 571.

apparently valid cheque card) is in fact paying as required, by discharging the original liability and creating in its stead a liability on the issuing company or bank. The case of the unsupported cheque is again more dubious. Even if the customer tendering such a cheque is not regarded as having paid, can he be said to be *making off* if the payee is satisfied with the cheque and is content that the customer should leave? If the draftsman merely meant "leaves" or "goes away" he would hardly have used the graphic expression "makes off"; presumably, therefore, the choice of that expression reflects some nuance of meaning. It has been suggested (correctly, it is submitted) that the phrase carries a connotation of "guilty haste" and is therefore confined to the case where the customer does not have the creditor's permission to leave without paying.[95] A debtor does not make off if for any reason, including the fact that he has practised a deception, his creditor is happy to see him go.[96] On this view the offence would not be committed where the customer pretends to pay the bill in any way, valid or otherwise, nor where he pretends to have already paid[97] or makes his escape by means of any other deception. These cases should be charged under section 2(1)(*b*) of the Theft Act 1978, which provides that a person is guilty of an offence if, with intent to make permanent default on an existing liability, he induces his creditor by deception to wait for or forgo payment.[98] A creditor who accepts a cheque by way of conditional satisfaction is deemed to be waiting for payment.[99]

9.45 This conclusion is reinforced by a consideration of the *mens rea* required by section 3. Not only must the defendant know that payment on the spot is required or expected, and make off dishonestly,[1] but he must intend to avoid payment of the amount due. In *Allen (Christopher)*[2] the House of Lords held that this requirement refers to an intent *never* to pay and that it is not sufficient that the defendant intends merely to avoid payment for the time being. This decision is somewhat surprising. A comparison with section 2(1)(*b*), the offence of deceiving one's

---

95 Francis Bennion [1980] Crim.L.R. 670, [1983] Crim.L.R. 205. This view appears to have been accepted in *Hammond* [1983] Crim.L.R. 571. In *Brooks* (1983) 76 Cr.App.R. 66 the Court of Appeal said that in most cases the phrase "makes off" requires no elaboration; but, with respect, if it means something different from "goes away" (as it presumably does) the difference needs to be explained.

96 Mr Bennion points out that if the creditor consents to the customer's fetching the means of payment he is not thereby consenting to the customer's disappearance. This view would catch the person who evades paying for a ride in a taxi by telling the driver that he is going into his house to get some money.

97 *Cf. Holt* [1981] 1 W.L.R. 1000.

98 *Supra*, para. 3.29.

99 s. 2(3).

1 *Supra*, para. 1.04ff.

2 (1985) *The Times*, 14 June, affirming [1985] 1 W.L.R. 50.

creditor into forgoing payment,[3] can be invoked in support of either view. That offence does expressly require an intent to make permanent default; it can therefore be argued on the one hand that the policy was to exempt the "stalling debtor" from criminal liability, and on the other that the reference to permanent default is conspicuously absent from section 3. The latter argument appears the stronger, since section 3 is clearly intended to differentiate between the ordinary debtor and the person who is merely allowed to defer payment until he leaves the premises. The latter view also derives support from authority on the same phrase in a different statute.[4] However, given the decision in *Allen*, the effect is that it is pointless (even if it is possible) to charge the section 3 offence in a case of cheque or credit card fraud. The offence of securing the remission of an existing liability by deception,[5] which it is submitted is sufficiently wide to cover the payment of a debt with a credit card or a cheque backed by a cheque card,[6] does not require an intent to make permanent default. The offence of inducing the creditor by deception to forgo payment[7] does require such an intent; but if the offence of making off without payment does too, the latter offers no advantage to the prosecution where a deception can be proved.[8] And the maximum penalty for an offence under section 2 is five years' imprisonment, compared with two years in the case of section 3.

---

3 *Supra,* para. 3.29.
4 *Corbyn v. Saunders* [1978] 1 W.L.R. 400.
5 Theft Act 1978 s. 2(1)(*a*); *supra,* para. 3.29.
6 Para. 2.25ff. (deception), 2.53 (causation), 3.34 (remission).
7 Theft Act 1978 s. 2(1)(*b*); *supra,* para. 3.29.
8 In *Hammond* [1982] Crim.L.R. 611, where the defendant had tendered bad cheques, the prosecution conceded that the reason for including a count under s. 3 was the difficulty of proving an intention to make permanent default as required by s. 2(1)(*b*).

CHAPTER 10

Frauds on the State

10.01   Frauds committed on the public at large, in the shape of the state (or in some cases the E.E.C.), fall into two basic types: the evasion of one's liabilities to the state, and the fraudulent obtaining of money from it. The main form taken by the first type is the evasion of taxes, duties and levies of various kinds; the second may involve either the obtaining of tax rebates or the fraudulent abuse of the social security system[1] or of schemes providing subsidies for particular industries[2] (such as the Common Agricultural Policy). The second type will almost invariably involve a deception of the authorities, and will therefore constitute the offence of obtaining property by deception contrary to section 15 of the Theft Act 1968;[3] the first may well involve deception (though it may consist simply in the failure to make contact with the authorities at all) and, if so, will normally amount to one or more of the offences of evading liability by deception under section 2 of the Theft Act 1978.[4] Often the particular means of deception adopted will give rise to liability for false accounting,[5] forgery[6] or the making of false statements contrary to section 5(*b*) of the Perjury Act 1911.[7] Sometimes a tax fraud is essentially no more than an insolvency fraud in which the defrauded creditors happen to be the revenue departments, and in that case some of the offences considered in the previous chapter may be relevant: fraudulent trading, in particular, may be a useful charge where the defaulting business is a company.[8] Insolvency fraud may in turn consist in the looting of a company by its controllers, to the detriment of shareholders and creditors alike, and in that event the possibilities discussed in chapters 4 and 5 should be borne in mind. In this chapter we consider some further offences relating specifically to these types of fraud.

CHEATING THE PUBLIC REVENUE

10.02   The common law recognises an offence of defrauding the public,

---

1   See Steve Uglow, "Defrauding the Public Purse" [1984] Crim.L.R. 128.
2   *e.g. Griffiths* [1966] 1 Q.B. 589.
3   *Supra,* para. 3.02ff.
4   *Supra,* para. 3.29ff.
5   *Supra,* para. 6.41ff.
6   *Supra,* para. 6.03ff.
7   *Supra,* para. 6.59.
8   *Supra,* para. 9.03ff.

sometimes known as cheating. The classic statement of the principle involved is that of Lord Mansfield in *Bembridge*:[9]

". . .where there is a breach of trust, a fraud, or an imposition in a subject concerning the public, which, as between subject and subject, would only be actionable by a civil action, yet as that concerns the King and the public (I use them as synonymous terms), it is indictable."[10]

The offence is distinct from that of conspiracy to defraud,[11] being narrower in that it is confined to frauds on the public at large, but wider in that it can be committed by one person acting alone. In modern times its application has been largely confined to frauds on the public revenue, but its continuing existence in that context at least was confirmed by *Hudson*.[12] The defendant was charged with submitting false accounts to an inspector of taxes with intent to defraud. The Court of Criminal Appeal held, approving a ruling by Bray J. in *Bradbury and Edlin*,[13] that the indictment disclosed an offence.

10.03 The decision in *Hudson* is not affected by the Theft Act 1968, which abolishes the offence of cheating "except as regards offences relating to the public revenue".[14] Although the offence has traditionally been used by the Inland Revenue, there seems no reason why the expression "the public revenue" should not embrace all taxes and duties levied by central[15] government, including those administered by the Board of Customs and Excise such as VAT.[16] Being a creature of the common law, the offence is punishable at large; it is therefore a powerful weapon not only where no statutory offence seems appropriate but also where the statutory maximum penalty seems insufficient. At the time of writing this is particularly so in the case of large-scale VAT fraud[17] (though it is expected that the statutory penalties will be increased by the Finance Act 1985). But it is not entirely clear whether the offence extends to every form of conduct which results in loss to the revenue and which falls within the concept of fraud discussed in chapter 1. In *Tonner*[18] it was argued that there must be some positive action (such as deception), and that a mere failure to act (such as the failure to account for tax due) did not amount to a cheat. The Court of Appeal was not persuaded of this

9 (1783) 22 St. Tr. 1.
10 At p. 155.
11 *Fountain* [1965] 2 All E.R. 671n.; *Scott v. Metropolitan Police Commissioner* [1975] A.C. 819.
12 [1956] 2 Q.B. 252.
13 [1956] 2 Q.B. 262n.
14 s. 32(1)(*a*).
15 But not local: *Lush v. Coles* [1967] 1 W.L.R. 685.
16 This seems to have been assumed in *Tonner* [1985] 1 W.L.R. 344.
17 *Infra*, para 10.16ff.
18 [1985] 1 W.L.R. 344.

proposition but found it unnecessary to decide the point. It is submitted that deception is clearly not a necessary ingredient: the offence is not strictly one of "cheating" but of fraud, and fraud does not require deception.[19] On the other hand it may be that even fraud requires *some* positive action. *Quaere* whether the mere failure to pay one's debts could ever be described as fraudulent.

FRAUDS ON THE INLAND REVENUE

10.04   The evasion of income and corporation tax generally involves an element of deception, either by understating income or by overstating deductions and allowances. It will normally therefore constitute an offence of evading liability by deception contrary to section 2 of the Theft Act 1978.[20] A taxpayer who submits a false return, so as to pay less tax than he should, may not be securing the "remission" of part of his liability (as required by section 2(1)(*a*)) or obtaining an "abatement" of it (as required by section 2(1)(*c*)), because the liability remains until the tax is paid in full; but he is certainly inducing the Revenue to "forgo payment" as required by section 2(1)(*b*), and the requisite intention to make permanent default will normally be clear. If the false return enables him to obtain a rebate, he will be guilty of obtaining property by deception.[21] He will almost certainly be committing offences of false accounting[22] (since a tax return is clearly a document required for an accounting purpose) and of making a false statement contrary to section 5(*b*) of the Perjury Act 1911,[23] and possibly even of forgery[24] (since a return which misstates the taxpayer's circumstances arguably "purports to have been made . . . in circumstances in which it was not in fact made").[25] Moreover he will of course be guilty of cheating the revenue.[26] In view of the availability of these charges, the Inland Revenue has seldom felt any pressing need for specific criminal offences of tax evasion: the "penalties" recoverable under the tax legislation are purely civil in character.[27] The Committee on Enforcement Powers of the Revenue Departments (the Keith Committee)[28] has, however, recommended the creation of criminal offences of tax evasion broadly comparable to those under section 39 of the Value Added Tax Act 1983.[29]

19   *Scott v. Metropolitan Police Commissioner* [1975] A.C. 819; *supra* para. 1.38.
20   *Supra,* para. 3.29ff.
21   *Supra,* para. 3.02ff.
22   *Supra,* para. 6.41ff.
23   *Supra,* para. 6.59; *Bradbury and Edlin* [1921] 1 K.B. 562.
24   *Supra,* para. 6.03ff.
25   Forgery and Counterfeiting Act 1981 s. 9(1)(*g*), *supra,* para. 6.16.
26   *Supra,* para. 10.02.
27   Taxes Management Act 1970 s. 100(3).
28   Cmnd. 8822 at para. 19.5.1.
29   *Infra,* para. 10.16ff.

"Lump" frauds

10.05 Apart from the theft of payable orders, the majority of prosecutions brought by the Inland Revenue concern abuses of the statutory machinery relating to the taxation of sub-contractors in the construction industry (the "lump").[30] Casual workers, who prefer the status of an independent sub-contractor to that of an employee, have often proved elusive when allowed to claim their remuneration in full without deduction of tax. Hence section 69 of the Finance (No. 2) Act 1975 requires the main contractor to deduct a percentage by way of provision for the sub-contractor's tax liability. In recognition of the difficulties which this would cause for honest sub-contractors, however, section 70 provides an exception: a sub-contractor is entitled to be paid in full if, on application to the Inland Revenue, he has been issued with a certificate and a book of vouchers. Both the certificate and the vouchers will bear the name of the person to whom they are issued. The certificate also bears his photograph. In order to claim payment in full he is required to present his certificate to the contractor (though this requirement is sometimes waived by less meticulous contractors) and to hand over a voucher, filled in with the details of the payment and signed, which the contractor will then pass on to the Revenue. A sub-contractor who has no intention of meeting his tax liabilities will therefore find it profitable to acquire a stock of vouchers, preferably with the corresponding certificate. With or without the connivance of the contractor, he can then receive his pay gross and avoid the necessity of accounting for the tax due. A dishonest contractor, moreover, can use vouchers improperly obtained so as to exaggerate his outgoings with totally fictitious payments.

10.06 Thus there are two stages in a typical "lump" fraud: the illicit acquisition of certificates and vouchers, and the misuse of them. Both stages will involve criminal offences. There are essentially three ways in which a dishonest sub-contractor can get his hands on the certificate and vouchers he requires. In the first place he may try to persuade the Revenue to issue them to him. This course may involve an element of deception as to his history and present circumstances. An offence is committed by a person who, for the purpose of obtaining a certificate, knowingly or recklessly makes any statement or furnishes any document which is false in a material particular;[31] but this is a summary offence, punishable with a fine of up to £5,000. Presumably such conduct would also constitute a cheat on the revenue at common law.[32] As we have seen,

---

30 S. Uglow, *op. cit.*
31 Finance (No. 2) Act 1975 s. 70(9).
32 *Supra,* para. 10.02.

deceiving a public official into doing something which he would not otherwise have done is an established form of criminal fraud.[33] Alternatively, the dishonest sub-contractor may beg, borrow, buy or steal the necessary certificate and vouchers from someone else. It is a summary offence (punishable with a fine of up to £5,000) to dispose of a certificate or voucher, or to possess one (or a document purporting to be one), without lawful authority or excuse.[34] A person supplying a certificate or vouchers will· also be at least an accessory to the offences committed through their misuse.[35] Moreover it was held in *Downes*[36] that a person who sells vouchers (or rather parts with them for cash, since they remain the property of the Inland Revenue at all times) may be convicted of stealing them. Although he knows that they will eventually find their way back to the Revenue, he is deemed to have the necessary intention permanently to deprive the Revenue of them:

> ". . . by parting with them, his action, which it is admitted amounts in these circumstances to an appropriation, also inevitably carries with it the effect that the documents cease to be in substance the same thing as they were before. They are no longer part of the statutory machinery for the collection of tax, but have deliberately been made available to be used as forgeries by dishonest sub-contractors and contractors to evade tax. It seems to this Court that in those circumstances there is a sufficient intent to deprive the Inland Revenue permanently of the documents to support the charge of theft on normal principles."[37]

It follows that the "purchaser" is guilty of handling stolen goods.[38] A third way of acquiring certificates and vouchers is simply to counterfeit them: this would constitute not only the summary offence of possessing a document purporting to be a certificate or voucher, but also forgery.[39]

10.07   The actual use of a certificate or vouchers (or both) by someone other than the person to whom they were issued may amount to various offences. Since a voucher is clearly a document made or required for an accounting purpose, the falsification of it will constitute false accounting.[40] Signing it in a false name will also be forgery,[41] because it will purport to have been signed by a person who did not in fact sign it. Even if it was signed by the authorised holder before he parted with it, it will

---

33   *Welham v. D.P.P.* [1961] A.C. 103; *supra* para. 1.40.
34   Finance (No. 2) Act 1975 s. 70(10).
35   *Infra*, para. 10.07.
36   (1983) 77 Cr.App.R. 260.
37   At p. 266, *per* Nolan J.
38   Theft Act 1968 s. 22.
39   *Supra*, para. 6.03ff.
40   *Supra*, para. 6.41ff.
41   *Supra*, para. 6.03ff.

still be a false instrument if someone else subsequently fills in the name of the contractor to whom it is presented and the amount and date of the payment: the wording of the voucher makes it clear that these details are to be filled in by the holder of the certificate to which it corresponds, and a completed voucher will therefore purport to have been completed by him. This is probably so even if the details are in a handwriting which bears no resemblance to that of the signature:[42] this would not necessarily be fatal to the fraud's chances of success because in practice vouchers are often filled in by the contractor instead of the sub-contractor. Of course, the contractor would not accept a voucher which was obviously not filled in by the appropriate person unless he was himself a party to the fraud. This too would not rule out a charge of forgery (indeed it might well ground a conspiracy charge), since, although there must be an intention to induce someone to accept the voucher as genuine, the intended victim of the deception may be the Revenue rather than the contractor. A charge of obtaining the gross pay by deception[43] would be harder to make out, since it would have to be proved both that the contractor did not know the vouchers had been issued to someone else and that he would not have paid the money in full if he had known; it may be that he would in any case have been willing to turn a blind eye. Finally a charge of cheating the Revenue would again be possible.[44]

Migration of companies

10.08 Section 482 of the Income and Corporation Taxes Act 1970 is directed at the practice of reducing a company's tax liability by transferring its residence overseas or by similar devices. Breach of these provisions does not merely render the manoeuvre ineffective but constitutes a serious criminal offence (albeit one which cannot be charged without the consent of the Attorney-General).[45] The existence of a criminal sanction is perhaps unnecessary, and the Keith Committee has recommended that if section 482 is to be retained it should give rise to a civil penalty only.[46]

10.09 Section 482(1) renders the following transactions unlawful if they are carried out without the consent of the Treasury:[47]

(a) For a company[48] resident in the U.K. to cease to be so resident.[49] A

---

42 *Supra,* para. 6.09.
43 *Supra,* para. 3.02ff.
44 *Supra,* para. 10.02.
45 s. 482(11).
46 Cmnd. 8822 at para. 7.2.7.
47 For Treasury consents, see s. 482(4).
48 Strictly speaking, a body corporate; but the term "company" will be used for the sake of brevity.
49 s. 482(1)(*a*).

company is resident in the U.K. if the central management and control of its trade or business is exercised here, but once its U.K. residence is established for tax purposes there is a rebuttable presumption that it continues to be resident here.[50] The offence is not committed if a company ceases to be resident in the U.K. merely because it has ceased to exist.[51]

(b) For a company resident in the U.K. to transfer its trade or business (or any part of it) to a person not so resident.[52] Where the functions of a company consist wholly or mainly in the holding of investments or other property, that function is deemed to be a business carried on by the company.[53] This provision is capable of reaching beyond the sphere of tax evasion to the practice of looting a company by transferring its assets overseas. However, a mere transfer of assets does not constitute a transfer of part of a company's trade or business unless it results in a substantial change in the character or extent of that trade or business.[54]

(c) For a company resident in the U.K. to cause or permit a non-resident company over which it has control[55] to create or issue any shares or debentures.[56] This provision does not apply to:

(i) the giving to the bankers of the non-resident company of any security for the payment of any sum due or to become due from it to them by reason of any transaction entered into with it by them in the ordinary course of their business as bankers;[57] or

(ii) the giving by the non-resident company to an insurance company[58] of any security for the payment of any sum due or to become due from the former to the latter by reason of any transaction between them entered into in the ordinary course of the insurance company's business by way of investment of its funds.[59]

(d) For a company resident in the U.K. to transfer (or cause or permit to be transferred) to any person (whether or not a U.K. resident) any shares or debentures of a non-resident company over which it

---

50 s. 482(7).
51 s. 482(10).
52 s. 482(1)(*b*).
53 s. 482(8).
54 s. 482(9).
55 Defined as the power of a person to secure by means of holding shares or the possession of voting power or by any powers conferred by the articles of association or analogous document that the affairs of the company are conducted in accordance with that person's wishes: s. 482(10), s. 534.
56 s. 482(1)(*c*).
57 s. 482(2).
58 Defined as a body corporate lawfully carrying on business as an insurer, whether in the U.K. or elsewhere: s. 482(10).
59 s. 482(3).

has control,[60] being shares or debentures which it owns or in which it has an interest,[61] or any beneficial interest therein.[62] There is an exception in the case of transfers for the purpose of enabling a person to be qualified to act as a director.[63]

10.10   Section 482(5) of the Income and Corporation Taxes Act 1970 provides:

"Any person who, whether within or outside the United Kingdom, does or is a party to the doing of any act which to his knowledge amounts to or results in, or forms part of a series of acts which together amount to or result in, something which is unlawful under subsection (1) of this section shall be guilty of an offence under this section, and in any proceedings in respect of such an offence against a director[64] of the body corporate in question (that is to say, the body corporate which is or was resident in the United Kingdom) or against any person who was purporting to act in that capacity:—

(*a*) it shall be presumed that he was a party to every act of that body corporate unless he proves that it was done without his consent or connivance; and

(*b*) it shall, unless the contrary is proved, be presumed that any act which in fact amounted to or resulted in, or formed part of a series of acts which together amounted to or resulted in or would amount to or result in, something which is unlawful under subsection (1) of this section was to his knowledge such an act."

The offence is punishable on conviction on indictment with two years' imprisonment or a fine of £10,000[65] or both.[66]

FRAUDS ON THE CUSTOMS AND EXCISE

10.11   By way of contrast with the legislation relating to the Inland Revenue, that concerning the administration of Customs and Excise duties and prohibitions contains a plethora of criminal offences. The evasion of prohibitions lies outside the scope of this work,[67] and even as regards the evasion of duty we shall confine ourselves to a handful of the most important offences under the Customs and Excise Management Act

---

60   *Supra*, n. 55.
61   s. 482(1)(*d*).
62   s. 482(10).
63   s. 482(1)(*d*).
64   "Director" includes any person occupying the position of director, by whatever name called: s. 482(10), Companies Act 1985 s. 741(1).
65   Or, in the case of a company which is or was resident in the U.K., three times the corporation tax, profits tax, capital gains tax and income tax paid or payable which is attributable to the income, profits or gains (including any chargeable gains) arising in the 36 months immediately preceding the commission of the offence, if that sum is greater than £10,000.
66   s. 482(6).
67   See para. 1.45.

1979. Offences of evading VAT and car tax, the administration of which is assigned to the Commissioners of Customs and Excise, will also be considered. The provisions of section 171(4) of the 1979 Act should be noted at the outset:

> "Where an offence under any enactment relating to an assigned matter[68] which has been committed by a body corporate is proved to have been committed with the consent or connivance of, or to be attributable to any neglect on the part of, any director,[69] manager, secretary or other similar officer of the body corporate or any person purporting to act in any such capacity, he as well as the body corporate shall be guilty of that offence and shall be liable to be proceeded against and punished accordingly."

The corresponding provision in section 18(1) of the Theft Act 1968 has already been discussed.[70]

False documents and statements

10.12   Section 167(1) of the Act provides as follows:

> "If any person knowingly or recklessly—
>
> (*a*) makes or signs, or causes to be made or signed, or delivers or causes to be delivered to the Commissioners[71] or an officer, any declaration, notice, certificate or other document whatsoever; or
>
> (*b*) makes any statement in answer to any question put to him by an officer which he is required by or under any enactment to answer,
>
> being a document or statement produced or made for any purpose of any assigned matter, which is untrue in any material particular, he shall be guilty of an offence under this subsection and may be detained . . ."

The offence is punishable on conviction on indictment with two years' imprisonment or a penalty of any amount, or both.[72] There is a corresponding offence,[73] summary only, which does not require proof of *mens rea*.[74] As usual the possibility that the main offence may be committed "recklessly" raises the question whether the recklessness referred to is subjective or objective—*i.e.* must the prosecution prove that the defendant realised the statement might be untrue? Or is it sufficient if

---

68 Defined as any matter in relation to which the Commissioners of Customs and Excise are for the time being required in pursuance of any enactment to perform any duties (s. 1(1)), and therefore including VAT and car tax.

69 "Director", in relation to any body corporate established by or under any enactment for the purpose of carrying on under national ownership any industry or part of an industry or undertaking, being a body corporate whose affairs are managed by the members thereof, means a member of that body corporate: s. 171(4).

70 *Supra*, para. 3.46.

71 *i.e.* the Commissioners of Customs and Excise: s. 1(1).

72 s. 167(2). On summary conviction the offence carries six months' imprisonment or a penalty of the prescribed sum or both.

73 s. 167(3).

74 *Patel v. Comptroller of Customs* [1966] A.C. 356, *Comptroller of Customs v. Western Lectric Co. Ltd* [1966] A.C. 367.

it never occurred to him to check? In the context of the Prevention of Fraud (Investments) Act 1958 the latter view has been adopted,[75] and it would also seem to be consistent with the House of Lords' interpretation of the word "reckless" (albeit in a quite different setting) in *Caldwell*.[76] It is clearly sufficient if the document or statement is literally true but conveys a false impression by virtue of what is left unsaid.[77]

Counterfeiting and falsification of documents

10.13 Section 168(1) provides:

> "If any person—
>
> (a) counterfeits or falsifies any document which is required by or under any enactment relating to an assigned matter or which is used in the transaction of any business relating to an assigned matter; or
>
> (b) knowingly accepts, receives or uses any such document so counterfeited or falsified; or
>
> (c) alters any such document after it is officially issued; or
>
> (d) counterfeits any seal, signature, initials or other mark of, or used by, any officer for the verification of such a document or for the security of goods or for any other purpose relating to an assigned matter,
>
> he shall be guilty of an offence under this section and may be detained."

The penalties are the same as for an offence under section 167(1). The offence has an affinity with that of forgery,[78] but is probably wider in scope. It may be that a "document" for the purposes of section 168 is not necessarily an "instrument" for the purposes of the Forgery and Counterfeiting Act 1981, though this view is not easy to reconcile with the definition of "instrument" in section 8(1) of that Act.[79] It is also likely that a person may "counterfeit or falsify" a document which is not *ipso facto* "false" within section 9(1) of the 1981 Act, because it does not "tell a lie about itself" but is merely inaccurate.[80] Possibly a "counterfeit" document would be false in this sense,[81] but not necessarily one which was "falsified". Certainly in the context of false accounting a document can be falsified without being forged, and although the Theft Act provides a definition it is submitted that the same would be true on the basis of the word's ordinary meaning.[82]

---

75 *Bates* [1952] 2 All E.R. 842, *Grunwald* [1963] 1 Q.B. 935; *supra,* para. 8.07.
76 [1982] A.C. 341.
77 *Kylsant (Lord)* [1932] 1 K.B. 442.
78 *Supra,* para. 6.03ff.
79 *Supra,* para. 6.04.
80 *Supra,* para. 6.08; but *n.b. Donnelly (Ian)* [1984] 1 W.L.R. 1017 (para. 6.17).
81 *Cf.* Forgery and Counterfeiting Act 1981 s. 28(1), which defines a "counterfeit" of a currency note or protected coin as a thing which resembles such a note or coin to such an extent that it is reasonably capable of passing for such a note or coin.
82 *Cf. Edwards v. Toombs* [1983] Crim.L.R. 43; *supra,* para. 6.44.

Evasion of duty

10.14 The Customs and Excise Management Act creates several over-lapping offences of being concerned in the evasion of duty payable on goods.

(1) Under section 50(2) it is an offence for any person, with intent to defraud Her Majesty of the duty payable, to unship, land or unload any goods[83] chargeable with a duty which has not been paid;[84] or to remove such goods from their place of importation or from any approved wharf,[85] examination station,[86] transit shed[87] or customs and excise station;[88] or to assist or be otherwise concerned in such unshipping, landing, unloading or removal.

(2) Under section 159(6) it is an offence to remove from Customs and Excise charge, without the authority of the proper officer and with intent to defraud Her Majesty of any duty chargeable, any imported goods which an officer has power under the Customs and Excise Acts 1979[89] to examine and which have not yet been examined.

(3) Under section 170(1) it is an offence knowingly to acquire possession of goods which are chargeable with a duty which has not been paid,[90] or to be in any way knowingly concerned in carrying, removing, depositing, harbouring, keeping, concealing or in any manner dealing with such goods, with intent to defraud Her Majesty of any duty payable.

(4) Under section 170(2) it is an offence to be in any way knowingly concerned in any fraudulent evasion, or attempt at evasion, of any duty chargeable on any goods.

All four offences are punishable on conviction on indictment with two years' imprisonment or a penalty of any amount.[91] The references to "duty" would appear at first sight to exclude VAT and car tax; but VAT chargeable on the importation of goods is deemed to be a duty for the

---

83 Including stores or baggage: s. 1(1).
84 Where goods have been mistakenly undervalued by a customs officer (without misrepresentation or concealment) and duty has been paid on the basis of that valuation, no further duty is payable: *Customs and Excise Commissioners v. Tan* [1977] A.C. 650.
85 See s. 20.
86 See s. 22.
87 See s. 25.
88 See s. 26.
89 *i.e.* the Customs and Excise Management Act 1979, the Customs and Excise Duties (General Reliefs) Act 1979, the Alcoholic Liquor Duties Act 1979, the Hydrocarbon Oil Duties Act 1979, the Matches and Mechanical Lighters Duties Act 1979 and the Tobacco Products Duty Act 1979: s. 1(1).
90 See n. 84, *supra*.
91 s. 50(4), s. 159(7), s. 170(3). On summary conviction the offences carry six months' imprisonment or a penalty of the prescribed sum or, if greater, three times the value of the goods (*i.e.* the price which they might reasonably have been expected to fetch, after payment of any duty or tax chargeable, if they had been sold in the open market at or about the date of the commission of the offence: s. 171(3)).

purposes of the 1979 Act,[92] and a similar rule applies where car tax on a vehicle is payable by a person who imports it but is not registered under the Car Tax Act 1983.[93]

10.15 The offences under section 50(2) and section 170 are wide in scope, due to the possibility of committing them by merely being "concerned in" the illegal activities referred to. This phrase is sufficiently vague to cover not only acts done before the goods are imported (and outside the jurisdiction)[94] but also dealings with them at any time after the importation.[95] The prosecution must, however, establish a "link or nexus" between the defendant's act and the importation[96] (though he need not be "connected with the original smuggling team"),[97] and it must be proved that at the time of his contribution[98] he intended to defraud[99] the Crown of the duty payable, or in the case of section 170(2) that another party intended to do so and that the defendant knew of that intention. The word "knowingly" in section 170(1) and (2) does not imply that he must know the exact nature of the goods in question, but he must know that a fraudulent evasion of duty is taking place.[1] On a charge of being knowingly concerned in the evasion of a Customs and Excise prohibition (which also falls within section 170(2)) it is not sufficient that the defendant believes it is the payment of duty which is being evaded,[2] and presumably the reverse is also true: a defendant who thought he was smuggling prohibited goods would not intend to defraud the Crown of duty. Nor is it sufficient, it seems (again by analogy with the position regarding the evasion of prohibitions),[3] if he mistakenly believes the goods to be of a type which is not in fact dutiable, even if he is under the impression that goods of that type *are* dutiable.

VAT fraud

10.16 Apart from the Customs and Excise offences mentioned above, the common law offence of cheating the public revenue[4] and general offences of deception and false documentation, a VAT fraud may involve

---

92 Value Added Tax Act 1983 s. 24(1).
93 Car Tax Act 1983 s. 5(4).
94 *Wall* [1974] 1 W.L.R. 930.
95 *Ardalan* [1972] 1 W.L.R. 463.
96 *Watts and Stack* (1979) 70 Cr.App.R. 187 at p. 192 *per* Bridge L.J.
97 *Neal* [1984] 3 All E.R. 156.
98 Not necessarily at the time of importation: *Jakeman* (1982) 76 Cr.App.R. 223.
99 Not necessarily by deception of customs officers: *Attorney-General's Reference (No. 1 of 1981)* [1982] Q.B. 848, *supra,* para. 1.45.
 1 *Hussain* [1969] 2 Q.B. 567.
 2 *ibid.*
 3 *Taaffe* [1984] A.C. 539.
 4 *Supra,* para. 10.02.

the commission of several offences under the Value Added Tax Act 1983.[5] Some of these offences do not require an element of fraud, but three of them do. Section 39(1) provides:

> "If any person is knowingly concerned in, or in the taking of steps with a view to, the fraudulent evasion of tax[6] by him or any other person, he shall be liable . . . on conviction on indictment to a penalty of any amount or to imprisonment for a term not exceeding 2 years or to both."[7]

There is presumably an "evasion" of tax if the tax is not paid when it should be, even if the person liable for it is eventually required to pay it; there would be little point in an offence which was not committed unless the fraud escaped detection. Moreover an evasion of tax may be "fraudulent" even if there is no deception of Customs and Excise officers.[8] Thus in *Fairclough*[9] it was held that the defendant had been guilty of fraudulent evasion by failing to register, using invoices bearing his father's cancelled registration number and charging his customers VAT for which he failed to account.

10.17 It is sufficient if the defendant is knowingly concerned in the taking of steps with a view to the fraudulent evasion of tax, rather than in the fraudulent evasion itself. One cannot be concerned in the evasion of tax unless tax is in fact evaded, whereas the taking of steps with a view to evasion is clearly in the nature of an inchoate offence.[10] Hence this will be the appropriate charge where the fraud is detected before the false return is due to be submitted. It is arguable that the phrase "the taking of steps" denotes some more positive action than mere "evasion", but it will seldom be difficult to establish some positive action on the defendant's part. In *McCarthy*[11] the defendant carried on business without registering for VAT although his turnover exceeded the threshold. Charged with taking steps with a view to the evasion of tax, he argued that his failure to register could not be described as the taking of steps: it was a *failure* to take steps. The Court of Appeal held that even if the non-registration was not a taking of steps, the carrying on of business without registering was. It would seem that there was in any event an actual evasion. It should also be noted that the defendant need not be the taxable person himself: it is sufficient if someone else knowingly co-operates in the fraud, *e.g.* by supplying false invoices.

5 In force on 26 October 1983, replacing Finance Act 1972 s. 38.
6 *i.e.* VAT: s. 48(1).
7 On summary conviction the offence carries six months' imprisonment, or a penalty of the statutory maximum or three times the amount of the tax (whichever is the greater), or both: s. 39(1)(a).
8 *Attorney-General's Reference (No. 1 of 1981)* [1982] Q.B. 848.
9 25 October 1982, C.A., unreported.
10 *Robertson v. Rosenberg* [1951] 1 T.L.R. 417.
11 [1981] S.T.C. 298.

10.18   Section 39(2) provides:

> "If any person—
>
> (*a*) with intent to deceive produces, furnishes, or sends for the purposes of this Act or otherwise makes use for those purposes of any document which is false in a material particular; or
>
> (*b*) in furnishing any information for the purposes of this Act makes any statement which he knows to be false in a material particular or recklessly makes a statement which is false in a material particular,
>
> he shall be liable. . . . on conviction on indictment to a penalty of any amount or to imprisonment for a term not exceeding 2 years or to both."[12]

This offence corresponds to that under section 167(1) of the Customs and Excise Management Act 1979,[13] and similar considerations apply. There is, however, the additional requirement in paragraph (*a*) (but not paragraph (*b*)) of an intent to deceive. This requirement has given rise to some difficulty because VAT returns are processed by computer, and it has been held by a trial judge that a false return is not therefore intended to deceive.[14] The Keith Report proposes an amendment along the lines of section 10(3) of the Forgery and Counterfeiting Act 1981,[15] which in effect deems a deception to take place if false information is fed into a computer.[16] Like section 10(3), the amendment would be confined to the particular mischief in question and would not affect the general law of deception.

10.19   Section 39(3) provides:

> "Where a person's conduct during any specified period must have involved the commission by him of one or more offences under the preceding provisions of this section, then, whether or not the particulars of that offence or those offences are known, he shall, by virtue of this subsection, be guilty of an offence and liable . . . on conviction on indictment to a penalty of any amount or to imprisonment for a term not exceeding 2 years or to both."[17]

This provision is intended to cover a case where it is clear that an offence has been committed during a period spanning several accounting periods, but it is impossible to prove exactly when it was committed: at least one of the defendant's returns must be false but it is not clear which. It was intended that the offence should not be charged in cases of minor evasion

---

12 On summary conviction the offence carries six months' imprisonment or a penalty of the statutory maximum or both: s. 39(2)(i).
13 *Supra,* para. 10.08.
14 *Moritz* (1981, unreported); *cf. supra,* para. 2.30.
15 *Supra,* para. 6.22.
16 Cmnd. 8822 at para. 18.4.24.
17 On summary conviction the offence carries six months' imprisonment, or a penalty of the statutory maximum or three times the amount of the tax evaded or to be evaded (whichever is the greater), or both: s.39(3)(*a*).

by small taxpayers but should be used as an alternative to conspiracy charges in cases of large-scale fraud, and undertakings were given in Parliament to that effect.

10.20 Doubts have been expressed as to whether the offences created by section 39 are sufficiently wide. A trader is liable to account to the Customs and Excise for the "output tax" charged by him to his customers minus any deduction for the "input tax" paid by him to his suppliers. A fraud may therefore be committed either by exaggerating the input tax paid (an "input fraud") or by understating the output tax collected or failing to account for it at all (an "output fraud"), or by a combination of both. As a result of such methods the trader may either avoid paying the full amount of tax for which he is liable or even obtain a repayment of tax (if the input tax paid appears to exceed the output tax collected). Representations were made to the Keith Committee to the effect that the offences under section 39(1) to (3) were inappropriate for input frauds, which therefore had to be charged as the evasion of liability by deception as regards any reduction in the trader's tax liability, and as obtaining property by deception as regards any repayment obtained.[18] But the difficulty is not apparent. An input fraud will normally involve an offence of submitting false returns contrary to section 39(2) of the Value Added Tax Act, and, if the trader's liability is reduced or extinguished, an offence of fraudulent evasion under section 39(1).

10.21 Similarly it was suggested to the Committee that a trader who absconds with the output tax collected would not be guilty of an offence under section 39 and would have to be charged under the Theft Acts.[19] This argument seems dubious on both counts. In the light of *McCarthy*[20] and *Fairclough*[21] it seems that to carry on business with no intention of accounting for the tax collected is sufficient to constitute fraudulent evasion contrary to section 39(1); and on the other hand it is debatable whether any offence under the Theft Acts would in fact be committed. The output tax would not be stolen by the absconding trader, because it would not be property "belonging to another". The trader is not a trustee for the Customs and Excise, nor is he obliged to keep the tax separate from the rest of his money so as to bring section 5(3) of the Theft Act 1968 into play:[22] his obligation is merely to account for an equivalent sum at the appropriate time. The only possible charge under the Theft

---

18 Cmnd. 8822 at para. 18.3.14.
19 *Ibid.*
20 [1981] S.T.C. 298; *supra,* para. 10.13.
21 Unreported; *supra,* para. 10.12.
22 *Supra,* para. 4.07ff.

Acts would seem to be one of obtaining the tax by deception,[23] *i.e.* by inducing the customers to believe that the trader intended to account for the tax. Such a charge would require proof that he intended all along to keep the tax for himself, and also that the customers would have refused to pay it if they had known that that was his intention.[24] A charge of fraudulent trading[25] would no doubt be appropriate in the case of a company, but would not be available in the case of an unincorporated business. Whether or not it is strictly necessary, the Keith Report recommends that section 39 be extended to cover the fraudulent claiming of repayments or input tax credits and the making of taxable supplies with intent to defraud the Customs and Excise of the output tax concerned.[26] It is also proposed that the maximum sentence be increased from two years to seven.[27]

Evasion of car tax

10.22 The Car Tax Act 1983[28] creates offences very similar to those under section 39 of the Value Added Tax Act 1983, but with no offence corresponding to that in section 39(3) which dispenses with the need to prove particulars of the fraud. An offence is committed, punishable on conviction on indictment with two years' imprisonment or a penalty of any amount or both,[29] in the following cases:

(1) If any person is knowingly concerned in, or in the taking of steps with a view to, the fraudulent evasion of car tax by him or any other person.[30]

(2) If any person

(a) with intent to deceive produces, furnishes or sends for the purposes of the Car Tax Act 1983 or regulations made under it,[31] or otherwise makes use for those purposes of, any document which is false in a material particular; or

(b) in furnishing any information for the purposes of the Act or regulations made under it makes any statement which he knows to be false in a material particular or recklessly makes a statement which is false in a material particular; or

---

23 *Supra,* para. 3.02ff.
24 *Supra,* para. 2.49ff.
25 *Supra,* para. 9.03ff.
26 Cmnd. 8822 at para. 18.4.23.
27 *Ibid.* at para. 18.4.26.
28 In force on 26 October 1983.
29 On summary conviction the offences carry six months' imprisonment or a penalty of the statutory maximum (or, in the case of the first offence, three times the amount of the tax, if greater) or both.
30 s. 1(4), Sch. 1 para. 8(1). *Cf. supra,* para. 10.12.
31 Or made by virtue of Sch. 1 para. 13.

(c) with intent to deceive uses or allows to be used any certificate issued in pursuance of regulations under the Act.[32]

Again the general Customs and Excise offences, and that of cheating the public revenue,[33] may be available.

SOCIAL SECURITY FRAUD

10.23   The fraudulent obtaining of social security benefits (*e.g.* by giving false details of one's domestic and financial situation) will usually constitute the offence of obtaining property by deception,[34] and a large-scale fraud should be charged as such, or as a conspiracy, if trial on indictment is desired. There are also several summary offences which may be relevant. A typical example is section 146(3)(*c*) of the Social Security Act 1975, which provides that it is an offence punishable with three months' imprisonment or a fine of level 5 on the standard scale,[35] or both, if a person

> "for the purpose of obtaining any benefit or other payment under this Act, whether for himself or some other person, or for any other purpose connected with this Act—
> (i) knowingly makes any false statement or false representation, or
> (ii) produces or furnishes, or causes or knowingly allows to be produced or furnished, any document or information which he knows to be false in a material particular."

There are offences in virtually identical terms relating to child benefit,[36] family income supplement[37] and supplementary benefit.[38] Prosecutions under the Social Security Act and the Child Benefit Act may only be brought with the consent of the Secretary of State or by an officer authorised by him for that purpose.[39] The *mens rea* required is limited: provided that the claimant's purpose is to obtain benefit, it is no defence that he has no intention of obtaining more benefit than he is entitled to.[40]

---

32 s. 1(4), Sch. 1 para. 8(2).
33 *Supra,* para. 10.02.
34 Theft Act 1968 s. 15(1); *supra,* para. 3.02ff.
35 Criminal Justice Act 1982 s. 46.
36 Child Benefit Act 1975 s. 11(1).
37 Family Income Supplements Act 1970 s. 11.
38 Supplementary Benefits Act 1976 s. 21, substituted by Social Security (Miscellaneous Provisions) Act 1977 s. 14(5).
39 Social Security Act 1975 s. 147(1), Child Benefit Act 1975 s. 11(3).
40 *Clear v. Smith* [1981] 1 W.L.R. 399, *Barrass v. Reeve* [1981] 1 W.L.R. 408; not following *Moore v. Branton* (1974) 118 S.J. 405. See S. Uglow [1984] Crim.L.R. 128 at p.130ff.

CHAPTER 11
Jurisdiction

11.01 Fraud, more than most forms of crime, is frequently complicated by the existence of an international dimension: the fraudsman and his victim may, for example, be in different countries, and the property which is the target may even be in a third. The problems created by this factor are generally thought of as relating to the jurisdiction of an English court, though strictly speaking this is not the case. A Crown Court to which a defendant has been duly committed for trial undoubtedly has jurisdiction to determine whether he is guilty of the offence with which he is charged; the question is simply whether he is. The difficulties arise because his liability may depend not only on what he has done but also on where he did it. Acts done outside England[1] are not normally prohibited by English law, though they may of course be prohibited by the law of another country. It is therefore incorrect (though convenient) to formulate the issue as one of whether an English court has jurisdiction over a particular offence: the real question is whether what was done amounted to an offence under English law at all.[2]

11.02 The basic principle applied by the courts in this area is straightforward (though its application may be less so). It is that English criminal law is territorial in its extent; in other words, no offence is committed under English law unless it is committed within the jurisdiction. The rule is not absolute: Parliament can and sometimes does legislate with extra-territorial effect, either expressly or by implication. The main examples within the scope of this work are the offence of participating ("whether within or outside the United Kingdom") in certain transactions prohibited by section 482 of the Income and Corporation Taxes Act 1970,[3] and offences (such as those under sections 50(2) and 170(2) of the Customs and Excise Management Act 1979)[4] of assisting or being concerned in offences committed within the juris-

---

1 Throughout this chapter the expression "England" includes Wales (but not, of course, Scotland or Northern Ireland).
2 See *Treacy v. D.P.P.* [1971] A.C. 537 at p. 559, *per* Lord Diplock; *D.P.P. v. Stonehouse* [1978] A.C. 55 at p. 90, *per* Lord Keith.
3 *Supra*, para. 10.08ff.
4 *Supra*, para. 10.14ff.

diction.[5] In the latter case the assistance would probably in any event constitute participation in the offence under the general principles of secondary liability and would therefore be triable in England: the offence is committed within the jurisdiction even if the defendant is abroad.[6] But these cases are the exception. Generally speaking the defendant must commit an offence in England before he can be criminally liable under English law. In order to appreciate the implications of this rule it will be convenient to distinguish between three types of offence: first those consisting of conduct which brings about a specified result ("result crimes"); secondly those which consist simply of prohibited conduct, with no need for any particular consequences to follow ("conduct crimes"); and finally the inchoate crimes of conspiracy and attempt.

RESULT CRIMES

11.03 Many offences consist not only of specified conduct on the defendant's part but also of specified consequences which must result from it. In the context of fraud the most important examples are the offences of obtaining various benefits by deception:[7] there is no substantive offence of deceiving another person *simpliciter*, only of deceiving a person *and* thereby obtaining a benefit. It is clearly possible for the deception to be effected in one place and the obtaining in another. If one of these elements occurs in England and the other elsewhere, is there an offence under English law? Lord Diplock has expressed the view that the offence is made out unless neither the deception *nor* the obtaining occurs in England,[8] but this view has not yet found widespread acceptance. The courts have preferred to apply the basic principle referred to above, *viz*. that there is no offence under English law unless the offence is committed within the jurisdiction; and they have taken the view that, since the offence is not committed *until* the benefit in question is obtained, it is committed *where* the benefit is obtained. Therefore it is not sufficient that the deception occurs in England if the benefit is obtained elsewhere.[9] But if the benefit is obtained in England it is immaterial that the deception took place abroad.[10]

11.04 Unfortunately a rule which focuses on the *result* of the defendant's conduct may prove difficult to apply, since there may be

---

5 *Wall* [1974] 1 W.L.R. 930.
6 *Robert Millar (Contractors) Ltd* [1970] 2 Q.B. 54.
7 *Supra*, ch. 3.
8 *Treacy v. D.P.P.* [1971] A.C. 537 at p. 558 ff.
9 *Harden* [1963] 1 Q.B. 8; *Tirado* (1974) 59 Cr.App.R. 80; *R. v. Governor of Pentonville Prison, ex p. Khubchandani* (1980) 71 Cr.App.R. 241.
10 *Ellis* [1899] 1 Q.B. 230.

room for argument as to precisely when and where the stipulated result occurred. In *Secretary of State for Trade v. Markus*,[11] for example, a company with offices in London obtained money from investors in West Germany by arranging for salesmen to call on them and show them brochures relating to a bogus investment trust in Panama. A director of the company was charged with conniving at the offence of fraudulently inducing a person to take part in an arrangement of a type specified by section 13(1)(b) of the Prevention of Fraud (Investments) Act 1958.[12] It was argued, plausibly enough, that since the victims were in West Germany throughout, they could not have "taken part" in the arrangement (the stipulated result) within the jurisdiction. The House of Lords held that they had indeed done so: although they had handed over their application forms and their money in West Germany, the documents were sent to London for processing by the company. In carrying out this processing the company was acting as the investors' agent. Therefore they had taken part in the arrangement within the jurisdiction, and the offence was made out. A somewhat similar case is *Beck*,[13] where the defendant used forged traveller's cheques in France. The cheques had been issued by an English bank and were duly honoured by it. The Court of Appeal dismissed the defendant's appeals against convictions of procuring the execution of valuable securities by deception. Although the immediate effect of his deception was to procure the acceptance (and therefore the "execution") of the cheques in France, they were accepted a second time when the bank honoured them in England. The defendant had therefore procured their "execution" within the jurisdiction as well as outside it.

11.05 Similarly, if the offence charged is one of obtaining property by deception it may be difficult to establish at what stage, and therefore in which jurisdiction, the property was obtained. In *Harden*[14] the defendant deceived a Jersey company into sending him certain cheques. The Court of Criminal Appeal held that he had obtained the cheques outside the jurisdiction, because title passed to him as soon as each cheque was posted in Jersey; therefore he was not guilty of obtaining by false pretences under English law. Delivering the judgment of the court, Widgery J. (as he then was) disclaimed any intention of laying down a general rule as to the time and place of the obtaining in such cases:

"In our judgment, there is no single and universal rule which decides that a cheque transmitted by the victim through the post is to be treated as having

11 [1976] A.C. 35.
12 *Supra*, para. 8.05.
13 [1985] 1 W.L.R. 22.
14 [1963] 1 Q.B. 8.

been obtained by the prisoner at the moment of posting, but it is clear that this will be the case if the prisoner has agreed with the victim that receipt by the postmaster should be equivalent to the receipt by himself."[15]

The court was prepared to find such an agreement on the facts, since the defendant's letters to the Jersey company expressly stated that the offers contained in them could be accepted by the sending of a cheque for the appropriate amount.

11.06   *Harden* was distinguished in *Tirado*,[16] where the defendant ran an employment agency in Oxford and fraudulently induced a number of Moroccans to send him money in the belief that he would find them jobs. He suggested to the victims that they could either post the money to him or transfer it *via* a Moroccan bank, which would send him a banker's draft drawn on a bank in London. There was no basis for the inference drawn in *Harden*, that the posting of the money was *agreed* to constitute delivery to the defendant. But the defence sought to extend *Harden* by arguing that there is no need for such an agreement, and that posting constitutes delivery if the recipient has merely prescribed or even recommended that the postal service be used. The Court of Appeal held that even if the civil law recognised such a rule it was not to be applied to the criminal law:

> " . . . we are not minded to take the law an inch beyond that which *Harden* determined, namely, that if a recipient of a valuable security wishes to show that he obtained it when it was posted to him, he has to be able to show an agreement, express or implied, whereby he had undertaken and accepted that posting should be equivalent to personal delivery as far as he was concerned. Of course, as a matter of first principles, a person does not normally obtain money or valuable securities sent to him until they reach his hands. *Harden* is an exception to that principle . . . "[17]

11.07   However, the court which decided *Tirado* was not referred to the Court of Appeal's earlier decision in *Baxter*.[18] In that case the defendant had sent fraudulent claims from Northern Ireland to football pool companies in Liverpool, without success. He was charged in England with attempting to obtain property by deception. It was argued on his behalf that even if the fraud had succeeded he would not have obtained the money in England but in Northern Ireland, and that by the same token he had not committed an attempt within the jurisdiction either. The court rejected both arguments, citing *Harden* as authority on the former point as if that case had laid down a general rule that money sent to the defendant is obtained where it is posted. *Harden* is not in fact

---

15   At p. 21.
16   (1974) 59 Cr.App.R. 80.
17   At p. 85, *per* Lord Widgery C.J.
18   [1972] 1 Q.B. 1.

authority for such a rule, but *Baxter* presumably is: although the case concerned an attempt rather than the full offence, the view taken on the question of the full offence is essential to the decision. If the court had not thought that the fraud would have been indictable in England had it succeeded, it could hardly have been held that the unsuccessful attempt *was* indictable. It is therefore submitted that the court's view on the full offence constitutes part of the *ratio*; and in that case it would seem to follow that *Tirado* was decided *per incuriam*. This is not to say that the courts can be expected to follow *Baxter* in preference to *Tirado*, and to regard *Harden* as representing not the exception but the rule. *Baxter* is a most unsatisfactory decision in which the court appears simply to have misunderstood the reasoning in *Harden*; in *Tirado* the point was carefully considered, and the actual decision was consonant with the ordinary meaning of the word "obtain". There can be little doubt that *Tirado* now represents the law.

11.08 It is in fact arguable that *Harden* itself would now be decided differently. It was concerned with the old offence of obtaining by false pretences, which was committed only when the defendant obtained *ownership* of the property. For the purposes of the new offence of obtaining property by deception, a person "obtains" property not only if he obtains ownership but also if he obtains possession or control.[19] On the facts of *Harden* it might now be argued that even if the defendant obtained ownership when the cheques were posted in Jersey he did not obtain control of them until he received them in England. It would of course be necessary to show that they were still "property belonging to another" at that stage, and Harden had already acquired title to them; but for the purposes of the Theft Act property "belongs" not only to the owner but also to anyone with possession or control.[20] If Harden did not obtain control of the cheques until he received them, it must follow that until that moment they were in the control of someone else (*viz.* the Post Office). On the other hand it might be said that he did not obtain control of the cheques *by* the deception, since the postman would presumably have delivered them even if he had known of the fraud; what Harden obtained by the deception was the *posting* of the cheques, and they were delivered to him not because the Jersey company had been deceived but because they had been duly posted.[21] In any event the facts of *Harden* must since *Tirado* be regarded as exceptional. In the normal case, where there is no agreement that mere posting will be sufficient to pass title, the defendant will not obtain the property in any sense until he actually receives it.

19 Theft Act 1968 s. 15(2).
20 s.5(1).
21 *Cf. supra*, paras. 2.49ff.

CONDUCT CRIMES

11.09 Where an offence consists solely of certain specified conduct on the defendant's part, irrespective of its consequences, the offence is not committed unless that conduct occurs within the jurisdiction. Even if the reason for prohibiting the conduct is that it is likely to result in harmful consequences, it is not sufficient that those consequences ensue in England if the prohibited conduct occurs elsewhere: it is the conduct, not the consequences, which constitutes the offence. In *Tarling (No. 1) v. Government of the Republic of Singapore*,[22] for example, the House of Lords held that it is not theft under English law to appropriate property outside the jurisdiction merely because it belongs to a company within the jurisdiction. Similarly it would seem that there is no offence under English law if an English company enters into a transaction abroad which would be prohibited if it were effected within the jurisdiction, such as a loan to one of its directors.[23] There may well be damage to the company's capital structure in England, and the possibility of such damage may well be the reason for the prohibition; but unless the transaction takes place in England there is no offence under English law, because it is not the damage which constitutes the offence but the transaction itself. Even if the offence requires an *intent* to bring about certain consequences as a result of the conduct in question, it is still the conduct which is prohibited rather than the intended consequences; hence the offence of forgery is not committed if a false instrument is made in France with the intention of using it to carry out a fraud in England. But if it were made in England for the purpose of committing a fraud in France, the offence would be made out.[24]

11.10 Generally speaking it will be clear, once the facts are established, whether or not the prohibited conduct took place within the jurisdiction. But in some cases the application of this test may present difficulty. The problem is that the concept of conduct is a somewhat ambiguous one: it may refer either to physical actions alone, or it may include certain direct consequences of those actions. In other words, what appears to be a conduct crime may on closer examination prove to be a kind of result crime. Forgery, for example, is commonly regarded as a conduct crime because there is no requirement that anyone be deceived by the false instrument or indeed that it be used at all, only that it be made with the *intention* that it is to be used.[25] Yet forgery does not consist simply of

22   (1978) 70 Cr.App.R. 77.
23   *Supra*, para. 5.02ff.
24   *Hornett* [1975] R.T.R. 256; *El Hakkaoui*]1975] 1 W.L.R. 396. See also *Grantham* [1984] Q.B. 675.
25   *Supra*, paras. 6.03ff.

carrying out certain physical actions with a pen or a typewriter: it consists of acting in such a way as to achieve a particular *result, viz.* the making of a false instrument. Usually this result is so inseparable from the conduct which brings it about that it is natural and convenient to think of it as *part* of that conduct. But once we extend the notion of conduct beyond the defendant's physical actions to include the direct consequences of those actions, it becomes possible to argue, without absurdity, that his conduct is not necessarily in the same place as he is. If, for example, he used a telex machine or a computer network so as to cause some distant terminal to generate a false instrument, his actions would have occurred in one place but the conduct constituting the offence (*sc.* the making of the false instrument) in another. And if the instrument were produced in England, with the necessary intention, the offence would be committed in England irrespective of the whereabouts of the defendant himself.

11.11 Similar reasoning might be employed if the effect of the defendant's communication were to interfere with an accounting system: *e.g.* he might gain access to an English bank's computer, *via* a terminal in another country, and arrange for an account controlled by him to receive a fictitious credit. He would then be falsifying an account within the jurisdiction, and could be charged with the offence of false accounting.[26] If the effect of the fraud were to transfer credits from other accounts to his own, he might perhaps be charged with the theft of those credits (although it was suggested above that he is unlikely to have the required intention of depriving the other customers of their property, *viz.* their rights against the bank).[27] The question would then arise whether his actions at a computer terminal outside the jurisdiction could amount to an appropriation within the jurisdiction. It is submitted that they could. Appropriation, *i.e.* the assumption of the rights of an owner,[28] must surely involve not merely the defendant's actions but also the effect of those actions on the property in question. If for any reason his communication failed to achieve the intended transfer of funds he would not have appropriated those funds but only attempted to do so.[29] If he did not interfere with the system directly but programmed it to make the transfer at a later date,[30] he would not have appropriated the funds until the program came into operation. It is submitted that theft is committed where the property is, not where the defendant is.[30a]

---

26 *Supra*, paras. 6.41ff.
27 *Supra*, para. 3.05.
28 Theft Act 1968 s.3(1).
29 In that case he might be guilty of an attempt, but probably only if his communication at least *reached* England: *infra*, paras. 11.22ff.
30 *Cf. Thompson* [1984] 1 W.L.R. 962.
30a This was apparently assumed to be so in *Tomsett* [1985] Crim.L.R. 369.

11.12   There is a lack of direct authority for the suggestions put forward above, which is hardly surprising: computer fraud is a comparatively recent development. But the courts have long recognised that something done in one place may sometimes be attributed, for the purposes of criminal liability, to a person in another place. This is most clearly so in the case of an innocent agent. In *Oliphant*[31] the defendant was employed in the Paris office of a London firm. It was his duty to send regular accounts of his receipts so that they could be entered in the cash-book in London, but he sent accounts which were incomplete. It was held that he had omitted material particulars from the cash-book, within the jurisdiction. It was immaterial that he did not personally make the entries in London: he made them through the innocent agency of the clerk. In *Treacy v. D.P.P.*[32] the defendant posted a blackmailing letter from England to a woman in Germany, and the question arose whether he had made a demand with menaces[33] in England. Lord Reid and Lord Morris were of the opinion that he did not make the demand until the letter was received in Germany, *i.e.* that he made it through the innocent agency of the postal service. The majority of the House disagreed on the construction of the word "demand", but it was not suggested that there is anything contrary to principle in the idea of a man in England making a demand in Germany. And if this is possible where the defendant acts through an innocent agent, there seems no reason why it should not be possible where he acts through the medium of telecommunications equipment with no human intervention at all.

INCHOATE CRIMES

11.13   The inchoate offences of conspiracy and attempt[34] are clearly conduct crimes, since it is in the nature of inchoate liability that the defendant need not have succeeded in achieving any results at all. It might therefore be expected that the position would be the same as for other conduct crimes, *i.e.* that the offence is committed if (and only if) the conduct in question occurs within the jurisdiction; and to some extent this is true. But there are certain complications, arising partly from the characteristics of inchoate liability in general and partly from the anomalous position of conspiracy to defraud. It will be convenient to consider first the case where the intended fraud is to take place abroad, but the conduct alleged to constitute the inchoate offence has taken place in England, and secondly the converse situation.

31   [1905] 2 K.B. 67.
32   [1971] A.C. 537.
33   Theft Act 1968 s.21.
34   The common law offence of incitement is comparatively rarely invoked and is not
     specifically considered here, but similar principles would no doubt be applicable.

Conduct in England directed at fraud elsewhere

11.14 Since the general rule is that a conduct crime is committed in England if the conduct in question takes place in England, it is tempting to assume that steps taken in England towards the commission of a fraud elsewhere must be indictable as inchoate offences under English law. In *Harden*,[35] for example, it was argued for the Crown that even if the full offence of obtaining by false pretences had been committed in Jersey, the defendant's conduct in England constituted an *attempt* to commit that offence. The court held that it was not possible to substitute a conviction of an attempt, because under section 9 of the Criminal Procedure Act 1851 the jury could not return such an alternative verdict unless it appeared to them upon the evidence that the defendant did not complete the offence charged; and in the court's view "the offences were in fact completed".[36] If this were the only obstacle to a conviction of an attempt it would presumably have been removed by section 6(3) of the Criminal Law Act 1967, which permits an alternative verdict if the jury find the defendant not guilty of the offence charged: there is no requirement that he must not in their view have *committed* that offence. But in any case the court was wrong, on its own view of the facts, in saying that Harden *had* committed the full offence. It fell into the trap of supposing that, because the obtaining was in Jersey, therefore the English courts had no jurisdiction to try Harden for the offences with which he was charged and which (in the court's view) he had clearly committed. It has already been pointed out that this is incorrect.[37] The court which tried Harden clearly did have jurisdiction to do so, but (on the Court of Criminal Appeal's interpretation of the facts) it was wrong to find him guilty of obtaining by false pretences because he had not committed that offence (*sc.* under English law) at all. He may have been guilty of the corresponding offence under the law of Jersey, but not of the offence with which he was charged.

11.15 Nevertheless the court was clearly right to conclude that Harden could not be convicted of an attempt, although it did so for the wrong reasons. The real objection to such a conviction was that it is not an offence under English law to attempt to commit an offence under foreign law. What Harden was attempting to do (and indeed succeeded in doing) was not an offence under English law; therefore under English law he was not committing an offence by attempting to do it. It is now expressly provided by section 1 of the Criminal Attempts Act 1981 that an act does not constitute the offence of attempt unless it is done with intent to commit an offence which, if it were completed, would be triable in

---

35 [1963] 1 Q.B. 8; *supra*, para. 11.05.
36 At p. 22.
37 *Supra*, para. 11.01.

England.[38] Although section 1(2) goes on to provide that an attempt may be committed even though the facts are such that the commission of the full offence is impossible, it is submitted that this does not extend to the case where the defendant will not be committing any offence even if he achieves his intended object. If this is correct it would make no difference that Harden did not know the law and supposed that if his plan succeeded he would be guilty of the full offence: in spite of his misapprehension he could not be said to have the required intention of committing an offence triable in England.

11.16 Similarly section 1 of the Criminal Law Act 1977 provides that the statutory offence of conspiracy is committed only if the course of conduct agreed upon will necessarily amount to or involve the commission of an offence triable in England.[39] Therefore an agreement made in England to commit a fraud elsewhere is not indictable in England as a conspiracy to commit an offence.[40] If the agreement were that the fraud might be committed either within the jurisdiction or outside it, depending on the circumstances, there would have been an indictable conspiracy at common law;[41] but this possibility would appear to be ruled out by the wording of section 1(1). The agreed course of conduct will not *necessarily* involve the commission of an offence in England.

11.17 On a charge of attempting or conspiring in England to commit an offence by carrying out a fraud elsewhere, it must therefore be determined (according to the principles already discussed) whether the intended fraud would in fact have constituted an offence under English law. There is however an additional complication in the case of conspiracy to defraud. On a charge of conspiracy to defraud it is unnecessary to prove that the fraud would have involved a substantive offence at all.[42] Indeed if it *would* have involved an offence, the charge must be one of conspiring to commit that offence, not of conspiracy to defraud.[43] It might therefore be thought that the possibility of a charge at common law offers the prosecutor an attractive solution to the difficulties mentioned above. Unfortunately the advantages of this tactic have been severely restricted. In *Board of Trade v. Owen*[44] the House of Lords held that it is not an offence under English

---

38   s.1(1), (4).
39   s.1(1), (4). There is an exception in the case of conspiracy to murder.
40   *Cf. Cox* [1968] 1 W.L.R. 88; *R. v. Governor of Brixton Prison, ex p. Rush* [1969] 1 W.L.R. 165.
41   *Kohn* (1864) 4 F.& F. 68; *Board of Trade v. Owen* [1957] A.C. 602 at p. 629, *per* Lord Tucker.
42   *Supra*, ch. 1.
43   *Ayres* [1984] A.C. 447; *Tonner* [1984] Crim.L.R. 618; *infra*, para. 12.34ff.
44   [1957] A.C. 602.

law to conspire to defraud persons outside the jurisdiction, whether or
not the fraud would have constituted a substantive offence if it were
carried out in England. More recently the Court of Appeal has held in
Attorney-General's Reference (No. 1 of 1982)[45] that, even if persons
within the jurisdiction would have been defrauded, the conspiracy is still
not indictable in England if that would have been a side-effect and the
true objective was to defraud persons abroad. Thus a scheme to sell
whisky in Lebanon bearing labels resembling those of an English
company was not indictable in England: although it was likely to cause
loss within the jurisdiction by infringing the company's trade marks, the
real object of the exercise was to defraud the prospective purchasers in
Lebanon. It is submitted with respect that the decision confuses the
conspirators' motive with their intention. No doubt their motive was
simply to obtain money from the purchasers in Lebanon. But if they
knew that the execution of their plan would inevitably cause loss in
England, they intended to cause that loss.[46]

11.18   What these decisions establish is that an agreement does not
amount to a conspiracy to defraud, indictable in England, unless its main
objective is to defraud some person or persons within the jurisdiction. It
may therefore be necessary to determine whether the defrauding was
intended to take place in England or elsewhere. One possible view is that
the place of the defrauding is the place where the victim is. As Professor
J.C. Smith has put it,

> "Whereas theft and obtaining by deception are defined in terms of the
> effect of the defendant's act on property, 'defraud' prima facie relates to the
> effect on the victim. It is something that happens to him . . . Just as a man
> can be killed or wounded only in the place where he is, so arguably, he can
> be . . . defrauded only in the place where he is."[47]

But (as Professor Smith goes on to point out) it can hardly be the law that
a conspiracy to obtain property outside the jurisdiction by fraud is
indictable in England merely because the owner of the property happens
to be here, or is expected to be here when the fraud is to be carried out.
An argument to this effect was in fact rejected by the Court of Appeal in
Attorney-General's Reference (No. 1 of 1982).[48] It was held not to be
sufficient merely that the English distillers would inevitably suffer loss as
a result of the infringement of their trade marks in Lebanon. They would
not thereby have been defrauded in England.

---

45   [1983] Q.B. 751.
46   *Cf.* J.C. Smith [1983] Crim.L.R. 534.
47   [1979] Crim.L.R. 220 at p. 223.
48   [1983] Q.B. 751, *supra*.

11.19 It does not follow that the victim's whereabouts are irrelevant. The concept of fraud encompasses a multitude of sins,[49] and it may be that the place of the defrauding depends on the particular type of fraud involved. If it consists simply of a direct infringement of the victim's proprietary rights (*e.g.* theft), it seems from *Attorney-General's Reference (No. 1 of 1982)*[50] that the victim is defrauded in the place where the infringement occurs, whether or not he is there at the time. But if the fraud consists of a deception which induces the victim to act to his detriment, *e.g.* by parting with property, it seems more natural to regard it as occurring where the victim is when he does the act in question.[51]

11.20 This possibility appears to have influenced the drafting of the charges in *Tarling (No. 1) v. Government of the Republic of Singapore*,[52] where it was alleged that Tarling, the chairman of a Singapore company, had purchased from it shares in a Hong Kong company at a considerable undervalue. The Singapore government took proceedings for his extradition. Under the Fugitive Offenders Act 1967 the crucial question was whether Tarling could have been committed for trial in England if those events which the evidence disclosed to have taken place in Singapore had taken place in England instead. It was therefore essential to draft the charges in such a way that, with the substitution of England for Singapore, the offences charged would have been committed within the jurisdiction of the English courts. One of the charges alleged a conspiracy to defraud the shareholders of the Singapore company by concealing the transaction from them and thus inducing them to refrain from demanding an account of the proceeds. It would of course have been simpler to particularise the fraud as consisting in the purchase itself, *i.e.* in depriving the shareholders of profits which were rightfully theirs; but a charge framed in this way would have been open to the objection that the transaction took place in Hong Kong and related to shares in a Hong Kong company. It could not then be said that the fraud took place in Singapore (*i.e.*, hypothetically, in England), unless the law is that a person is defrauded in the place where he is, rather than the place where his interests are infringed. This position was presumably thought to be untenable, and the decision in *Attorney-General's Reference (No. 1 of 1982)*[53] bears out that view.[54] The effect of focusing on the alleged

---

49   *Cf. supra*, para. 1.31ff.
50   [1983] Q.B. 751, *supra*.
51   Not, presumably, when he is *deceived*, since deception alone is not fraud: *cf.* para. 1.33.
52   (1978) 70 Cr.App.R. 77.
53   [1983] Q.B. 751, *supra*.
54   Another charge alleged a conspiracy to *steal* the shares, and the House was unanimous that even if there was evidence of theft (which the majority denied: see *supra*, para. 4.33), it was committed in Hong Kong, not Singapore.

deception of the shareholders rather than on the transaction itself was that the fraud could more plausibly be presented as having taken place in Singapore.

11.21 Unfortunately the decision is inconclusive on this point because the majority of the House of Lords held that there was no evidence of the conspiracy alleged; it was therefore unnecessary to decide where, if anywhere, the shareholders were defrauded. Nevertheless Lord Salmon expressed the view that if there had been a fraud it would in any case have been committed in Hong Kong.[55] The minority, on the other hand, were of the opinion not only that there was evidence of the alleged conspiracy but that (if England were substituted for Singapore) it would have been committed within the jurisdiction. This view is implicit in Lord Edmund-Davies' dissent, since he would have allowed the Singapore government's appeal on the charges of conspiracy to defraud,[56] and it was expressly stated by Viscount Dilhorne. Indeed Viscount Dilhorne was prepared to regard the purchase itself, and not merely the deception of the shareholders, as a fraud committed in Singapore.[57] This view is hard to reconcile with *Attorney-General's Reference (No. 1 of 1982)*.[58] But the dissenting speeches lend some support to the argument that certain types of fraud are committed where the victim is, rather than where the offending transaction takes place.

Conduct abroad directed at fraud in England

11.22 We have seen that steps taken in England towards the commission of a fraud abroad do not normally constitute an inchoate offence under English law because there is no intention of committing a *substantive* offence under English law. It might then seem reasonable that the English courts should accept jurisdiction in the converse situation, where steps are taken abroad towards the commission of a fraud in England. The difficulty here is that attempt and conspiracy are conduct crimes, and on principle are not indictable in England unless the conduct in question takes place in England. In practice, however, this problem is seldom insuperable, because the fraudsmen will normally have succeeded in achieving some part of their object in England and to that extent may be regarded as having acted within the jurisdiction. Indeed there appears to be no reported case in which an English court has declined jurisdiction over an attempt or conspiracy to commit an offence in England solely on the ground that the conduct in question took place abroad.

55 At p. 132.
56 He appears to have been under the impression that the only issue dividing the House on these charges was that of dishonesty (at p. 134).
57 At p. 124.
58 [1983] Q.B. 751; *supra*, para. 11.17.

11.23 It will be recalled, for example, that in *Baxter*[59] the sending of fraudulent football pool claims from Northern Ireland to Liverpool was held to be indictable in England as an attempt to obtain property by deception. The defence had argued that even if the full offence would have been committed in England,[60] the attempt consisted simply of the defendant's conduct in posting the claims in Northern Ireland. The decision was not that conduct abroad was indictable in England if directed at an offence in England, but that although the defendant had not left Northern Ireland the attempt was in fact committed in England. Sachs L.J., delivering the judgment of the court, said:

> "An attempt to commit a crime is established by proving an intent to commit it and in addition proving that in pursuance of that intent something has been done that is more than a mere preparation and is sufficiently proximate to the intended offence . . . Obviously the period between the moment the proximate act or acts commence and the time they finally fail may vary immensely. At any moment of that period, however, it is plainly true to say of the offender, 'He is attempting to commit that crime'. It matters not whether on any particular set of facts the attempt is best described as a continuing offence (as where a time bomb set to explode at a given hour in this country is being sent by rail) or as a series of offences (as where there are a series of blows on a cold chisel to force a door open). If the time bomb is discovered on the train, it matters not whether it is known on which side of some border it was placed there. At the moment of discovery it can plainly be said of the person who put it there that he is attempting to cause an explosion. The position is no different if what is being transmitted is a letter and the moment when its contents come to light occurs on the premises where it is meant to produce the intended result, an obtaining by deception of money from someone within the jurisdiction. The attempt has occurred within the jurisdiction. On those principles it is accordingly manifest that there is no reason why the jurisdiction of the courts here should not attach to the offence. An alternative but no less effective way of expressing the matter is to say that he who despatches a missile or a missive arranges for its transport and delivery (essential parts of the attempt) and is thus committing part of the crime within the jurisdiction by the means which he has arranged. The physical personal presence of an offender within this country is not, according to our law, an essential element of offences committed here."[61]

11.24 *Baxter* was applied in *D.P.P. v. Stonehouse*,[62] where a prominent politician had taken out several life assurance policies and then disappeared in Miami in such circumstances as to give the impression that he had drowned. His intention was to enable his wife (who was not a party to the fraud) to collect the proceeds of the insurance policies while

---

59 [1972] 1 Q.B. 1; *supra*, para. 11.07.
60 *Supra*, paras. 11.05ff.
61 At p. 11f.
62 [1978] A.C. 55.

he made a new life in Australia. However he was arrested before his wife had made a claim. He was charged, *inter alia,* with attempting to obtain[63] property by deception. The defence argued that the conduct alleged to constitute the offence, *i.e.* the fake drowning, had taken place entirely outside the jurisdiction. Unlike Baxter, Stonehouse had not even sent a deceptive communication to England. He had simply disappeared. The House of Lords held that he had nevertheless committed the attempt in England by causing the news of his "death" to be communicated there. As Lord Edmund-Davies put it:

> "The appellant was no obscure person, but a Member of Parliament, well-known both in politics and in the business world, and he knew as surely as if he had arranged matters himself that news of his disappearance would immediately be flashed back home. Indeed, [counsel for the appellant] accepted that the appellant had that very thing in mind, and events fulfilled his expectations up to the hilt. The law must keep in step with technical advances in international communications and the dissemination of news, and one who has it in mind that they will be utilised by others and, indeed, banks on their doing so must, in my judgment, be treated no differently from one who himself posts a letter or telephones a message or makes a personal broadcast, in which events learned counsel accepted that the issue of justiciability could not be in doubt."[64]

Lord Diplock went as far as to suggest that there is no need for any conduct within the jurisdiction at all, provided that there is the necessary intention to commit an offence in England; he thought, for example, that in *Baxter* there would still have been jurisdiction even if the claims had been intercepted in the post before leaving Northern Ireland.[65] But this view found no support, and Lord Keith expressly disagreed.[66]

11.25 The courts have adopted a similar approach in the context of conspiracies formed abroad to commit offences in England. In *D.P.P. v. Doot*[67] five Americans entered into an agreement in either Belgium or Morocco to import cannabis into England, and proceeded to carry the agreement out. They were charged not only with substantive offences of importing the cannabis but also with conspiracy to do so. The Court of Appeal held that the conspiracy, having been made outside the jurisdiction, was not indictable in England; the House of Lords disagreed and restored the convictions. Again the House stopped short of saying that there was no need for any conduct within the jurisdiction,[68] but it held that the conduct necessary to constitute the conspiracy had in fact

---

63 "Obtain" includes enabling another to obtain: Theft Act 1968 s. 15(2).
64 At p. 84.
65 At p. 67.
66 At p. 93.
67 [1973] A.C. 807.
68 Though Lord Salmon hinted at this possibility (at p. 832ff.).

occurred in England when the defendants arrived in pursuance of the agreement and began to carry it out. Although originally formed abroad, the conspiracy had continued in existence in England. Lord Pearson, with whom Lord Wilberforce agreed, put the matter thus:

> "A conspiracy involves an agreement, expressed or implied. A conspiratorial agreement is not a contract, not legally binding, because it is unlawful. But as an agreement it has its three stages, namely (1) making or formation, (2) performance or implementation, (3) discharge or termination. When the conspiratorial agreement has been made, the offence of conspiracy is complete, it has been committed, and the conspirators can be prosecuted even though no performance has taken place . . . But the fact that the offence of conspiracy is complete at that stage does not mean that the conspiratorial agreement is finished with. It is not dead. If it is being performed, it is very much alive. So long as the performance continues, it is operating, it is being carried out by the conspirators, and it is governing or at any rate influencing their conduct. The conspiratorial agreement continues in operation and therefore in existence until it is discharged (terminated) by completion of its performance or by abandonment or frustration or however it may be. On principle, . . . I think . . . a conspiracy to commit in England an offence against English law ought to be triable in England if it has been wholly or partly performed in England."[69]

Indeed it would seem to follow from his Lordship's reasoning that there is a conspiracy within the jurisdiction not only if something is done in England in pursuance of the agreement but even if the conspirators are simply present in England during the currency of the agreement; and Viscount Dilhorne was apparently prepared to accept this conclusion.[70] It might even be sufficient if only *one* of the conspirators were present in England. Lord Salmon objected that in that case the sole representative could not be said to be "agreeing with himself, whilst here, on behalf of each of the other conspirators".[71] But he might still be conspiring *with* the others. If an agreement were reached by telephone between a person in England and one abroad, it could surely be said that the agreement was made in England (though it could equally be said that it was made abroad). Similarly, it is submitted, there is a continuing conspiracy in England if, during the currency of the agreement, one of the conspirators comes to England.

69   At p. 827.
70   At p. 823.
71   At p. 835.

CHAPTER 12

Presenting a Fraud Case

12.01 Fraud cases vary enormously in complexity. This chapter is concerned principally with the presentation of a case alleging large-scale fraud, though much of what is said will apply to fraud cases in general.

CURBING THE LENGTH OF A TRIAL

12.02 Fraud trials are often inevitably long; the photocopier has made them longer. There is often a tension between prosecution and defence which the court has to resolve. The prosecution feels that its best chance of achieving a conviction of the maximum number of defendants is to try them all together and subject them to a mass of evidence. If they are tried separately, then those tried may blame those who are absent. If only part of the picture is presented, then the jury are less likely to be convinced of overall fraud. For precisely corresponding reasons defendants will want to be tried separately with as little evidence as possible called against them. Their fears may be not merely the natural trepidation of the guilty, but the genuine concern of the innocent. Trying a large number of people together, with a vast amount of evidence, may make it difficult for the tribunal (particularly a lay one) to distinguish the guilty from the innocent, and may present it with the difficult task of considering certain evidence against some of the accused but not against all.

12.03 In a number of modern cases the courts have stressed the need to curb the length of trials. Some are fraud cases, others are not; the principle remains good throughout. The courts do recognise that where serious large-scale crime is involved a long trial may be a necessity. Since the danger to the community is great, the community must be prepared to undertake the burden of averting it. Thus in *Simmonds*[1] Fenton Atkinson J. said in relation to a purchase tax fraud:

". . . the ever-mounting intricacy of the legislation imposing taxes has been followed by ever-increasing ingenuity on the part of numbers of persons conspiring together fraudulently to evade the taxation. Such are the

1 [1969] 1 Q.B. 685.

complexities of these fraudulent schemes and the devices used in them that only too often the only way that the interests of justice can be served is by presenting to a jury with the aid of schedules an overall picture of the scheme and charging a conspiracy to cheat and defraud. Obviously every effort should be made to present instead to the jury a relatively small series of substantive offences—but that cannot always be done and this case is one of those where only a conspiracy charge can provide for the protection of the interests of the community when once the legislature produces intricate laws."[2]

On the other hand the courts discourage long trials whenever they can be avoided. Thus in *Novac*[3] Bridge L.J. said:

"Some criminal prosecutions involve consideration of matters so plainly inextricable and indivisible that a long and complex trial is an ineluctable necessity. But we are convinced that nothing short of the criterion of absolute necessity can justify the imposition of the burdens of a very long trial on the Court."[4]

12.04   In *Simmonds*[5] the Court of Appeal gave advice on means to reduce the length of fraud trials. Some of these procedures are now followed as a matter of course, but they may conveniently be summarised:

(1) The prosecution should seek to simplify the issues to be tried and verdicts given, and include a number of defendants and counts in the same indictment only where that is absolutely necessary. In this context it is useful to remember the words of Bridge L.J. in *Novac:*[6]

"It is quite wrong for prosecuting authorities to charge, in a single indictment, numerous offenders and offences, simply because some *nexus* may be discoverable between them, leaving it to the Court to determine any application to sever which may be made by the defence. If multiplicity of defendants and charges threatens undue length and complexity of trial then a heavy responsibility must rest on the prosecution in the first place to consider whether joinder is essential in the interests of justice or whether the case can reasonably be sub-divided or otherwise abbreviated and simplified. In jury trial brevity and simplicity are the hand-maidens of justice, length and complexity its enemies."[7]

(2) The prosecution should supply the trial judge in advance of the trial with an opening note, so that he may consider how best to control the length of the trial.

(3) There should be a pre-trial summons for directions at which questions as to the form of the indictment and severance of defendants

2   At p. 689f. *Cf. Thorne* (1978) 66 Cr.App.R. 6 at p. 13, *per* Lawton L.J.
3   (1976) 65 Cr.App.R. 107.
4   At p. 118. *Cf. Thorne, supra,* at p. 13f., *per* Lawton L.J.
5   [1969] 1 Q.B. 685.
6   (1976) 65 Cr.App.R. 107.
7   At p. 118f.

and counts may be argued. It may be necessary at this stage to argue the admissibility of evidence: for example, the question whether a piece of evidence on one count is admissible on another may bear upon the question whether there is a true nexus between counts or defendants.[8]

(4) The trial judge should be given sufficient time before such a summons to form his own independent view as to the best way to present the case to the jury in the interests of the administration of justice as a whole.

(5) If the trial judge disagrees with the form in which the prosecution seeks to present the case, he should ask it to recast it. The extent, if any, to which he can compel it to do so is considered later.[9]

(6) Schedules of evidence which it is anticipated will be given should be prepared in advance of the trial. Not all evidence can or should be scheduled. The ingenuity of prosecuting counsel to produce schedules is never-ending—in one celebrated case a schedule of orgies was drawn. In a fraud case, however, there will often be repetitive evidence based on documents which need not be produced if a schedule is made of them. This can usually be done by agreement between counsel and often by admission. It is rarely suitable to schedule evidence which is at the heart of the case and disputed by the defence. The written word may have an over-persuasive effect. In many instances, however, a schedule may go to the jury with a suitable warning and room on the schedule to note alternative submissions or evidence. By agreement a schedule may replace the evidence on which it is based if the defence admits it. If it does not admit it and the judge takes the view that disputes on it are on minor matters, then there would seem no reason why he could not order it to go before the jury, even if the defence objects. In such an event the evidence supporting the schedule would have to be called and the jury warned strongly that the schedule itself is not evidence.

(7) Interviews between investigators and defendants should be pruned. In *Simmonds* the court commented that "there is vast scope for those engaged in the preparation of a case for trial so to bring out the evidence in chief as to extract the essence of the interviews without going into every word of them."[10] The defence may always put them in a wider context if they wish. If the defence requests the full context at the outset it is usually given, but the prosecution need not accede to the request provided it makes it clear that only part of an interview is presented.

(8) Defence counsel should not raise untenable points or cross-examine away from the issue.

---

8 *Cf. D.P.P.* v. *Boardman* [1975] A.C. 421 at p. 459, *per* Lord Cross; *Novac, supra,* at p. 110.
9 *Infra,* para. 12.58ff.
10 At p. 692.

SELECTION OF CHARGES

The need for precision

12.05 A criminal trial should seek to convict the guilty and acquit the innocent. In order to ensure the latter it has long been recognised that the prosecution should bring a precise charge so that an accused may know in advance exactly what it is he has to meet. If the indictment is over-precise, however, the guilty may escape on a technicality. The tension between the need for precision and the desire to avoid over-technicality is frequently present in a fraud trial. The prosecution has usually accumulated evidence which on the face of it reveals dishonest conduct and which calls for an answer. Very often, however, it lacks inside information that would reveal to it the precise nature of the fraud. It may, and very often in a complicated case will, have drawn a false inference in some particular area. It may be right in the inference of dishonest conduct but wrong in its deductions about the method employed. Whilst, therefore, the prosecution must formulate its charges with reasonable precision, it also desires to stretch them as wide as possible. It wishes to allow itself room for manoeuvre during the ensuing trial. The defence, on the other hand, will want in most cases to pin the prosecution down to as narrow and precise a charge as possible. It is conscious that the adversarial system offers it distinct advantages. It need not show its hand until the prosecution has committed itself to a particular charge. Once that is done, it may escape because the prosecution has chosen the wrong charge; or it may succeed in excluding evidence which, whilst it possibly indicates fraud, is irrelevant to the particular fraud charged.

Substantive charges and conspiracy

12.06 Very often in a fraud case there are a multiplicity of charges the prosecution may make. To bring them all would be oppressive to an accused and overcomplicate the trial. The prosecution has a number of ways of meeting this problem. It may choose sample charges, adducing evidence of other acts amounting to offences as evidence of dishonesty. Instead of charging the actual offences committed, it may charge a conspiracy to commit them. The acts which constitute the substantive offences then become evidence from which the antecedent criminal agreement may be inferred. Sometimes the prosecution tries to have its cake and eat it by including both a conspiracy charge and charges of substantive offences. In general the courts have discouraged the use of a conspiracy charge where substantive charges will do, and the inclusion of both conspiracy and substantive charges in one indictment.

12.07   Before considering the cases in which these rules have evolved, it may be useful to consider in general the advantages and disadvantages to either side of conspiracies and substantive charges. Defendants generally prefer to meet substantive charges. The word "conspiracy" has a sinister ring which many defendants fear. It is more difficult for a defendant in a conspiracy trial to sever his trial from that of other defendants. On a joint trial co-defendants who might exculpate a particular defendant may choose not to give evidence, though they could be compelled in a separate trial. If the prosecution elects substantive charges, there is always the chance that it may choose the wrong charge, though this danger has been greatly reduced since the technicalities of the old Larceny Acts were discarded. If the prosecution picks sample counts, then it may choose an instance for which the defendants happen to have an explanation. On the other hand, if there has been fraudulent conduct and the prosecution picks a sufficiently wide selection of sample counts, conviction ought to ensue in at least some instances. If sample counts are chosen, then a defendant may be able to argue successfully that other conduct is inadmissible because it lacks the striking similarity necessary for its admission in evidence or because it is not relevant to any issue raised by the substantive charges.[11] The defendant may in a conspiracy case be exposed to evidence which would not be admissible on a substantive charge. For instance, it is frequently held that in a conspiracy case the act of any conspirator in furtherance of the conspiracy is the act of all conspirators.[12]

12.08   What is seen as disadvantage to the defence is often seen as advantage to the prosecution, and so prosecutors often favour a conspiracy charge. Such a charge gives them the maximum room for manoeuvre during the trial. The fact that they fail to prove one part of their case is immaterial if they adduce other evidence which still goes to prove the general agreement. No difficulties as to similar fact evidence are likely to arise, since all relevant conduct goes to the conspiracy. Evidence inadmissible on a substantive charge may become admissible on a conspiracy. Where the organisers of crimes have deliberately kept themselves in the background, a jury may more readily understand their guilt of conspiracy than their involvement in individual offences committed by others. If sample counts are laid, the accused can only be sentenced on the basis of those counts (unless he asks for other offences to be taken into consideration). If a conspiracy count is included, the agreement will cover all the offences which are subsequently committed,

---

11 *Cf. infra*, para. 13.12ff.
12 *Luberg* (1926) 19 Cr.App.R. 133 at p. 136f., *per* Sankey J.; *Griffiths* [1966] 1 Q.B. 589 at p. 594, *per* Paull J.; *infra*, para. 13.05ff.

and the trial judge may form his own view whether to sentence on the basis that the accused committed all or only some of the offences in pursuance of the general agreement. In the result an accused may qualify for a criminal bankruptcy order on a conspiracy charge for which he would not qualify on the aggregate of sample substantive counts.[13] On the other hand, a prosecutor may find a conspiracy count has its disadvantages. He must define his conspiracy precisely and particularise it. He must not charge two conspiracies in one count. He may find that the defendants can escape on technicalities even more easily on a conspiracy charge than on substantive counts.

12.09   The court may have interests independent of both prosecutor and defendant. Where trial is by jury, a conspiracy verdict may be too wide to be an adequate guide to sentence. A judge may prefer to avoid any vital fact-finding exercise independent of the jury's verdict. The court will also want to ensure that the trial is kept within reasonable bounds and that the jury is not overburdened with detail or the public with expense. In any event if there is one conspiracy count covering a number of identical substantive counts, the maximum sentence available is limited to the maximum for one of the substantive counts.[14] The court may feel this is inadequate.

Substantive charges preferable
12.10   The relationship between conspiracy and substantive counts involves two separate questions: (a) Should there be a conspiracy count at all? (b) If so, should it co-exist with substantive counts or be tried alone? In *Verrier v. D.P.P.*[15] the House of Lords stated the general rule that, where there is an effective and sufficient charge of a substantive offence, the addition of a charge for conspiracy is undesirable. In *Selsby*[16] Lord Cranworth (then Rolfe B.) expressed the view that where possible it was more satisfactory to indict for a substantive offence rather than conspiracy. This view was adopted and greatly reinforced by Cockburn C.J. in *Boulton.*[17] That was a case so weak it required six counsel, including two Law Officers, to prosecute it to acquittal. Two men were found walking in public in women's clothing. A medical examination produced some evidence of buggery.[18] In addition, at their lodgings were found letters from a number of other men with apparent references to dressing in women's clothing. There was also evidence that some (though

---

13   *Cain* [1985] A.C. 46.
14   Criminal Law Act 1977 s. 3(3).
15   [1967] 2 A.C. 195 at p. 223f., *per* Lord Pearson.
16   (1851) 5 Cox 495n. at p. 497.
17   (1871) 12 Cox 87.
18   The report is somewhat coy about the "unnatural act".

not all) of the accused had lived in the same premises and had occasionally shared a bed. They were indicted with a general conspiracy to commit felonious and unnatural crime (presumably buggery), a general conspiracy to incite persons unknown to commit the same offence, and, in a series of twelve other counts, a number of smaller conspiracies to commit the same crime (these last being based principally upon the letters that passed from one to another). Cockburn C.J. was strongly critical of the way the police had behaved in the investigation. As to the form of the indictment, he said:

> "I am clearly of opinion that where the proof intended to be submitted to a jury is proof of the actual commission of crime, it is not the proper course to charge the parties with conspiring to commit it; for that course operates, it is manifest, unfairly and unjustly against the parties accused; the prosecutors are thus enabled to combine in one indictment a variety of offences, which, if treated individually, as they ought to be, would exclude the possibility of giving evidence against one defendant to the prejudice of others, and deprive defendants of the advantage of calling their co-defendants as witnesses."[19]

Despite expressing himself so strongly the learned Lord Chief Justice nevertheless left the counts to the jury, though his comments on the facts, adverse to the Crown, must have contributed to the defendants' acquittal.

12.11 In *West*[20] the Court of Criminal Appeal quashed a count of conspiracy as duplicitous. Humphreys J., giving the judgment of the court, added:

> "The most serious aspect of the present case was the creation of false documents brought into being and used for the purpose of deceiving the Board of Trade. The law of this country is not so futile that such conduct, if proved, cannot be criminally punished without recourse to a vaguely worded general charge of conspiracy extending over six years. There is a growing tendency to charge persons with criminal conspiracy rather than with the specific offences which the evidence shows them to have committed. It is not to be encouraged."[21]

In *Cooper and Compton*[22] two police officers were charged with conspiracy to steal and in four substantive counts of robbery and four alternative counts of larceny. The allegation against them was that they had used their position as police officers to force four named witnesses to hand over property under threats of police action of one sort or another against them. Their defence was that in three of the four cases they had not taken any property, and that in the fourth they had done so but only

19 (1871) 12 Cox 87 at p. 93.
20 [1948] 1 K.B. 709.
21 At p. 720.
22 (1947) 32 Cr.App.R. 102.

at the request of the complainant. The jury convicted them of conspiracy but acquitted them on the substantive counts. The Court of Criminal Appeal quashed the conviction as unreasonable, because the only material on which it could be based was the evidence of the four incidents and the jury had acquitted the defendants on the substantive charges relating to those incidents. Humphreys J., delivering the judgment of the court, said:

> "In this case it appears to us that there was no necessity from any point of view for the insertion of any charge of conspiracy. A verdict of Guilty could be supported only if the jury believed the general story, and the general story was one told by four different persons, each of whom, if he was believed, proved conclusively a charge of stealing which, from the point of view of the punishment, is actually a more serious offence than that of conspiracy, and it is owing to the insertion of that count that this trouble has arisen. Counsel for the prosecution was doing his duty in considering whether it was desirable or not to insert a count for conspiracy in this indictment. He thought that it was. In a similar case in future counsel for the prosecution will probably think, and think very long, before he clogs a perfectly simple case of stealing in one or more instances with a count for conspiracy, because it is so well known that juries not infrequently fail to understand what the lawyer finds so simple to understand, the difference between conspiracy and larceny."[23]

12.12 These cases, and others which followed them, were also concerned with the inclusion of conspiracy and substantive counts in the same indictment and with rolled up or duplicitous conspiracy counts. To these topics we shall have to return.[24] But these cases do discourage the use of conspiracy counts which do no more than rehearse in different form allegations that could as well be made in substantive counts, or which amount to an improper attempt to launch a prosecution on evidence too nebulous to support substantive counts. It is to be noted, however, that while the use of conspiracy counts in such circumstances is discouraged, in none of these cases was a count quashed on that ground alone. Whether the court has power to quash a conspiracy count on the ground that it is an improper form of indictment on particular facts, even though there is evidence to support it, must be considered under a separate head.[25]

Circumstances where conspiracy charges may properly be laid
12.13 There is in any event another side to the coin. The courts have recognised that the conspiracy charge has a legitimate place in an indictment for fraud. In many cases it is the organisation of crime that is

---

23 At p. 111.
24 *Infra*, para. 12.19ff., 12.24ff.
25 *Infra*, para. 12.58ff.

the greater evil than the individual crimes committed under its aegis, and a conspiracy charge may legitimately aim at that. In *Verrier v. D.P.P.*[26] the House of Lords approved two passages from R. S. Wright J. on Conspiracy.[27] At one point he says:

> "To permit two persons to be indicted for a conspiracy to make a slide in the street of a town, or to catch hedge sparrows in April, would be to destroy that distinction between crimes and minor offences which in every country it is held important to preserve. On the other hand, there may be cases in which the concurrence of several persons for committing an offence may essentially change its character, and so enhance its mischief that the joint act may properly be treated as a crime."[28]

Earlier he points out that:

> "There may be cases in which the agreement or concurrence of several persons in the execution of a criminal design is a proper ground for aggravation of their punishment beyond what would be proper in the case of a sole defendant. Such would be cases in which the co-operation of several persons at different places is likely to facilitate the execution or the concealment of a crime, or in which the presence of several persons together is intended to increase the means of force or to create terror, or cases of fraud in which suspicion and ordinary caution are likely to be disarmed by the increased credibility of a representation made by several persons."[29]

12.14 *Verrier* was a case in which the substantive offence had not been consummated so that conspiracy had to be charged. Their Lordships nevertheless expressed the view that it was only in exceptional cases that conspiracy should be substituted for substantive counts.[30] Moreover they held that the sentence for conspiracy could be greater than for the substantive offence or offences which it was agreed to commit. This rule is now reversed by section 3 of the Criminal Law Act 1977, but the general observations of R.S. Wright are still apt in this context. Lord Coleridge C.J. made a similar point in *Mogul Steamship Co. Ltd. v. McGregor, Gow and Co.*[31] He drew a distinction between the tort of conspiracy, where damage must be proved, and the crime of conspiracy where proof of the agreement is sufficient:

> ". . . in an indictment it suffices if the combination exists and is unlawful, because it is the combination itself which is mischievous, and which gives the public an interest to interfere by indictment."[32]

26 [1967] 2 A.C. 195.
27 *The Law of Criminal Conspiracies and Agreements* (1873).
28 At p. 83; *cf. Blamires Transport Services Ltd* [1964] 1 Q.B. 278 at p. 282f., *per* Edmund Davies J.
29 At p. 81f.
30 At p. 223f., *per* Lord Pearson.
31 (1888) 21 Q.B.D. 544.
32 At p. 549. *N.b.* that, with certain exceptions (*e.g.* conspiracy to defraud), a conspiracy to commit an unlawful act is no longer a crime unless the unlawful act is itself criminal: Criminal Law Act 1977 s. 1(1), *infra* para. 12.34.

12.15 There are other criminal cases in which the Court of Criminal Appeal has stressed that the fact of combination may make a crime more serious. They were, like *Verrier,* concerned with the appropriate sentence in conspiracy cases and like *Verrier* must now be read subject to section 3 of the Criminal Law Act 1977. Thus in *Morris*[33] the defendant had been engaged in the wholesale smuggling of watches over an eight month period. Lord Goddard C.J. observed:

> "Where the evidence showed that the only matter in which the defendant had been concerned was one definite offence, it would obviously be wrong, by means of indicting him for conspiracy, to impose on him a longer sentence than he could have received if he had been indicted merely for the substantive offence. But in the present case the appellant has been engaged in a traffic which obviously has been going on for many months; he has had four motor-cars fitted so that this traffic can be carried on, and was smuggling on a very extensive scale. Those considerations do not therefore apply to this case."[34]

Similarly in *Field*[35] it was argued that the defendants, who had conspired to obstruct the course of justice, had in effect done no more than wilfully obstruct the police and should be sentenced on that basis. Lawton J., delivering the judgment of the court, disagreed.

> "Even if the object of the conspiracy had been the obstruction of the police, which it was not, in the circumstances of this case the fact of the unlawful combination of these appellants to achieve that end would have changed its character and so enhanced its mischief that the joint act might properly be treated as a different and more serious crime."[36]

12.16 The seriousness of conspiracy may lie not only in the organisation involved, but also in the aggregate of the acts committed in pursuance of the agreement. In *Jones*[37] this was described as the "overall criminality" of the acts alleged. The six defendants were union shop stewards in the building trade and members of a strike action committee. They organised a picket of two hundred and fifty people at five building sites in Shrewsbury and three sites in the nearby town of Telford. Their intention was to bring about a stoppage of work at all the building sites, some of which were themselves extensive in area. At each site there was a terrifying display by pickets of force and violence, actually committed or threatened, against buildings, plant and equipment; at some sites there were also acts and threats of personal violence. The indictment charged conspiracy to intimidate, unlawful assembly and affray. In addition there were thirty-nine substantive counts against some of the defendants, some

---

33 [1951] 1 K.B. 394.
34 At p. 399.
35 [1965] 1 Q.B. 402.
36 At p. 423; *cf. supra,* para. 12.13 at n. 28.
37 (1974) 59 Cr.App.R. 120.

being for offences of intimidation. The defence sought to quash the conspiracy count on the ground that it was unnecessary, the intimidation involved being sufficiently covered by the substantive counts. James L.J., delivering the judgment of the Court of Appeal, said:

> "It is not desirable to include a charge of conspiracy which adds nothing to an effective charge of a substantive offence. But where charges of substantive offences do not adequately represent the overall criminality, it may be appropriate and right to include a charge of conspiracy . . . In the present case the alleged criminality disclosed by the witness statements could not be represented by charges of substantive offences alone, the Crown case could not be adequately presented in the interests of justice by preferring a small number of charges of substantive offences of intimidation, and the task of the judge and the jury was simplified by proceeding upon one count of conspiracy instead of a large number of counts alleging substantive offences."[38]

Three separate points are involved in this judgment:

(1) The nub of the case against the accused was their overall organisation of the picketing at all the sites involved. It was that organisation which distinguished their culpability from that of the other pickets who merely acted on their orders.

(2) The aggregate of violence at all six sites was a truly aggravating aspect of the case.

(3) Those propositions established, it was simpler to represent the overall criminality in one conspiracy count.

These propositions are often applicable in fraud cases. Very often it is the organisation of the fraud which is the nub of the case. Frequently the organisers ensure that they remain in the background while the front men commit the substantive offences. Usually the fraud consists of a very large number of identically repeated substantive offences. It is their aggregate which makes the fraud serious, not their individuality.

12.17 There may be cases where the evidence that the accused committed substantive offences is thin, but the evidence taken as a whole clearly indicates that he conspired with others to commit substantive offences. In *Cooper and Compton*[39] Humphreys J. gave an example of conspiracy to steal being a proper count where the evidence supporting individual thefts is nebulous, but the jury are likely to infer the existence of a general conspiracy. In *Greenfield*[40] the accused were charged with a general conspiracy to cause explosions and a number of substantive counts of possessing explosive substances and firearms. There had been twenty-five explosions which on the basis of scientific evidence were

38 At p. 124.
39 (1947) 32 Cr.App.R. 102 at p. 109f.
40 [1973] 1 W.L.R. 1151.

alleged to have had one source. One group of explosions was declared to be the work of the Angry Brigade, one group was aimed at Spanish targets and another at Italian. There was a good deal of argument at the trial as to whether all the explosions could be attributed to a common source. Beyond the general pattern of explosions and explosive devices the prosecution had evidence that the appellants all lived together in premises where explosive substances were found together with publicity material for the Angry Brigade. They had all been associated over a long period. The fingerprints of two of the defendants linked them to particular explosions. The defence contended that the conspiracy count made the trial unfair and that the defendants should have been charged with substantive counts. In this way and only this way would the judge and the defendants have known which overt acts had been proved against which defendant. Lawton L.J., delivering the judgment of the court, rejected that argument, although acknowledging that there was some substance in it.

> "If there has been a series of criminal overt acts which can be shown by clear evidence to be the acts of identifiable individuals, in most cases there is no need for a charge of conspiracy. But in some cases there may be clear evidence of conspiracy but little evidence that any of the conspirators committed any of the criminal overt acts. Those who instigated the criminal acts can only be brought to justice by means of a charge of conspiracy. In such cases a charge of conspiracy is both justifiable and necessary . . . Between those extremes there are cases in which there is evidence that some of the defendants, but not all, committed a few, but not all, of the criminal overt acts. [Counsel for the Crown] submitted that this was just such a case and that a conspiracy charge was justified. We agree."[41]

12.18 Although *Greenfield* was not a fraud case, the principles there enunciated are often relevant to fraud cases, which frequently consist of a very large number of individual instances. In some instances it will be unclear at the outset (and often finally as well) which defendant committed the individual fraud, whilst it is plain that some of the defendants committed some of them. Usually the organisers distance themselves from the public and are not involved directly in the individual instances of fraud. What is plain is that all are members of the same organisation, bent to a greater or lesser degree on the same fraudulent ends. In the same way it mattered not in *Greenfield* that only two of the defendants could be directly implicated in only two of the explosions. To have charged only those two with those two offences would (as the jury's verdict demonstrated) not have adequately represented the true criminality of all the defendants' actions. What mattered was not the particular identity of a particular actor, but the fact that all were prepared to join an

41 At p. 1158.

organisation bent on causing explosions, thereby giving encouragement and succour to those who committed the individual acts. By joining, they technically made themselves guilty of all the acts of the organisation. That, the defence said, was unfair. Lawton L.J. rejected that criticism:

"... what usually matters when assessing what sentence to pass is not when a defendant joined a conspiracy but what part he played in furthering it. Many a dangerous conspiracy has been near to ending when a man of strong personality has joined and given it more vigour."[42]

Trial of conspiracy and substantive charges together discouraged
12.19 If a conspiracy count is properly laid, it may be accompanied by other counts, either substantive or conspiracy. Should the conspiracy count or counts be tried alone or together with substantive counts? In 1977 Lord Widgery C.J. issued a practice direction in these terms:

"1. In any case where an indictment contains substantive counts and a related conspiracy count, the judge should require the prosecution to justify the joinder, or, failing justification, to elect whether to proceed on the substantive or on the conspiracy counts.
2. A joinder is justified for this purpose if the judge considers that the interests of justice demand it."[43]

In *Griffiths,*[44] where the Court of Criminal Appeal quashed a conviction on a general conspiracy count which was bad for duplicity, Paull J., delivering the judgment of the court, expressed the view that except in simple cases a conspiracy count should be tried separately from substantive counts.[45] That was a fraud case in which the court took the view that not only should there not have been a general conspiracy count, but not even one trial. There were in all twenty-five counts involving the jury returning seventy-eight verdicts. Paull J.'s reasons for urging the separate trial of conspiracy and substantive counts were (1) that the sum of the two over-complicated the trial, and (2) that juries found it difficult to comprehend that evidence which was admissible on a conspiracy count was inadmissible on substantive counts.

12.20 It is plainly undesirable to include a conspiracy count when its ambit is no wider than substantive counts in the same indictment. To do so risks the problems that arose in *Cooper and Compton,*[46] where a conspiracy to steal depended upon allegations of four separate thefts which were covered by substantive counts in the same indictment. The jury acquitted on the substantive counts and convicted on the conspiracy.

42 *Ibid.*
43 Practice Direction (Crime: Conspiracy) [1977] 1 W.L.R. 537.
44 [1966] 1 Q.B. 589.
45 At p. 594.
46 (1947) 32 Cr.App.R. 102; *supra,* para. 12.11.

The verdicts could not stand together and the conspiracy verdict was quashed. Sometimes the prosecution seeks to include sample substantive counts and a general conspiracy which covers a whole course of fraud, including other instances of fraudulent conduct which could have been the subject of identical substantive counts. Technically a conspiracy verdict might be justified on the basis that the jury, though not satisfied of fraud on the particular sample charges, were so satisfied in other instances. Where, however, the conduct relied upon is identical, the same dangers of confusion and inconsistency will arise and it will generally be better that the prosecution be put to its election. In other instances the prosecution may seek to include in a conspiracy count subsidiary examples of fraud different in kind from those charged in the substantive counts. Provided it is clear that the conspiracy count embraces only matters different in kind, it may be justifiable to join it with substantive counts. In a complicated case, however, it is probably better to simplify the issues and again put the prosecution to its election.

Circumstances where conspiracy and substantive charges may be tried together
12.21   There are plainly cases where joinder of a conspiracy count with substantive counts is justified. The clearest instance is where the conspiracy and substantive counts are truly alternative counts. In many cases there may be matters of form or substance which warrant an acquittal on one charge without precluding a conviction on another. This was recognised in *Cooper and Compton* itself, where Humphreys J. said:

> "In a great many cases there is no doubt at all that a verdict of Guilty of conspiracy but Not Guilty of the particular acts charged is a perfectly proper and reasonable one. In such cases it would be very wrong not to insert in the indictment a charge of conspiracy. Criminal lawyers know that often while a general conspiracy, for example, a conspiracy to steal, is likely to be inferred by the jury from the evidence, it may be that the evidence of the particular acts forming the larcenies, which are charged in the indictment, are supported by rather nebulous evidence. In such a case the jury may say, and very likely will say, Not Guilty of larceny, but Guilty of conspiracy to commit larceny."[47]

This line of reasoning was followed in *Greenfield*,[48] where there was evidence (a) that two of the accused had been involved in causing an explosion or explosions, (b) that a number of the defendants had been involved in a general conspiracy to cause twenty-five explosions (though it was possible that a jury might at the end of a trial acquit some or all of the defendants of that allegation), and (c) that certain of the defendants

47   At p. 109f.
48   [1973] 1 W.L.R. 1151; *supra*, para. 12.17.

had explosives (*viz.* firearms) in their possession. The Crown charged all the defendants with a general conspiracy to cause explosions. It did not charge any substantive counts of causing explosions, but did charge substantive counts of possessing firearms and explosives. The Court of Appeal approved that course. They did not give detailed reasons but it is plain that the possession counts (being different in kind) were true alternatives, and that their joinder was justified by the danger that the defendants, though acting illegally, might not have been convicted on the general conspiracy.

12.22 Similarly in *Jones*[49] the defendants were indicted for a general conspiracy to intimidate persons working on a number of building sites, unlawful assembly, affray and a large number of substantive counts of intimidation. The substantive counts of intimidation were severed but the other counts remained joined. Clearly the three remaining counts were different in kind from one another. They might have been open to the objection that they all covered precisely the same ground, but on the other hand there might have been grounds to acquit on one and convict on another: the jury might have found that there was unlawful fighting but not intimidation, or that there was unlawful assembly but not fighting, or that there was fighting but it was not to the terror of the public. There was also legal argument as to the correct definition of intimidation. The trial proceeded on all three counts and in the event the jury convicted on all three. The prosecution may often be tempted to hedge its bets with alternative counts in this way, and the extent to which it should be allowed will always be a question of degree. *Jones* may well have been a case where three alternative counts were too many: in a complicated case the jury should be presented with simple issues. However, the Court of Appeal said nothing to disapprove the course taken. It is not difficult to think of other examples where joinder of a conspiracy and a substantive count would be justified. If there is a charge of attempt but it is doubtful whether the acts alleged are sufficiently proximate, and more than two are involved, an alternative conspiracy count should be charged. If there are only two conspirators a substantive count may be necessary in case the jury take the view that one is guilty and the other is not.

Simplification of issues
12.23 It should always be remembered that at the end of the day it is desirable that the jury should be left with as few and as simple issues as possible. Issues which the prosecution should be allowed to cover at the

---

49 (1974) 59 Cr.App.R. 120; *supra,* para. 12.16.

outset may prove to be non-issues; if so, they may properly be abandoned at the close of the evidence. In *Jones* it is unlikely that three alternatives were really required and they could probably have been pruned. If a number of alternatives covering substantially the same ground are left to a jury, it may be oppressive to take verdicts on all of them. The jury can be told that if they convict on alternative number 1, they need not consider number 2, and that they should only go on to number 2 if they have acquitted on number 1 on a specified ground which does not apply to number 2. If they then convict on number 1 they can be discharged from giving a verdict on number 2. Another way to simplify alternatives is for the prosecution to charge them all but to elect to proceed on only one, with the warning that if at the close of its case (or even later) a specific point is taken, then it will fall back on a count included in the indictment but not immediately proceeded upon. On the other hand all the alternatives may be placed before the jury, but they can be told that some are there for technical reasons which in the event may not arise and that they should therefore concentrate their minds on one particular count.

General and separate conspiracies

12.24　One problem that frequently arises when conspiracy is charged is the exact description of the particular conspiracy. On a general conspiracy charge defendants often argue that, even if it be proved that they have acted fraudulently in association with the general conspirators, they are nevertheless not party to the general conspiracy but only to some separate subsidiary conspiracy. If a conspiracy count on its face alleges two separate agreements it is bad for duplicity and will be quashed;[50] but duplicity is a matter of form, not substance.[51] If a count on its face charges only one conspiracy, it cannot be quashed at the outset of the trial, though a submission of no case will succeed if the prosecution prove that a defendant is guilty not of the agreement charged but of a separate though associated one.[52] The Crown may guard against this eventuality by including alternative conspiracy counts. If the defence wishes to quash a count at the outset which on its face alleges only one agreement, it may force the prosecution to reveal that it in fact alleges two by obtaining particulars of it.[53] If the prosecution fails to deliver particulars when it should, it may be permissible for the judge to look at the depositions as constituting particulars. On the other hand it may be to the advantage of the defence to allow the count to run in the hope of escaping on a

50　*West* [1948] 1 K.B. 709; *Davey* [1960] 1 W.L.R. 1287.
51　*Greenfield* [1973] 1 W.L.R. 1151 at p. 1156, *per* Lawton L.J.
52　*Griffiths* [1966] 1 Q.B. 589; *Greenfield, supra*, at p. 1156f., *per* Lawton L.J.
53　*Infra*, para. 12.48ff.

submission of no case; but this tactic may fail if the judge allows the count to be amended, or an additional count added, at the close of the prosecution case.

12.25   The case of *Griffiths*[54] illustrates the dangers involved in a failure to analyse the true nature of an agreement. Griffiths and his accountant were alleged to have devised a scheme to defraud the Ministry of Agriculture, which had instituted a scheme to give subsidies to farmers who spread agricultural lime on their fields. It was alleged that in a number of instances Griffiths had greatly exaggerated the quantity of lime which had been spread. Seven farmers were allegedly induced to take part in this scheme, but there was no evidence that any one farmer knew that any of the others were involved or knew that Griffiths was doing this with other farmers at all. The prosecution charged a general conspiracy to defraud. The Court of Criminal Appeal held that there was no general agreement, but a central agreement between Griffiths and his accountant and a series of separate agreements with each farmer. Paull J., delivering the judgment of the court, said:

> ". . . all must join in the one agreement, each with the others, in order to constitute one conspiracy. They may join in at various times, each attaching himself to that agreement; any one of them may not know all the other parties but only that there are other parties; any one of them may not know the full extent of the scheme to which he attaches himself. But what each must know is that there is coming into existence, or is in existence, a scheme which goes beyond the illegal act or acts which he agrees to do . . . The matter can be illustrated quite simply. I employ an accountant to make out my tax return. He and his clerk are both present when I am about to sign the return. I notice an item in my expenses of £100 and say: 'I don't remember incurring this expense.' The clerk says: 'Well, actually I put it in. You didn't incur it, but I didn't think you would object to a few pounds being saved.' The accountant indicates his agreement to this attitude. After some hesitation I agree to let it stand. On those bare facts I cannot be charged with 50 others in a conspiracy to defraud the Exchequer of £100,000 on the basis that this accountant and his clerk have persuaded 500 other clients to make false returns, some being false in one way, some in another, or even all in the same way. I have not knowingly attached myself to a general agreement to defraud. Similarly, the Post Office clerk who agrees to alter a date stamp in a case where a bookmaker has been swindled must know that the alteration is to be used for a fraudulent purpose. He therefore joins a scheme to defraud that bookmaker, of whom he may not have heard, but he cannot be indicted, merely because he has agreed to alter that stamp, on a charge of a conspiracy to alter date stamps and cheat bookmakers all over the country. We venture to say that far too often this principle is forgotten and accused persons are joined in a charge of conspiracy without any real evidence from which a jury may infer that their

54   [1966] 1 Q.B. 589.

minds went beyond committing with one or more other persons the one or more specific acts alleged against them in the substantive counts, or went beyond a conspiracy to do a particular act or acts."[55]

12.26 The court distinguished the earlier case of *Meyrick and Ribuffi*,[56] where the defendants were the owners of separate clubs in Soho. Each bribed the same police officer to give a falsely favourable report to his superiors on the conduct of his or her club. They were charged in substantive counts and also with a conspiracy to obstruct the police and prevent the due administration of the law. The judge directed the jury that they should not convict on the conspiracy count unless they were satisfied that the defendants had entered into an agreement with a common design. The Court of Criminal Appeal upheld their conviction. In *Griffiths* this case was distinguished because the incidents had occurred in the small geographical area of Soho in circumstances which indicated that night club proprietors in that district well knew what was happening generally in relation to the police. It may be doubted whether this is a valid ground of distinction. If I make an agreement with A, the mere fact that I know A has made similar agreements with B, C and D does not make me party to those agreements. If I buy a suit from a West End store, my knowledge that the same store has sold many suits to other customers does not make me party to those other contracts of sale. To speak of a common design may be misleading: a number of different agreements may all have an object in common, but that does not make them one agreement.

What constitutes a general agreement
12.27 What then is required, beyond knowledge of the conduct of other conspirators, to make a defendant party to a general agreement? In order to answer this question we must bear in mind some of the basic principles of the law of conspiracy. All conspirators are guilty of any criminal acts committed pursuant to the conspiracy.[57] A conspirator need not be party to the agreement at its inception, but may join it at some later stage.[58] To become a party to a general agreement the particular defendant must be party to the same criminal plan or agreement as his fellow conspirators. Since this requirement is a matter of agreement, its fulfilment must depend upon the common intention of the conspirators; and that intention may be inferred from the surrounding circumstances. Thus in *Parnell*[59] Fitzgerald J. said:

---

55 At p. 597ff.
56 (1929) 21 Cr.App.R. 94.
57 Hawkins' *Pleas of the Crown* Book II, p. 442; applied in *Greenfield* [1973] 1 W.L.R. 1151 at p. 1158, *per* Lawton L.J.
58 *Simmonds* [1969] 1 Q.B. 685 at p. 696, *per* Fenton Atkinson J.; *Murphy* (1837) 8 C. & P. 297; *Greenfield, supra,* at p. 1158, *per* Lawton L.J.
59 (1881) 14 Cox 508.

"It may be that the alleged conspirators have never seen each other, and have never corresponded, one may have never heard the name of the other, and yet by the law they may be parties to the same common criminal agreement. Thus in some of the Fenian cases tried in this country, it frequently happened that one of the conspirators was in America, the other in this country, that they had never seen each other, but that there were acts on both sides which led the jury to the inference, and they drew it, that they were engaged in accomplishing the same common object, and, when they had arrived at this conclusion, the acts of one became evidence against the other."[60]

12.28 In the case of a political conspiracy it is easy to see that an individual who joins in to commit a specific act will also intend to subscribe to the aims of the entire conspiracy: he will intend by his modest part to further the general aim of the organisation. A similar line of argument may be applied in fraud cases. Knowledge of the acts of fellow conspirators is not in itself enough to make a defendant party to a general agreement, but knowledge may be one of the facts from which the necessary intent can be inferred. To take some examples:

(1) A conspirator may know that his limited act is essential to the success of the conspiracy; without him it will fail. If he commits it, he plainly intends to further the general scheme.

(2) He may know that a general scheme exists and that, though his act is not crucial to its success, the scheme is nevertheless dependent on a number of persons like himself subscribing to it. He may thus intend to further the general scheme.

(3) He may know that the success of his individual fraud depends in part on a large number of people doing the same thing under the general scheme: *e.g.* it may further the general scheme if a particular fraudulent form is supplied many times to the party defrauded, who is likely thereby to be deluded into thinking that the scheme is not fraudulent.

(4) Although his interest is primarily in his individual benefit, he may know that the effect of his joining in the scheme will be to aid the perpetrators. In this way he may intend to further its ends, particularly if there is a possibility that he himself may join in again later.

These examples might be multiplied. They all come down to the same question, which must be answered on the facts of the individual case: did the defendant intend to become party to the general, as opposed to a particular, agreement? On this point it may be doubted if the facts of *Meyrick and Ribuffi,*[61] as reported, were sufficient to draw that inference.

12.29 If the conspirators have quite different objects, there will clearly

---

60 At p. 515.
61 (1929) 21 Cr.App.R. 94; *supra,* para. 12.26.

be more than one agreement, if one exists at all. Thus in *Dawson*[62] a man was alleged to have conspired with a total of twelve other men, of whom six were charged and three convicted of conspiring to cheat and defraud. The subject matter of the alleged agreement was orange juice, buses, bogies, landing vehicles and bills of exchange. On the facts the Court of Criminal Appeal took the view that there were several separate agreements relating to the various types of goods. Similarly in *Jackson*[63] there was alleged a conspiracy to take over two separate companies in a fraudulent manner. There were differences in the method employed in each case. The Court of Criminal Appeal held that there were two separate agreements. In *Davey*[64] a count was brought against seven persons for conspiracy to defraud the creditors of a large number of companies over a period of eleven years. Some of the persons charged had nothing to do with the affairs of some of the companies involved, and indeed some of the companies had been wound up before some of the defendants appeared on the scene. The Court of Criminal Appeal held that this constituted more than one agreement. It must always be a question of fact whether a general agreement can be inferred from particular details in the case. The fact that the conspirators have different objects at different times may not matter if the essence of the fraud is a single method employed in differing circumstances. On the other hand if a particular defendant is interested in only one of these objects, he may be party only to an agreement relating to that object. Similarly it is not uncommon for fraudsmen to employ, at one and the same time or in succession, a series of companies which effectively exist only to disguise the fraud or give substance to it. If the methods used are the same, the existence of the individual companies does not negate the general agreement. The case of *Jones*[65] is an example where a common agreement to intimidate workmen on a number of separate building sites at different times was properly indicted as one agreement.

Change in law resulting in separate agreements

12.30 It may be that a change in the law results in an inference of separate agreements. Thus in *West*[66] the appellants were charged with conspiracy to contravene Regulation 55 of the Defence Regulations 1939. Between 1940 and 1946, which were the pleaded limits of the conspiracy, the Board of Trade made a number of Orders under the Regulation controlling (*inter alia*) the manufacture of toilet preparations. The orders were successive and were not in force at the same time. The later orders

---

62   (1960) 44 Cr.App.R. 87.
63   [1959] Crim.L.R. 839.
64   [1960] 1 W.L.R. 1287.
65   (1974) 59 Cr.App.R. 120; *supra,* para. 12.16.
66   [1948] 1 K.B. 709.

were obviously not in force at the inception of the conspiracy. In one instance a succeeding order replaced its predecessor in virtually identical terms. Other orders substantially altered the system of control which the conspirators contravened. The Court of Criminal Appeal held that this was not one agreement but successive agreements relating to the different orders. If the substance of the law had remained the same throughout and only the form had changed, a general conspiracy to contravene such orders as were from time to time in force might perhaps have been alleged; but the court did not encourage this view. Where there is a change in the substance of the law, adjustments in the method may be vital even if the overriding object of the fraud remains the same. It may be prudent for the prosecution at least to include counts alternative to a general conspiracy.

Subsidiary agreements

12.31   On the facts of a particular case there may be a general agreement between certain conspirators, but separate subsidiary agreements between them and other defendants. This is illustrated by *Griffiths*,[67] where Griffiths and his accountant entered into a general agreement between themselves to defraud the Ministry of Agriculture but then entered into a series of individual agreements with different farmers to defraud the Ministry in particular cases. In such circumstances a general conspiracy count can be preferred against the principal conspirators with separate smaller conspiracies against the others. The principals may be named as defendants in the subsidiary counts or simply as persons with whom the subsidiary defendants conspired. If the former course is adopted and the principal conspirators are convicted on the main conspiracy, the jury can be discharged from giving a verdict in their case on the lesser conspiracies.[68]

Core agreement

12.32   It matters not that the prosecution fails to prove the entire conspiracy alleged against all the alleged conspirators, provided there is a core conspiracy to which all are shown to be party. Thus in *Greenfield*[69] the prosecution alleged a general agreement to cause twenty-five explosions. There was argument at the trial as to whether, even if it were shown that the defendants were involved in some explosions, there was sufficient proof that they were involved in all. The Court of Appeal endorsed the view that it was enough if there were a core of explosions for which they were all responsible.

67   [1966] 1 Q.B. 589; *supra,* para. 12.25.
68   *Cf. supra,* para. 12.23.
69   [1973] 1 W.L.R. 1151; *supra,* para. 12.17.

Alternative conspiracy counts

12.33　There may be cases in which the prosecution wishes to insert alternative conspiracy counts, *e.g.* to cover the eventuality that a general conspiracy count will fail because the jury take the view that it in fact constituted separate agreements. Such an eventuality might also be covered by alternative substantive counts, but the point is probably made more clearly by alternative conspiracies. There is nothing wrong in principle with charging alternative conspiracies in an appropriate case.

Conspiracy to defraud

Effect of Criminal Law Act 1977

12.34　Section 1(1) of the Criminal Law Act 1977, as substituted by section 5(1) of the Criminal Attempts Act 1981, defines the offence of conspiracy as follows:

> "Subject to the following provisions of this Part of this Act, if a person agrees with any other person or persons that a course of conduct shall be pursued which, if the agreement is carried out in accordance with their intentions, either—
>
> (*a*) will necessarily amount to or involve the commission of any offence or offences by one or more of the parties to the agreement, or
>
> (*b*) would do so but for the existence of facts which render the commission of the offence or any of the offences impossible,
>
> he is guilty of conspiracy to commit the offence or offences in question."

Section 5(1) of the 1977 Act abolishes the offence of conspiracy at common law, but section 5(2) contains this saving:

> "Subsection (1) above shall not affect the offence of conspiracy at common law so far as relates to conspiracy to defraud, and section 1 above shall not apply in any case where the agreement in question amounts to a conspiracy to defraud at common law."

12.35　There has been much controversy as to the effect of these provisions, particularly as to the exclusion of section 1 where a conspiracy to defraud could formerly have been charged. Read literally this would mean that a conspiracy to commit any offence within the description of fraud, *e.g.* a conspiracy to steal or even to rob, would have to be charged as a conspiracy to defraud. This would make a nonsense of the Act. An alternative approach was that by confining conspiracy to agreements to commit a crime, rather than (as hitherto) to commit an unlawful act, section 1(1) left gaps in the law which could conveniently be filled by preserving conspiracy to defraud. The Law Commission, in its draft proposals which led to the 1977 Act, clearly had these lacunae very much in mind in preserving conspiracy to defraud at common law. Thus the opposite view was that conspiracy to defraud was preserved only to cover those fraudulent conspiracies which were not caught by section 1(1). The middle view was that conspiracy to defraud was preserved in its entirety and that the prosecution had the choice of charging either a section 1 conspiracy or a conspiracy to defraud. That interpretation faced the difficulty of accommodating that part of section 5(2) which provides that section 1 shall not apply where the agreement amounts to a conspiracy to defraud at common law. There were conflicting decisions of the Court of Appeal as to which view was correct.[70]

12.36 The matter was finally settled by the House of Lords in *Ayres*.[71] Their Lordships held first that the middle view (that conspiracy to defraud was preserved in its entirety as an alternative charge) was clearly precluded by the wording of section 5(2). Lord Bridge, delivering a speech in which the House concurred, said:

> "According to the true construction of the Act, an offence which amounts to a common law conspiracy to defraud must be charged as such and not as a statutory conspiracy under section 1. Conversely a section 1 conspiracy cannot be charged as a common law conspiracy to defraud."[72]

Their Lordships went on to hold that the purpose of section 5(2) was to preserve conspiracy to defraud merely so as to cover those instances of combined fraudulent conduct which could not be covered by a section 1 conspiracy. In cases of doubt they suggested the inclusion of alternative counts under section 1 and at common law, leaving the trial judge to rule which one should be left to the jury.

12.37 This decision resulted in certain practical difficulties for prosecutors. The Law Commission had pointed out that there is no generalised offence of criminal fraud in English law.[73] That being so, what should the prosecution charge (a) where part but not all of the offending conduct could be encompassed by a conspiracy to commit a substantive offence, and (b) where all of the offending conduct could be encompassed by charging a number of conspiracies to commit substantive offences, but one charge of conspiracy to defraud could more conveniently encompass the whole? The Court of Appeal considered both of these situations in *Tonner*[74] and held that in neither could a conspiracy to defraud be charged. In their view the House of Lords in *Ayres* had sought to clarify the effect of sections 1 and 5(2) of the 1977 Act. To allow the arguments

---

70 *Walters* (1979) 69 Cr.App.R. 115; *Duncalf* [1979] 1 W.L.R. 918.
71 [1984] A.C. 447.
72 At p. 455.
73 Working Paper No. 56 (1974).
74 [1985] 1 W.L.R. 344.

advanced by the Crown would be to return this area of the law to a state of uncertainty. It was now beyond doubt that if a conspiracy involved the commission of any substantive offence, it could only be charged as a conspiracy under section 1 of the 1977 Act and not as a conspiracy to defraud.

Lacunae

12.38   The effect of these decisions is to confine conspiracy to defraud to situations where its abolition would have left lacunae in the existing law. These potential lacunae may be identified by comparing the general concept of fraud, discussed in chapter 1 above, with the network of substantive offences considered in succeeding chapters (as well as others not dealt with in this work). Such a comparison suggests that there will be very few cases of "fraudulent" conduct (even in the wide, technical sense of that word) which involve no substantive offence at all. Indeed, in the great majority of frauds there is no need to look further than the Theft Acts. It may be helpful to summarise the circumstances in which it would not be possible to charge either theft or one of the deception offences:[75] these are the only circumstances where conspiracy to defraud is not immediately ruled out, though of course it will still be unavailable if any other substantive offence is involved.

12.39   (1) The benefit procured by the fraud may fall outside the categories of benefit enumerated in the Theft Act offences, *viz.*:

(a) property;[76]

(b) "services" as defined by section 1(2) of the Theft Act 1978;[77]

(c) the various ways of evading a liability set out in section 2(1) of the Theft Act 1978;[78]

(d) the forms of "pecuniary advantage" covered by the surviving portion of section 16 of the Theft Act 1968;[79] and

(e) the execution of a valuable security within the meaning of section 20(2) of the Theft Act 1968.[80]

We have seen that certain types of benefit are not regarded as property for the purposes of theft and obtaining property by deception (*e.g.* services, information, computer time), but these benefits may well fall within one of the other categories set out above. In particular it would seem that virtually any benefit constitutes "services" within the meaning

---

75   *Supra,* ch. 3.
76   *Supra,* para. 3.03ff.
77   *Supra,* para. 3.25ff.
78   *Supra,* para. 3.29ff.
79   *Supra,* para. 3.37ff.
80   *Supra,* para. 3.40ff.

of section 1 of the 1978 Act if it is conferred on the understanding that it has been or will be paid for; therefore a fraudulent scheme to obtain a non-gratuitous benefit will almost inevitably be a conspiracy to commit the offence under section 1 unless no element of deception is involved. One example of a benefit which is not necessarily understood to be paid for is the action of a public official who is deceived into failing to do his duty;[81] but the deception would often involve offences such as forgery,[82] false accounting[83] or the making of a false statement contrary to section 5 of the Perjury Act 1911.[84]

12.40   (2) It may be that the benefit obtained is a form of property, but there is no offence of theft or obtaining property by deception because the property does not technically "belong to another" at the time of the appropriation or obtaining.[85] Thus a prospective bankrupt who disposes of his assets so as to keep them from his creditors is guilty of fraud[86] but not of theft, because the assets are legally his; but of course such conduct would normally fall within one or more of the specific offences created by the insolvency legislation.[87] Conversely it may be that although the property does technically belong to another, it might not be so regarded by a criminal court, *e.g.* where it is obtained in breach of a fiduciary duty and is in consequence held subject to a constructive trust.[88] But often the property would have *originally* belonged to the beneficiary, so that a theft charge might be possible, or else would be received by way of a bribe contrary to the Prevention of Corruption Acts.[89] Alternatively, a deception might result in the obtaining of property which did not previously belong to another; *e.g.* the victim is induced by deception to create a fresh chose in action in favour of one of the fraudsmen. The recipient obtains intangible property by deception, but that property has never belonged to anyone but him.[90] It would seem, however, that if the chose in action is represented by a document which is handed over (*e.g.* a cheque, a share certificate), there is technically an offence of obtaining the *document* by deception. Moreover there will normally be an execution of a valuable security and therefore an offence under section 20(2) of the 1968 Act.[91]

---

81   *Welham v. D.P.P.* [1961] A.C. 103; *supra,* para. 1.40.
82   *Supra,* para. 6.03ff.
83   *Supra,* para. 6.41ff.
84   *Supra,* para. 6.59.
85   *Supra,* para. 3.13ff.
86   *Hall* (1858) 1 F. & F. 33; *Heymann* (1873) L.R. 8 Q.B. 102 at p. 105, *per* Blackburn J.
87   *Supra,* para. 9.16ff.
88   *Supra,* para. 4.03ff.
89   *Supra,* ch. 7.
90   *Supra,* para. 3.13.
91   *Supra,* para. 3.40ff.

12.41   (3) The benefit obtained, though falling within one of the
categories covered by the Theft Act offences, may not have been obtained
in either of the ways stipulated, *viz.* (a) by deception or (b) (in the case of
property belonging to another) by appropriation. The Law Commission
suggested various types of fraudulent conduct which might fall short of
deception, but in view of the courts' readiness to infer deception by
conduct,[92] some of the examples given would probably constitute
deception offences: *e.g.* the creation of a false impression of solvency by a
bank or similar institution,[93] the buying of shares at an inflated price so
as to create a false market,[94] and gambling swindles involving the fixing
of football matches or the doping of racehorses (which in any event
would probably constitute offences of corruption).[95] In other cases it may
be more debatable whether any deception would be involved, *e.g.* where
there is a mere failure to disclose material facts rather than positive
misrepresentation,[96] or where the "victim" is a computer.[97] Deception is
not of course essential where the benefit obtained is property belonging to
another: appropriation will do. Between them these two concepts cover
most ways of fraudulently obtaining property. But there may be some
cases where, though there is clearly no deception, the property is in a
sense obtained with the owner's consent: *e.g.* where it is disposed of by an
agent, company director or other fiduciary with authority to dispose of it.
In such a case it is arguable that because of the owner's consent there is
no appropriation and therefore no theft.[98] But there might well be an
offence of corruption or one of the transactions specifically prohibited by
the companies legislation.[99]

12.42   (4) Even if the scheme involves the *actus reus* of one of the Theft
Act offences, the necessary *mens rea* may be absent. A charge of
conspiracy to defraud can never be permissible merely on the ground that
the scheme may not be dishonest, because dishonesty is an essential
element of criminal fraud;[1] but it might be available in the absence of
some other required mental element. Thus it might be fraud to procure
the execution of a valuable security by deception without any view to
gain or intent to cause loss, as required by section 20(2) of the 1968 Act.[2]
Similarly the unauthorised use of property, with no intention of

---

92 *Supra,* para. 2.06.
93 *Esdaile* (1858) 1 F. & F. 213.
94 *Scott v. Brown, Doering, McNab & Co.* [1892] 2 Q.B. 724.
95 *Supra,* ch. 7.
96 *Supra,* para. 2.10.
97 *Supra,* para. 2.30.
98 *Supra,* para. 4.19ff.
99 *Supra,* ch. 5.
 1 *Supra,* para. 1.04ff.
 2 *Supra,* para. 3.45.

permanently depriving the owner, is fraud[3] but not theft.[4] For the same reason we have suggested that theft will not normally be committed where a computer fraud involves the illicit transfer of funds from other people's bank accounts, because the victims are not deprived of their property (*viz.* their rights against the bank).[5] But there would almost certainly be an offence of false accounting,[6] and possibly also an obtaining of the proceeds by deception.[7]

12.43 It will be apparent from this summary that there will be very few frauds which fall outside even the Theft Acts, let alone the whole of the substantive criminal law. For most purposes conspiracy to defraud is effectively a dead letter. Whether or not Parliament intended this result, the wording of section 5(2) (as interpreted in *Ayres*)[8] appears to have achieved it. The retention of conspiracy to defraud was in any event an interim measure, designed to preserve the scope of the existing law until the promised review of fraud could be carried out and further legislation enacted. In the wake of *Tonner*[9] this is plainly a matter of urgency. What is now required is a comprehensive implementation of the policy underlying the Criminal Law Act 1977, *viz.* to restrict the law of conspiracy to agreements to commit substantive offences. There can be few circumstances, if any, where conduct which is not an offence if committed by one person should be an offence if committed by two. But before conspiracy to defraud can be finally dispensed with it will be necessary to decide how far (if at all) the resulting lacunae should be filled by substantive offences. On the one hand it might be sufficient to create certain specific offences to cover some of the possibilities outlined above. Some lacunae would no doubt remain: there is no end to human ingenuity, and unless fraudulent conduct is illegal *per se* there will be occasional instances which go unpunished. But clarity and certainty are legal virtues. Concepts as ill-defined as that of fraud in its present form should have no place in the definition of criminal offences.

12.44 On the other hand there might be something to be said for a general offence of fraud, provided it were adequately defined and not merely an amorphous safety-net. Such a charge would be useful not only where there would otherwise be a lacuna but also where, though a substantive offence has been committed, it fails to represent the essence of the fraud. An example is the case put by the Law Commission of railway

---

3 *Scott v. Metropolitan Police Commissioner* [1975] A.C. 819.
4 *Supra*, para. 3.17ff.
5 *Supra*, para. 3.05.
6 *Supra*, para. 6.41ff.
7 *Thompson* [1984] 3 All E.R. 565.
8 [1984] A.C. 447; *supra*, para. 12.36.
9 [1985] 1 W.L.R. 344; *supra*, para. 12.37.

employees who resell used but uncancelled tickets for their own profit. They have stolen the piece of card on which the tickets are printed, and they have probably obtained the passengers' money by deception; but the gravamen of the offence is the fraud on the railway, which has been deprived of money which it would otherwise have received. However diligently lacunae are filled, there will be cases where the reality of the situation would be best represented by an allegation of fraud. It follows that the decision in *Tonner,* that conspiracy to defraud cannot be charged where part but not all of the fraudulent scheme is covered by a substantive offence, will produce unreal charges. In addition there may be cases where the conduct complained of can be covered by a variety of charges of conspiracy to commit substantive offences, but to do so would present an unnecessarily complicated picture and would involve findings of fact on issues which are not to the main point. Now that particulars of fraud are required,[10] a general allegation of fraud with clear but simple particulars may often be the best way of presenting a fraud case.

Fraudulent trading

12.45 It may be that we already have a general fraud offence, which is not subject to the same restrictions as conspiracy to defraud, in the offence of fraudulent trading under section 458 of the Companies Act 1985.[11] As we have seen, this offence is committed where a company carries on business with intent to defraud its creditors, or anyone else's creditors, "or for any fraudulent purpose". Read literally, section 458 extends to any fraud whatsoever for which a company is the vehicle; and in practice prosecutors sometimes use this type of charge as a kind of one-man conspiracy to defraud, thus evading both the requirement of an agreement and the problems created by section 5(2) of the Criminal Law Act 1977. But it must be remembered that the predecessor of section 458, section 332(3) of the Companies Act 1948, appeared in the part of the Act concerned with winding up, and in that context it seems improbable that Parliament intended to create a general offence embracing any form of fraudulent conduct by a company.[12] Admittedly it is no longer necessary for the company to be in liquidation before the offence can be charged, and (presumably for this reason) the section no longer appears among the provisions on winding up. It is arguable that this change effectively frees the section from any contextual restriction connecting it with liquidation. But if the offence was originally confined to certain types of fraud, one

10 *Infra,* para. 12.49.
11 Replacing Companies Act 1948 s. 332(3) with effect from 1 July 1985; *supra,* para. 9.03ff.
12 *Cf. supra,* para. 9.05.

would not expect Parliament to extend it to cover *all* types of fraud without saying so. Moreover it would clearly be anomalous if there were a general offence of fraudulent conduct on the part of a company but not on the part of an individual or an unincorporated business.

General deficiency counts

12.46   Generally a charge in an indictment must be specific as to the property stolen or otherwise dishonestly obtained, and the time and place of its appropriation or obtaining. There are, however, exceptional cases where the prosecution are entitled to lump together a number of appropriations. This may be on one of two grounds. Firstly the appropriations may properly be regarded as one continuous appropriation. Thus in *Firth*[13] a mill owner diverted gas supplied to his mill so that for some years it was not metered. He was charged with stealing an aggregate amount of gas on one day, and the count was held good. Similarly in *Shepherd*[14] the defendant was employed to fell trees over a period of a month. It could be shown that in the course of that month he had dishonestly felled an additional eight trees for his own purposes, though the precise date on which any one tree had been felled could not be proved. He was charged in one count with stealing eight trees, and the count held good. In *Henwood*[15] the defendant had been in the service of the prosecutor for nine years and was found to have a number of articles belonging to the prosecutor in a box at his own lodgings. Although the articles were different in kind, there was no evidence as to when they had been stolen. One count alleging theft of all of them was held good. Bovill C.J., relying on the cases cited above, said that it would have made no difference had there been evidence of distinct takings. In *Wilson v. Read*[16] two defendants stole coal and coke from their employers over three and a half years, but there was no evidence as to any precise amount on any one occasion. They were charged in aggregate and the charge held good. In *Cain*[17] the defendant received £20,000 which was either stolen or the proceeds of stolen goods. She admitted receiving this sum over a period from her husband, who was a burglar, but there was nothing to indicate when she had received any particular sum. An aggregate count was upheld on the basis that it reflected a continuous series of closely linked offences.

12.47   The second justification for such a count is that the appropriation cannot be split up because the prosecution do not have enough

13   (1869) L.R. 1 C.C.R. 172.
14   (1868) L.R. 1 C.C.R. 118.
15   (1870) 11 Cox 526.
16   [1956] Crim.L.R. 418.
17   [1983] Crim.L.R. 802.

information to do so. This ground could clearly have justified the aggregate counts in some of the earlier cases considered above, and in *Henwood,* at least, might have been a preferable approach: it is difficult to regard the theft of different types of articles as a continuous appropriation. In *Tomlin*[18] the defendant was bound to account on a particular day for monies received by him in small amounts over a period. The prosecution could not show when any individual amount had been taken or what the total deficiency was at any one time. An aggregate count was upheld by the Court of Criminal Appeal because the Crown could not particularise further. This case was relied on in *Cain,* where it was said that it would affront common sense to require the prosecution to give particulars they could not give.

PARTICULARS

Overt acts

12.48   In cases of treason in former times the law required proof of an overt act of the defendant to ground a conviction, and these overt acts were commonly set out in the indictment. In conspiracy cases proof of overt acts was not necessary in law, but if the prosecution relied upon them to prove the conspiracy it became the custom to particularise them or provide particulars on request. The advent of depositions to a large extent circumvented the need for such particulars but they continued to be ordered, and it is now usual to provide particulars of a conspiracy under the Indictments Act 1915. A particular is not the same as an overt act (though in many cases particulars will describe overt acts): a particular is a reasonably precise assertion of the prosecution's case against the defendants. It need not be an act at all. The provision of particulars dispenses with the need to set out overt acts, but they are referred to in some of the earlier cases cited below and for this reason they are explained here.

The need for particulars

12.49   Section 3(1) of the Indictments Act 1915 provides:

> "Every indictment shall contain, and shall be sufficient if it contains, a statement of the specific offence or offences with which the accused person is charged, together with such particulars as may be necessary for giving reasonable information as to the nature of the charge."

In substantive counts it has long been customary to provide particulars of, for instance, deceptions alleged. In conspiracy cases it became

18   [1954] 2 Q.B. 278.

customary, on application for particulars, for the Crown to reply that sufficient particularity was to be found in the depositions and counsel's opening address. This practice was sanctioned by the courts until the Court of Appeal indicated in *Landy*[19] that particulars of fraud ought to be supplied as a matter of course. They gave two reasons for requiring particulars: (1) to enable the defendants and the trial judge to know precisely, and on the face of the indictment itself, the nature of the prosecution's case, and (2) to stop the prosecution shifting their ground during the course of the trial without leave of the judge and the making of an amendment.

The drafting of particulars

12.50　　The Court of Appeal stressed in *Landy* that the indictment should not resemble a civil statement of claim: what is required is conciseness and clarity. In particular the court discouraged the use of phrases such as "falsely representing" and "to the prejudice of" and forbade the use of a general allegation of "divers other false and fraudulent devices". The draft particulars suggested by the court as appropriate to the facts of *Landy* itself warrant detailed scrutiny. They read as follows:

"[A, B and C] on divers days between____and____conspired together and with [X, Y and Z] to defraud such corporations, companies, partnerships, firms and persons as might lend funds to or deposit funds with Israel British Bank (London) Ltd ('the bank') by dishonestly

(i) causing and permitting the bank to make excessive advances to insubstantial and speculative trading companies incorporated in Liechtenstein and Switzerland, such advances being inadequately secured, inadequately guaranteed and without proper provision for payment of interest

(ii) causing and permitting the bank to make excessive advances to its parent company in Tel Aviv, such advances being inadequately secured, inadequately guaranteed and without proper provision for payment of interest

(iii) causing and permitting the bank to make excessive advances to individuals and companies connected with [X] and his family, such advances being inadequately guaranteed and without proper provision for payment of interest

(iv) causing and permitting the bank's accounts and Bank of England returns to be prepared in such a way as (a) to conceal the nature, constitution and extent of the bank's lending and (b) to show a false and misleading financial situation as at the ends of the bank's accounting years

(v) causing and permitting the bank to discount commercial bills when (a) there was no underlying commercial transaction, (b) the documents evidencing the supposed underlying transactions were false and (c) the transactions were effected in order to transfer funds to the bank's parent company in Tel Aviv."[20]

19　[1981] 1 W.L.R. 355.
20　At p. 362.

It will be noted that the particulars suggested are relatively short, given that the trial lasted some 90 days. They nevertheless state the essential allegations in some detail. Those allegations all related to dealing in funds deposited with the bank without any of the normal safeguards for the protection of those funds. In that sense particulars (i), (ii), (iii) and (v) are homogeneous. Particular (iv) is an allegation of cooking the books to disguise the alleged fraudsmen's operations. In fraud cases there will often be a wide variety of fraudulent methods, sometimes very different in kind, though with a common aim. The particulars suggested in *Landy* do not encourage the insertion of a long list of fraudulent devices in the hope that some will stick. The inclusion of too many particulars may cause difficulty when it comes to a verdict.

12.51 It is particularly noticeable that the *Landy* particulars not only include no allegation of false representation, but no allegation of deception. No doubt the investors who were alleged to have been defrauded were deceived into thinking that the bank intended to operate in accordance with normal prudent banking practice, and may in particular have been deceived by false or misleading accounts. Some of the transactions are alleged to have been false; others are merely alleged to have been insufficiently secured. A simple departure from normal commercial standards might be evidence of fraud, but not necessarily so. The various undersecured advances are all alleged to have been excessive; the alleged departure from normal practice is gross. The absence of an allegation of deception, and the presence of an allegation of gross departure from standard practice, necessarily place a great importance on the word "dishonestly". A man who persistently deals in a manner which he knows would be wholly unacceptable in ordinary commercial terms to those who entrust money to him will usually be dishonest. He puts himself forward as a banker, receives money from people who naturally expect that he will follow certain prudent commercial practices, and deliberately drives a coach and horses through those practices. Whether he is dishonest or not may depend on the extent to which he departs from normal practice. If he were dealing with his own money he could act as he chose; when he deals with monies which others have entrusted to him, the investors can reasonably expect a certain minimum standard of conduct. A slight departure from that standard would not warrant a finding of dishonesty; a substantial departure would. It must always be a matter of degree when dishonesty occurs.

Must all the particulars be proved?

12.52 Some particulars are essential to the proof of a charge: for instance, appropriation must be proved to establish theft. In other cases there may be particulars the proof of which is not essential. Thus on a charge of obtaining by deception the prosecution may particularise a number of deceptions; the proof of one only is essential to the conviction. Difficulties may arise in this respect upon a joint charge. Suppose A and B are charged with obtaining by deception, with particulars of deceptions x and y. The jury find that they were both instrumental in obtaining the property, but A used deception x and B deception y. If it can be shown that there was a joint venture, and that it was in contemplation that each could use several deceptions, there may be a conviction. Otherwise it would seem that they have committed separate offences.

12.53 Problems may also arise on a conspiracy charge. In *O'Connell*[21] a number of defendants were indicted for a conspiracy which was alleged to have a large number of objects. The jury convicted some of the defendants of conspiring to effect all the objects, some of conspiring to effect some only and not others, and one with conspiring to effect an even smaller number. At the invitation of the House of Lords, the judges of the Queen's Bench indicated that in their opinion the verdicts were bad. Tindal C.J. gave their reasons:

> ". . . though it was competent to the jury to find one conspiracy on each count, and to have included in that finding all or any number of the defendants, yet it was not competent for them to find some of the defendants guilty of a conspiracy to effect one or more of the objects stated, and others of the defendants guilty of a conspiracy to effect others of the objects stated, because that is, in truth, finding several conspiracies on a count which charges only one."[22]

Such difficulties may often arise on a conspiracy charge in a fraud case. Over the full period of the conspiracy numerous fraudulent devices may be used. Whether or not all the defendants are guilty will depend upon the proof of a core agreement to which they are all party. Provided there is such a core agreement, the various devices used may be evidence from which the individual defendants' guilt may be inferred, or evidence of the general intent of the agreement, or evidence from which it may be inferred that a particular device was within the general contemplation of the agreement. The prosecution should take care to ensure that the particulars define an agreement to which all are party. The fact that an act or device is not particularised does not make it inadmissible in evidence: it may be relevant in any of the ways set out above. If it is particularised but it cannot be shown to be part of the agreement in

---

21 (1844) 1 Cox 365.
22 At p. 473f.

which all the defendants joined, the particular may be regarded as surplusage (if it is inessential to guilt) and evidence of it as relevant in some subsidiary manner, as explained above. In *Esdaile*[23] there was a conspiracy to defraud shareholders of the Royal British Bank. The defendants were alleged to have represented that the Bank was solvent when it was not. Thereafter there was a new share issue to which shareholders subscribed on the basis of the misrepresentation. Only some of the defendants could be shown to be party to that issue. It was objected that it could not in those circumstances be an overt act of the conspiracy. The court held that an overt act laid and proved against some but not all of the conspirators may be admissible to prove the object or intent of the conspiracy.

CHANGING THE INDICTMENT

Severance

12.54 The joinder of defendants is governed by common law.[24] The alleged wrongdoing of the individual defendants must be sufficiently related that the interests of justice will best be served by trying them together. The relationship between the offenders rarely presents a problem in a fraud case since there is usually alleged some joint offence or some form of participation in a fraudulent organisation. The difficulty which does arise is the number of defendants who ought to be in the dock at one time in order to produce a fair trial. On the one hand the case must be presented in a form which a jury can reasonably be expected to understand. If the jury are asked to consider the case against too many defendants, they may be unable to distinguish sufficiently between them, and an innocent man may be sucked down with the guilty.[25] There may be evidence admissible against one defendant, but inadmissible and prejudicial against another.[26] At the same time the absence of one defendant may enable another to cast all the blame on him, and so escape justice.[27] A jury may speculate unwisely on the absence of a potential defendant. Plainly the court has to strike a balance between these rival considerations. As these are matters of practice, the court has a complete discretion to sever defendants either on application or on its own motion. In *Miller*[28] Devlin J. observed that it would be rare that defendants on a

---

23 (1858) 1 F. & F. 213; *cf. infra,* para. 13.04.
24 *D.P.P. v. Merriman* [1973] A.C. 584; *Assim* [1966] 2 Q.B. 249.
25 *Novac* (1976) 65 Cr.App.R. 107; *Thorne* (1978) 66 Cr.App.R. 6; *Dawson* [1960] 1 W.L.R. 163.
26 *Griffiths* [1966] 1 Q.B. 589; *supra,* para. 12.19.
27 *Moghal* (1977) 65 Cr.App.R. 56; *Miller* (1952) 36 Cr.App.R. 169 at p. 174, *per* Devlin J.
28 *Supra* n. 27; *cf. Boulton* (1871) 12 Cox 87, *supra* para. 12.10.

conspiracy charge should be severed: the reasons which he cogently advances are those already put forward for trying any joint offenders together. But there would seem to be no reason in principle why defendants in a conspiracy trial should not be severed if to try them all together would produce an unmanageable trial.

12.55 Joinder of counts is governed by section 4 of the Indictments Act 1915 and rule 9 of the Indictment Rules 1971: the effect of these provisions is that offences may be joined in the same indictment if those charges are founded on the same facts, or form or are a part of a series of offences of the same or a similar character. This plainly leaves a wide discretion. But again there are practical limits to the scope of an indictment. Thus in *King*[29] Hawkins J. said:

> "The defendant was tried for obtaining and attempting to obtain goods by false pretences upon an indictment containing no fewer than forty counts; and I pause here to express my decided opinion that it is a scandal that an accused person should be put to answer such an array of counts containing, as these do, several distinct charges. Though not illegal, it is hardly fair to put a man upon his trial on such an indictment, for it is almost impossible that he should not be grievously prejudiced as regards each one of the charges by the evidence which is being given upon the others. In such a case it would not be unreasonable for the defendant to make an application that each count or each set of counts should be taken separately."[30]

12.56 In addition to any inherent power to sever counts as a matter of practice, there is specific statutory authority for such severance. Section 5(3) of the Indictments Act 1915 provides:

> "Where, before trial, or at any stage of a trial, the court is of opinion that a person accused may be prejudiced or embarrassed in his defence by reason of being charged with more than one offence in the same indictment, or that for any other reason it is desirable to direct that the person should be tried separately for any one or more offences charged in an indictment, the court may order a separate trial of any count or counts of such indictment."

The subsection appears to be aimed at the severance of counts rather than of defendants, though severance of a count may result in severance of defendants. The relationship between section 5(3) and the predecessor of rule 9 of the Indictment Rules was considered in *Ludlow v. Metropolitan Police Commissioner*.[31] Lord Pearson, delivering a speech in which the House concurred, stated the following propositions:

(1) If counts are not based on the same facts, then, to be capable of

29 [1897] 1 Q.B. 214.
30 At p. 216.
31 [1971] A.C. 29.

joinder, they must be part of a series of offences of the same or a similar nature.

(2) Two offences can constitute a series.

(3) Whether the nature of offences is similar is a question of both law and fact.

(4) For the similarity to be sufficient there must be a nexus between the offences. The offences should exhibit such similar features as to establish a *prima facie* case that they can properly and conveniently be tried together.

(5) The fact that evidence in relation to one count is admissible on others may be a ground for joining with them; but joinder is not restricted to such a situation.

(6) Section 5(3) gives the trial judge power to sever even when counts are properly joined.

12.57 These propositions leave the definition of the required nexus or connection rather vague. There will inevitably be a connection where both offences are alleged to have been committed by the same person, but this in itself would not be enough. The House of Lords approved the decision in *Clayton-Wright,*[32] where a defendant was charged with arson, arson with intent to defraud insurers, and attempting to obtain money from insurers by false pretences. All three counts were concerned with an attempted fraud on insurers by burning a boat. There was added a count which alleged that some nine months earlier the defendant had obtained money from insurers by the false pretence that a mink coat had been stolen from his car. The Court of Criminal Appeal held that both types of charge were of swindling underwriters and that they were properly joined. The decision in *Ludlow* itself, however, makes it plain that the discretion to join goes much further than the type of circumstances which arose in *Clayton-Wright.* In *Ludlow* the defendant had been into the private part of a public house where, it was alleged, he had attempted to steal. Sixteen days later he entered another public house, had an argument with a barman, punched him and snatched money from him. He was charged on two counts, one of attempted theft and one of robbery. The House of Lords held that they were properly joined because they had the common ingredient of actual or attempted theft, and they involved stealing or attempting to steal in neighbouring public houses at a time interval of only sixteen days.

Power of the court to order other changes

12.58 Beyond the court's powers to order an indictment to be quashed or severed or amended on the application of the prosecution, it is an open

32 [1948] 2 All E.R. 763.

question whether the court may order the prosecution to amend the indictment in some particular way. Suppose, for example, that the prosecution indicts for conspiracy: can the judge order it to substitute substantive counts if he considers the conspiracy count unfair to the accused? Can he order the prosecution to include in an indictment counts which are not there but which in his opinion ought to be there? Can he quash a count which is in proper form but which he considers inappropriate for the trial of the accused? If he has such powers, it must follow that the defence may ask him to exercise them. In *Simmonds*[33] Fenton Atkinson J., after consultation within the Criminal Division of the Court of Appeal, said:

> "If upon examination of material before him the judge considers that the presentation of the case in the way proposed by the prosecution involves undue burdens on the court in general and jurors in particular, and is for this or other reasons contrary to the interests of justice, he has a right and, indeed, a duty to ask that the prosecution recast their approach in those interests, even if a considerable adjournment is entailed."[34]

This does not make it entirely clear whether the prosecution is to be merely requested to alter its approach or ordered to do so.

12.59   The House of Lords has considered *obiter* on a number of occasions the existence and extent of any general discretion in the judge to secure a fair trial. There are powerful dicta in support of such a general discretion from (amongst others) Lord Pearce in *Connelly*[35] and *Selvey*,[36] Lord Devlin in *Connelly*,[37] Lord Salmon in *Humphrys*[38] and *Sang*[39] and Lord Scarman in *Sang*.[40] Viscount Dilhorne in *Humphrys*[41] was less willing to recognise its existence. The jurisdiction was exercised in *Riebold*,[42] a fraud case in which the defendants were indicted on two conspiracy counts and 27 counts of larceny and obtaining by false pretences. The Crown elected to proceed on the conspiracies, and the accused were convicted. Subsequently both defendants' convictions were quashed: the trial judge had wrongly refused to let one cross-examine the other as to character, and once his conviction was quashed there was on the facts no one left for the other defendant to have conspired with. The prosecution then sought to proceed on the substantive counts, but the

33   [1969] 1 Q.B. 685.
34   At p. 692.
35   [1964] A.C. 1254 at p. 1361.
36   [1970] A.C. 304 at p. 360.
37   [1964] A.C. 1254 at p. 1347 and p. 1354.
38   [1977] A.C. 1 at p. 45f.
39   [1980] A.C. 402 at p. 444.
40   *Ibid.* at p. 457.
41   [1977] A.C. 1 at p. 23f.
42   [1967] 1 W.L.R. 674.

trial judge refused to let them and quashed the remaining counts. In *Smith*[43] the defendants were charged with manslaughter in one indictment and offences of dishonesty in another. Glyn Jones J. took the view that the two indictments ought to be tried together, and granted a voluntary bill combining them in one indictment. It is not entirely clear whether this was done of his own motion. Technically it would seem possible for the court to grant such a bill of its own motion. But this was simply a case of combining existing counts in one indictment; it was not a case of forcing the prosecution to proceed on counts that were not drawn by it.

12.60 If there is any general power to compel the prosecution to proceed on certain counts or in a certain manner, it should be exercised with caution. In *D.P.P. v. Humphrys*[44] Viscount Dilhorne said:

> "A judge must keep out of the arena. He should not have or appear to have any responsibility for the institution of a prosecution. The functions of prosecutors and of judges must not be blurred."[45]

Lord Salmon concurred in that view:

> ". . . a judge has not and should not appear to have any responsibility for the institution of prosecutions; nor has he any power to refuse to allow a prosecution to proceed merely because he considers that, as a matter of policy, it ought not to have been brought. It is only if the prosecution amounts to an abuse of the process of the court and is oppressive and vexatious that the judge has the power to intervene."[46]

---

43   [1958] 1 W.L.R. 312.
44   [1977] A.C. 1.
45   At p. 26.
46   At p. 46.

CHAPTER 13

Evidence

13.01 This is not a general treatise on the law of evidence and it would not be appropriate to consider every type of evidential problem that may arise in the course of a fraud trial. Nevertheless, certain points of evidence do arise with particular frequency in such cases and merit detailed consideration. They may be expressed by the following questions:

(1) On a conspiracy charge may general evidence of the conspiracy be admitted before the defendant's adherence to the agreement is proved?

(2) Are all acts or declarations by one conspirator in furtherance of a conspiracy admissible against all conspirators? Does this rule entail the admissibility of hearsay evidence? Does it apply equally to all joint offences?

(3) When is evidence admissible of a defendant's similar conduct on occasions other than that charged?

GENERAL EVIDENCE OF CONSPIRACY

13.02 In any joint crime the problem may arise that an act or declaration of one defendant may prove his intention to commit the crime charged, but it may not prove the intentions of others. If he is tried with others, then the jury will require direction on the probative force, if any, of the evidence against those others. If those others are tried separately, then the question will arise whether the evidence is admissible at all. In *Queen Caroline's case*[1] the judges were asked the following question by the House of Lords:

> "Supposing that, according to the rules of law, evidence of a conspiracy against a Defendant for any indictable offence ought not to be admitted to convict or criminate him, unless as it may apply to himself or to an agent employed by him, may not general evidence, nevertheless, of the existence of the conspiracy charged upon the record, be received in the first instance; though it cannot affect such Defendant, unless brought home to him, or to an agent employed by him . . . ?"[2]

1   (1820) 2 Br. & B. 284.
2   At p. 303f.

To that question Abbott C.J. delivered the following unanimous opinion of the judges:

> "We are of opinion, that on a prosecution for a crime to be proved by conspiracy, general evidence of an existing conspiracy may in the first instance be received, as a preliminary step to that more particular evidence, by which it is to be shewn that the individual Defendants were guilty participators in such conspiracy. This is often necessary to render the particular evidence intelligible, and to show the true meaning and character of the acts of the individual defendants; and, on that account, we presume it is permitted. But, it is to be observed, that, in such cases, the general nature of the whole evidence intended to be adduced is previously opened to the Court, whereby the Judge is enabled to form an opinion as to the probability of affecting the individual Defendants by particular proof applicable to them, and connecting them with the general evidence of the alleged conspiracy; and if, upon such opening, it should appear manifest, that no particular proof sufficient to affect the Defendants is intended to be adduced, it would become the duty of the judge to stop the case *in limine*, and not to allow the general evidence to be received, which, even if attended with no other bad effect, such as exciting an unreasonable prejudice, would certainly be a useless waste of time."[3]

13.03 This general principle should be approached with a certain caution. The notion that the Crown may prove (a) that there is an agreement between A and B to commit x, (b) that C was party to that agreement, is logically impeccable. Nevertheless the danger may exist that, because A and B agreed to do x, and C was associated with them or had some common objectives, the tribunal of fact may be too ready to assume that C was party to that very agreement. He may not have been party to any agreement at all, or only to a subsidiary but different agreement. The opinion of the judges in the Queen's case recognises the power of a trial judge to stop a case *in limine* if need be; but it omits an intermediate position which is probably more important, *viz.* that evidence of what other conspirators agreed may be more prejudicial than probative and may therefore be excluded at the judge's discretion. In the example given the real question is: to what did C agree? In general what A and B agreed will have only limited relevance; its prejudicial effect upon a jury may be considerable.

13.04 That is not to say that there may not be cases where the evidence of the general conspiracy is sufficiently relevant to be admitted. In *Esdaile*[4] there was a conspiracy to defraud the shareholders of the Royal British Bank. The defendants were alleged to have fraudulently represented that the Bank was solvent when it was not. Some but not all of the defendants were party to a new share issue. The evidence of the

3   At p. 310.
4   (1858) 1 F. & F. 213.

issue was held admissible against all of them to show the object of the conspiracy. Obviously the misrepresentation of solvency would not be fraudulent unless it were made with a dishonest purpose. If it could be shown that A and B intended to profit from the proceeds of the new issue which shareholders were to be induced by the misrepresentation to purchase, and that C was party to the misrepresentation, then it might be inferred that C must have known the dishonest purpose of the misrepresentation (*viz.* the new issue). The fact of the new issue could therefore be evidence against him. It could not prove his guilt, however, unless the jury were satisfied that he must have known it was the purpose of the misrepresentation. If he did not know that, then the fact that A and B had profited independently would prove nothing against him.

ACTS IN FURTHERANCE OF CONSPIRACY

13.05 It is often stated that any act or declaration in furtherance of a conspiracy is admissible against all the conspirators. In this context a distinction is drawn between conspiracies and joint substantive offences. In *Griffiths*[5] Paull J., delivering the judgment of the Court of Criminal Appeal, said:

> "The practice of adding what may be called a rolled-up conspiracy charge to a number of counts of substantive offences has become common. We express the very strong hope that this practice will now cease and that the courts will never again have to struggle with this type of case, where it becomes almost impossible to explain to a jury that evidence inadmissible against the accused on the substantive count may be admissible against him on the conspiracy count once he is shown to be a conspirator. We do not believe that most juries can ever really understand the subtleties of the situation. . . . [In] two counts upon which the appellant Bishop was convicted, there was literally no receivable evidence at all against him, the evidence being entries in Griffiths' books of account, evidence in the conspiracy count once Bishop is brought into a conspiracy but not evidence upon which he can be brought into the conspiracy."[6]

It is not only juries who may find this proposition difficult to understand. There can be no reason in principle why evidence should be admissible on a charge of conspiracy to commit a given offence but not on a joint charge of committing that offence. Often enough conspiracies are charged where substantive offences have been committed. It would be absurd if the prosecution could circumvent the ordinary rules of evidence by charging a conspiracy to commit a substantive offence rather than the offence itself. Plainly the rule ought to be the same for all joint offences.

5 [1966] 1 Q.B. 589.
6 At p. 594.

Either, therefore, the rule is more limited in its application to conspiracy trials than is commonly supposed, or it ought equally to apply to all trials of joint offences.

13.06 Moreover, in its application to conspiracy the rule runs two serious dangers. In the first place it may be fallaciously circular. All conspirators are responsible for all acts done in furtherance of the conspiracy, whether they knew about them or not. By agreeing to an end, one is responsible for what is done to that end (though not, of course, for acts outside the contemplation of the agreement). But acts done in furtherance of the conspiracy by others do not prove that one is party to the conspiracy; that must be achieved independently. Since all conspirators are responsible in law for the acts of their fellow conspirators, the point at issue in a conspiracy trial is never to which acts an individual defendant was party, but whether he was a party to the general agreement. The second difficulty with the rule is that it may be interpreted as involving the admissibility of hearsay evidence. It would be an odd situation if conspiracy were the only charge on which hearsay were admissible.

13.07 In view of these difficulties it may be illuminating to examine the case on which the supposed rule is founded. In *Blake and Tye*[7] the defendants were charged with various conspiracies which in sum amounted to agreements to evade the payment of customs dues on certain goods imported into the United Kingdom. Tye was the agent for the importer. He was under a statutory duty to record in official customs records the quantity and value of goods imported. He had to take an official copy of that entry to Blake, who was a landing waiter. Blake had to certify the correctness of the entry. The prosecution case was that the defendants had agreed to understate (and had in fact understated) the value of the goods so that Tye need only account for a limited amount of customs duty. Tye, it was alleged, then passed the goods to the importer, charging him the true amount of duty, and split the difference with Blake. Tye failed to appear on trial and Blake was tried alone. The entries made by Tye and acknowledged by Blake in official records were admitted without objection. Blake's acknowledgement made them an admission. Even if he had not acknowledged them they might have been admissible, not as hearsay but as establishing as a fact the declared value of goods. That was truly an act in furtherance of the conspiracy. It was admitted not to prove the truth of its contents (on the contrary, it was alleged to be false), but to prove the fact of the undervaluation by Tye to which it was

7   (1844) 6 Q.B. 126.

alleged Blake was party. There will be many occasions when an entry in a document will be admissible for a similar purpose.

13.08 The prosecution however went further. It sought to prove that Tye had made an entry in his daybook showing the true value of the goods he passed to the importer. The case does not suggest that the daybook was any form of official record. As against Tye it would have been an admission; as against Blake it must have been hearsay. The fact that a greater quantity of goods was supplied to the importer would have been relevant, and could have been proved by calling the importer. Could it equally be proved against Blake by the entry in Tye's daybook? The prosecution also sought to prove an entry on a cheque counterfoil by Tye purporting to show that he had made out a cheque to Blake for an amount equal to half the difference between the duty paid to customs and that acquired from the importer. The payment of a sum equal to half the proceeds would again have been relevant, and might have been proved by direct evidence. Could it be proved against Blake by Tye's entry on the cheque stub?

13.09 At the trial both these items of disputed evidence were admitted. Motion was made to the Court of Queen's Bench for a new trial on the ground that the evidence was inadmissible. The court held that the evidence as to the entry on the cheque counterfoil was not properly admitted, and granted the motion. The ground for the rejection of the evidence was that the paying of the cheque was not an act in furtherance of the conspiracy, since the conspiracy was to evade the payment of customs dues and that evasion was already complete at the time the counterfoil was written. Hearsay evidence was not admissible to prove an act that was not done in furtherance of the conspiracy. Lord Denman C.J. said:

> "The conspiracy was fully effected before that was done. The evidence, therefore, is on the same footing as evidence that Tye told some other party that he had paid Blake money on account of the fraud. . . . If we received every statement of a party shewn to be a conspirator, we should often find ourselves embarrassed by a party relying upon a statement of his own, to exonerate himself."[8]

The other judges concurred in this reasoning, Coleridge J. adding the observation that the note was simply made out for Tye's own use.[9] Lord Denman C.J. put forward the classic objection to hearsay evidence, *viz.* that it may be fabricated. However, to say (as Coleridge J. did) that the division of plunder was not part of the common object seems to fly in the

8 At p. 137.
9 At p. 140.

face of common sense. The whole purpose of the agreement was the eventual division of plunder and it must have continued until that was effected.

13.10 The question of the admissibility of the daybook was never fully argued. Counsel for the applicant was stopped in argument, and Coleridge J. in his judgment made it plain that counsel had not been heard on this issue. The court nevertheless made observations, *obiter*, to the effect that the entry in the daybook was admissible. It is upon these observations that the supposed rule is founded. Lord Denman C.J. said:

> "The day book was evidence of something done in the course of the transaction, and was properly laid before the jury as a step in the proof of the conspiracy."[10]

Patteson J. said:

> " . . . the concert may be shewn by either direct or indirect evidence. The day book here was evidence of what was done towards the very acting in concert which was to be proved. It was receivable as a step in the proof of the conspiracy."[11]

Williams J. said:

> " . . . the existence of a conspiracy may be shewn by the detached acts of the individual conspirators. Therefore, the entry made by Tye in his day book was admissible, in order to shew one act done with the common purpose."[12]

Coleridge J. indicated that he thought the entry was probably admissible.[13]

13.11 So far as the report shows, the daybook was merely Tye's private record. He was under no statutory obligation to make it. He did not show it to the customs officers or to Blake to secure payment of the full dues. Had he done so, it might have been admissible to show the fact that it was made, but not the truth of its contents. Moreover, in all probability, it was made after the goods had entered. In principle, therefore, it seems to be in no different position from the cheque counterfoil. Of course, the judges' observations may confuse two issues. The fact that Tye had given the importer a higher value and charged him greater dues than he had declared or paid to the customs was clearly *relevant*: these acts would have been a necessary part of the conspiracy, or acts in its furtherance. The real question was how they could be *proved*. They could clearly be

10   At p. 137.
11   At p. 138f.
12   At p. 139.
13   At p. 140.

proved by the direct evidence of the importer, or by admission against an individual defendant. A hearsay statement, however, ought to be just as objectionable in this case as in the case of the cheque counterfoil. Conspiracy may be inferred from the detached acts of conspirators, but those acts must be properly proved by admissible evidence. This view is to some extent borne out by the case of *Steward*.[14] The defendant was convicted of conspiring to defraud by doping racehorses. A fellow conspirator gave evidence (without objection) that Steward had doped a particular horse. He also said that another conspirator had told him that Steward had doped a number of other horses. The evidence of this statement was held inadmissible because it was not made in furtherance of the conspiracy.

SIMILAR CONDUCT

13.12 Evidence of conduct other than that charged may sometimes be admissible provided it is relevant. The classic statement of the rule is to be found in the speech of Lord Herschell L.C. in *Makin v. Attorney-General for New South Wales*.[15]

> "It is undoubtedly not competent for the prosecution to adduce evidence tending to shew that the accused has been guilty of criminal acts other than those covered by the indictment, for the purpose of leading to the conclusion that the accused is a person likely from his criminal conduct or character to have committed the offence for which he is being tried. On the other hand, the mere fact that the evidence adduced tends to shew the commission of other crimes does not render it inadmissible if it be relevant to an issue before the jury, and it may be so relevant if it bears upon the question whether the acts alleged to constitute the crime charged in the indictment were designed or accidental, or to rebut a defence which would otherwise be open to the accused."[16]

13.13 Lord Herschell's dictum makes it clear that evidence is not admissible merely because it relates to conduct similar to that charged: it must be relevant to a specific issue in the case. Thus in *Holt*[17] the defendant had authority to take orders on his employer's behalf but not to accept payment. He was charged with obtaining money from a customer by the false pretence that he was authorised to collect it; evidence was admitted that at about the same time he had obtained money from another customer by the same pretence. His conviction was quashed by the Court for Crown Cases Reserved. No reasons were given, but the decision was explained by Blackburn J., *arguendo*, in *Francis*:[18]

14 [1963] Crim.L.R. 697.
15 [1894] A.C. 57.
16 At p. 65.
17 (1860) 8 Cox 411.
18 (1874) L.R. 2 C.C.R. 128.

"There the alleged false pretence was an assertion of authority to receive the money, and the question was, authority or no authority. The evidence was wholly irrelevant."[19]

Assuming that Holt did not deny receiving the money, his defence might have been either that he was in fact authorised to do so, or that (having misunderstood his instructions) he believed that he was. The fact that he had also obtained money from another customer was entirely consistent with either defence, and was therefore irrelevant.

13.14   Of course, the prosecution cannot always anticipate the nature of the defence. If it appears reasonably likely that an issue may arise to which the evidence is relevant, then the prosecution may adduce it. If the prosecution were forced to wait until the defendant raised the issue in evidence, it might be put at a disadvantage. It might cross-examine about the other conduct, but if the defendant denied it, it might be prevented from calling evidence in rebuttal because the matter did not arise *ex improviso*. If the defence asserts that the issue is not a live one, it may circumvent the need for the evidence by making a suitable admission. Nevertheless the prosecution should not be allowed to tilt at windmills so as to prejudice the defence. It must also be remembered that, even if the evidence is relevant, the trial judge will in any event have the power to exclude it on the grounds that its probative value is outweighed by its prejudicial character. With these caveats in mind, we now consider some of the ways in which evidence of similar conduct may be relevant to the issues raised.

Essential background

13.15   In the first place there may be cases where the evidence of misconduct on other occasions is so inextricably bound up with that relating to the occasion charged, so closely associated with it in time and place, that it is impossible to understand the position without hearing the whole story: the other conduct is an essential part of the background to the case. Thus in *Ellis*[20] a shop assistant was suspected of stealing from the till. On a particular day marked coins were put into it. The assistant was watched and on a number of occasions was seen apparently taking something from the till. Each time a check on the till revealed a deficiency. Eventually the marked coins were found in his possession and he was charged only with stealing those. Evidence was admitted, on that charge, of all the apparent takings. Bayley J. in the King's Bench took the view that the trial judge had discretion to admit the evidence of all the takings because they were all part of one entire transaction:

---

19   At p. 130.
20   (1826) 6 B. & C. 145.

"[The evidence] went to shew the history of the till from the time when the marked money was put into it up to the time when it was found in the possession of the prisoner."[21]

The decision may be explicable on the basis that the prosecution had no way of knowing on which occasion the defendant had taken the marked coins; it was therefore essential for them to adduce evidence of each occasion on which it might have been done.

13.16   *Ellis* was followed in *Salisbury*,[22] where a postman was charged with stealing banknotes from a letter posted by A. It was alleged that he had also stolen notes from another letter posted by B, and had replaced B's notes with A's. In support of this allegation evidence was adduced that A's notes had been found in B's letter and that B's notes had been traced to the defendant. Patteson J. held this evidence admissible:

"I think that the evidence respecting [B's] notes is essential to the chain of facts necessary to make out the case."[23]

Once the thief of B's notes was identified, the presence of A's notes in B's letter obviously tended to prove who stole A's notes.

13.17   The line of reasoning in these cases was taken even further in *Cobden*.[24] Three men were charged with breaking into the booking office of Nether Whitacre railway station. Three other stations on the same line had been broken into on the same night, and jemmies were found on each of the defendants which corresponded with marks on doors or drawers which had been broken open at one station or another. Property taken from Nether Whitacre station was found on two of the defendants, and property from one of the other stations on the third. Bramwell B. admitted all the evidence:

"I think that evidence of the acts of the prisoners during the same night is admissible, in order to explain why none of the property taken from Nether Whitacre was found upon one of the prisoners. If it is proved that he was in possession of other property stolen from another station on the same night, that, with other circumstances, might be evidence that all the men had been engaged in each burglary, and that the third man had received his share of the booty wholly from what was taken from the other station. The events of that night, relating to these burglaries, are so intermixed that it is impossible to separate them."[25]

If there was evidence that the booty had been shared that would be highly probative of a joint enterprise. However, that inference could only be

21   At p. 148.
22   (1831) 5 C. & P. 155.
23   At p. 157.
24   (1862) 3 F. & F. 833.
25   At p. 834.

drawn once it was shown (by the jemmies) that all three were associated together on the same night.

Proof of particular knowledge

13.18 In a fraud case it is more likely that the defendant will admit the acts alleged but deny that he acted with the necessary mental element. If he denies knowledge of certain relevant information, evidence of previous transactions may serve to refute his denial. If, for example, he is charged with obtaining money by misrepresenting the quality of goods sold, and claims to have believed that the goods were as he described them, it will clearly be relevant that he had already received complaints from other customers about similar goods. In *Patel*[26] the defendant was charged with being knowingly concerned in taking steps with a view to the fraudulent evasion of purchase tax, which was payable on stockings purchased for resale within the United Kingdom. The defendant financed the purchase by a company of large quantities of nylon stockings and paid for their transport to unregistered traders within the United Kingdom, to whom they were sold on for further sale on the United Kingdom market. The appellant's defence was that he had been deceived by a director of the company, and did not know to whom the stockings were sold or that they were sold on for eventual sale in the United Kingdom. Evidence was admitted that six months earlier the defendant had purchased a large quantity of nylon stockings as agent on behalf of another firm, saying that the stockings were bound for Pakistan. The Court of Criminal Appeal held that evidence of the earlier transactions was admissible.

> "Since [the defendant's] business apparently consisted of financing other companies with which he was not directly concerned in cases in which those companies were placing orders for nylon stockings which purported to be orders for export, could the jury believe that in the cases charged he in fact made no inquiries and took no interest in what became of the goods ordered and paid for by him?"[27]

It was not in fact suggested that he had made no inquiries, but that he had been deceived. Even so, his knowledge of the trade and of the workings of purchase tax was plainly relevant to his state of mind in the second series of transactions: it cast doubt on his assertion that he did not know what was going on. It does not in fact appear to have been alleged that the previous transaction was illegal or that the stockings did not go to Pakistan, and indeed some of them were unsuitable for the British market. The evidence cannot therefore have been relevant on the grounds

26 (1951) 35 Cr.App.R. 62.
27 At p. 67f., *per* Byrne J.

that the earlier transaction was similar to the one alleged, and tended to prove dishonesty, but solely as revealing knowledge of a particular trade.

13.19 In certain cases there appears to have been some confusion between the relevance of similar conduct to the defendant's knowledge of material facts and its tendency to suggest a course of systematic fraud—a distinction which may be crucial because the evidence will not be admissible for the latter purpose unless it satisfies the criteria discussed below.[28] In *Porter*[29] the appellant was charged with obtaining money by falsely representing that a business carried on by him under the name Approved Hotels, Cafés and Restaurants of Great Britain was a *bona fide* association honestly carried on to offer advantages to subscribers. His defence was that, while he had indeed obtained money on such representations, he had no intent to defraud. Two years earlier he had carried on a business and obtained money in a way that was remarkably similar, and had been convicted of obtaining by false pretences. He was questioned in cross-examination about the circumstances of that previous business. He was not asked about the conviction, though he volunteered it. The Court of Criminal Appeal held that the evidence of the earlier business was admissible to show that the defendant must have known from his experience that carrying on such a business would only result in its failure and in subscribers being defrauded of their money. This reasoning is unconvincing. There was no reason to suppose that a business of that description was necessarily doomed to failure even if it were carried on in good faith. No doubt the second business was equally likely to fail if the defendant made no attempt to give the subscribers value for money; but the issue was whether he intended to do so, not whether he appreciated the commercial realities of running such a business. The evidence might indeed have been admissible as tending to prove that the defendant made a habit of running bogus businesses of this kind, but it should have been justified on that basis rather than as proof of particular knowledge.

13.20 Similar confusion may be detected in *Ollis*.[30] The defendant had a bank account that had lain dormant for three years. On July 5 he drew a cheque on the account for £5. It was dishonoured, and he was charged with obtaining money by false pretences. His defence was that he expected money to be paid into the account by a solicitor. The evidence of the solicitor was that money would have been paid in if certain property had been sold but that it had not at that date been sold. The

---

28 Para. 13.22ff.
29 (1935) 25 Cr.App.R. 59.
30 [1900] 2 Q.B. 758.

defendant was acquitted. The next day he was put on trial for obtaining property by false pretences that cheques drawn on June 24 and 26 and July 6 were good and valid orders. At this trial the prosecution were allowed to adduce evidence of the transaction on July 5 to negative any belief on the defendant's part that there was money in the bank to meet any of the cheques. The Court for Crown Cases Reserved held by a majority of six to two that this evidence was admissible, but the court's reasoning is obscure: much of it is directed to the question whether the evidence was inadmissible because of the acquittal in the first trial, rather than the logically prior question of whether it was relevant at all. Lord Russell C.J. said:

> " . . . it was relevant as shewing a course of conduct on the part of the accused, and a belief on his part that the cheques would not be met."[31]

Mathew J. concurred. Wright J. said:

> "The evidence tended to shew that the conduct of the prisoner, in tendering drafts on a bank at which he had no living account, was not inadvertent or accidental, but was part of a systematic fraud . . . "[32]

But it is hard to see how the writing of several bad cheques could be evidence of a "systematic fraud", when the defence was that the defendant was expecting money to be paid into his account:[33] if that defence were true, there was no reason why he should not write cheques. Provided that the aggregate of the cheques drawn did not exceed the amount which he anticipated would be paid in, the *number* of cheques drawn was beside the point.

13.21   The alternative reason for holding the evidence to be relevant was that it proved the defendant's knowledge of the state of his account. Darling J. said:

> " . . . this evidence . . . was material, for it went some way to shew that the defendant knew he had no assets at the bank on which he gave a cheque, as this had already been brought to his notice in regard to another cheque given by him but a very short time before."[34]

If it had been proved that the defendant knew one of his cheques had been dishonoured, this would certainly have been relevant to the issue of whether he knew the state of the account.[35] But two of the cheques which were the subject matter of the second trial had been drawn *before* the one on which the defendant had been acquitted; and according to Bruce J.

---

31   At p. 764.
32   At p. 768.
33   Bruce J. thought (at p. 772) it could be assumed that the defence was the same as in the first trial.
34   At p. 779.
35   *Cf.* Channell J. at p. 783.

(who dissented) there was no evidence that when the defendant wrote the cheque on July 6 he knew that the cheque written on July 5 had been dishonoured.[36] It is submitted that, at any rate on the facts as reported, the evidence of the transaction on July 5 was irrelevant to any issue before the court.

Proof of system

13.22 There is a deceptive simplicity in Lord Herschell's dictum in *Makin*,[37] that evidence of similar conduct is not admissible as proof of the defendant's criminal propensities but only if it is relevant to an issue before the court. The difficulty is that similar conduct may be logically relevant *because* it suggests certain propensities.[38] People who have committed crimes before are more likely to commit crimes than people who have not. But not all evidence which is logically relevant is legally admissible. Evidence of similar conduct is generally excluded, not because it is irrelevant but because such probative value as it does have is outweighed by its likely prejudicial effect. In some cases, however, the probative force of the evidence may be such that to ignore it would be an affront to common sense, and in such a case it may be admissible. The reasoning which the jury are invited to accept is that it would be a remarkable coincidence if the defendant had acted on previous occasions in a manner similar to that now alleged, but was not in fact guilty on the occasion charged. The more remarkable the coincidence would be, the less reason there is to exclude the evidence:

> "If the jury are precluded by some rule of law from taking the view that something is a coincidence which is against all the probabilities if the accused person is innocent, then it would seem to be a doctrine of law which prevents a jury from using what looks like ordinary common sense."[39]

13.23 The problem is to define how improbable the coincidence must be. A test which met with the broad approval of the House of Lords in *D.P.P. v. Kilbourne*[40] and *D.P.P. v. Boardman*[41] was whether the conduct relied upon bore a "striking similarity" to that charged. But here we must draw an important distinction. Both cases were concerned with

---

36 At p. 778.
37 [1894] A.C. 57 at p. 65; *supra*, para. 13.12.
38 *D.P.P. v. Kilbourne* [1973] A.C. 729 at p. 757, *per* Lord Simon; *D.P.P. v. Boardman* [1975] A.C. 421 at p. 456, *per* Lord Cross; P. B. Carter, "Forbidden Reasoning Permissible" (1985) 48 M.L.R. 29.
39 *Robinson* (1953) 37 Cr.App.R. 95 at p. 106f., *per* Hallett J.
40 [1973] A.C. 729.
41 [1975] A.C. 421.

homosexual assaults on boys, and with the question whether evidence on one count alleging sexual misconduct against one boy could be admissible on a similar count alleging misconduct against another; the issue was not the nature of the defendants' intentions, but whether the misconduct had occurred at all. In such a case there is plainly sense in requiring something like a hallmark before the evidence has sufficient probative force to be admissible. But if (as is more likely in a fraud case) the act is admitted, and what is in issue is the intent with which it was committed, different considerations may apply. Whether there must be a "striking similarity" in this case depends upon the interpretation of that phrase. There may be conduct which is in itself striking and unusual, in which case the coincidence of another piece of conduct bearing the same hallmark will obviously be highly probative. It may be, however, that the conduct is not in itself striking, but that there are a number of other acts which are very similar to it. If a person has carried out some everyday action, which might be dishonest but might on the other hand be accidental or the result of a misunderstanding, the fact that he has acted similarly on another occasion may help to prove that he was acting dishonestly on the occasion in issue; and in that case the evidence of the other occasion may be admissible. It may be the similarity which is striking rather than the conduct itself.

13.24   Less fashionable, but possibly more helpful in the present context, is the notion of system. If a person is charged with committing a murder in unusual circumstances, and he has previously committed murders in similar circumstances,[42] it would no doubt be odd to say that evidence of the earlier murders was admissible to prove a course of systematic murder. In a fraud case, however, the issue is usually not one of identity but of intention, and proof of other transactions similar to the one charged may tend to suggest that the defendant acted dishonestly throughout. To disappoint one customer may be regarded as a misfortune; to have disappointed twenty looks suspiciously like fraud. In *Fisher*[43] Channell J. put the matter thus:

"The principle is that the prosecution are not allowed to prove that a prisoner has committed the offence with which he is charged by giving evidence that he is a person of bad character and one who is in the habit of committing crimes, for that is equivalent to asking the jury to say that because the prisoner has committed other offences he must therefore be guilty of the particular offence for which he is being tried. But if the evidence of other offences does go to prove that he did commit the offence charged, it is admissible because it is relevant to the issue, and it is

42   *Cf. Straffen* [1952] 2 Q.B. 911.
43   [1910] 1 K.B. 149.

admissible not because, but notwithstanding that, it proves that the prisoner has committed another offence. For example, on a charge of embezzlement, if the defence is that the failure to account for the money is due to a mistake on the part of the prisoner, evidence is admissible to prove other instances of the same kind, because that evidence tends to prove that in the particular case the prisoner had not made a mistake. Another instance is where a person obtains goods by paying for them with a cheque which is subsequently dishonoured, in which case evidence is admissible to prove other cases in which the prisoner has obtained goods by cheques which were dishonoured. In other words, whenever it can be shewn that the case involves a question as to there having been some mistake or as to the existence of a system of fraud, it is open to the prosecution to give evidence of other instances of the same kind of transaction, notwithstanding that the evidence goes to prove the commission of other offences, in order to negative the suggestion of mistake or in order to shew the existence of a systematic course of fraud."[44]

This passage must not be read as suggesting that evidence of systematic fraud is admissible *per se*: we have already pointed out that it must be relevant to a specific issue in the case.[45] It may well be relevant to the defendant's knowledge or his good faith, but its relevance should be established before it is admitted.

13.25 A case where the similar conduct was clearly relevant to the issue of dishonesty is *Wyatt*,[46] where the defendant was charged with obtaining board and lodging at a boarding house by means of an implied representation that he intended to pay. In the period immediately preceding this incident he had left other boarding houses without paying. The Court for Crown Cases Reserved held that evidence of the earlier transactions was rightly admitted to prove a system practised by him. In *Francis*[47] the defendant was charged with attempting to obtain an advance from a pawnbroker in Northampton on the security of a ring, by the false pretence that it was a diamond ring. His defence was that his employer had instructed him to pawn the ring and had told him that it was a diamond ring. Evidence was admitted that two days earlier he had obtained an advance from a pawnbroker in Bedford on a chain which he falsely represented to be gold, and had attempted to do the same in Leicester with a ring which he falsely represented to be a diamond ring. The Court for Crown Cases Reserved held this evidence admissible. Lord Coleridge C.J. said:

"It seems clear upon principle that when the fact of the prisoner having done the thing charged is proved, and the only remaining question is,

44   At p. 152.
45   *Supra*, para. 13.13.
46   [1904] 1 K.B. 188.
47   (1874) L.R. 2 C.C.R. 128.

whether at the time he did it he had guilty knowledge of the quality of his act or acted under a mistake, evidence of the class received must be admissible. It tends to shew that he was pursuing a course of similar acts, and thereby it raises a presumption that he was not acting under a mistake. It is not conclusive, for a man may be many times under a similar mistake, or may be many times the dupe of another; but it is less likely he should be so often, than once, and every circumstance which shews he was not under a mistake on any one of these occasions strengthens the presumption that he was not on the last . . . Evidence that he, . . . at Bedford, obtained money from another pawnbroker on the pledge of a chain which he represented to be gold, when it in fact was not gold, was surely matter from which the jury might infer that he was in a course of cheating pawnbrokers by knowingly passing off on them false articles under the pretence that they were genuine . . . "[48]

13.26 Obviously the more often an act is repeated, the easier it will be to draw the necessary inferences; but there is no reason in principle why a single similar act should not be sufficient. As we have already pointed out, the degree of similarity may be crucial.[49] In *Fisher*[50] the defendant was charged with obtaining a pony and cart by the false pretence that they were for his wife, who was too sick to inspect them, that a bill which he delivered as security was good and genuine, and that he had an account at a specific bank. Evidence was admitted that on two occasions within a month of this transaction he had obtained provender by falsely pretending he had a business which involved keeping horses. The Court of Criminal Appeal held that that conduct was not sufficiently similar to justify its admission. As Channell J. put it:

" . . . if a man is charged with swindling in a particular manner, his guilt cannot be proved by shewing that he has also swindled in some other manner."[51]

But evidence that the defendant had obtained a horse three days earlier, on a false promissory note which was not honoured, was in the court's opinion rightly admitted.

Subsequent conduct

13.27 The question has occasionally arisen of whether it is permissible to rely on similar conduct occurring after the conduct charged. For some purposes, *e.g.* to establish the defendant's knowledge at the time of the alleged offence, subsequent conduct is clearly irrelevant (though we have seen that in *Ollis*[52] this point was apparently overlooked). It may

---

48 At p. 131f.
49 *Supra,* para. 13.23.
50 [1910] 1 K.B. 149.
51 At p. 153.
52 [1900] 2 Q.B. 758; *supra,* para. 13.20.

however be relevant as tending to prove a dishonest course of conduct. In *Rhodes*[53] the defendant advertised in newspapers for new-laid eggs for his dairy. The prosecutor responded to the advertisement and sent him over six hundred eggs. The defendant was indicted for obtaining the eggs on the false pretence that he was carrying on a business as dairyman or farmer, required them for that business and was then in a position to pay for them. The report does not indicate the defence raised to this allegation. The advertisement continued to appear in the newspapers, and two more suppliers sent the defendant eggs for which they were not paid. The Court for Crown Cases Reserved thought it clear that the evidence of these transactions would have been admissible as proof of a fraudulent scheme if they had occurred before the transaction charged,[54] and went on to hold that they were not rendered inadmissible merely because they had taken place subsequently. In the course of argument Wright J. drew attention to a passage in Roscoe's *Criminal Evidence* which doubted whether subsequent conduct could be admitted, since it would be possible that the guilty intention might not have arisen until after the acts upon which the charge was founded. That passage was relied upon and followed in *Boothby*.[55] The defendant was charged with obtaining food by false pretences. The victim had a business for sale. The defendant was alleged to have called upon him and represented that he had certain money, was connected with a company in the Isle of Man and was in a position to buy the victim's business. He persuaded the victim to give him food and lodging for a short period. Immediately on leaving the victim he visited a farmer who wished to sell his farm; he represented that he wished to buy the farm and would get the money in a few days, and again he obtained food and lodging. All the representations were alleged to be false. The detailed representations as to his means differed in each case. Relying on the passage in Roscoe and distinguishing *Rhodes* as decided upon its particular facts, the Court of Criminal Appeal held that the evidence of the subsequent transaction with the farmer ought not to have been admitted on the trial of the charge relating to the businessman. But there does seem to have been a remarkable similarity in the method used to obtain food and lodging in two instances occurring one after the other. On the face of it, unless there is a rule that subsequent conduct may not be relied upon, the evidence ought to have been admitted.

13.28 Other decisions of the Court of Criminal Appeal suggest that subsequent similar conduct may be admitted. Thus in *Mason*[56] the

---

53 [1899] 1 Q.B. 77.
54 *Per* Lord Russell C.J. at p. 81, Wills J. at p. 84.
55 (1933) 24 Cr.App.R. 112.
56 (1914) 10 Cr.App.R. 169.

defendant was charged with forgery and uttering a forged instrument. The instrument was a deed. His defence was that he was the dupe of another and had no knowledge that the document was forged when he uttered it. Evidence was admitted that he had subsequently forged other deeds. The Court of Criminal Appeal specifically held that subsequent similar conduct was admissible. Similarly, in *Hurren*[57] the accused were charged in two counts of obtaining money from householders on the false pretence that they would do building work. Their defence was that they were genuine but inefficient builders. Evidence was admitted that they had subsequently obtained money from others in a similar way, to show that they had a fraudulent scheme and were not genuine builders. The Court of Criminal Appeal held that the evidence had been rightly admitted. *Boothby* was not cited. On principle there would seem to be no reason why subsequent similar conduct should not be admissible, provided it is relevant, in the same way as previous conduct. A defendant's intentions may have changed by the time of subsequent conduct, but for that matter they may have changed since previous conduct. The likelihood of this possibility will depend largely on the degree of similarity and the length of time separating the occasions in question. But if the evidence is relevant according to these criteria, the accident of chronological priority ought to be immaterial.

Previous acquittals

13.29   The question has occasionally arisen whether it is permissible to adduce evidence of similar conduct where the defendant has previously been charged in respect of that conduct and has been acquitted. It seems that the admissibility of such evidence depends upon the precise purpose for which it is sought to adduce it. In *Ollis*[58] the defendant, having been acquitted of dishonestly passing a bad cheque, was then charged with dishonestly passing other bad cheques over the same period. Evidence of his passing the cheque in respect of which he had been acquitted was admitted to show that he knew the other cheques would not be honoured. We have already considered the application of the general principles of similar conduct evidence to this case and suggested that the evidence should not have been admitted because it was irrelevant.[59] But it was further held that, if the evidence was relevant, it was not rendered inadmissible merely because the defendant had been acquitted in respect of the transaction to which it related. Lord Russell C.J. said:

57   (1962) 46 Cr.App.R. 323.
58   [1900] 2 Q.B. 758.
59   *Supra*, para. 13.20f.

"It is clear that there was no estoppel; the negativing by the jury of the charge of fraud on the first occasion did not create an estoppel; nor is there any question arising upon the maxim '*Nemo debet bis puniri pro uno delicto*'. The evidence was not less admissible because it tended to shew that the accused was, in fact, guilty of the former charge. The point is, was it relevant in support of the three subsequent charges?"[60]

13.30 *Ollis* should be contrasted with *G. (an infant) v. Coltart*,[61] where a domestic servant was charged with stealing property belonging to her employer and to a guest. The property was found in the servant's room; she claimed that she had intended to return it, but she had failed to return the guest's property although she knew that the guest was about to leave the country. In view of the guest's unavailability the prosecution offered no evidence in respect of her property, and that charge was accordingly dismissed. The prosecution then adduced evidence, on the charge relating to the employer's property, of the finding of the guest's property and of the defendant's knowledge of the guest's imminent departure: these facts were relied upon as disproving the defendant's claim that she intended to return the property. The Divisional Court held that this evidence should not have been admitted, because its purpose was to establish the defendant's guilt on the charge of which she had already been acquitted. Salmon L.J. said:

" . . . on general principles . . . it would be quite wrong to allow the prosecution in order to obtain a conviction in case B to seek to show that the defendant was guilty in case A, after the defendant has been acquitted in case A. I have no doubt that, even although the defendant is acquitted in case A, evidence called against the defendant in case A could be relevant in case B, for example, to show what his intent was in case B. But it can never be permissible in case B to rely on the guilt of the defendant in case A if he has been acquitted in case A."[62]

Ollis was distinguished on the ground that there was no attempt in that case to prove that the defendant was in fact guilty of the offence of which he had been acquitted:

" . . . the distinction between that case and the present one is that in the present case the only relevance of the evidence tendered was to prove guilt in the [guest's] case, whereas in *R. v. Ollis* the prosecution were able to say: we are not alleging, let alone relying on, the accused's guilt of the first cheque; we are relying on the fact that the first cheque was not met only to show what the accused's knowledge or state of mind was when he gave the other three cheques."[63]

60   At p. 764.
61   [1967] 1 Q.B. 432.
62   At p. 439f.
63   At p. 440.

13.31 The view expressed in *Ollis*, that the criminal law knows no doctrine of issue estoppel, has now been confirmed by the House of Lords in *D.P.P. v. Humphrys*:[64] a defendant who secures his acquittal by perjured evidence may be tried for perjury even if the evidence shows that he was guilty of the offence of which he was acquitted. An acquittal does not prove conclusively that a man is innocent; it merely records that a jury on a particular day were not satisfied of his guilt. Their Lordships referred to *G. v. Coltart* and did not regard it as inconsistent with their decision, but the two are not easy to reconcile. In both cases the evidence was directly relevant on the second charge but suggested that the defendant should have been convicted on the first charge too. Possibly the explanation is that in *G. v. Coltart* the court was tilting at the wrong target. The prosecution had no need to suggest that the defendant was guilty on the second charge *because* she was guilty on the first. The evidence was relevant because it revealed a conjunction of circumstances which would be improbable if the defendant were innocent on the second charge: on that hypothesis she would have appropriated the property of her employer and of the guest, in similar circumstances, with the intention of returning the former but not the latter. What was relied upon was not her *guilt* on the first charge but the circumstances giving rise to it (which did incidentally suggest that she was guilty). On this view the decision is of marginal significance. Similar conduct is admissible if it is relevant in itself, according to the principles discussed above, even if it proves guilt on another occasion and even if the defendant has been acquitted in respect of that occasion. The only relevance of the acquittal is that the prosecution may not use the defendant's *guilt* on the other occasion as an essential plank in their argument—which they could hardly do in any event, because it would be irrelevant.

---

64 [1977] A.C. 1.

Specimen Indictments

1. Theft
STATEMENT OF OFFENCE
Theft contrary to section 1 of the Theft Act 1968.

PARTICULARS OF OFFENCE
John Doe, on a day unknown between 1st and 31st January 1986, stole a cheque no. 12345 drawn on the Moneybags Bank for £7,000, the property of Robert Roe.

Note: a cheque is a valuable security and therefore more valuable than a mere piece of paper.

STATEMENT OF OFFENCE
Theft *etc.*

PARTICULARS OF OFFENCE
John Doe on 5th January 1986 stole £3,000 the property of Robert Roe being part of the proceeds of cheque no. 12345 drawn by Jane Smalls on the Moneybags Bank in favour of the said Robert Roe.

2. Theft—General Deficiency
STATEMENT OF OFFENCE
Theft *etc.*

PARTICULARS OF OFFENCE
John Doe, between 1st January and 6th June 1986, stole £14,000 the property of Robert Roe.

3. Obtaining Property by Deception
STATEMENT OF OFFENCE
Obtaining Property by Deception contrary to section 15(1) of the Theft Act 1968.

PARTICULARS OF OFFENCE
John Doe on 15th March 1986 dishonestly obtained a banker's draft for £10,000 from Robert Roe, with the intention of permanently depriving the said Robert Roe thereof, by deception, namely by falsely stating to the said Robert Roe that he was an agent for the Careful Carriage Company and authorised to receive the said draft on their behalf.

STATEMENT OF OFFENCE
Obtaining Property *etc.*

PARTICULARS OF OFFENCE
John Doe on 1st March 1986 dishonestly obtained an overcoat from Robert Roe, with the intention of permanently depriving the said Robert Roe thereof, by deception, namely by inducing the said Robert Roe by words and conduct falsely to believe that a cheque no. 12345 drawn on the Bountiful Bank for £100 by the said John Doe was a good cheque.

Note: a "good cheque" in these circumstances means one which the drawer has no reason to doubt will be honoured in the ordinary course. This could be specifically pleaded thus—"by deception, namely by inducing Robert Roe by words and conduct falsely to believe that the said John Doe then had no reason to doubt that the said cheque would be honoured in the ordinary course." This is, however, a little clumsy, so the form above is preferred.

STATEMENT OF OFFENCE
Obtaining Property *etc.*

PARTICULARS OF OFFENCE
John Doe on 1st March 1986 dishonestly obtained an overcoat from Robert Roe, with the intention of permanently depriving the said Robert Roe thereof, by deception, namely by presenting to the said Robert Roe a Plasticash Credit Card no. 7895 and signing a debit slip thereon in purported payment of the sum of £50, thereby inducing the said Robert Roe falsely to believe that the said John Doe then had the authority of Plasticash plc to present the said card in payment of the said sum.

4. Evasion of a Liability by Deception

STATEMENT OF OFFENCE
Evasion of a Liability by Deception contrary to section 2(1)(*a*) of the Theft Act 1978.

PARTICULARS OF OFFENCE
John Doe on 1st March 1986 dishonestly secured the remission of a debt of £100 he then owed to Robert Roe by deception, namely by presenting to the said Robert Roe a Plasticash credit card no. 7895 and signing a debit slip thereon in purported payment of the said debt, thereby inducing the said Robert Roe falsely to believe that the said John Doe then had the authority of Plasticash plc to present the said card in payment of the said sum.

STATEMENT OF OFFENCE
Evasion of a Liability by Deception contrary to section 2(1)(*b*) of the Theft Act 1978.

PARTICULARS OF OFFENCE

John Doe on 1st March 1986 with intent to make permanent default on a debt of £100 he then owed to Robert Roe dishonestly induced the said Robert Roe to wait for payment by deception, namely by falsely stating to the said Robert Roe that he the said John Doe needed the £100 to pay for medical treatment for his grandmother Ada Buckit.

5. Common Frauds based on Deception

(i) *The Long Firm Fraud*

This is a type of fraud in which the fraudsmen set up a bogus business and induce suppliers to supply goods on a false promise of payment and/or customers to pay for goods on a false promise of delivery. The fraudsmen disappear before the time for payment/delivery arrives.

STATEMENT OF OFFENCE

Conspiracy to Obtain Goods by Deception contrary to section 1(1) of the Criminal Law Act 1977.

PARTICULARS OF OFFENCE

John Doe and Robert Roe between 1st January and 31st December 1986 conspired together and with other persons unknown dishonestly to obtain furniture and household goods, with the intention of permanently depriving the owners thereof, by deception, namely by inducing by words and conduct such persons as might be induced to part with goods to Bent Productions Limited falsely to believe that Bent Productions Limited was a genuine and honest business and that they then intended that the said Bent Productions Limited would pay for any goods so supplied.

STATEMENT OF OFFENCE

Conspiracy to Obtain Property by Deception contrary to section 1(1) of the Criminal Law Act 1977.

PARTICULARS OF OFFENCE

John Doe and Robert Roe between 1st January and 31st December 1986 conspired together and with other persons unknown dishonestly to obtain monies, with the intention of permanently depriving the owners thereof, by deception, namely by inducing by words and conduct such persons as might be induced to pay monies to Bent Productions Limited falsely to believe that the said Bent Productions Limited was a genuine and honest business and that they then intended that furniture and household goods would be delivered by Bent Productions Limited to the said persons in return for the said monies.

(ii) *Carbon Paper Frauds*

These frauds depend on selling goods which are in continuous demand in large quantities such as carbon paper or adhesive tape. Often an initial order is genuinely obtained. Then the fraudsmen deceive the customer into thinking that a larger order has been placed than actually was, or that a repeat order has been placed. Very often the prices charged are exorbitant. Care has to be taken in framing charges to remember the maxim *caveat emptor*. Only actual deceptions should be charged.

STATEMENT OF OFFENCE

Conspiracy to Obtain Property by Deception contrary to section 1(1) of the Criminal Law Act 1977.

PARTICULARS OF OFFENCE

John Doe and Robert Roe between 1st January and 31st December 1986 conspired together and with other persons unknown dishonestly to obtain monies, with the intention of permanently depriving the owners thereof, by deception, namely by inducing by words and conduct such persons as might be persuaded to pay the said monies to the Curious Carbon Company falsely to believe that they had ordered or repeated an order for a quantity of carbon paper equal in value to the said monies and that the price charged therefor was a competitive market price.

(iii) *Cross-Firing Cheques*

Here the fraudsmen transfer cheques rapidly between different bank accounts in order to make it appear that certain of the accounts are at any given moment more in credit than they actually are. Withdrawals are then made against the supposed credits.

STATEMENT OF OFFENCE

Conspiracy to Obtain a Pecuniary Advantage by Deception contrary to section 1(1) of the Criminal Law Act 1977.

PARTICULARS OF OFFENCE

John Doe and Robert Roe between 1st January and 31st December 1986 conspired together and with other persons unknown dishonestly to obtain a pecuniary advantage, namely increased borrowing by way of overdraft in excess of agreed drawings limits in respect of an account no. 123456 held by Bent Productions with Moneybags Bank plc, by deception, namely by inducing by words and conduct the employees of the said Moneybags Bank plc falsely to believe that transfers by cheque or telegraph between the said account and other accounts held by or on behalf of Bent Productions with Skinflint Bank plc and Generosity Bank plc were good orders for the payment of the sums stated therein and that they intended, at the time the said transfers were drawn, that they would be met on presentation and that the said transfers were made in the course of ordinary business transactions.

(iv) *Commodity Frauds*

These are usually based upon the ignorance of the public as to the relationship between a commodity broker and his client and the very risky nature of the commodity market. Care must be taken in settling an indictment to ensure that positive deceptions are relied on. The maxim *caveat emptor* may apply where the broker is silent and the customer deceives himself.

STATEMENT OF OFFENCE

Conspiracy to Obtain Property by Deception contrary to section 1(1) of the Criminal Law Act 1977.

PARTICULARS OF OFFENCE

John Doe and Robert Roe between 1st January and 31st December 1986 conspired together and with other persons unknown dishonestly to obtain monies, with the intention of permanently depriving the owners thereof, by deception, namely by inducing by words and conduct such persons as might be induced to send monies to Corkscrew Commodities in order to invest the said monies in the purchase of options to buy gold bullion from Corkscrew Commodities, falsely to believe that Corkscrew Commodities were dealers on the floor of the London Metal Exchange, that Corkscrew Commodities would act as agents for any such purchaser, and that any investment in the said options would be as safe as houses.

(v) *Villa Frauds*

In recent years there have been a number of these frauds, where members of the public have been induced to pay monies for the purchase of a villa abroad on the basis that the fraudsmen own the land on which it is to be built, or are agents for a foreign company, when neither is the case.

STATEMENT OF OFFENCE

Conspiracy to Obtain Property by Deception contrary to section 1(1) of the Criminal Law Act 1977.

PARTICULARS OF OFFENCE

John Doe and Robert Roe between 1st January and 31st December 1986 conspired together and with other persons unknown dishonestly to obtain monies, with the intention of permanently depriving the owners thereof, by deception, namely by inducing by words and conduct such persons as might be induced to send the said monies to Over the Rainbow Villas falsely to believe that the said Over the Rainbow Villas owned a plot of land called Los Platos at Benidorm in Spain and that they intended that villas would be constructed on the said land and sold in perpetuity to any purchaser.

6. False Accounting
STATEMENT OF OFFENCE
False Accounting contrary to section 17(1)(*a*) of the Theft Act 1968.

PARTICULARS OF OFFENCE
John Doe on 1st March 1986 dishonestly with a view to gain by himself or another or with intent to cause loss to another falsified a record required for an accounting purpose, namely an invoice purporting to show that Robert Roe had paid £25 for a pair of shoes.

STATEMENT OF OFFENCE
False Accounting *etc.*

PARTICULARS OF OFFENCE
John Doe on 1st March 1986 dishonestly with a view to gain by himself or another or with intent to cause loss to another falsified a record required for an accounting purpose, namely a sales day book which he was required to keep by his employers Boobs Boutique, by omitting or concurring in omitting from the said book an entry recording that Roberta Roe had bought a dress from Boobs Boutique for £200.

STATEMENT OF OFFENCE
False Accounting contrary to section 17(1)(*b*) of the Theft Act 1968.

PARTICULARS OF OFFENCE
John Doe on 1st March 1986 dishonestly with a view to gain by himself or another, in furnishing information to Add and Subtract, accountants to Tasty Deals, produced a document required for an accounting purpose, namely a cash book, which was to his knowledge misleading false and deceptive in a material particular, in that it falsely purported to show that a total of £156 had been properly expended on petty cash transactions on behalf of Tasty Deals for the week ending 2nd February 1986.

7. Revenue Frauds
These can be charged as the common law offence of cheating the revenue.

STATEMENT OF OFFENCE
Cheating the Public Revenue.

PARTICULARS OF OFFENCE
John Doe between 1st April and 31st December 1986 with intent to defraud cheated Her Majesty the Queen and Her Commissioners of Inland Revenue of public revenue, namely income tax, by failing to submit an income tax return to the said Commissioners or to account to the said Commissioners for income tax due from him upon his income for the year ending 1st April 1986.

The most common type of Inland Revenue fraud prosecuted is the "lump" fraud, where subcontractors in the construction industry use stolen or false tax exemption certificates to obtain payment from main contractors without tax deductions.

STATEMENT OF OFFENCE

Conspiracy to Cheat the Public Revenue contrary to section 1(1) of the Criminal Law Act 1977.

PARTICULARS OF OFFENCE

John Doe and Richard Roe between 1st January and 31st December 1986 conspired together to cheat Her Majesty the Queen and Her Commissioners of Inland Revenue by:
  (i)   the unauthorised use of a subcontractor's tax exemption certificate issued to Bog Contractors Limited;
  (ii)   the provision of false documents, namely invoices from Bog Contractors Limited to Rickety Construction Limited, purporting to show that Bog Contractors Limited had performed work for Rickety Construction Limited to the amount shown on the said invoices;
  (iii) arranging for the making of payments by Rickety Construction Limited to John Doe ostensibly for the benefit of Bog Contractors Limited in respect of construction works carried out by the said John Doe for the said Rickety Construction Limited without the deductions retentions and payments on account of tax required by section 69 of the Finance (No. 2) Act 1975.

STATEMENT OF OFFENCE

False Accounting contrary to section 17(1)(*a*) of the Theft Act 1968.

PARTICULARS OF OFFENCE

John Doe on 1st March 1986 dishonestly and with a view to gain for himself or another or with intent to cause loss to the Commissioners of Inland Revenue falsified a record required for an accounting purpose, namely an invoice of Bog Contractors Limited, by concurring in the making of an entry therein purporting to show that the said Bog Contractors Limited had carried out building operations for Rickety Construction Limited to the value of £2,500.

STATEMENT OF OFFENCE

Obtaining by Deception contrary to section 15(1) of the Theft Act 1968.

PARTICULARS OF OFFENCE

Robert Roe on 1st April 1986 dishonestly obtained from Rickety Construction Limited the sum of £1,500 with the intention of permanently depriving Rickety Construction Limited thereof by deception, namely by falsely stating that John Doe was employed by Bog Contractors Limited, was entitled to use a tax exemption certificate issued to Bog Contractors Limited and was entitled to payment by Rickety Construction Limited of the sum of £1,500 without any deduction therefrom under the provisions of section 69 of the Finance (No. 2) Act 1975.

VAT frauds are usually perpetrated by understating the amount of tax received (output tax) or inflating the amount properly offset as paid out by the taxpayer (input tax). There is a specific offence under section 39 of the Value Added Tax Act 1983. Because this has a low maximum sentence it has become customary to charge such offences as cheating the revenue. In most cases this will become unnecessary when the Finance Bill 1985 comes into force and increases the maximum sentence.

STATEMENT OF OFFENCE

Conspiracy to Cheat the Public Revenue contrary to section 1(1) of the Criminal Law Act 1977.

PARTICULARS OF OFFENCE

John Doe and Richard Roe between 1st January and 1st July 1986 conspired together and with other persons unknown to cheat Her Majesty the Queen and Her Commissioners of Customs and Excise of public revenue, namely value added tax, by submitting value added tax returns to the said Commissioners which falsely stated the amount of input tax paid by Bullion Enterprises Limited and/or failing to submit value added tax returns or properly to account for value added tax received by Bullion Enterprises Limited.

STATEMENT OF OFFENCE

Fraudulent Evasion of Value Added Tax contrary to section 39(1) of the Value Added Tax Act 1983.

PARTICULARS OF OFFENCE

John Doe on 1st May 1986 was knowingly concerned in the fraudulent evasion of value added tax by submitting to Her Majesty's Commissioners of Customs and Excise a value added tax return falsely purporting to show that his total input tax for the quarter ended 1st April 1986 was £2,557 and that the said sum being in excess of his output tax for the said period the said Commissioners owed him £52.

8. False Statements to Induce Investments

STATEMENT OF OFFENCE

Making a False Statement to Induce Investment contrary to section 13(1) of the Prevention of Fraud (Investments) Act 1958.

PARTICULARS OF OFFENCE

John Doe on 1st March 1986 attempted to induce Robert Roe to enter into an agreement to acquire the shares of Nosedive plc by making a statement or forecast which he knew to be misleading, false or deceptive, or was reckless whether it was misleading, false or deceptive, namely that the shareholders of Nosedive plc were about to receive an offer for their shares from Purgatory Press plc at a price at least £1 above their current stock market price.

Index

accounting practice (*see also*
    accounts; deception;
    dishonesty; false accounting)
    dishonesty and, 1.30
    misleading accounts and, 6.47f.
accounts (*see also* accounting
    practice; auditor, false statements
    to; bank account; client accounts;
    deception; documents; false
    accounting; statements, false)
    bankrupt failing to keep, 9.24ff.
    company, 6.61ff.
    falsification of, 6.39ff.
    forgery of, 6.06f., 6.40
agent (*see also* corruption; director;
    fiduciary)
    corruption of, 7.11ff.
    deception of or by, 6.60, 7.15ff.
    disclosure, duty of, 2.10
    disposal of principal's property by,
    4.19ff.
    false statements, to or by, 6.60, 7.15ff.
    principal, distinguished from, 4.15ff.
    secret profit by, 4.03ff.
alias, use of (*see also* deception;
    forgery), 6.14
appropriation, *see* theft
auditor, false statements to, 6.64

bank account (*see also* cheque; cheque
    card; computer fraud; deposits)
    balance, obtaining by deception, 3.20
    balance, theft of, 3.05ff.
    cheque, theft of, 3.09, 3.19
    opening of, procuring by deception,
    3.26
    overdraft, obtaining by deception,
    3.38
    overdraft facility, theft of, 3.08
bankruptcy, 9.16ff.
    absconding with property, 9.19
    accounts, failure to keep, 9.24ff.

company, participating in manage-
    ment of, 9.30
concealment of property, 9.17f.
credit, obtaining, 9.32ff.
deception of creditors, 9.21
disposal of property, 9.17f.
documents, falsification of, 9.20
gambling, 9.27ff.
losses, failure to explain, 9.27ff.
omissions in statements, 9.22
speculations, rash and hazardous,
    9.27ff.
trade or business, engaging in, 9.31
bribery, *see* corruption

car tax (*see also* Customs and Excise)
    duty, deemed to be a, 10.14
    evasion of, 10.22
causation
    deception, in, 2.31ff., 2.49ff.
    forgery, in, 6.27
    reliance and, 2.56ff.
cheating the public revenue (*see also*
    Customs and Excise; tax evasion),
    10.02f.
cheque (*see also* bank account; cheque
    card; deception; forgery; theft)
    evasion of liability, 3.35f.
    making off without payment, 9.43ff.
    misdated, whether forgery, 6.16
    obligation to accept, 2.51
    obtaining by deception, 3.13, 3.19
    representation, implied, 2.40ff.
    risk of dishonour, payee aware of,
    2.23
    stagging, 2.41
    stop list, consultation of, 2.32
    theft of, 3.09, 3.19
    valuable security, as, 3.40
cheque card (*see also* bank account;
    cheque; deception; forgery)
    bank not deceived, 2.60